SUGAR AND SPICE

ABOUT THE AUTHOR

Jon Stobart is Professor of History at Manchester Metropolitan University. He has published widely on the history of consumption, retailing, and leisure in eighteenth-century England, and has a particular interest in the spatiality of consumption and the marketing of goods. His recent publications include *Selling Textiles in the Long Eighteenth Century* (2014), co-edited with Bruno Blonde, *The Country House: Material Culture and Consumption* (2015), co-edited with Andrew Hann, and *Consumption and the Country House* (2016), co-authored with Mark Rothery.

Sugar and Spice

Grocers and Groceries in Provincial England, 1650–1830

JON STOBART

OXFORD
UNIVERSITY PRESS

OXFORD

UNIVERSITY PRESS

Great Clarendon Street, Oxford, OX2 6DP,
United Kingdom

Oxford University Press is a department of the University of Oxford.
It furthers the University's objective of excellence in research, scholarship,
and education by publishing worldwide. Oxford is a registered trade mark of
Oxford University Press in the UK and in certain other countries

Published in the United States of America by Oxford University Press
198 Madison Avenue, New York, NY 10016, United States of America

British Library Cataloguing in Publication Data
Data available

Library of Congress Cataloging in Publication Data
Data available

ISBN 978–0–19–957792–7 (Hbk.)
ISBN 978–0–19–879596–4 (Pbk.)

For Jane

Acknowledgements

There are many people and organizations that have assisted in the research and production of this book. Grants from the Leverhulme Trust and the AHRC have made possible much of the archival work for this project, and I am grateful for their support. Undertaking this work would have been impossible without the assistance of archivists and search-room staff in a large number of places: the record offices in Bedford, Chester, Hanley, Lichfield, Maidstone, Northampton, Norwich, Oxford, Preston, Shrewsbury, Stafford, Stratford-upon-Avon, Truro, Warwick, York, and at the British Library, the Central Library in Manchester, the John Rylands Library, Northamptonshire Central Library, and The National Archives. I would like to thank Lucy Bailey, Amy Barnett, and Andrew Hann for generously making available some of their data and thus enriching various sections of the book. Thanks also to the following for permission to reproduce images: the Bodleian Library, University of Oxford, John Johnson Collection; the Cheshire Archives and Local Studies; the Norfolk Library and Information Service, and Northamptonshire Central Library.

There are numerous colleagues who have helped to refine my thinking about groceries, retailing, consumption, and material culture. These include the organizers and participants at a wide range of conferences and seminars in Amsterdam, Antwerp, Berlin, Cambridge, Exeter, Ghent, Jyvaskyla, Leeds, Leicester, Lisbon, Liverpool, London, Lyon, Northampton, Nottingham, Oxford, Paris, Rouen, Telford, Warwick, and Wolverhampton. Particular thanks go to Amy Barnett, Bruno Blondé, Nancy Cox, Sheryllynne Haggerty, Ian Mitchell, Mark Rothery, and Sara Pennell for reading drafts and talking about groceries and grocers. They encouraged me to think broadly and to be rigorous in my analysis. The quality of the final text owes much to the care and attention of Hilary Walford and Andrew Hawkey, who helped to correct my grammatical, typographical, and presentational errors. Finally, thanks to my family, who have, more or less convincingly, shown an interest in the grocery trade of eighteenth-century England. They have been very patient.

Contents

List of Tables

List of Figures

Whilst every effort has been made to secure permissions, we may have failed in a few cases to trace the copyright holders. We apologize for any apparent negligence. Should the copyright holders wish to contact us after publication, we would be happy to include an acknowledgement in subsequent reprints.

Abbreviations

BL	British Library
BLA	Bedfordshire and Luton Archive
BM	British Museum
Bodl., JJC	Bodleian Library, University of Oxford, John Johnson Collection
CALS	Cheshire Archives and Local Studies
CRO	Cornwall Record Office
HRL	Hanley Reference Library
JRL	John Rylands Library
KAS	Kent Archive Services
LiRO	Lichfield Record Office
LMA	London Metropolitan Archives
LRO	Lancashire Record Office
MCL	Manchester Central Library
NCL	Northamptonshire Central Library
NLIS	Norfolk Library and Information Service
NoRO	Norfolk Record Office
NRO	Northamptonshire Record Office
OBP	Old Bailey Papers
ORO	Oxfordshire Record Office
SA	Shropshire Archives
SCLA	Shakespeare Central Library and Archive
TNA	The National Archives
WRO	Warwickshire County Record Office
WSL	William Salt Library

Introduction

In May 1742, the Norwich grocer Robert Baret advertised a range of teas recently acquired at the East India Company sales, along with coffee, chocolate, sago, capers, anchovies, and spirits. Around the same time, Molly Brooks was buying tea, sugar, fruit, spices, nuts, and chocolate from the Worcester grocer Thomas Dickenson.[1] As these examples make clear, consumers in eighteenth-century England were firmly embedded in an expanding world of goods, one that incorporated a range of novel foods (tobacco, chocolate, coffee, and tea) and new supplies of more established commodities, including sugar, spices, and dried fruits. Such was the attraction of these imported groceries that they went from being novelties or expensive luxuries in the mid-seventeenth century to central elements of the British diet a century or so later. Much has been written about this transition. The trade in these goods has been linked to the rise of Britain as a commercial and imperial power, and sometimes to discussions of slavery, while their consumption is seen as transforming many aspects of British society and culture, from mealtimes to gender identity.[2] Indeed, the combined attention of economic, social, and cultural historians has placed onto imported groceries an enormous weight of conceptual, historical, and empirical significance. Few have stopped to consider whether these goods can really carry such a heavy explanatory load or to think about the everyday practicalities of selling, buying, and consuming sugar, tea, spices, or tobacco. This book attempts to do both of these things—and more. The explicit focus is the character and development of the grocery trade in provincial England between the spread of new 'exotic' goods in the mid-seventeenth century and the emergence of Co-Operative Society stores and multiples in the middle decades of the nineteenth century. In tracing the lines of supply that carried groceries from merchants through retailers to consumers, I demonstrate how changes in retailing and shopping were central to the broader transformation of consumption and consumer practices.

---

[1] *Norwich Mercury*, 8 May 1742; WSL, D1798 HM 29/2-4.
[2] The most influential book on exotic produce and empire is Walvin, *Fruits of Empire*, but see also Blackburn, *New World Slavery*, 363–76; Mintz, *Sweetness and Power*, 19–73; Smith, 'Complications'. For discussion of the growing taste for such goods see, *inter alia*, Coe and Coe, *History of Chocolate*; Cowan, *Social Life of Coffee*; de Vries, *Industrious Revolution*, 154–77; Mintz, *Sweetness and Power*, 74–150; Schivelbusch, *Tastes of Paradise*; Shammas, 'English and Anglo-American Consumption'; Smith, *Consumption*; Bickham, 'Eating the Empire'.

NOVELTY, LUXURY, AND PLEASURE

In recent years, consumption has emerged as a meta-narrative in historical enquiry, especially for the eighteenth century, where it has eclipsed the Industrial Revolution as the dominant explanatory framework for social, cultural, and economic transformation.[3] This surge of interest has coincided with a contemporary spending boom that has placed the consumer at the heart of modern society; but it draws on a much longer tradition of academic interest in the relationship between consumption and modernity. At the turn of the twentieth century, Sombart and Veblen wrote about consumption as the 'decisive force behind modern capitalism'; seventy-five years later, Baudrillard could argue that it was 'the semiotic code constituting post-modernity itself'.[4] This enduring interest reflects the broad and malleable nature of consumption as a concept and process—a flexibility that allows it to be moulded to a wide variety of viewpoints and historical processes. For eighteenth-century England, it has been variously portrayed as a key catalyst for industrialization (for example, through processes of import substitution); a central tenet of social and cultural structures (most notably, politeness); an integral part of the modernization of urban environments; and a driving force in the development of colonial trade and, ultimately, imperialist agendas.[5] Each study, of course, carries its own reading of the relationship between the consumer, the practices and spaces of consumption, and the commodities being consumed.[6] Often drawing on or reacting against Sombart and Veblen, many historians have seen the consumer as being defined by gender or class. Others have suggested that they were moulded by their spatial environment. Such ideas have been brought together most completely in studies of nineteenth-century department stores that highlight the powerful nexus of consumption created by drawing together elite and middle-class women in a dream world of goods. Yet such analyses rob the individual of agency and sometimes, it seems, of the ability even to think for themselves. In response, historians of consumption are rightly starting to draw on work by geographers and others to highlight the individual's ability to shape his identity and environment

---

[3] Berg, *Luxury and Pleasure*, 5.

[4] Trentmann, 'Beyond Consumerism', 373.

[5] On links to industrialization, see McKendrick, 'Consumer Revolution'; Berg, *Luxury and Pleasure*, 79–116; Styles, 'Product Innovation'; Riello and Parthasarathi (eds), *Spinning World*. Politeness, urban change, and consumption are discussed in Carter, *Men and Polite Society*; Klein, 'Politeness for Plebes'; Stobart, Hann, and Morgan, *Spaces of Consumption*, 57–110; Sweet, 'Topographies of Politeness'; Borsay, *English Urban Renaissance*, 115–96; Berry, 'Polite Consumption'; Stobart and Schwarz, 'Leisure, Luxury and Urban Specialization'. Consumption and empire are central themes in Walvin, *Fruits of Empire*; Blackburn, *New World Slavery*, 363–76; Mintz, *Sweetness and Power*, 44–60; Norton, 'Tasting Empire'; Bickham, 'Eating the Empire'. The emergence of a common culture of consumption across the British Empire is discussed in Breen, 'Empire of Goods'; Shammas, *Pre-Industrial Consumer*; Berg, *Luxury and Pleasure*, 279–325.

[6] See, e.g., Berg, *Luxury and Pleasure*; Carter, *Men and Polite Society*; Glennie and Thrift, 'Consumers, Identities and Consumption Spaces'; Peck, *Consuming Splendor*; Stobart, Hann, and Morgan, *Spaces of Consumption*; Walsh, 'Shops, Shopping and the Art of Decision Making'.

through his consumption choices and practices. Here, the notion of spatiality is sometimes deployed to capture the complexities of the social–spatial interaction.[7]

A focus on agency places great emphasis on the motivations underpinning consumption and, more particularly, the meanings that goods and practices carried for consumers. Three broad sets of ideas have dominated historians' thinking in this area: novelty, luxury, and utility. Novelty is central to many readings of consumer change in the eighteenth century and is still recognized as a driving force of consumption today.[8] Berg argues that novelty forms a key element of fashion, since it creates the possibility for constant change—the energy behind fashion's 'caprice and valorization of ephemerality'.[9] What is it, though, that makes fashion so attractive to consumers? Why the constant craving for the new? Drawing on Scitovsky's analysis of human satisfaction and consumer dissatisfaction, Berg suggests that one reason is that the pursuit of novelty is pleasurable. Along with variety and complexity, it stimulates and arouses the senses and alleviates the boredom that results from the needs of a body being satisfied.[10] Novelty, in this sense, can be tied into the so-called Diderot effect: the restless renewal of goods resulting from progressive dissatisfaction with the *status quo ante*.[11] At the same time, novelty offered the opportunity to redefine one's position in relation to the prevailing social order. If notions of the individual were only slowly emerging in the seventeenth and eighteenth centuries, then novel goods provided at least some opportunity to define and project 'self' within and sometimes in opposition to hierarchical social groupings.[12] They were important because they allowed new practices and identities to be carved out, from the soberly dressed coffee-drinking man of business to the snuff-taking dilettante of high-society London.[13] Yet novelty is also a problematic category, both intrinsically and in its use by historians. It is itself ephemeral, being exhausted through the process of consumption and thus in need of constant renewal. While possible with toys, clothes, and tableware, this is less easily achieved with groceries. Variety can be sustained up to a point, through different blends of tea or different combinations of spices, but is ultimately limited by the very nature of the commodities. Moreover, there is a tendency to assume that novelty made goods desirable without much thought being given to how this attraction might play out in practice. Indeed, Campbell, Bianchi, and others have argued that novelty was a difficult idea for consumers, new goods needing to be incorporated

---

[7] On department stores and consumption, see Miller, *Bon Marché*; Rappaport, *Shopping for Pleasure*; Williams, *Dream Worlds*. For discussion of spatiality and consumption, see Glennie and Thrift, 'Consumers, Identities and Consumption Spaces'; Miller et al., *Shopping, Place and Identity*; Stobart, Hann, and Morgan, *Spaces of Consumption*.

[8] See McKendrick, 'Consumer Revolution'; Blondé and Van Damme, 'Fashioning Old and New', 3–4; McCracken, *Culture and Consumption*, 18–20, 79–83.

[9] Berg, *Luxury and Pleasure*, 250.

[10] Berg, *Luxury and Pleasure*, 250. See also Scitovsky, *Joyless Economy*.

[11] See de Vries, *Industrious Revolution*, 32–3.

[12] Campbell, 'Understanding Consumption'; Styles, *Dress of the People*, 8–16; Cowan, *Social Life of Coffee*, 10–12, 16–47.

[13] Schivelbusch, *Tastes of Paradise*, 34–9, 131–46.

into existing systems of consumption or sets of goods before they became know-able and desirable.[14]

Novelty, then, does not explain all consumer behaviour. Many historians have, instead, seen luxury as a more compelling system for understanding consumption. Luxury is a slippery and relative term: contingent upon time and space, as well as culture and wealth. Building on a lengthy debate over the virtues and vices of luxury that had run through much of the early modern period, Adam Smith distin-guished two types of luxury consumption: that which does not endure and that which does. He noted a switch from one to the other as taking place in the early eighteenth century, with elite consumers increasingly seeking new indicators of status: 'For a pair of diamond buckles perhaps, or for something as frivolous and useless, they exchanged the price of the maintenance of a thousand men for a year, and with it the whole weight and authority which it could give them.'[15] Historians have confirmed this transition, although Peck and others have pushed the timing back into the seventeenth century or earlier.[16] They have also broadened out the scope of luxury consumption, moving beyond Smith's rather pejorative emphasis of fripperies and Sombart's emphasis on the gratification of individual sensuous desires to encompass a broad range of material goods. Yet luxury remains a category closely bound to elite consumption: neither the flouting and subsequent abandonment of sumptuary laws, nor the stretching of the concept to encompass semi-luxury, new luxuries, populuxe, or customary luxuries has entirely broken this link.[17] It has stretched it, though; and in ways that make it necessary to consider what luxury actually meant to consumers, both rich and poor. For Sombart, it was bound up with sensuality, an association developed by Nef, who noted the sump-tuousness, beauty, and delight of luxury goods, and more recently by Smith, Berg, and many others.[18] In this way, luxury is linked to the idea of pleasure.

This association is written into the title of Berg's book about eighteenth-century production and consumption, and forms an important subtext. Yet it never receives the detailed conceptual analysis afforded to luxury—she seems to take as read its meanings and implications for consumption.[19] This is unfortunate, because it is a complex category most readily understood as part of Scitovsky's conception of utility.[20] Far from bringing a narrow focus onto the usefulness of objects, utility can be thought of more broadly as a search for comfort and a search for pleasure. The latter, Scitovsky argued, was linked to stimulation and arousal of the senses, and was an inherently open-ended process, since the desire

[14] Campbell, 'Desire for the New'; Bianchi, 'Taste for Novelty'.

[15] Smith, *Wealth of Nations*, 418–19.

[16] See, e.g., Peck, *Consuming Splendor*, 10–22; Berger, *Most Necessary Luxuries*; Goldthwaite, *Wealth and the Demand for Art*.

[17] Berg, *Luxury and Pleasure*, esp. 117–92; de Vries, *Industrious Revolution*, 44–7; Fairchilds, 'Production and Marketing of Populuxe Goods'; Smith, *Consumption*, esp. 92–103.

[18] Sombart, *Luxury and Capitalism*; Nef, *Cultural Foundations*; Smith, *Consumption*, 63–104; Berg, *Luxury and Pleasure*, esp. 21–45.

[19] Berg, *Luxury and Pleasure*. There is no mention of pleasure in the index.

[20] Scitovsky, *Joyless Economy*. See also de Vries, *Industrious Revolution*, 20–5.

for pleasure could never be satiated. This links back to the stimulating effect of novelty, but also on to other factors that could afford pleasure. Hedonism and the search for new corporeal stimulants might form an obvious link to the consumption of coffee, tea, chocolate, and sugar, but we should also be mindful of more sentimental associations that tied owners and particular goods, especially those linked to family or friends.[21]

These ideas have been brought together by de Vries, but steered in a particular direction: the contextualization of shifting household economics that lay at the heart of his industrious revolution. If we stand back a little further is it possible to see how these conceptions of novelty, luxury, and pleasure have been fitted into broader theorizations of consumption?

UNDERSTANDING CONSUMPTION

From the perspective of neoclassical economics, consumption can be explained in terms of rational choices on the part of the individual and/or society. Davis, for example, argued that the surges in demand that he identified in English foreign trade were the result of reduced prices that introduced larger sections of society to a new range of goods and consumption practices. Once established, he suggested, these were not easily 'shaken by subsequent vicissitudes in prices, but continued to grow rapidly'.[22] These ideas have been developed much further by de Vries, who has looked into the black box of household economies and argued that many became increasingly dependent upon the market to supply their needs and wants, and reoriented their spending around a new set of goods.[23] Crucial in these developments was the bundling of goods in which the consumption of tea, for example, encouraged the acquisition of kettles, cups, teapots, and so on. Writ large, the spread of a new domestic material culture across Europe in the late seventeenth and early eighteenth centuries is thus partly attributable to falling prices and rising incomes, which created favourable demand conditions for tea, coffee, tobacco, sugar, and chocolate.

De Vries in particular offers a sophisticated and wide-ranging theorization of these processes. However, the danger is that such arguments, when reduced to their essence, see demand simply as a function of price relative to income, with little thought being given to what might make the goods themselves attractive to consumers. Yet consumers had a wide range of goods from which they could choose: why should sugar or tobacco, for instance, be favoured over beer or meat? One functionalist answer to this question is that consumption—and especially the consumption of certain novel or luxury goods—served the needs of Western capitalism. For Sombart, consumption was the very foundation of capitalist economies, because economies cannot grow without a sustained rise in demand and growth is funda-

[21] Berg, 'Women's Property'.
[22] Davis, 'English Foreign Trade'.
[23] De Vries, *Industrious Revolution*, 23–37, 186–237.

mental to capitalism. More nuanced versions of this argument have been rehearsed, *inter alia*, for sugar and coffee. Mintz views the former as a central prop to consumer demand and a key element of working-class diets. Indeed, he sees the first time that a worker added sugar to his tea as a revolutionary moment. Rather more measured, but no less profound, are the arguments of Smith and Schivelbusch, who associate coffee with both sober propriety and a bourgeois work ethic.[24]

The problem with all these accounts is their lack of clarity about how individual behaviour related to the grand sweep of historical change. They may be long on rhetoric and the polemic of contemporary commentators, but relatively little is said about everyday consumption practices or the motivations that underpinned them. The second of these is addressed head-on by perspectives on consumption that focus on its rational use in differentiating individuals and groups. For Veblen, the social status of the leisured classes was cemented and communicated through their conspicuous consumption. The emphasis was on luxury and display which linked both to material goods and personal accomplishments. In late nineteenth-century America, Veblen identified the latter as a knowledge of 'dead languages', the correct handling of grammar, and an understanding of the proprieties of dress; he also emphasized the conspicuous employment of male servants as symbols of 'waste' or unnecessary expenditure. Servants held a similar symbolic significance in the eighteenth century, as did the cultivation of gentlemanly manners and tastes, which ensured that goods were consumed in a seemly manner, appropriate to the leisured lifestyle of the elite.[25] Above all, though, it was the nature of the goods being consumed that differentiated the leisured classes. In Veblen's words, their consumption 'undergoes a specialisation as regards the quality of the goods consumed. Since the consumption of these more excellent goods is an evidence of wealth, it becomes honorific; and conversely the failure to consume in due quantity and quality becomes a mark of inferiority and demerit.'[26] Naturally, the character of these positional goods changed over time, but the emphasis remained on luxury, defined in terms of cost, complexity of acquisition, and association with appropriately exclusive systems of knowledge.[27] Through the Middle Ages and early modern periods, spices played a key role in displays of wealth and power—they were costly, came from distant lands, and were often associated with notions of paradise. If their importance declined in the eighteenth century, chocolate, high-grade tea, and elaborate sugar confections emerged as novel and luxurious goods associated with wealthy elites.[28] The ability to display this luxury was important, but so too was the need to maintain the social distinctions marked by conspicuous consumption, because failing to keep up appearances implied slippage from the social elite.

[24] Sombart, *Luxury and Capitalism*; Mintz, *Sweetness and Power*, 183–6; Smith, *Consumption*, 140–61; Schivelbusch, *Tastes of Paradise*, 15–84; Cowan, *Social Life of Coffee*, 9.

[25] Veblen, *Theory of the Leisure Class*, 25, 57, 75.

[26] Veblen, *Theory of the Leisure Class*, 73–4. See also Sombart, *Luxury and Capitalism*, 99–100.

[27] On the definition of luxury, see Appadurai, *Social Life of Things*, 3–63; Berg, *Luxury and Pleasure*, 21–45. On positional goods, see Hirsch, *Social Limits to Growth*.

[28] See, e.g., Dawson, *Plenti and Grase*, 160–73; Schivelbusch, *Tastes of Paradise*, 4–13; Coe and Coe, *History of Chocolate*, 129–64; Mintz, *Sweetness and Power*, 88.

This fear of falling down the social ladder was not restricted to the elite. Smith argues that the middling sorts deployed respectability as a defensive mechanism, consuming in particular ways in order to bolster their position in relation to those lower down the social scale.[29] This challenges Simmel's assertion that goods and tastes would 'trickle down' to those of lower social status, implying instead a much more active process of 'chase and flight' or, perhaps more correctly, chase and *fight*.[30] The driving force came from below, with individuals and groups seeking to imitate the consumption practices of their social superiors and thus appropriate them as status symbols. This idea was developed by McKendrick into a model of emulative consumption.

In imitation of the rich the middle ranks spent more frenziedly than ever before, and in imitation of them the rest of society joined in as best they might...Spurred on by social emulation and class competition men and women surrendered eagerly to the pursuit of novelty, the hypnotic effects of fashion and the enticements of commercial propaganda...The closely stratified nature of English society, the striving for vertical social mobility, the emulative spending bred by social emulation, the compulsive power of fashion begotten by social competition—combined with the widespread ability to spend to produce an unprecedented propensity to consume.[31]

The driving force behind this emulative spending was social competition, fuelled by fashion and facilitated by the fine grading of both society and consumer goods. Greig, for example, identifies London's *Beau Monde* as an elite group whose membership was defined by fashionable consumption and social cachet or, as Lord Chesterfield described it, 'through a certain je ne scay quoy which other people of fashion acknowledge'. This links closely to Simmel's conception of fashion as a coding of objects which defines membership or allegiance.[32] Those who aspired to membership of the *Beau Monde* had to consume in an appropriate manner and drew their inspiration from people who were already part of the privileged circle. Such aspirational and emulative behaviour was apparent to contemporary commentators. McKendrick quotes Forster, who wrote in 1767 about the 'perpetual restless ambition' felt within each class 'to raise themselves to the level of those immediately above them'. He also notes Wedgwood's strategy of selling first to the elite since one must 'begin at the *Head* first, & then proceed to the inferior members'.[33] Novelty was central to such fashion-based emulative consumption, be it of Wedgwood porcelain, patterned chintz, or exotic groceries such as tea or tobacco. It introduced constant change and offered fine distinctions to be drawn in terms of the character or quality of goods.

Whilst persuasive and highly influential, this emulation model has been subjected to a growing body of criticism, which falls into two main groups. The

[29] Smith, *Consumption*, esp. 189–222. See also Bailey, 'Maintaining Status'.
[30] Simmel, *On Individuality*, 293–323; McCracken, *Culture and Consumption*, 94–5.
[31] McKendrick, 'Consumer Revolution', 11.
[32] Greig, 'Leading the Fashion', 297; Berg, *Luxury and Pleasure*, 251–2; Campbell, 'Desire for the New', 247; Simmel, 'Fashion'.
[33] McKendrick, 'Consumer Revolution', 11; McKendrick, 'Josiah Wedgwood', 110.

first builds on Veblen's belief that accomplishments such as manners and deportment were the product of an education in taste. He argued that

> a knowledge of good form is *prima facie* evidence that that portion of the well-bred person's
> life which is not spent under the observation of the spectator has been worthily spent in
> acquiring accomplishments that are of no lucrative effect. In the last analysis the value of
> manners lies in the fact that they are the voucher of a life of leisure.[34]

The significance of this is that appropriate consumption was not purely a product
of spending power or successful imitation—it had to be learned. This was because,
as Bourdieu argues, goods and practices carried meanings that could be properly
understood only by those who possessed knowledge of the code in which those
meanings were written.[35] To an extent, the necessary learning could be purchased
along with material goods (for example, through conduct manuals or cookery
books[36]); but it was largely dependent upon existing status and access to resources.
Writing about France in the 1960s and 1970s, Bourdieu emphasized formal education in the Grand Écoles; in the eighteenth century this equated with university or
the Grand Tour, but it was also linked to time spent assembling and reading a
gentlemanly library, and to opportunities for discoursing with peers about art,
science, and the classics. The attributes that this brought to an individual were
both a mark of social distinction and a mechanism for perpetuating privilege.
Investment in cultural capital was not, as Veblen supposed, of 'no lucrative effect';
rather, it served to distinguish the individual from the rest of society. Moreover,
consumption of this nature took a more subtle, detached, and inconspicuous form
to be appreciated only by those sufficiently cultivated.[37] The late seventeenth-
century uptake of tea, coffee, and chocolate among discerning social elites might
be viewed in this way. Certainly, the manners and mannerisms required of those
taking snuff in the middle decades of the eighteenth century were closed to anyone
unable to learn the mysteries of the art.[38]

A second critique of the emulation model focuses on the actual motivations of
consumers. Utility was a powerful influence on many, with goods offering comfort
and pleasure, and being 'frequently ascribed with values of usefulness, civility and
ingenuity'.[39] These practical and emotional qualities are too easily obscured in theorizations that rarefy goods into systems of meaning, overlooking their intrinsic characteristics and usefulness. Tea and coffee were stimulants, valued among other
reasons because they induced alertness and wakefulness; sugar was a useful addition
to the ingredients available for cooking and made plain meals more palatable, and
Jamaica pepper was an excellent substitute for a number of eastern spices. From a

[34] Veblen, *Theory of the Leisure Class*, 49.
[35] Bourdieu, *Distinction*, 2, 228.
[36] Klein, 'Politeness for Plebes'; Pennell, 'Perfecting Practice'.
[37] Miller, *Material Culture*, 149.
[38] Schivelbusch, *Tastes of Paradise*, 131–2; Fennetaux, 'Toying with Novelty', 24–5.
[39] Berg, 'New Commodities', 69. See also Weatherill, *Consumer Behaviour*, 145–57; Overton et al.,
Production and Consumption, 98–108.

different perspective, Campbell has argued that the trickle-down of goods or practices should not be read as emulative or even imitative behaviour. A lady's maid, for
example, may have copied her mistress's hairstyle, taken snuff, and drunk tea without claiming social equality or emulating her lifestyle.[40] In any case, emulation offers
only a partial explanation for consumption: it is an aspiration for which deeper
motivations must be sought. Campbell finds this in a shift in eighteenth-century
values and attitudes towards a Romantic ethic that was marked by 'a distinctive
form of hedonism, one in which the enjoyment of emotions as summoned through
imaginary or illusory images is central…combined with the ranking of pleasure
above comfort'. Within this, longing for goods and experiences was just as important as their actual consumption: it helped to generate the ceaseless new wants that
Campbell sees as being characteristic of modern consumerism.[41]

What this meant in practical terms is not always spelt out very clearly. However,
the possibilities become a little clearer when Cowan draws on this model in linking
the initial uptake of coffee to the hedonism of a group of virtuosi, and much the
same has been argued for tobacco, smoking being associated with a certain character type.[42] Such motivations tie consumption closely to personal identity: goods
and practices acting as markers of character rather than status. Indeed, it is possible
to see consumption as a process through which the meanings of goods are sorted
and organized into a coherent system that communicates something of the identity
and character of the consumer. For Douglas and Isherwood, this is perhaps the key
role of consumption, because, 'without some conventional ways of selecting and
fixing agreed meanings, the minimum consensual basis of society is missing'.[43]
From this perspective, consumption is a shared social experience, the significance
of which runs far deeper than a simple concern for competitive display; rather, it is
an active process, a continual acting out and redefining of culture and social meaning. In this way, consumption can be viewed as a performance that draws on and
gives meaning to a range of material objects, and that serves to define identity. As
Campbell asserts: 'the self is built through consumption [and] consumption
expresses the self.'[44] Thus, for example, we can see Elizabeth Shackleton consuming
in a way that reflected and reinforced her identity as an elderly provincial gentlewoman or Glasgow's arriviste colonial merchants engaging in a 'spectacular form
of self invention' through the consumption of 'elaborate and symbol-laden possessions'. More generally, Smith links the growing consumption of imported groceries
to the construction of respectability among an expanding middling sort—an
attempt to carve out a social status based on virtue and manners, but bolstered by
material goods and consumption practices.[45] In this way, we can extend the idea of

[40] Campbell, 'Understanding Consumption', 41.
[41] Campbell, 'Understanding Consumption', 48; Campbell, *Romantic Ethic*, 203.
[42] Cowan, *Social Life of Coffee*, 11–14; Smith, *Consumption*, 161–2.
[43] Douglas and Isherwood, *World of Goods*, 65.
[44] Campbell, *Romantic Ethic*, 288.
[45] Vickery, *Gentleman's Daughter*, esp. 183–94; Nenadic, 'Middle-Rank Consumers', 127; Smith,
Consumption, 189–222.

consumption bundles beyond the material and into the behavioural: consuming tea meant not just teacups, kettles, and so on, but also the ritualistic performances of pouring, drinking, socializing, and displaying self.

Whether such performances are conscious mechanisms of identity construction is a contested point. Goffman distinguishes front-stage from back-stage spaces as the arena in which self is consciously performed—a dichotomy that has been highly influential in analyses of the domestic space.[46] However, simple binaries of front or back stage, public or private, are inadequate in communicating the complexities of everyday life. And there are more fundamental questions about the link between identity and action, with a growing number of historians emphasizing the importance of repeated mundane activities in shaping identity. In short, they argue, identity is constructed through practice. In terms of consumption, we might contrast the self-conscious performances of promenading, taking tea, or discoursing in the coffee house with the repeated and routinized practices of shopping, cooking, or eating.[47] In both cases, however, it is through action that the meanings of practices and goods are mobilized in the construction of identity.

Like ours today, the practices and motivations of eighteenth-century consumers were complex and are not amenable to simple explanatory models, not least because an individual might be driven by different motives according to the context or goods being consumed. Whatever their motivation, it is clear that durable and consumable goods held important meanings for consumers. Yet there is a danger in focusing too closely on these issues and neglecting the processes of supply that linked commodities and consumers. Their importance has long been recognized, Fine and Leopold exemplifying how an understanding of the routes and mechanisms through which goods passed on their way from producer to consumer brought a fuller understanding of the wider meanings and significance of particular commodities.[48] A similar concern prompted Walvin and Mintz to interrogate the links between exotic produce and colonial systems of production.[49] They emphasize the power of consumer demand in shaping the ways in which tea, sugar, tobacco, and so on were produced and traded, and ultimately the ways in which Britain grew and operated as a colonial power. In this way, they use analysis of the production and consumption of colonial goods as a critique of slavery, imperialism, and global trade. However, these inspiring studies say little about the ways in which empire was made real for everyday consumers through advertising, recipes, or nomenclature. These topics are picked up by Bickham, who argues that, 'by the

---

[46] Goffman, *Presentation of Self*. Applications of and variations on his model can be found in Weatherill, *Consumer Behaviour*, esp. 8–9; Overton et al., *Production and Consumption*, 134–6; Kross, 'Mansions, Men, Women'; Andersson, 'A Mirror of Oneself'; Vickery, *Behind Closed Doors, passim*; Barnett, 'In with the New', 84–91.

[47] Rappaport, *Shopping for Pleasure*, 74–107; Stobart, Hann, and Morgan, *Spaces of Consumption*, 98–109; Glennie and Thrift, 'Consumers, Identities and Consumption Spaces', 39–40.

[48] Fine and Leopold, *World of Consumption*.

[49] Walvin, *Fruits of Empire*; Mintz, *Sweetness and Power*.

close of the eighteenth century, food was at the heart of the British imperial experience', linked closely to a growing public interest in empire.[50] But his analysis is too
closely focused on empire and fails to see it as just one part of a much wider set of
reference points by which consumers negotiated a growing world of goods. Moreover, none of these studies is really concerned with and convincing in its analysis
of domestic supply systems: the mundane practices of retailing and shopping. Yet
retailers played a vital role in bringing the world of goods to the home of the individual consumer—responding to and feeding growing demand, but also helping
to shape that demand through advertising, relative pricing, and service provision.
The way in which the retail sector accommodated and promoted novel or luxury
goods is particularly important in this regard. Shoppers were engaged in a relational and reflective activity through which identity was constructed and communicated: how and where goods were acquired can be just as important as what was
being bought.[51] The ways in which shoppers connected with groceries and other
goods—inspecting, choosing, buying, and paying—is therefore central to understanding changing consumption practices.

RETAILING, SHOPS, AND SHOPPING

Retailing was long seen as underdeveloped and primitive before the advent of
department stores, multiple retailers, and cooperatives in the middle decades of the
nineteenth century. The first two of these were seen by Jefferys, Matthias, and others
as especially important in revolutionizing the ways in which groceries were bought
and sold.[52] They brought with them apparently innovatory practices such as fixed
prices and cash sales that helped to improve the efficiency of retailing by speeding
the shopping process. At the same time, retail spaces were modernized, with a
greater emphasis on display, while the goods being sold were increasingly branded
with the name of the producer or distributor—a process in which cooperative societies played a key role.[53] From this perspective, any changes occurring before these
monumental transitions were minor and situated within a dark, atavistic, and backward retail environment. This myth of underdevelopment was challenged by Alexander's analysis of retailing during the Industrial Revolution, which pointed towards
important changes in the early decades of the nineteenth century. It was effectively
exploded by the work of Willan, Mui and Mui, and Shammas, who demonstrated
the existence of a growing, dynamic, and complex retail sector in eighteenth-century
England. More recent work by Walsh, Cox, Glennie and Thrift, Berry, Stobart, and

[50] Bickham, 'Eating the Empire', 107. See also Wilson, *Sense of the People*; Bowen, 'British Conceptions of Global Empire'.
[51] See Shields, 'Spaces for Consumption', 1–6; Stobart, Hann, and Morgan, *Spaces of Consumption*,
13, 160–8.
[52] Jefferys, *Retailing in Britain*; Mathias, *Retailing Revolution*. See also Purvis, 'Co-Operative Retailing'; Stobart, *Spend, Spend, Spend*, 133–43; Alexander, *Retailing in England*, 103–7, 159–228.
[53] On retail space, see Morrison, *English Shops*, 145–57, 193–6; on branding, see Jefferys, *Retailing
in Britain*, 38–41, 218–20, 259–60, 270–1, 333–4, 381–3.

Peck has thrown open the shutters of seemingly gloomy and unappealing shops to reveal sophisticated social and economic spaces.[54]

Contemporaries were well aware of the importance of retailing, even if their figures were little more than educated guesses. In 1688 King thought that there were about 50,000 shopkeepers and tradesmen; Postlethwayt estimated 100,000 in 1757, while just two years later Massie suggested a figure of 162,500. The numbers are large and the reality of growth is apparent: a reflection of population expansion, increased trade, urbanization, and a growing commercialization of the household. More telling than this numerical growth—which could, of course, be achieved simply by spreading demand more thinly across a larger number of shop-keepers—is the expanding variety of goods available in shops, including novelties, imported wares, and semi-luxuries.[55] Thus, while fairs, markets, and pedlars contin-ued to play an important part in supplying the needs of both urban and rural consumers, they were gradually eclipsed by fixed shop retailing. In the eighteenth century, Stourbridge fair still carried on an extensive trade in Nottingham glass, Sheffield cutlery, and hardware from the west Midlands, but many others were increasingly associated with agricultural produce or livestock. If they remained attractive as places to go, people often visited 'out of curiosity only, to partake of the usual diversions of these public places'.[56] Pedlars persisted longer and were clearly seen by shopkeepers as important, if 'unfair' competition against which they raised a chorus of complaints.[57] In contrast, a more symbiotic relationship developed between markets and shops—the latter were often clustered around the marketplace and did much of their trade on market days, when the town was filled with visitors coming to buy provisions at the market.

Cox rightly warns of taking an overly Whiggish view of fixed shops as modern and progressive, but it is clear that they grew in importance as points of supply and as agents of a new kind of shopping. One underlying cause, Walsh argues, is that shops were replacing street markets as the mental focus for consumers. It was in shops that the newest, most fashionable items were to be found and, by extension, where consumer desires were created and indulged—a role that made them the subject of a stinging critique from some contemporary commentators.[58] They were, in effect, windows onto a world of goods that helped to open up the mental hori-zons of townspeople and country folk alike.[59] Another reason for the rise of the

[54] Alexander, *Retailing in England*; Willan, *Inland Trade*; Mui and Mui, *Shops and Shopkeeping*; Shammas, *Pre-Industrial Consumer*; Walsh, 'Shop Design'; Cox, *Complete Tradesman*; Glennie and Thrift, 'Consumers, Identities and Consumption Spaces'; Berry, 'Polite Consumption'; Stobart, Hann, and Morgan, *Spaces of Consumption*; Stobart and Hann, 'Retailing Revolution'; Peck, *Consuming Splendor*.

[55] See Mui and Mui, *Shops and Shopkeeping*, 29; de Vries, 'Purchasing Power'.

[56] Postlethwayt, 'Fairs', quoted in Berg, *Luxury and Pleasure*, 258; Everitt, 'Marketing of Agricul-tural Produce', 537. The relative decline of fairs was patchy, but occurred across Europe—see Berg, *Luxury and Pleasure*, 258; Welch, 'Fairs of Early Modern Italy'; Blondé et al., *Buyers and Sellers*, 17.

[57] Mui and Mui, *Shops and Shopkeeping*, 73–105.

[58] Cox, *Complete Tradesman*, 17–37; Walsh, 'Stalls, Bulks, Shops'.

[59] Reed, 'Cultural role of small towns'.

shop was that its physical space could be consciously moulded around the display of goods, and the social and economic practices of buying and selling. Glazed and bow windows became increasingly common through the eighteenth century, and fittings and furnishings were introduced to display goods and create appropriate environments for the polite rituals of shopping. People were encouraged to enter the shop, which was transformed into a place for display and marketing.[60] Along-side these changes, shopkeepers adopted new practices in order to encourage sales. The more prestigious retailers cultivated the shop as a leisure environment, encouraging browsing and sociability.[61] Linked to this was the development of the show-room as a specialist space designed for displaying goods to their best advantage. These were most famously used by Wedgwood, but early eighteenth-century retailers were deploying similar strategies to sell higher-order goods in a more private environment. As Cox argues, entry to these spaces was reserved for privileged customers—a differentiation echoed in the use of private back rooms or even the parlour as a space to entertain customers. This use of the 'home as showcase' blurred the line between commercial and domestic space, and carried implications for the ways in which the shopkeeper's home was decorated and perceived.[62]

In other shops, the process of selling was made as efficient as possible, with fixed prices and cash sales becoming more widespread. The advantages of this were clear to contemporaries. Robert Owen wrote that 'not much time was allowed for bargaining...the article being asked for was presented, taken at once, and paid for all with great dispatch'. Furthermore, as James Lackington noted when later describing his decision to establish his bookseller's business without offering credit, it obviated the problems of unsettled bills and the time spent chasing creditors, and freed capital for investment in stock.[63] Shopkeeping was also becoming more businesslike, with a burgeoning number of guides for tradesmen—paralleling the proliferation of conduct manuals. Some of these offered practical instruction on how to improve accounting systems, so that shopkeepers could start to assess the profitability of their businesses. Most, though, centred on the ways in which they should behave towards their customers. According to Defoe, the shopkeeper had 'to bear with all sorts of impertinence, and the most provoking curiosity that it is possible to imagine', and must have 'no passions, no resentment; he must never be angry; no not so much as seem to be so'. He also had to be able to deliver an informed and polite patter as goods were presented on the counter for inspection. The shopkeeper thus trod a fine line between persistence, deference, and sociability.[64]

---

[60] Cox, *Complete Tradesman*, 79–98; Walsh, 'Advertising'; Walsh, 'Newness of the Department Store'; Hann and Stobart, 'Sites of Consumption'; Stobart, Hann, and Morgan, *Spaces of Consumption*, 123–32.

[61] Walsh, 'Shop Design'; Cox, *Complete Tradesman*, 76–115; Hann and Stobart, 'Sites of Consumption'.

[62] Cox, *Complete Tradesman*, 127–39; Stobart, 'Accommodating the Shop'.

[63] Owen, *Life*, i. 18–19; Lackington, *Memoirs*, 214.

[64] Defoe, *Compleat English Tradesman*, 103.

The eighteenth-century retail system was varied, dynamic, and sophisticated. A large range of goods could be bought from even fairly modest village shops, while urban shopping streets offered enormous choice. But there is a danger in becoming overly concerned with the shop rather than shopping, not least as it privileges supply- over demand-led changes. Indeed, recent work has suggested that more novelty and choice could create problems for shoppers, as it made it more difficult for them to judge the quality of wares and make informed choices between different goods. The problem was made worse by the growing spatial separation of producer and consumer. Under such circumstances, Blondé and Van Damme argue, a close relationship with a trusted shopkeeper was invaluable, since it helped customers negotiate the options available. In this way, changes in consumption could cement traditional modes of selling.[65] That said, consumers did not become the passive victims of attractive and artful displays, the 'seductive ambience of pleasing and dramatic interiors', or the pressure of persistent sales patter. The fictional Evelina may have worried that she 'thought I should never choose a silk; for they produced so many…and they recommended them all so strongly, that I fancy they thought I only wanted persuasion to buy everything they showed me'.[66] In reality, however, shoppers were under no obligation to buy. Indeed, Berry has suggested that a lengthy process of inspecting goods and questioning the shopkeeper was central to a mode of polite shopping, which involved browsing before striking a bargain. While it remains unclear how far such modes of shopping extended down the social scale, it is clear that such practices were widespread, prompting some shopkeepers to complain that their customers would 'tumble over my goods, and deafen me with a round of questions'.[67] Worse, they might leave without buying anything at all—a possibility that was very real, as shopping became a polite and respectable way of passing time; of seeing and being seen. Glennie and Thrift rightly argue that it is unlikely that eighteenth-century consumers had a 'complete intellectual framework through which they articulated their motives and which they deployed when encountering commodities, other consumers, and consumption sites'; but they made active choices to engage in shopping and to visit particular shops.[68] In this way, shopping gave agency to the consumer and was important in the construction of personal identity. It drew on specific sets of social and economic skills that were important enough to be taught, and yet were learned and honed through repeated performance.[69] In short, shopping for goods could be just as significant as owning them and merits the same level of scrutiny and theorization.

---

[65] Blonde and Van Damme, 'Retail Growth'. See also Cox, *Complete Tradesman*, 116–45.
[66] Burney, *Evelina*, 25.
[67] Defoe, *Compleat English Tradesman*, 64.
[68] Glennie and Thrift, 'Consumers, Identities and Consumption Spaces', 39.
[69] Peck, *Consuming Splendor*, 27; Miller et al., *Shopping, Place and Identity*, 15.

KEY THEMES

There is a mismatch between analyses of consumption and those of retailing in terms of the role played by groceries. While Schivelbusch, Mintz, Smith, and de Vries, among many others, argue that groceries had the power to transform society in many different ways, we know very little about the ways in which they were bought and sold. Histories of retailing in the eighteenth century have largely focused on durable goods, groceries being seen as everyday items, the buying and selling of which was unremarkable and mundane. Can this be true? Can goods such as tea, sugar, and tobacco, which apparently revolutionized domestic practices and shaped identities, really have been purchased in a casual and routine manner? If they were, what does this tell us about attitudes to such goods and about the link between shopping and consumption? To fully understand the impact of groceries, we need to develop a more rounded appreciation of the relationship between supply and demand, not in any abstract, econometric sense, but in terms of the actions and reactions of those engaged in buying and selling. More generally, we need to ground the cultural interpretations of consumption that have tended to dominate in recent years much more thoroughly in the social and economic practicalities of everyday life. My aim in this book is to provide an integrated analysis of the grocery trades in England from the middle decades of the seventeenth century to the early nineteenth century—one that follows groceries through the hands of merchants, into the retail shop and thence to the consumer. In doing this, I highlight the importance of groceries and grocery retailers to wider processes of social and economic change, and engage critically with a number of broader themes.

The first of these is the fundamental reorientation of trade that took place in the late seventeenth and especially the eighteenth century. This commercial revolution was closely linked to the trade in and consumption of groceries and to Britain's developing colonial ambitions. We have already noted the connections drawn between new groceries and empire by Walvin, Mintz, and Bickham, and the relative lack of research on the ways in which this relationship was played out through advertising and marketing practices, and how it was perceived by consumers. These are issues that are discussed in more detail in Chapters 2, 7, and 9. Of central concern here is the fact that many 'colonial' groceries came from beyond the formal reach of empire—most notably tea, but also a wide range of spices and dried fruits—while other goods came from much closer to home. This raises three important issues. The first relates to consumer choice and the frameworks within which particular decisions were made: what importance was accorded to the provenance of goods by both retailers and consumers, and how significant were such considerations when judging quality and making purchases? The second centres on the more general significance of the commercial revolution: to what extent did new goods and new supplies supplant older ones, and how far were consumers' mental horizons shifted by changing patterns of trade? The third is concerned with the relationship between food and empire: to what extent did the consumption of groceries link into broader interest in empire among ordinary people?

Second is the nature of retail change during the long eighteenth century and how we might define and identify retail revolution. At a basic level, this means knowing more about the changing number, geography, and supply of (grocery) shops—developments that are charted in Chapters 3 and 4. It also involves developing a better understanding of the physical premises and retail practices of those dealing in groceries (covered in Chapter 5 and Chapters 6 and 7 respectively). From this, it is possible to gauge how grocers fitted into wider processes of retail change, but also to assess what the grocery trade might tell us about the extent, nature, and impact of any eighteenth-century retail revolution. Critical in this respect is the question of how novelties were accommodated within existing retail systems and ranges of goods: were they simply slotted in alongside familiar spices, dried fruits, and so on, or did they prompt profoundly different modes of promotion and selling? This leads to more fundamental questions about supply- and demand-driven change that have long preoccupied economic historians. Here, the balance has recently tipped towards the latter, but crucial role of retailing is often ignored. It is hugely important, therefore, to understand whether grocers' retail techniques influenced consumer attitudes to new (and traditional) foods, and whether we see grocers playing an active role in the spread of new goods and new forms of consumption. In essence, this boils down to the question of whether retail change was a response or stimulus to consumer change.

The third theme centres on the extent and nature of household engagement with the market—a key component of de Vries's industrious revolution. In focusing on the consumer through such a lens, we need to consider who bought groceries, in what quantities, and in what ways. The extent to which consumption (especially of new groceries) permeated all levels of society can tell us much about the penetration of the market, but also about the depth of any transformation in consumer behaviour and attitudes. The obvious dividing lines here are between different social strata, but gender differences are also significant, especially given the strong associations drawn by Smith, Schivelbusch, Vickery, and others between particular commodities and gender identities. Looking into people's shopping baskets and cupboards to see the types of goods that they were purchasing and consuming (Chapters 8 and 9) reveals something of their identity and domestic consumption practices. It also provides insights into the everyday reality of 'consumption bundles', seen by de Vries as instrumental in shaping consumer behaviour. Shopping practices too are seen as dividing along class lines, especially in Berry's model of polite consumption, but these apparent divisions need to be examined more closely and the sociability of the shop explored in more detail. How did different people and social groups behave in shops, and what does this tell us about their attitudes and motivations as consumers?

Linked closely to this is the question of what made goods attractive to consumers. Here, the need is to examine in detail the relative merits of novelty, luxury, and pleasure as explanatory concepts in terms of both the uptake of groceries and consumer changes more generally. Novelty can usefully be juxtaposed with continuity and tradition, but we need to consider how goods moved from one category to the other, and how novel items were incorporated within existing groups of goods and established practices and processes of consumption. Luxury is often associated with the intrinsic qualities of goods, so we need to think how this could play out with groceries (what made spices, chocolate, or green tea luxuries?) and what comprised luxury for different social groups. Perhaps surprisingly, comfort and pleasure have been afforded less attention in the context of new groceries and require proper critical analysis. These issues are explored in the context of provincial shops, but also in the store cupboards and on the tables of consumers (Chapters 1, 9, and 10). While all three ideas are seen as dynamic, driving forward change in consumer behaviour and material culture, we need to consider the extent to which they operated within value systems that remained steady across time and different social groups. This means critically engaging with theorizations, such as the new 'cultural contexts' seen by Smith as framing the consumption of imported groceries. We need to question how far social change was driven by the availability of new goods and deploy some healthy scepticism about the extent to which consumers operated as part of some grand scheme, such as the making of respectability.

Last, and perhaps most important, is the contribution that can be made to debates about the nature of consumer change in eighteenth-century England: is it possible to rescue the idea of consumer revolution? Three aspects of this are particularly important: the shift towards a new material culture; the motivations that underpinned consumption, and the link between consumption and identity. If we take these in turn, there is little doubt that material culture was transformed during the early modern period, but the precise timing and character of any changes remain open to debate, as does the extent to which they penetrated all levels of society. Analysing the changing ownership of goods linked to the consumption of groceries (Chapter 10) provides an opportunity to engage in these broader debates and to assess the importance of 'consumption bundles' within this process. The question of consumer motivation (Chapters 1, 9, and 10) takes us back to ideas of novelty, luxury, and utility, but also forwards to think about how consumption practices were driven by emulation, taste, and distinction, a restless desire for new experiences, and so on. In assessing what motivated the consumption of (new) groceries, we need to think whether it is possible to generalize across different social groups and also whether we can transfer these insights into consumer change in general. In short, were consumer motivations specific to particular commodities and groups? If so, what does this tell us about the link between consumption and identity? Much has been written about the knowing consumer, but to what extent is it possible to identify such a figure, in terms of either the goods they owned or their shopping practices?

In addressing these various themes, this book places the grocer and the grocery trade at the centre of changes in retailing and consumption. It grounds the cultural analysis of novelties such as tea and coffee in the day-to-day activities of buying and selling, and links the world of global politics and international trade to the shop counter and the dinner table.

1

Ancient and Modern: The Grocery Trade in Early Modern England

INTRODUCTION

The traditional picture of retailing before 1650 portrays a system that was underdeveloped and highly dependent upon periodic forms of exchange. Most households were able to supply many of their own needs: all but the very poorest could raise some livestock or grow some food, and some could spin their own yarn and make clothing. Markets were the chief source of fresh food and other necessities, and were closely regulated to ensure fair trading and protect what were sometimes uncertain supplies. Fairs gave access both to staples and to a wide range of semi-luxuries, providing a window onto an expanding world of goods; but they were present for only a few days in the year. More permanent, if highly specialized, were direct sales from guild-controlled craftsmen. Only later did retail shops and pedlars provide households with the ability to make regular purchases of a wide range of consumer goods—a development that, de Vries argues, coincided causally with increasing market orientation of households engaged in Z-consumption.[1] This picture is partial at best: pre-modern retail systems had long been characterized by a large number and variety of shops and selds, which formed a permanent presence for retailers in towns and helped to make shopping an everyday occurrence, especially in London and the major provincial cities.[2] In less urbanized areas, fairs continued to provide a greater choice of goods and perhaps keener prices than those generally available in small towns and villages, but their significance gradually declined through the sixteenth and seventeenth centuries.[3] Renewed urban growth, increasingly reliable systems of long-distance trade, an influx of novel goods from both the Old and the New World, and, above all perhaps, changing attitudes to shopping all placed greater emphasis on the fixed shop well before the mid-seventeenth century.[4]

---

[1] De Vries, *Industrious Revolution*, 169–70, 26–37. In its timing, this switch matches McKendrick's argument for an eighteenth-century birth of consumer society; see McKendrick, 'Consumer Revolution'.

[2] Selds were larger structures housing a number of traders, each with their own retail space. Keene, 'Sites of Desire'.

[3] Addison, *English Fairs*, 120–51; Davis, *History of Shopping*, 25–54, 100–55; Mitchell, 'Changing Role of Fairs'.

[4] A useful overview of the retail trade at this time is found in Stobart, *Spend, Spend, Spend*, 21–40. See also Morrison, *English Shops*, 5–29; Davis, *History of Shopping*, 3–24; Farmer, 'Marketing the Produce'.

The position of the grocery trade within these wider processes of retail change is of considerable importance, not least because of the close association between groceries and the construction of 'consumption bundles' which marked Z-commodities.[5] To what extent was the retailing of groceries a specialized and shop-based activity in the early modern period, and what are the implications of this for the timing and completeness of the switch to market-oriented households theorized by de Vries? Addressing these questions and assessing long-term change and continuity in the retailing of groceries focuses our attention onto three main areas. First is the issue of what constituted and defined a grocer during the medieval and early modern periods. Retail trades—indeed all trades—are usually defined in terms of the goods being sold, distinctions sometimes being enshrined in guild regulations. Yet grocers were different: there were guilds that defined and delimited the trade in terms of the goods being sold, but there were other definitions that focused on the nature of retailing, most obviously the notion of selling gross or in bulk. These distinctions are important, as they have an impact on the standing of those identified as grocers, which, in turn, links to their ability to shape consumption practices and the development of retailing in England. Second, and linked to this, is the more general issue of the grocer's position in broader processes of consumer revolution and thus to long-term shifts in the nature of grocers' business and stock-in-trade. The widespread availability of novel or exotic goods during the early modern period would suggest an earlier and deeper penetration of consumer culture than has previously been suggested, especially if these goods were being bought by 'ordinary' households. Third is the rise of a set of new groceries that are often seen as transforming both the grocer's stock and the consumption practices of people across Europe: sugar, tobacco, chocolate, coffee, and tea. Much has been written about these commodities and about the motivations that lay behind their rapid rise in popularity, from de Vries's model of the changing household economy to Schivelbusch's notion of bourgeois sobriety and Smith's 'making of respectability'.[6] Of particular significance to my argument through the rest of the book is the extent to which these goods were viewed as exotic luxuries, vehicles for augmenting status or shaping identity, or pleasurable additions to the diet, and how they were incorporated into or transformed existing frameworks of consumption.[7]

STATUS AND STANDING

Rees traces the origins of grocers to the London Pepperers' Guild, chartered in 1180. Their ordinances reveal that they sold a range of spices and confectionary and generally sold in gross; indeed, one or two of the members were referred to as

---

[5] De Vries, *Industrious Revolution*, 31–7.

[6] See, e.g., Mintz, *Sweetness and Power*; Smith, *Consumption*; Cowan, *Social Life of Coffee*; Coe and Coe, *History of Chocolate*; Norton, 'Tasting Empire'; Bickham, 'Eating Empire'; Schivelbusch, *Tastes of Paradise*; de Vries, *Industrious Revolution*, 122–86.

[7] These are themes that are explored briefly in this chapter, but discussed more fully in Chs 9 and 10.

'grossarius' in City and Guild records.[8] Following the failure of the Pepperers' Guild in 1345, twenty-two of its members founded a new fraternity, which was, by 1373, referred to as the Company of Grossers—a title amended three years later when their ordinances were revised and extended to the Company of Grocers of London. This included the pepperers of Sopers Lane, the spicers of Cheapside, and the canvassers of the Ropery (who dealt in goods related to shipping).[9] From the outset, then, grocers were a diverse group, dealing in a range of goods. They added to this over the years, with apothecaries and later tobacconists also coming under the jurisdiction of the Company of Grocers. The skills or mysteries that they sought to protect were those of 'garbling' (that is, sifting and cleaning spices) and preparing these and other commodities for sale. These were periodically renewed and refined through a series of ordinances that frequently sought to link these practices to consumer protection. Thus, in 1447, the Company of Grocers petitioned the king, arguing that a wide range of goods, including dried fruits, treacle, oils and confections, were 'daily sold to the subjects not at all cleansed, garbled and searched, to the manifest deceit and hurt of our subjects'. In his reply, the king granted these powers to the grocers, so that 'none of our subjects may be deprived of benefit in buying any of the aforesaid spices, drugs and merchandise, nor by the buying of these kind to be in any wise hurt in their bodily health'.[10]

These privileges were peculiar to the City of London, but similar arrangements were established in many provincial towns—at least those with corporations that could sanction and enforce such regulations. However, the diversity of stock and skills that came under the remit of the grocers sometimes brought them into conflict with other tradesmen and guilds over the right to sell certain goods. Perhaps the most significant in terms of the nature of the grocery trade was that between the grocers' and physicians' companies over control of apothecaries. Tensions began in the 1560s and came to a head in the early seventeenth century, when apothecaries began agitating for their own company, arguing in a petition of 1614 that:

many imperfect and unskilful persons do make and sell, without restraint, false and corrupt medicines...to the disgrace and prejudice of the noble science of physic and of the learned physicians and of such as are skilful in the art of apothecaries, and to the imminent danger of your subjects healths and lives which abuses by your said subjects remaining one body politic with the Company of Grocers, hath not hitherto nor cannot receive any due reformation.[11]

Here again we have arguments about the link between proper regulation and public health. Despite counterclaims from the grocers, the king granted the apothecaries their own company in 1617, subsequent legal judgments drawing the fine line

[8] Rees, *Grocery Trade*, i. 16–19. Rees finds evidence of spicers' guilds in Newcastle, York, and elsewhere around the same time, while Priestly and Fenner, *Shops and Shopkeepers*, 6, suggest that spicers were an established part of the retail trade in Norwich from the fourteenth century.
[9] Rees, *Grocery Trade*, i. 31–40.
[10] Quoted in Rees, *Grocery Trade*, i. 67.
[11] Quoted in Rees, *Grocery Trade*, i. 222.

between apothecaries' and grocers' areas of trade. The former were licensed to make and sell medicines, and to sell seeds and roots used for medicines, distilled waters, pills, syrups, conserves, and ointments. They also had the first offer to buy other drugs 'peculiar to ye Apothecaries' and the right to sell grocers' goods, but not 'in grosse'. Grocers, meanwhile, were allowed to continue selling sweets, scents, spices, wax, 'wormed tobacco', painters' and dyers' materials, vermillion, isinglass, gum Arabic, mercury, quicksilver, and arsenic.[12] In short, there was considerable overlap between the goods in which London's apothecaries and grocers were licensed to trade.

Guild regulations and ordinances thus identified the grocer as a distinct and dignified tradesman, and one of some standing—at least within corporate towns. Yet there were other understandings of the grocer's trade that owed less to the range of goods being sold and more to the ways in which the retailers operated. Cox argues that the term grocer was generally used either for someone who sold in gross or for small shopkeepers selling everyday items to the poorer sections of society.[13] The first of these links to the practices of the London pepperers and grocers who acted as wholesalers as well as retailers; but it carries other connotations, since engrossing (that is, the buying and hoarding of large quantities of a commodity in order to push up prices) was expressly outlawed. In this sense, unless they were importing merchants, those dealing in bulk might be seen as profiteering and circumventing the moral economy of the marketplace. The incorporated London grocers were largely immune from such accusations since they dealt primarily in imported goods, which required the middle man to break bulk and process the commodities being shipped. With other tradesmen, especially those in smaller provincial towns, this was more problematic. Some undoubtedly dealt in bulk, but the term grocer was often used more loosely and in some cases interchangeably with mercer.[14] Equating grocers with small shopkeepers puts them on an altogether different footing—something more akin to the ubiquitous provisions dealer of the early nineteenth century.[15]

What, then, are we to make of the term 'grocer' in the medieval and early modern periods? At one level, we might draw a distinction between the London grocers, described by Rees as 'ministers of luxuries to the rich', and the lowlier provincial dealer, supplying everyday goods to a local clientele.[16] The contrast here probably comes in terms of the customers being served rather than the stock carried, although the scope and range of the London grocer were clearly far greater, not least because of their close connections with the Italian merchants who supplied

---

[12] Star Chamber Judgement, 4 Aug. 1620, copied into Apothecaries Ordinance Book, London Metropolitan Archive, MS 8251, fo. 81. For fuller discussion, see Parkinson, *Nature's Alchemist*, 177–8.

[13] Cox, *Complete Tradesman*, 204.

[14] See Stone, 'Grocers and Groceries', 42–8, for some seventeenth-century examples of provincial wholesaling grocers.

[15] Alexander, *Retailing in England*, 59–60, 110–11, 127–8; Blackman, 'Retail Grocery Trade', 116; Burnett, *Plenty and Want*, 55.

[16] Rees, *Grocery Trade*, i. 51.

so many of their goods. A contrast might also be drawn between the substantial tradesman located on major thoroughfares and their counterparts on the back streets. Again, the customers served would have been very different, as would the degree of specialization—back-street shops selling groceries as part of a wider array of everyday goods. In reality, though, all these tradesmen made a growing range of groceries available to a wide variety of consumers across the country, helping to transform the consumption practices of even modest households.[17]

It is clear that grocers were never a closely defined set of tradesmen, the mixed profile found in the early nineteenth century being a feature common to earlier periods.[18] In corporate towns, all tradesmen were supposed to be freemen. This status could sometimes be purchased from the corporation, but it was usually gained through serving an apprenticeship with a guild member, who charged a premium in return for inducting the apprentice into the mysteries of the trade. The rates charged by different trades give us an idea of their relative attraction in terms of social standing, wealth, and profitability. The usual premium charged by London grocers in the medieval period was £10, rising to £100 by the early seventeenth century. Rates were much lower in the provinces, William Stout being apprenticed to a Lancaster grocer and ironmonger in 1679 for a premium of just £20.[19] These rates put grocers somewhere in the middle of retail trades, a position confirmed by Campbell's assessment of London trades in the mid eighteenth century (Table 1.1). The most costly apprenticeships were with mercers and drapers, where set-up costs were also highest. Grocers were bracketed with apothecaries, hosiers, and booksellers; earthenware shops, stationers, and haberdashers being far cheaper trades to enter.[20]

When setting up their children in trade, families had to take a variety of costs into consideration and balance these against the likely returns. Indeed, Campbell's book (and others like it[21]) was in part directed at assisting in these choices and it contained a scathing commentary on the value of apprenticeship. Of oilmen he wrote that it was 'worth no lad's while to slave seven years in this dirty shop for any knowledge he can reap from his Master on his practice', while grocers had 'nothing to learn but the market price of goods, and to be so cunning as not sell for less than they buy'.[22] Defoe was just as critical, believing that the value of apprenticeship lay in learning about running a business—a skill that involved being acquainted with processes of buying as well as selling stock, and being incorporated into his master's network of contacts.[23] Inevitably, some apprentices were unhappy with their lot,

[17] De Vries, *Industrious Revolution*, 154–64.
[18] See Alexander, *Retailing in England*, 59–60; Mui and Mui, *Shops and Shopkeeping*, 129–32; Priestley and Fenner, *Shops and Shopkeepers*, 6–7.
[19] Stout, *Autobiography*, 73. Rees, *Grocery Trade*, i. 87, 252, suggests that country grocers would charge premiums of £35–£50.
[20] Campbell, *London Tradesman*. For fuller discussion of these costs, see Cox, *Complete Tradesman*, 165–9; Earle, *English Middle Class*, 106–12.
[21] See, e.g., Defoe, *Compleat English Tradesman* (1726); Clare, *Youth's Introduction to Trade* (1758); Collyer, *Parents and Guardians Directory* (1761).
[22] Campbell, *London Tradesman*, 283, 335.
[23] Defoe, *Compleat English Tradesman*, i. 10, 15, 35.

Table 1.1. Start-up costs and income levels for selected trades in London, 1747, and York, 1797 (£)

| Trade | London, 1747 | | York, 1797 | |
	Apprenticeship	Set-up costs	Average income	Range
Mercer	50–200	1,000–10,000	—	—
Woollen draper	50–200	1,000–5,000	184	100–400
Hosier	20–200	500–5,000	—	—
Apothecary	20–200	50–200	218	100–400
Grocer	20–100	500–2,000	200	100–350
Bookseller	20–100	50–100	180	80–350
Ironmonger	30–100	500–2,000	149*	70–200
Tobacconist	30–100	100–5,000	110	70–150
China shop	5–100	100–2,000	225	200–300
Haberdasher	10–50	100–2,000	149	60–250
Stationer	20–30	100–2,000	—	—
Confectioner	10–40	100–300	119†	80–150
Earthenware shop	5–20	100–300	—	—
Slop shop	<5	—	—	—
Petty grocers	—	—	77	60–100

* hardware dealer; † confectioner and fruiterer.

Sources: Campbell, *London Tradesman*, 331–40; Mui and Mui, *Shops and Shopkeeping*, 129.

Roger Lowe recording in 1664 that he 'thought it sad for me to be ingaged 9 years to stay in Ashton to sell my Master's ware and get no knowledge'.[24] Despite such reservations, grocers continued to advertise for apprentices well into the nineteenth century. A 'grocer and tea-man' named William Wood, for example, placed a notice in the Liverpool press in 1820 asking for an apprentice: 'one from the Country, and of the Society of Friends, will be preferred. As he will board in the House and be treated as one of the Family, a premium will be expected.'[25] Even at this date, then, an apprenticeship was seen as an undertaking in which it was worth investing time and money.

Premiums varied within as well as between trades, as did incomes. By the end of the eighteenth century, grocers were among the wealthiest retailers in York, with average incomes exceeded only by chemists and china dealers (Table 1.1), but there was clearly a long tail in terms of income, 'petty grocers' or provisions dealers being considerably less wealthy. Such variations were long-standing. In medieval London, grocers had been among the leading citizens: thirty-nine served as Lord Mayor in the period 1231–1500, some on a number of occasions.[26] Elsewhere, grocers appear on town corporations, often in growing numbers. In Norwich, they were among the trading elite, with individuals such as Augustine Briggs (alderman,

[24] Lowe, *Diary*, 16 Oct. 1664.
[25] *Liverpool Mercury*, 29 Dec. 1820. See also *Bristol Mercury*, 25 Aug. 1821.
[26] Rees, *Grocery Trade*, i. 73–4.

mayor, and Member of Parliament) being worth over £9,000 at his death in 1684.[27] Yet there were always those who operated at a lower social and economic scale, some working at the margins of regulated trade. The ordinances of the London Company of Grocers often railed against those who tried to interlope onto the privileges of its members. Centuries later, the corporation in York was similarly exercised by illegal trading. In 1775, a committee was established to pursue trades-men who were unwilling or unable to pay the £25 fee required to obtain their freedom and thus legally trade in the city. Among a total of 239 offenders, they prosecuted five grocers: one paid his fee after being sued; another agreed to give over trading; a third was thrown into debtors' prison for refusing to pay; a fourth managed to evade the committee, and the fifth was recognized as being too poor to pay more than 20 shillings.[28]

Such divisions were no doubt real, but they draw attention away from the more typical seller of groceries. This was characterized by Defoe as respectable rather than showy, living in a house that was comfortably furnished with tables from London, rugs from Westmorland, kitchenware from Birmingham and glassware from Stourbridge, rather than being filled with ostentatious imported luxuries.[29] This chimes with the evidence from probate inventories. In a small sample of sixteen retailers selling groceries in the late sixteenth and early seventeenth centu-ries, inventoried wealth ranged from £6 up to £122, but over half the shopkeepers had between £35 and £56. They were not rich and powerful, nor were they eking out a marginal existence: their houses were plainly but reasonably well furnished, with an emphasis on beds, bedding, linen, pewter and brassware—traditional forms of domestic material culture.[30] Occasionally, decorative items lightened the scene, as with John Cross of Huyton in Lancashire who had five wrought cushions. Lawrence Newall of Rochdale, meanwhile, had £12 worth of apparel and a sizeable collection of books valued at £1 6s. 8d. suggesting that he had some standing in the town.[31] These were respectable tradesmen whose household economies broadly mirrored those of their customers: they were part of a consumer culture that valued decent, pleasurable goods, rather than novelties and luxuries. Significantly, and in common with many of their neighbours, the majority of their wealth was held as stock-in-trade.

STOCKS, SUPPLIES, AND CUSTOMERS

From their inception, grocers were closely linked to the sale of imported foods, especially spices. The essential stock of the medieval grocer in London can be discerned from the goods with which the company's five porters were to be paid in

---

[27] Priestly and Fenner, *Shops and Shopkeepers*, 6.
[28] Mui and Mui, *Shops and Shopkeeping*, 131–2.
[29] Defoe, *Compleat English Tradesman*, i. 348–9. See Ch. 10 for more discussion of the material culture of the grocer's home.
[30] See Overton et al., *Production and Consumption*, 87–120.
[31] LRO, WCW 1639, John Cross; LRO, WCW 1649, Lawrence Newall.

1379. There were dyes such as alum, madder and woad; spices and seeds including pepper, ginger, cinnamon, cumin, anise, liquorice, and rice; currants and dates; soap and several kinds of wax; yarn, canvas, cotton, flax and paper, and sugar. In large provincial towns, a similar variety of goods was being sold by grocers. Rees quotes two legal cases involving mid-fifteenth-century Nottingham grocers who were seeking to secure payment for goods supplied. These included: pepper, saffron, ginger, cloves, mace, cinnamon, draget powder, frankincense, sanders, wax, salt, and currants.[32] From this, it is clear that exotic imported groceries were available from provincial suppliers from an early date, but it seems likely that retailers in smaller towns were able to provide only a more limited range of spices, seeds, and fruits. For example, while the stock of a fifteenth-century Leicester mercer incorporated a wide variety of cloth, haberdashery, and hardware, it included only honey, raisins, vegetable seeds, and salt by way of groceries.[33]

The range of stock held by grocers remained fairly stable through the early modern period, although sugar became increasingly important. In *A Winter's Tale* we have the shepherd's son deciding what to buy for the shearing feast:

Three pounds of sugar. Five pounds of currants. Rice. (What will this sister of mine do with rice?) I must have saffron to colour the warden pies. Mace, Dates, none—that is out of my note. Nutmegs, seven. A race or two of ginger (but that I may beg). Four pounds of prunes and as many of raisins of the sun.[34]

That all these came from the grocer indicates something of their status as purveyors of special foods: this is, after all, a shopping list for a feast. The goods listed might even be seen as luxuries, at least in terms of cost. While one of the flock cared for by this shepherd could have been bought for 1*s*. 5*d*., the pepper he was sent for cost 1*s*. 4*d*. per pound; mace was 8*s*., cloves 8*s*, sugar 4½*d*., currants 2*d*., and prunes 1½*d*. The ginger that he hoped to beg was 4*s*. per pound, suggesting that he had a good relationship with his grocer or real confidence in his ability to negotiate.[35] More importantly, these costly imported foods were all familiar to this shepherd (and his audience, in both the play and the theatre) and were clearly not the exclusive domain of the wealthy. There are also some indications that London grocers at least were becoming more specialized in their stock during this period. Davis suggests that they lost something of their 'marine store' character to concentrate more on non-perishable foods. Of particular importance here was the sale of sugar, the price of which fell through the later sixteenth and seventeenth centuries as New World supplies were developed (see Chapter 2). It was joined on the shelves of a growing number of grocer's shops by another New World commodity: tobacco. Demand for traditional wares such as spices and fruit was also buoyant during this period, imports of the latter increasing fourfold in the century leading up to the

---

[32] Rees, *Grocery Trade*, i. 26, 89–90.
[33] Cited in Davis, *History of Shopping*, 18–19.
[34] Shakespeare, *Winter's Tale*, IV. iii. Wardens are pears; race is the root of ginger.
[35] The prices come from Earl of Northumberland's Household Book of 1512. Costs increased markedly during Elizabeth's reign—part of a wider problem of inflation—and by 1577, sugar was 1*s*. 3*d*. per pound, currants were 4½*d*. and raisins 3*d*. See Rees, *Grocery Trade*, 119–20.

Table 1.2. Commodities stocked by grocery retailers, *c.*1660–1830

Commodity (no. of varieties)	% with commodity	Mean no. of varieties per shop
Sugar (11)	52.9	1.2
Tobacco (4)	64.7	0.9
Spices (19)	82.4	3.8
Apothecary wares (8)	52.9	1.3
Seeds (7)	41.2	0.8
Fruit and nuts (12)	70.6	1.7
Spirits (5)	29.4	0.3
Other culinary groceries (10)	41.2	0.9
Hops, cheese, grain, etc. (13)	23.5	0.2
Dyes, starch, etc. (15)	64.7	1.6
Soap, candles, etc. (14)	88.2	2.9

Source: probate inventories.

civil war. As one commentator observed: 'the very Greeks that sell them wonder what we do with such great quantities thereof, and know not how we should spend them except we use them for dyeing or to feed hogges'—a comment that again suggests that these were far from rarely consumed luxuries.[36]

By the early seventeenth century, then, the London grocer's shop was, above all, a place to buy imported food, although its stock still overlapped considerably with that of apothecaries and chandlers. Much the same was true of provincial retailers, lists of stock in probate inventories indicating that a wide variety of goods were being sold (Table 1.2).[37] The core of the grocer's stock was spices and chandlery ware (soap, candles, wax, pitch, and so forth), which were not only sold by the vast majority of grocery retailers, but also stocked in greatest variety. Across the seventeen shops analysed, there were fourteen different culinary spices, from grains of paradise to saffron, plus a number of seeds also used in cooking (including fennel and caraway); but pepper was easily the most common, being sold in nearly two-thirds of the shops. Other traditional lines were also widespread, as were some newer commodities. Dried fruits, dyestuffs, and tobacco were all found in around two-thirds of shops, the last representing impressive penetration for a product introduced to Britain only a generation or two earlier (see below). Sugar was less widespread, being found in only half the shops, as were apothecary wares. That said, they could both be found in impressive variety in certain shops: that of James Oldfield, a Macclesfield mercer who died in 1635, contained treacle, white and brown candy, and sugar in loaf and powdered form.[38] Perhaps more striking, though, is the absence of everyday foods such as flour, hops, and cheese, suggesting that these were still purchased primarily at the market and that grocers were not general provisions dealers.

[36] Quoted in Davis, *History of Shopping*, 93–4; Moryson, *Itinerary*, iv. 176.
[37] See also Willan, *Inland Trade*, 61.
[38] CALS, WS 1635, James Oldfield.

Few provincial retailers stocked any of these goods in large quantities. Lawrence Newall of Rochdale was fairly typical, his 1649 inventory listing, among other things: 2 lbs 14 oz of long pepper, 4 lb of grains, 16 lb of sweet soap, 4 lb of starch, 3 lb 8 oz of red lead, and 1 lb of bayberries. The combined value of these goods (17*s.* 3*d.*) was easily overshadowed by his stock of sugar loaves (worth £4 2*s.*), tobacco (£3 5*s.* 11*d.*) and indigo (£10 4*s.*).[39] These three were key commodities for Newall, but were themselves overshadowed by the woollen cloth, wool, yarn, and thread that also appeared in his shop. These were worth £83 14*s.* 5*d.* and appear to have been more important in defining his identity as a shopkeeper, since he is described as a mercer. Such combinations of stock were typical of provincial shops, groceries sometimes appearing very much as a sideline to another area of activity. For example, Simon Harbert of St Stephen in Cornwall was a tailor by trade. He had about 50 yards of cloth, 84 stockings, and a variety of threads, points, pins, and lace, but also sold soap and an unspecified range of spices, probably from the room in which he did his tailoring.[40] This questions the extent to which grocery selling was specialized, even if it was primarily shop based. But the true grocer stood out in terms of the range and depth of stock: the 1598 inventory of Thomas Finnies, a Coventry grocer, listed ten different spices, three sorts of dried fruit, and three grades of sugar. Coventry, of course, was a major urban centre; but even small town and village shops stocked an impressive range of groceries. The Charlbury mercer Thomas Harris (d. 1632) had six sorts of spices, four kinds of dried fruit, four different dyestuffs, three grades of sugar, and a wide variety of chandlery. His near contemporary Peter Harries sold groceries in the Warwickshire village of Grandborough. His shop contained, among other things: pepper, mace, nutmeg, cloves, ginger, turmeric, liquorice, sugar candy and loaves, logwood, verdigris, indigo, brimstone, soap, candles, wax, and tobacco pipes.[41] This level of provision gave consumers access to a wide variety of commodities, linking a broadening world of goods to towns and villages across the country, and suggesting that these goods were already a regular part of the diet of many provincial households in the seventeenth century.[42]

The shops from which these goods were sold appear to have been simply furnished.[43] Lawrence Newall, for example, had weights and balances, scales, boxes, chests, shelves, and a shop board worth an impressive £3 12*s.* 8*d.* Similarly, Thomas Harris had shelves, boxes and chests, barrels and firkins, weights and scales; John Capel of Birmingham also had a nest of boxes, as did Thomas Finnies and James Oldfield. The exact nature of these boxes is hard to determine, and it is likely that

---

[39] LRO, WCW 1649, Lawrence Newall. I am grateful to Nancy Cox for supplying a copy of this inventory.

[40] CRO, H123, Simon Harbert (1606). The only shopkeepers not selling other types of goods were the apothecary John Staine (LiRO, B/C/11, 1615) and the tobacconist John Loveday (LiRO, B/C/11 1635).

[41] LiRO, B/C/11, Thomas Finnies (1598); LiRO, B/M, Peter Harries (1614); ORO, Thomas Harris (1632).

[42] De Vries, *Industrious Revolution*, 154–64.

[43] For a fuller discussion of the furnishing of early shops, see Cox, *Complete Tradesman*, 87–8; Keene, 'Sites of Desire', 129–32, 144–9.

they varied considerably between and within shops. Oldfield had draw boxes, middle boxes, and old boxes; the fact that he had 'old ginger that is in the box without the lide' suggests that others were lidded in some way.[44] All these men had mortars and pestles, those of Newall and Harris being especially noteworthy as they weighed in at 31 lb and 16¾ lb respectively. These were used for grinding spices before sale, indicating that some time and skill were needed in preparing as well as selling groceries.[45] Elsewhere, effort was made to package up goods for sale, Oldfield having 15 oz of pepper 'that is made up in pennyworths and half penny-worth'. All this suggests a well-developed trade that reached into the smallest of towns, anticipating by half a century the commercial growth seen as essential in facilitating the industrious revolution.

It would be a mistake, however, to think of the fixed shop as the only venue from which these retailers might sell their wares. The 1606 inventory of Robert Bennett is particularly intriguing in this regard. No occupation is given on his inventory, but his lengthy list of highly varied stock suggests that his business was extensive and wide-ranging: it incorporated textiles, haberdashery, hardware, and groceries.[46] Bennett does not appear to have had a shop as such; rather he operated from a series of fairs spread across Cornwall. He had three fair boards, two trestles, and a fair pole in his house in Tregony. There were four more fair poles at Helston, about 20 miles away, and another three with a Mr Cowling in Madron in the far west of the county, whilst a further five boards were at Probus, just a few miles from his home. Whether he sold wholesale or retail is unclear, but the quantities of some items suggest that he was dealing directly with customers for some goods. It seems unlikely, however, that these periodic events could have been the only outlet for some of his groceries: almonds, raisins, currants, and figs would all have benefited from a more regular turnover, as is indicated by the presence in his inventory of a barrel of 'bad figs'.

In some respects, Bennett's business was an echo of an earlier age. In medieval times, the great fairs were major events, affording local consumers a rare opportunity to acquire a whole range of exotic goods. In 1226, for example, Henry III had requested the mayor of Winchester to buy Alexandrian sugar for him at the great Winchester fair. They continued to be important into the sixteenth century. From Wollaton Hall in Nottinghamshire, for example, the Willoughbys made purchases of sugar, comfits, dried fruits, spices, and many other goods at Stour-bridge and Lenton fairs. Around the same time, the Earl of Northumberland's Head Clerk visited a number of fairs in the north of England to buy salt, honey, oil, verjuice, mustard, and twenty-three types of spices.[47] While fairs had undoubtedly lost much of their importance by the seventeenth century, in less urbanized areas, such as Cornwall, they remained a significant part of retailing for much

[44] LiRO, B/C/11, John Capel (1631); see nn. 36 and 37 for other references.
[45] Harris's was explicitly labelled as a 'spice mortar'. Given that their value was calculated per pound in weight, it is likely that they were metal.
[46] CRO, B1531, Robert Bennett (1606).
[47] Mintz, *Sweetness and Power*, 82; Davis, *History of Shopping*, 43–51; Dawson, *Plenti and Grase*, 161–73.

longer. More generally, they provided an opportunity for local shopkeepers to restock, perhaps buying from men such as Bennett who acted as middlemen between the retailer and the merchant. This was particularly important with groceries, many of which came from overseas. Through to the sixteenth century, spices and various Mediterranean products came via the major Italian ports. The *Libel of English Policy*, written by Adam de Moleyns in 1436–7, refers among many other things to Seville oil and grain, white Castile soap, and Spanish iron and wool. It particularly notes:

> The grete galee of Venees and Florence,
> Be wel ladene wyth thynges of complacence,
> All spicerye and all grocers ward,
> Wyth swete wynes, and all manere chafare.[48]

On the basis of such trade, the Italian merchants were a major force in medieval London. However, their power declined along with their trade in the sixteenth century as first the Portuguese and later the Dutch opened up sea routes to the Far East.

The detailed development of this trade is beyond the scope of the present discussion.[49] What does concern us, however, is the impact that this change had upon the supply of groceries within England. Of particularly significance in this respect is the establishment in 1600 of the East India Company, which was granted a monopoly of this new direct trade with the orient. Their early interest was focused on pepper, nutmeg, and mace; but later voyages brought home a much larger range of spices, not least as the company developed factories in Sumatra, Java, Borneo, Malacca, Celebes, Siam, Malabar, India, and elsewhere.[50] The trade was highly profitable, bringing returns of up to 340 per cent to the Adventurers who invested in voyages. It also produced a shift in the pattern of supply. As large consignments of spices were landed, stocks held by the company increased greatly, as did those of the king, who had privately invested in the trade. This brought the problem of how best to release these stocks without lowering prices, with both company and king anxious that grocers should buy only their spices and not those re-exported from the Low Countries.[51] Correspondence between the company and the court makes clear that most sales of imported spices were to London grocers. They, in turn, retailed some in their own shops; but much was sent out to country shopkeepers, for whom the London grocers operated as wholesalers, or carried by London tradesmen to provincial fairs. Indeed, it was the presence of London dealers that helped to make Lenton and other fairs the key point of supply for wealthy consumers into the sixteenth century. However, the provincial elite also made purchases of exotic foods directly from London shops when they visited the metropolis or drew on supplies from local

---

[48] *The Libelle of Englyche Polycye*, quoted in Salzman, *English Trade*, 461. De Moleyns was critical of England's reliance on this overseas trade, imported groceries, drugs, and so on being unnecessary and ephemeral. He made an exception for sugar.

[49] See Chaudhuri, *Trading World*, 1–18.

[50] Rees, *Grocery Trade*, i. 200–1, 211–18.

[51] Rees, *Grocery Trade*, i. 206–10.

retailers. Henry Willoughby occasionally bought sugar, comfits, and aqua vitae in London during 1522 and 1523, while the Derbyshire gentleman Ralph Gell purchased a variety of groceries through his son at Clement's Inn, the goods then being dispatched by carrier. In contrast, the Vernons of Haddon Hall in Derbyshire chose to buy most of their groceries in nearby Chesterfield and Ashbourne.[52]

Such local supplies were, of course, the only option for most consumers. Fairs were important, but their infrequency made them less well suited for the modest, day-to-day pattern of purchasing that characterized most households. Such people were more reliant upon shopkeepers. It is clear from the lists of debts appearing in inventories that many provincial retailers offered their customers credit by allow-ing them to purchase goods on account.[53] Lawrence Newall was typical in this regard. Debts owing to him were split between a 'litle paper booke' and 'grate debt Bookes'—a nominal distinction that is borne out by the size of accounts recorded in each. The former included thirty-four entries, all but five of them for less than £1 and many amounting to just a few shillings; the latter contained forty-nine debts, twenty-one of which were for under £1, the remainder averaging about £3. These small debts suggest modest purchases and perhaps a degree of control over the amount of credit extended to customers—something that was important for the success of the retail business.[54] Thirteen of the debts recorded in Newall's shop books were for specific items, many of which were being bought in very small amounts. William Clegge owed 4*d.* for currants; Joseph Kaye 4*d.* for long pepper; Robert Brearlaye 7*d.* for tobacco and Abel Dearden 6*d.* for half a pound of soap.[55] These were most likely single purchases, probably made for immediate consump-tion, suggesting that such groceries were items of everyday consumption by the mid-seventeenth century, even among ordinary households in a small provincial town. Moreover, over half of these debts were for two items that were relatively new to the grocer's shop, or at least newly available to such modest consumers: tobacco and sugar. Does this indicate an early democratization of consumption of these small luxuries or pleasures? At the very least, it shows that they too had penetrated deep into the early modern household economy. But what was the basis of this growth; what made these and other new groceries so attractive?

NEW GOODS: EXOTIC NOVELTIES TO EVERYDAY ITEMS?

As we have seen already, sugar was by no means a new item on the shelves of grocers' shops or in the homes of wealthier consumers. It was present in England from at least the twelfth century and regularly used in elite households from the thirteenth. The Countess of Leicester, for example, bought 55 lb of 'ordinary' and

---

[52] Dawson, *Plenti and Grase*, 162, 171–2.

[53] See also Cox, *Complete Tradesman*, 147, 149, 154; Willan, *Inland Trade*, 91.

[54] Many inventories recorded large quantities of debts that were unrecoverable, while the shop-keeper might spend an inordinate amount of time trying to secure payment from debtors; see Lowe, *Diary*, 28 Aug. 1663, 22 July 1664.

[55] LRO, WCW 1649, Lawrence Newall.

Table 1.3. Imports into England of selected groceries, 1699–1701 to 1772–4

Commodity	1699–1701		1722–4		1752–4		1772–4	
	£000s	Set to base	£000s	Set to base	£000s	Set to base	£000s	Set to base
Tobacco	249	1.0	262	1.1	560	2.3	519	2.1
Sugar	630	1.0	928	1.5	1,302	2.1	2,364	3.8
Coffee	27	1.0	127	4.7	53	2.0	436	16.2
Tea	8	1.0	116	14.5	334	41.8	848	106.0

Source: Davis, 'English Foreign Trade', 300–3.

powdered sugar over a seven-month period in 1265, while Bishop Swinfield's household got through more than 100 lb of sugar in 1289.[56] At this time, Mintz argues, it was primarily viewed and employed as a spice. Contemporary cookbooks show how it was integrated within existing systems of cooking, sugar being combined with ginger, pepper, cinnamon, and even honey in a wide range of meat dishes.[57] Although the quantities in these recipes are rather vague, it is clear that sugar was being deployed to augment the flavour of dishes rather than sweeten them. In this context, sugar was a quintessential luxury: consumed by the wealthy alongside other expensive spices and condiments in a way that communicated economic and cultural capital. For Mennell, cooking during this period was much more about these spices than it was about the foods into which they were mixed. He argues that, as tastes and with them cooking practices changed in the seventeenth century, so the use of spices stagnated or even declined. Perhaps, as Schivelbusch suggests, this change in taste was linked to a loss in the mystery and allure of spices as new sea routes made them more readily available.[58] If this is true, it is striking that the same fate did not befall sugar. On the contrary, consumption rose enormously during the early modern period and into the nineteenth century (Table 1.3).

The continued and growing appeal of sugar came from its other uses. One of these was as a medicine.[59] In order to make sense of sugar in this context, it was necessary to bring it within the existing modes of understanding the properties of commodities and the way in which they would influence the body. Most influential was the Galenic system, in which sugar was generally seen as warm and moist. It was preferable to hot, dry honey, because it 'agreeth with all ages, and all complexions; but contrawise, Honie annoyeth many, especially those that are cholerick, or full of winde in their bodies'.[60] Sugar was most frequently recommended against

[56] Labarge, *Baronial Household*, 96–7.
[57] Mintz, *Sweetness and Power*, 85–7; Lehmann, *British Housewife*, 22–5.
[58] Mennell, *All Manners of Food*, 62–133; Smith, *Consumption*, 86–97; Schivelbusch, *Tastes of Paradise*, 4–13.
[59] Mintz, *Sweetness and Power*, 96–108.
[60] Venner, *Plaine Philosophical Discourse*, 103.

digestive complaints and in prescriptions for coughs and sore throats; but it was also added to many other cures to make them either more palatable or more efficacious. Gervase Markham, for example, included sugar in his cures for a new cough (sugar soaked in aqua vitae) and an old cough (betony, caraway, dried skirret, hound's tooth, and pepper mixed with honey taken for nine days; followed by sugar, liquorice, aniseed, and coriander ground together and taken as required). It also features in treatments for consumption and to staunch blood, and as a vehicle to ease the ingestion of tonics for colic and stones.[61] Despite dissenting voices, sugar remained central to the apothecary's art well into the eighteenth century, while newspaper advertisements carried home-spun cures to a wider audience. One correspondent to the Chester press in 1774 offered a cold remedy that comprised 'a large tea-cup full of linseed, two pennyworth of stick-liquorish, a quarter of a pound of sun raisins'. These were to be put into four pints of water and boiled until reduced by half. After adding a quarter of a pound of brown sugar candy, a tablespoon of old rum, and another of best white wine vinegar, the liquor was to be drunk before going to bed or whenever the 'cough is troublesome'.[62]

Its persistence as a medicine is notable, but the most important uses of sugar by this date—and the fundamental reasons behind the surge in consumption in this period—were as a sweetener and preservative. The former had two distinct dimensions. First was the construction of elaborate decorative pieces for the dinner table. In a practice that spread from the Middle East, sugar was combined with crushed almonds, oils, and vegetable gums to create marzipan. This could be moulded into almost any shape desired before being baked hard to create what were known as 'subtleties', used to mark voids: the intervals between courses.[63] By the sixteenth century, the use of sugar in creating decorative jellies, marzipan sculptures, and other confections was widespread among the wealthy. A hundred years later, cookbooks invariably included instructions for creating a wide range of such dishes, but thereafter the fashion shifted onto spun-sugar decorations: equally elaborate, but arguably more subtle and refined. Despite the popular appeal of many eighteenth-century cookbooks, these decorative uses of sugar remained largely the preserve of a wealthy minority: they were luxury and in some sense positional goods that allowed consumers to communicate their wealth and status. Indeed, it is possible to go further and see in these confections evidence for Sombart's assertion of sugar as a female luxury. This connection is at first confirmed, but then undermined by the second aspect of sugar's deployment as a sweetener.[64] There was a long-established English tradition of using sugar to sweeten wine, especially when it was old. This appears to have waned in the early

[61] Markham, *English Housewife*, ed. Best, 15, 26–7, 34–5.

[62] *Adams Weekly Courant*, 29 Nov. 1774. Significantly, all the ingredients could be had from the grocer's shop, maintaining the blurred line between grocer and apothecary. Another advertisement, for a patent medicine, recommended putting a few drops on a lump of sugar (*Adams Weekly Courant*, 5 May 1778).

[63] Hall, 'Culinary Spaces', 173–5; Mintz, *Sweetness and Power*, 88.

[64] Sombart, *Luxury and Capitalism*, 99. For a more subtle reading, see Hall, 'Culinary Spaces'.

seventeenth century, but any decline was far outweighed by the growing practice of adding sugar to tea and coffee.[65] It is unclear exactly when this grew to prominence. Smith argues that tea and coffee were taken without sugar when they were first introduced, the practice spreading only slowly until the early eighteenth century. Indeed, he links sugar directly to the growing popularity of these drinks, particularly among women.[66] The practice was apparently widespread by 1706, when a medical tract argued that 'coffee, tea and chocolate were at first used only as medicines, while they continued unpleasant; but since they were made delicious with sugar, they are become poison'.[67] Initially linked with female taste, sweetened tea became ubiquitous among both sexes by the second half of the eighteenth century, much to the chagrin of social commentators, who railed against the poor wasting their money on such luxuries, despite the falling price of both commodities (see Chapter 9). Sugar as a preservative had a much longer history. Preserved fruit was an established delicacy among the English elite by the fifteenth century, but remained an expensive luxury until the price of sugar fell in the 1600s. A century later, both manuscript and published cookbooks abounded with recipes for preserving fruit in sugar, again marking the transition of sugar from a luxury to an everyday commodity.[68]

Tobacco was introduced to Britain rather later than sugar, but was the first commodity from the New World to penetrate and transform British cultures of consumption. It was initially adopted in Spain and Portugal in the early sixteenth century, but its popularity quickly spread across the Mediterranean and subsequently to the Middle East and to northern Europe. The rapid assimilation of tobacco can be seen in the visual portrayal of smoking. Early images played on its exoticism, tattooed Native Americans being shown standing alongside the tobacco plant, with long pipes held to their mouths, ready to smoke. Yet these images were counterbalanced by others showing urbane Europeans puffing contentedly. In contrast, the language used to describe the process of smoking was slow to develop: as late as 1627, commentators were struggling to find the right words, people being described as drinking or imbibing the smoke.[69] If its provenance made it exotic and alluring, this was reinforced and nuanced by the channels through which it came to Britain. Brooks traces two routes: one was via the Spanish army serving in Flanders in the 1560s—their practices being imitated by other soldiers, including those from England; the second was through the example of sailors and adventurers returning from the New World or the Mediterranean. According to Smith, the

---

[65] This use is highlighted in an early seventeenth-century satire entitled *Wine, Beer, Ale and Tobacco,* fo. A4, which opens with the following exchange:

SUGAR. Nutmeg?
NUTMEG. Sugar? Well met, how chance you wait not upon your Master, where's Wine now?
SUGAR. Oh sometimes without Sugar, all the while he's well if I be in his company, 'tis but for fashion sake, I wait upon him into a room now and then, but am not regarded; marry, when he is ill, he makes much of me...

[66] Smith, *Consumption*, 121–4.   [67] Duncan, *Wholesome Advice*, 12.
[68] Mintz, *Sweetness and Power*, 123–7. For a fuller discussion of these uses, see Ch. 9.
[69] Schivelbusch, *Tastes of Paradise*, 96–8.

latter in particular helped to associate tobacco and smoking with adventure and manliness. More specifically, Sir Walter Raleigh's use of it in promoting his colonial schemes in North America helped to create a link between tobacco and imperialism.[70] Indeed, its role in England's imperial ambitions was perhaps critical in overcoming the aversion to smoking strongly held and expressed by James I. In a pamphlet published in 1604, he argued that tobacco was injurious to health and, more importantly perhaps, offended genteel politeness and good manners. Smoking at the table was particularly abhorrent, not least because the 'filthy smoke and stinke thereof' would 'athwart the dishes, and infect the aire'. Moreover, tobacco was a luxury that caused addiction and weakened the virtuous will.[71]

Despite or perhaps because of these qualities, tobacco was consumed and imported in ever greater quantities through the late sixteenth and seventeenth centuries. Production was promoted in the North American colonies and discouraged at home; while a favourable excise regime offered protection against imports of what was often seen as better-quality Spanish American tobacco.[72] If the pace of growth slackened in the eighteenth century, then it was only relative to the earlier booms and the extraordinary expansion in imports of other goods (Table 1.3). Notwithstanding Smith's arguments, the key to this growth lay not so much in colonial associations or notions of assertive nationalism, and more in the things that tobacco did and was believed to do to the body and mind. Quite apart from its very real addictive qualities, tobacco was seen from the outset as having specific and general medicinal effects. Some seventeenth-century medical writers saw smoking as a general panacea, similar in its benefits to spa waters, for which there was also a growing fashion; but tobacco was also seen as a cure for a range of specific diseases, most notably syphilis.[73] A more definite impact, observed by many commentators, was the calming effect of smoking—an association that encouraged its use as a treatment for headaches and for psychic disorders such as melancholy. Like sugar, tobacco was easily incorporated into the Galenic system, being seen as hot and dry; it removed mucus and phlegm, a property that was seen as making the brain steadier and thus beneficial to mental activity.[74] Combined with its calming effect, this created an image of the smoker as contemplative and linked smoking with cordial sociability. It was closely linked to coffee-house culture and particularly with what Smith terms rational masculinity.[75] However, tobacco was also consumed by women: sometimes in terms of pipe smoking, but far more often—in the eighteenth century at least—through the practice of snuff taking. Originating in Spain, this reached its apogee in the French court. While never being quite so fashionable in England, it gained considerable popularity among elite men and women, who drew their inspiration from across the Channel. Snuff

[70] Brooks, *Mighty Leaf*, 35–44, 60–6; Smith, *Consumption*, 161–2.
[71] James I, *Counter-Blaste*, D1. Other pamphlets showed the lance and book of old being replaced by pipes and goblets, cards and dice—see Schivelbusch, *Tastes of Paradise*, 108.
[72] Smith, *Consumption*, 164–5; Goodman, *Tobacco*, 149–50. The suppression of domestic production was common across Europe.
[73] Brooks, *Mighty Leaf*, 35–44.   [74] Schivelbusch, *Tastes of Paradise*, 103.
[75] Smith, *Consumption*, 166–7.

taking became an important social ceremony: a means of presenting self and judging others, and one that required careful attention to deportment and etiquette.[76] In its emphasis on elegance, snuff in some ways anticipated the early nineteenth-century rise of cigar smoking; but its physiological effects were the same as smoking pipes—it dried the body and brain and thus aided mental activity.

Chocolate arrived in Europe around the same time as tobacco, being adopted first and most enthusiastically in Spain in the sixteenth century. From the outset, chocolate was linked to empire, through both its provenance and its initial uptake by the conquistadors.[77] However, unlike tobacco, its adoption by Europeans involved a lengthy and complex series of cultural and practical adaptations. The Aztecs prepared their chocolate by flavouring it with a range of local spices (including vanilla and chilli peppers) and more occasionally honey. It was served with a froth produced by pouring the drink from one container to another and was drunk cold. Norton argues that those who turned to chocolate drinking in the sixteenth century 'embraced the beverage in the manner in which it was presented to them, having no alternative way to think or feel about it'. Indeed, they imported not just chocolate and cacao, but also the range of Mesoamerican spices needed for its preparation.[78] Increasingly, however, the Spanish adapted chocolate to their own tastes and convenience: sugar was used as a sweetener; Old World spices were used in place of those from the New World (although here the aim might have been to reproduce the same flavours), and the drink was served hot. Yet the importance of frothing was maintained, with special *molinillo* produced to create the desired foam.

At the same time, the social meanings and cultural significance of chocolate were also shifting, although here the process of transition is more difficult to trace with real certainty. For the Aztecs, chocolate was special: the drink was consumed by the elite and the cacao beans held great economic value and symbolic meanings—the cacao pod representing the human heart.[79] In its journey to the European table, only the first of these was transported more or less intact; the others were replaced by a new set of associations. As with other novel commodities, chocolate was seen as having medicinal benefits and was duly incorporated in the Galenic system. Cacao itself was judged to be cold, but the spices with which it was prepared were hot, making the qualities of chocolate complex and varied. Yet its medical qualities do not appear to have played a large part in the growing popularity of chocolate in Europe. Of more importance was its position as a nutritious drink, which clerics could consume during periods of fasting, and its growing favour among the Spanish elite. From Spain, the fashion for drinking chocolate spread to Italy and France, where it became closely associated with luxury and leisure.[80] Among the aristocracy, it was generally taken at breakfast, either in bed or

---

[76] Schivelbusch, *Tastes of Paradise*, 131–2; Fennetaux, 'Toying with Novelty', 24–5.
[77] Coe and Coe, *History of Chocolate*, 108–21; Norton, 'Tasting Empire', 10–12.
[78] Norton, 'Tasting Empire', 7–8, 13–14; Coe and Coe, *History of Chocolate*, 86–93.
[79] Coe and Coe, *History of Chocolate*, 93–103.
[80] Coe and Coe, *History of Chocolate*, 129–64.

in the boudoir: its consumption a study in cultivated idleness and playful eroti-
cism. This tied into chocolate's enduring reputation as an aphrodisiac, which had
particularly potent effects in 'supplying the Testicles with a Balsam, or a Sap'.[81]

When chocolate arrived in England in the 1650s, then, it already carried a heavy
load of cultural baggage: some from the New World; most from Catholic Europe.
Schivelbusch makes much of the distinction between the decadence of Catholic
and *ancien regime* chocolate, and the intellectual entrepreneurialism reflected in
the Protestant taste for coffee. Certainly, there was a rather different attitude to
chocolate in England. Pepys was an enthusiastic drinker, recording in his diary on
6 January 1663 that he was 'Up, and Mr Creede brought a pot of chocloatt ready
made for our morning draught' and on 3 May 1664 that he 'went by agreement to
Mr Blands and there drank my morning draught in good Chocolatte'.[82] While he
took his chocolate in the morning, these were not the leisurely breakfast encounters of the aristocracy; they had a sense of urgency reflected in English instructions
for making chocolate that ensured expedient preparation suitable for 'men of
business'.[83]

If chocolate never really caught on in eighteenth-century Britain, part of the
reason was the availability of coffee and tea as alternatives. The first reports of
coffee drinking probably came to England through Leonhard Rauwolf's travel
narrative based on his visit to the Levant in the 1580s, which circulated in manuscript form long before it was translated in 1593. This described the mode in
which the Turks drank their coffee and presented some of its qualities—themes
that characterized many of the travel accounts that followed.[84] By the time it
arrived in the 1650s, therefore, the English literati were well aware of coffee's qualities and the social contexts in which it was drunk. Despite this, neither the East
India nor Levant Company appears to have seen much of a market for coffee in
England. That they were unduly cautious is clear from its rapid uptake (Table 1.3),
a phenomenon that was sufficient to cause some consternation, since coffee could
only be bought for cash from Turkish-dominated territories in the Middle East—a
position that offended mercantilist sensibilities. The answer suggested by some,
including members of the Royal Society, was to encourage coffee production in
English colonies in America and the West Indies along the lines seen for sugar and
tobacco. Although this took many years to develop (see Chapter 2), such sentiments linked coffee into England's imperial ambitions. Growing demand also
brought the opportunity to impose excise duty, charged from 1660 at a rate of 4*d*.
per gallon.[85] The nature of this tax suggests that it was mostly consumed at the
coffee houses that spread rapidly across London and, to a lesser extent, provincial
towns in the second half of the seventeenth century. However, Pepys also records
drinking coffee at home and at his friends' houses, where it was often taken with a

---

[81] Stubbes, *Natural History of Coffee*, 18. It is significant that many images of chocolate drinking
from the eighteenth century show chocolate being served by women to men. See Schivelbusch, *Tastes
of Paradise*, 88–94.
    [82] Schivelbusch, *Tastes of Paradise*, 92; Pepys, *Diary*, iv. 5; v. 139.
    [83] See Coe and Coe, *History of Chocolate*, 173.
    [84] Cowan, *Social Life of Coffee*, 16–17.   [85] Ellis, *Coffee House*, 124.

little sugar.[86] This sweetener would have helped consumers acquire a taste for coffee—a process not made any easier by the complex and often rather uncertain process of roasting the beans, which could easily lead to them being burnt or underdone, either of which would spoil the flavour.[87]

That coffee grew in popularity almost despite its intrinsic qualities has been attributed to three broad factors. Cowan argues that its initial uptake was largely due to the attitudes of the English virtuosi—a group whose interests encompassed classical antiquity and the Italian renaissance, but who were, above all, driven by a set of sensibilities that they termed 'curiosity'.[88] To such men, coffee formed part of a wider interest in the exotic, but also an enthusiasm for experimentation with a wide range of new substances that were becoming available in the seventeenth century, including betel nuts and opium. Within this range of drugs, coffee ranked as a mild stimulant—one that facilitated mental activity and encouraged rational and sober thinking.[89] As with other new commodities, coffee was incorporated into the Galenic system, although there was disagreement about its qualities and where it should be placed. One thing was certain, however: coffee dried out the body's phlegm. Whether this was good or bad depended upon the temperament of the individual and herein lay the grounds for a medical controversy that surrounded coffee throughout the seventeenth and eighteenth centuries. Its advocates made wide-ranging claims about the benefits of coffee drinking, from curing headaches through preventing dropsy, gout, or even scurvy, to acting as an electuary. Such vagueness allowed coffee-house keepers to make extravagant claims about the virtues of the drink, which in turn gave satirists a field day.[90] A particular concern was that coffee was thought to have a deleterious effect on male virility. One pamphlet, written as *The Women's Petition against Coffee*, complained that men were 'not able to *stand* to it, and in the very first Charge fall down *flat* before us. Never did Men wear *greater breeches*, or carry *less* in them of any *Mettle* whatsoever.'[91]

The indisputable ability of coffee to stimulate the body and mind perhaps linked it to the most important factor in its growing consumption: its place in male sociability, especially in the coffee house. Smith argues that it played a central part in the construction of rational masculinity within the public sphere, helping to make coffee houses the focal point of public discourse and businesslike interchange.[92] Coffee houses certainly became important social and cultural institutions, and did much to stimulate as well as provide for public demand for coffee. However, they cannot have accounted for the continued growth of coffee imports and consumption in the later eighteenth century (Table 1.3). We have already seen that consumption in the home was an integral part of coffee drinking from its introduction to

[86] Pepys, *Diary*, v. 105.   [87] Ellis, *Coffee House*, 118–23.
[88] Cowan, *Social Life of Coffee*, 11.
[89] Cowan, *Social Life of Coffee*, 31–40; Schivelbusch, *Tastes of Paradise*, 110.
[90] Schivelbusch, *Tastes of Paradise*, 45–8; Ellis, *Coffee House*, 132–7.
[91] Anon., *The Women's Petition against Coffee*, 2.
[92] Smith, *Consumption*, 151–61. See also Schivelbusch, *Tastes of Paradise*, 49–61; Cowan, *Social Life of Coffee*, 89–112.

London society. Its integration into domestic rituals and sociability must also have played a part in its sustained growth. That said, from the early decades of the eighteenth century, coffee was increasingly eclipsed by tea, especially within the home.

Tea came to England last, but had perhaps the biggest impact on British consumption cultures. While the Dutch had imported Chinese tea as early as 1606, the first mention of its sale in England comes in 1658, when it was noted that: 'coffee, chocolate and a kind of drink called "Tee" was sold on every street'.[93] This suggests that coffee and chocolate were more familiar drinks, but also that tea was sufficiently established to be widely available, even if we allow for a touch of hyperbole. Two years later, demand was significant enough to allow tea to be taxed alongside coffee in the 1660 excise, the higher rate of 8*d.* per gallon indicating that it was seen as a luxury product, consumed only by the wealthy. It was the favourite drink of the court, perhaps reflecting the personal preferences of Queen Catherine, but certainly offering the opportunity for displays of conspicuous consumption.[94] Underpinning these attractions were the medical attributes accorded to tea, which, in essence, closely paralleled those of coffee. It was thought to be especially effective against headaches, a poem written in honour of Queen Catherine's birthday suggesting that 'The Muses' friend, Tea, does our fancy aid; Repress those vapours which the head invade'. Above all, though, it was a stimulant, which, according to a treatise from 1660, 'makes the body active and alert...It is good against nightmares, it eases the brain and strengthens the memory. It is especially good for sustaining wakefulness. One infusion is sufficient to allow one to work through the night, without doing injury to one's body.'[95]

Such qualities sustained demand during the initial fashion for tea drinking in the seventeenth century. From the early eighteenth century, however, imports grew dramatically (Table 1.3) and took tea beyond the realms of the medical and the elite table. It became the drink of choice first for the middling sort and later for the labouring classes as well. The reasons for this rapid rise remain uncertain. Price reductions were no doubt important in the long run, since they opened up the possibility of even the poorest being able to purchase lower grades of tea (see Chapters 2 and 9). Yet early growth took place in the face of steady or even rising prices, and tea remained significantly more expensive than coffee until well into the eighteenth century. Tea was not part of Britain's imperial project during this period, although imports were in the hands of the East India Company, which always promoted its interests with vigour, both to government and to the public. While it was consumed in coffee houses, the key to its rise in the early decades of the eighteenth century was probably its close association with women, often in conjunction with the home. The link was made in poems and paintings, the delicacy of the equipage being reflected in that of the female consumers and their polite conversation. Tied in with this, according to Smith, was the new practice of adding sugar to tea. This is often seen as a way of understanding the burgeoning demand for

---

[93] Quoted in Rees, *Grocery Trade*, ii. 2.   [94] Ellis, *Coffee House*, 124–5.
[95] Quoted in, respectively, Rees, *Grocery Trade*, ii. 3; Schivelbusch, *Tastes of Paradise*, 83–4.

sugar, but might also help to explain the sustained fashion for tea among the elite and its progressive spread to other social groups.[96]

CONCLUSIONS

The grocery trade was established as a distinct branch of retailing in the Middle Ages, defined by the goods sold and the skills required to prepare these for sale. Both stock and skills were enshrined by guild regulations, but these were often difficult to enforce and carried little weight outside the corporate town. Through much of the country, therefore, groceries were sold by a wide range of retailers whose nominal specialization lay elsewhere: mercers, chandlers, and the like. Nonetheless, the early modern grocery trade was predominantly shop based and supplied a mixed clientele with a growing variety of imported goods. Indeed, many of the goods with which we associate the grocer in the eighteenth or even the nineteenth century were already found on the shelves of sixteenth- and early seventeenth-century shops and were being consumed in ordinary households. In short, the grocery trade was already vibrant and geographically widespread well before the period of de Vries's industrious revolution—or, indeed, McKendrick's consumer revolution. But this does not, of itself, undermine either theory. Indeed, it could be argued that a well-developed and functional retail system is a necessary prerequisite to fundamental changes in consumer behaviour: if growing and shifting demand cannot by serviced by retailers, then any economic or cultural transformation will inevitably be muted.

This is not to say that grocery retailing in the early seventeenth century was already revolutionized and 'modern'; rather, it was suited to the needs of contemporary consumers and had the flexibility to incorporate new products and (as we shall see) new systems of selling. Indeed, some new products were already finding their way onto the shelves of early modern grocers' shops, most notably sugar and tobacco. Much has been made about the collective attractions of these and other colonial groceries, from Schivelbusch's ideas of bourgeois sobriety and Smith's notion of respectability, to the consumption bundles that lie at the heart of de Vries's industrious revolution.[97] These are powerful arguments, which put these goods in the vanguard of cultural and social transformation. However, as we have seen, these various goods had different, if sometimes complementary, attractions, which developed and changed over time and space. This has three important implications. The first is that the cultural meanings and associations of a particular commodity were rarely stable over the *longue durée*—a characteristic seen in sugar (spice, medicine, sweetener, and preservative) and tobacco (smoked in pipes and later in cigars and cigarettes, or taken as snuff). The second is that consumers sometimes made choices between commodities, so that growing demand for one

---

[96] Ellis, *Coffee House*, 125; Smith, *Consumption*, 121–30; Vickery, *Gentleman's Daughter*, 195–202.

[97] See Schivelbusch, *Tastes of Paradise*; Smith, *Consumption*; de Vries, *Industrious Revolution*, 31–7.

might suppress demand for another. This is apparent at a national scale, the English consuming 1.5 lb of tea and only 0.1 lb of coffee per head in 1780, whereas the Dutch consumed 1.1 lb and 6.2 lb respectively.[98] The third is that, while these new goods replaced demand for some existing products (such as beer), they were often integrated into established modes of cooking and living, and were thus consumed alongside a range of familiar commodities. This created long-term continuities in the consumption of groceries and therefore in the grocers' stock-in-trade. However, growing quantities of new imported groceries had a profound impact on both retailing and consumption practices—change as much as continuity marked the eighteenth-century grocery trade.

[98] De Vries, *Industrious Revolution*, 160.

2

A New World of Goods: Groceries in the Long Eighteenth Century

INTRODUCTION

Britain's overseas trade was transformed in the century or so after the Restoration: it grew in volume and value, realigned geographically, and became centred on a new set of commodities and products—not least the new groceries that began to penetrate European markets. Estimates vary, but the value of imports and exports increased three- or fourfold between the 1660s and 1770s.[1] This growth reflected changes in the domestic economy, with new industries emerging during the course of the eighteenth century to rival the traditional dominance of woollen textiles. Cottons, ironware, and ceramics all experienced their own version of industrial revolution, output expanding rapidly as a result of organizational as well as technical innovation.[2] Commercial growth was also linked to Britain's imperial ambitions, most particularly across the Atlantic and in the Far East, but also in west and southern Africa. In the east, the Dutch were largely successful in defending their monopolistic control over most of the Spice Islands, and British attention was focused primarily on India, the source of a large variety of manufactured goods as well as spices and other foodstuffs. The English East India Company (EIC) pursued vigorous military and commercial strategies, gradually expanding its territorial control in the Carnatic and Bengal, and enjoying a monopoly on the lucrative trade with both India and China—the latter remaining largely beyond Western imperial ambition.[3] Their ships carried textiles, porcelain, spices, and tea (among many other things) back to Britain, to be sold at the company auctions in London. The American and West Indian colonies received large amounts of manufactured goods from Britain, exports becoming increasingly reoriented around these new colonial markets.[4] In the opposite direction came a range of tropical goods, most notably sugar and tobacco (and later cotton), but also a growing range of spices, coffee, and chocolate. These were generally grown as part

---

[1] Harley, 'Trade', 176–81; Davis, 'English Foreign Trade'; Dean and Cole, *British Economic Growth*, 41–9, 315–22.
[2] See King and Timmins, *Industrial Revolution*, 68–101.
[3] See Chaudhuri, *English East India Company*; Bowen, *Business of Empire*.
[4] Deane and Cole, *British Economic Growth*, 87.

of a plantation economy, which was largely dependent upon the use of slaves brought from West Africa.[5]

In short, Britain's commercial revolution shifted the country's economic focus away from Europe and towards its growing empire to the east and west. It brought to British consumers new and/or increasingly affordable groceries, which together accounted for over one-third of British imports by the 1770s.[6] As we have already seen, these are viewed by historians as central to the transformation of consumption practices and material culture in the eighteenth century. Indeed, the link between commercial and consumer evolution is fundamental to our understanding of both processes.[7] What has received far less attention is the way in which these new goods were accommodated within or served to restructure established retail systems. Shammas argues that the task of selling these goods had a transformative impact on British retailing. For her, 'the demand for groceries only obtainable from abroad...stimulated the mercantile community to set up country shops'. Moreover, the line of causality is clear: 'once shopkeepers stocked tobacco, sugar and caffeine drinks that were bought frequently but in small amounts, it made sense to stock other provisions purchased in the same way, such as salt, soap, starch, candles, butter, cheese, flour and bacon.'[8] The rapid turnover and high margins on these goods made shops viable in greater numbers and in more places than ever before. It was the new tropical groceries, then, that led a retail revolution, at least in numerical terms. Bickham takes the argument further, suggesting that the imperial associations of these foods were central to the meaning they held for consumers—they were available locally, but their primary affiliations were with overseas colonies. In this way, they were central to public interest and interaction with empire, which, according to many historians, emerged during the Seven Years War and grew further during the American and French wars of the late eighteenth century.[9]

While persuasive in some respects, both of these contentions need to be examined in the light of what retailers actually sold by way of groceries—the ways in which 'imperial foods' related to other goods, and the language used to describe their provenance and qualities. The overall context for reappraising the impact of new groceries on English retailing is the shifting geography of supply and the growing importance of empire. However, the main focus of attention must lie in detailed analysis of the changing stock-in-trade of retail grocers, through which a number of related questions are addressed. First is the issue of who actually sold the new range of groceries: were grocers the key suppliers or were other retailers better placed to market these cornerstones of polite sociability? Second is the question of how these new commodities fitted into established lines of stock and the ways in

  [5] On the plantation economy, see Walvin, *Fruits of Empire*, 132–54; Mintz, *Sweetness and Power*, 46–60.

  [6] Berg, 'Consumption in Britain', 365.

  [7] See, e.g., Walvin, *Fruits of Empire*; Smith, *Consumption*; Berg, 'Consumption in Britain'.

  [8] Shammas, *Pre-Industrial Consumer*, 259.

  [9] Bickham, 'Eating the Empire', 75–81, 105–6. See also Walvin, *Fruits of Empire*, 155–73; Wilson, *Sense of the People*; Bowen, 'British Conceptions of Global Empire'.

which they facilitated expansion in the range of goods available. Were they, as Shammas argues, a stimulus to retail growth or did they encourage specialization so that the grocer becomes more narrowly defined as a retailer of imported food-stuffs, as Rees would have us believe?[10] Third is the extent to which these goods carried associations of empire for the shopkeeper and consumer through the language used to describe them in shopkeepers' inventories. Of particular interest here is use of place names: with which places were groceries associated, and did this communicate imperial affiliations or tell consumers about the nature and quality of the goods? Through this detailed analysis it is also possible to examine the broad relationship between food and empire, and between commercial and retail change. In particular, we can assess the penetration of empire into the everyday nomencla-ture of goods and the extent to which the introduction of new goods involved change in existing retail systems.

COMMERCIAL REVOLUTION AND CONSUMPTION

While the volume of trade and the relative importance of different trading partners were transformed during the late seventeenth and eighteenth centuries, the basic geography of the global trade in groceries was established rather earlier. In laying out the operations of the various trading companies, Lewes Roberts's *Merchants Mappe of Commerce* (1638) provides a detailed picture of the provenance of a wide range of groceries. Trading with India, Persia, and Arabia, the EIC brought back a range of spices and drugs as well as textiles, precious stones, and 'infinite other commodities'. The Turkey Company imported, among other things, 'muscadins of Gandia' and 'corance [currants] and oils of Zante, Cephalonia and Morea'; the Muscovy Company brought home honey, pitch, tax, wax, and rosin, and the French Company salt, wines, oils, and almonds. From Spain and Portugal came wine, rosin, olives, oils, sugar, soap, aniseed, liquorice, and so on, while Italy supplied oils and rice, as well as acting as a conduit for Eastern produce. Conclud-ing his survey, Roberts writes that he need not 'particularise the large traffic of this island to their late plantations of Newfoundland, Somers Islands, Virginia, Barba-does and New England'.[11] What Roberts so clearly recognized was the way in which the established trade routes that brought goods from the east and the Medi-terranean were already being augmented with others that drew on colonial produc-tion. This connection between the production and commerce in tropical groceries, the growth of British and other European empires, and shifting patterns of trade have become a familiar theme in both imperial and economic history.[12] Yet it is a story that both over- and underplays the importance of colonies in supplying a growing range of desirable foods.

---

[10] Shammas, *Pre-Industrial Consumer*, 259; Rees, *Grocery Trade*, ii. 31–52.

[11] Roberts, *Merchant's Mappe*, 258–61.

[12] The relationship is brought out most clearly in Walvin, *Fruits of Empire*; Mintz, *Sweetness and Power*; Chaudhuri, *English East India Company*.

There were also strong continuities of supply, Europe remaining an important source for the wide range of groceries that Roberts identified in the mid-seventeenth century. Dried fruit, oils, soap, rosin, wax, and salt are not the products that most excite historians, yet they were central to consumers and grocers alike—servicing basic needs and generating a regular flow of business at the shop. These goods were largely unaffected by the changing patterns of trade and the growth of colonial economies that occurred in the eighteenth century. By ignoring such commodities and continuities of supply, analyses of the geography of supply and the link between groceries and colonies is rendered too simplistic. That said, as Defoe was careful to note, colonies were central to the provision of a new range of goods.[13] Almost from its foundation, Virginia was linked to the production and trade in tobacco. Smith argues that it was the private introduction and growing of the plant that rescued the colony from collapse in the early seventeenth century and ensured its subsequent prosperity. English planters and merchants certainly became a powerful voice, lobbying for government support in the shape of tax concessions and protection from overseas and domestic production. But Virginia by no means monopolized the tobacco trade. Portuguese and especially Spanish colonies were also engaged in production, and much of the tobacco arriving in Europe in the sixteenth and seventeenth centuries came through Iberian towns. Indeed, it was only an advantageous excise regime that allowed Virginian tobacco to find a market in Britain in the first place, Spanish-American tobacco being preferred by many smokers.[14] Much the same story was true of sugar. This was grown through-out the Mediterranean in the Middle Ages, but production was progressively shifted by Spanish and Portuguese colonists: in the fifteenth century to the Canaries, Madeira, and Sao Tome, and a century later to the New World. In all these places, sugar was grown using slave labour—a system that was to characterize sugar production for the next 300 years. By the early seventeenth century Portugal was supplying much of Europe's demand for sugar, re-exporting supplies from its vast colony in Brazil.[15] This was noted by Roberts in his survey of 1638, but so too was the emergence of Barbados—a remarkably prescient observation, given that it was not until 1655 that Barbadian sugar began to have a real impact on the British market. Coupled with the opening-up of Jamaica for sugar production in the 1660s, this quickly led to British demand for sugar being largely met by its West Indian colonies.[16]

Of the new caffeine drinks, only chocolate was a New World product. Planta-tions were briefly established in Jamaica in the mid-seventeenth century, but were destroyed by disease in the 1670s, while later cultivation in Martinique was very

---

[13] Defoe, *Compleat English Tradesman*, i. 327–9; ii. 134–5.

[14] Smith, *Consumption*, 163–5; Goodman, *Tobacco*, 149–50; Brooks, *Mighty Leaf*, 81–120, 149–90.

[15] Mintz, *Sweetness and Power*, 32–8.

[16] Davis, 'English Foreign Trade', 152–3. The West Indian trade benefited greatly from the influence within British politics of wealthy (and often absentee) plantation-owners. Only in the mid-nineteenth century was the West Indian interest reduced and with it the trade in sugar, British consumers being increasingly supplied with sugar from Brazil. See Mintz, *Sweetness and Power*, 56–64.

small scale. The key sources of supply were Venezuela and various Central American colonies, which reflects the early and sustained Spanish enthusiasm for chocolate drinking.[17] Tea and coffee came from the east and initially lay mostly within the confines of powerful, non-European empires. Throughout our period, practically all tea consumed in Europe came from China. Supplies to Britain increased significantly after 1717, when the EIC negotiated the right to export tea directly from Canton; but it was not until the 1840s that plantations were developed in India. Mintz might be correct in describing this 'as a means not only of profit but also of the power to rule', but it came at a time when other colonial production systems were already declining in the face of free trade.[18] Coffee was rather different, with a switch to colonial production coming much earlier. Imports to Europe initially came from Arabia, either through the Yemeni port of Mocha in the ships of the EIC or via Turkey and the Levant Company's vessels. These supplies were supplemented around the turn of the eighteenth century, when the Dutch introduced coffee cultivation to their colonies on Java (in 1696) and Surinam (1712). The French followed suit, growing coffee in their West Indian colonies from 1715, as did the British from 1728, when plantations were established in Jamaica and Montserrat.[19] But coffee never supplanted sugar in the West Indian economy; nor did West Indian coffee dominate the British market, generally being regarded as inferior to Turkish coffee.

The West Indies also grew in importance as a source for spices and dyestuffs: some native to the new world, others being introductions on plantations. For example, Jamaica pepper, a native species, became important to British consumers in the seventeenth century because it combined the flavours of cinnamon, nutmeg, and cloves. Ginger and nutmegs were introduced to Jamaica and other islands in the late seventeenth century and formed significant secondary outputs, while indigo was grown in Georgia and Carolina.[20] Like coffee, they were far less important than sugar and tobacco to the plantation economies and rarely challenged the dominance of East Indian spices and dyes. In this context, the traditional sources of supply in the Spice Islands and India remained crucial. Systems of production varied across these areas, with Dutch plantations most closely resembling the production regimes seen in the West Indies.

Overall, then, supplies increasingly lay within the bounds of European empires; but how important to consumers were imperial provenance and associations? In terms of shaping overall levels of demand (not always in a positive manner), the links between product and colony were perhaps clearest in the case of sugar.[21] Long associated with plantation economies, the consumption of sugar became a significant thread within campaigns for the abolition of slavery, especially in the years

[17] Coe and Coe, *History of Chocolate*, 180–200. The importance of Trinidad in the production of chocolate came only later in the nineteenth century.
[18] Chaudhuri, *Trading World*, 388; Mintz, *Sweetness and Power*, 114.
[19] Cowan, *Social Life of Coffee*, 56–9, 75–7.
[20] Edelson, 'Characters of Commodities', 351.
[21] There was occasional rhetoric about boycotts of tea, such as that mooted in the *Poor Man's Guardian*, 14 Feb. 1835, but these never came to anything.

1791–2 and 1824–5.[22] The first call to abstain from consuming sugar came in a pamphlet written by W. B. Crafton following the defeat of Wilberforce's bill in 1791.[23] It argued for the rejection of slave-grown sugar on moral and humanitarian grounds, since it was tainted by the blood of slaves working on West Indian plantations—a theme that was rehearsed in numerous poems and pamphlets in the years that followed.[24] These arguments undermined the supposedly virtuous qualities of sugar and were linked with attempts to promote alternative sources. East Indian sugar was portrayed as being preferable because, as one card handed out by the Sheffield Female Anti-Slavery Society claimed: 'by six families using East India sugar instead of West India sugar one slave less is required.'[25] This was manifestly not an anti-imperial campaign: slavery was the target, not colonialism. Yet this differentiation was problematic on two grounds. First, the principled arguments of abolitionists were caught up in the self-serving character of the 'East India interest', several prominent campaigners being leading East India merchants with much to gain from a reorientation of trade.[26] Indeed, the choice between West and East Indian sugar fed into wider debates over the real economic competitiveness of slave-based plantation production. Second, there were problems in communicating to others the moral rectitude of the sugar being consumed. Although an array of material objects were produced to advocate East Indian over Caribbean produce, it was impossible to distinguish the provenance of sugar solely from its appearance. The only way to be certain was to abstain completely, sugar being recast as a luxury that was not simply unnecessary but 'pestilent'.[27] Yet here both campaigners and historians seem to have taken a very narrow view of the uses to which sugar might be put, focusing almost entirely on its consumption with tea. As Davies puts it: 'the only display abstention necessitated was the entirely private display of feminine refusal at the domestic tea table.'[28] Such a sacrifice may have been quite easy; rather harder to do without was sugar as a culinary ingredient and preservative (see Chapter 9).

Judging the impact of these campaigns is extremely difficult. Contemporaries estimated the number of abstainers at 400,000 by late 1792, but the thoroughness and duration of any abstention are less certain, and it is clear that attempts to spread the message to the working classes was met with limited enthusiasm.[29] Moreover, while East Indian sugar became more important during the early nineteenth century, it never challenged the Caribbean as a point of supply in Britain. Indeed, it is ironic that the eventual replacement of West Indian by Brazilian sugar involved buying from slave-based plantation production.[30]

---

[22] Mintz, *Sweetness and Power*, 51–4; Walvin, *Fruits of Empire*, 123–8, 134–54; Hall, 'Culinary Spaces', 177–81. For a fuller discussion of these campaigns and especially the role of women, see Midgeley, *Feminism and Empire*, 41–64; Davies, 'A Moral Purchase'.
[23] Crafton, *Short Sketch*.
[24] See, e.g., Coleridge, 'On the Slave Trade'; Birkett, *African Slave Trade*.
[25] Quoted in Midgeley, *Feminism and Empire*, 54.
[26] Most notable was James Cropper, a leading member of the Liverpool East India Association (see Carlton, 'James Cropper'). On the economics of sugar plantations, see Mintz, *Sweetness and Power*, 56.
[27] Coleridge, 'On the Slave Trade', 139; Crafton, *Short Sketch*, 20.
[28] Davies, 'A Moral Purchase', 145.
[29] Midgeley, *Feminism and Empire*, 54.   [30] Mintz, *Sweetness and Power*, 62–3.

There was also a less principled critique of some imported groceries that portrayed them as being injurious to health. Most of these critiques were linked to attempts to sell other goods—either variants on the commodity under attack or remedies for its supposedly harmful effects. This is nicely illustrated by an advertisement from the 1820s for 'English Tea', which was presented as a preferable alternative to 'Foreign Tea' because of its restorative effects. While this was available from the Patent Medicine Warehouse on Clare Street in Bristol, it was sold—like ordinary tea—in packets and canisters.[31] Patent medicines themselves were often marketed as general pick-me-ups, but were also seen as effective against the deleterious effects of tea, coffee, and the like. A notice for the 'Cordial Balm of Gilead', placed in the Bristol press in 1820, argued that it would 'relieve those persons who, by an immoderate indulgence of their passions, have ruined their constitutions'. Included in this category was 'the delicate female, whom an immured and inactive life, together with the immoderate use of tea...has, without any fault of hers, brought on the calamitous symptoms of a consumptive habit'.[32] Significantly, it was both tea and the associated lifestyle that brought about the downfall of such women—neither was seen as physically or morally healthy, echoing in part the contemporary campaigns against slave-grown sugar.[33] A generation earlier, John Wesley had voiced a similar critique, arguing that tea was 'an unwholesome and expensive food'.[34]

These health concerns focused on the impact of 'foreign' goods. There were also anxieties about domestic practices that threatened the purity and integrity of groceries, with tea again being the focus of attention. As early as 1710 there were concerns being expressed about the practice of mixing damaged with good tea;[35] but the real problem was that other leaves were being added by dealers to bulk up consignments. Legislation was enacted in 1725 and strengthened in 1731 explicitly outlawing the adulteration of tea with, among other things: terra-japonica, sugar, molasses, log-wood, sloe leaves, and liquorice leaves. Despite this, the practice continued, prompting Richard Twining to complain in 1785 about the production of 'smouch' using dried ash leaves—a practice that was both damaging his trade and undermining perceptions of the tea-blender's art.[36] Such products were also, he argued, injurious to health, a problem that came into sharp focus in the early nineteenth century when reports began to surface of the practice of 'reviving' tea or turning low-grade black tea into more expensive green tea by adding colouring agents such as Prussian blue or verdigris.[37] Significantly, the adulteration of tea was seen as a domestic problem, being carried out by dealers and manufac-

[31] *Bristol Mercury*, 12 Apr. 1824. There were also advertisements for English Herb Snuff (*Aris's Birmingham Gazette*, 8 Apr. 1782) and English Coffee, 'composed entirely of English herbs, roots, barks, plants &c' and to be drunk in the morning or evening, just like the ordinary coffee or tea it sought to replace; it was also cheaper, at only 2*s.* 6*d.* per canister (*Adams Weekly Courant*, 11 Oct. 1774).

[32] *Bristol Mercury*, 1 May 1820. Similar elixirs were available to restore the health after excessive use of tobacco (see, e.g., *Norwich Gazette*, 13 June 1741).

[33] Midgeley, *Feminism and Empire*, 52–3; Davies, 'A Moral Purchase', 141, 145–6.

[34] Letter dated 10 Dec. 1748, quoted in Rees, *Grocery Trade*, ii. 29.

[35] *Tatler*, 10 Oct. 1710.   [36] Rees, *Grocery Trade*, ii. 27, 59–62.

[37] Rappaport, 'Packaging China', 131. See also Burnett, *Plenty and Want*, 106–7.

turers in Britain. This is in stark contrast with developments later in the nineteenth century, when there was a growing perception that tea was being adulterated at source—a shift that was linked to changing attitudes to the Chinese, who were increasingly seen as dirty and deceitful.[38]

As with campaigns against sugar, these concerns over purity and adulteration brought the provenance of tea into sharper focus: they heightened awareness of *where* goods came from and connected British consumers to overseas production, and more arguably to empire.[39] However, there is little sign that they dented demand: by the third quarter of the eighteenth century, tea, sugar, and tobacco were central to the lives of a wide range of people. As early as 1670, tobacco was being used by 25 per cent of the population, while sugar, treacle, and tea were central elements of working-class diet by the 1760s.[40] As Smith suggests, growth in demand for spices was sluggish in the eighteenth century. Having reached perhaps 0.75 lb in the 1670s, annual per capita consumption fell back to around 0.3–0.4 lb. Similarly, demand for tobacco had peaked by the early eighteenth century, while that for coffee grew only slowly (see Table 2.1).[41] The latter was overtaken in popularity by tea in the 1720s, as the price of the latter declined significantly, if unevenly, in response to changing tax regimes as much as the growing efficiency of supply.[42] Per capita consumption grew fourfold between the 1730s and 1790s, outstripping in relative terms the phenomenal rise of sugar, which had experienced its own surge in the early decades of the eighteenth century.

The underlying causes of this growth have been extensively discussed elsewhere (see Chapter 1), much emphasis being placed on the ways in which new consumer goods became central to the practices of polite sociability across Europe.[43] As de Vries argues, this involved choices being made between different foods and drinks— colonial groceries increasingly being favoured over traditional consumer goods.[44] This process was facilitated by significant reductions in prices. Sugar, for example, experienced a long-term decline from about 2*s.* per pound in the Middle Ages to around 4*d.* per pound by 1680, before creeping up over the course of the eighteenth century. The price of tea, meanwhile, fell markedly in the 1720s–30s, helping to stimulate demand among a broader section of society (Table 2.2). In contrast, dried fruit appears to have increased considerably in price towards the end of the eighteenth century as supplies were disrupted by the revolutionary and Napoleonic wars. Even with this increase, currants and raisins remained within the reach of many ordinary consumers, while the cheaper teas such as bohea could be had for

---

[38] Rappaport, 'Packaging China', 136.

[39] See Walvin, *Fruits of Empire*. There are obvious parallels here with twenty-first-century concerns over the provenance of food and its relationship with quality.

[40] Shammas, 'English and Anglo-American Consumption', 178–85.

[41] Smith, *Consumption*, 86–9.

[42] See Mui and Mui, *Shops and Shopkeeping*, 250–4.

[43] Useful summaries can be found in Cowan, *Social Life of Coffee, passim*; Mintz, *Sweetness and Power*, 74–140; Smith, *Consumption*, esp. 86–92, 121–9, 140–50; Schivelbusch, *Tastes of Paradise, passim*.

[44] De Vries, *Industrious Revolution*, 154–64.

Table 2.1. Per capita consumption of selected groceries in England and Wales, eighteenth century

Pepper		Tobacco		Coffee		Sugar		Tea	
Date	lb	Date	lb	Date	lb	Date	lb	Date	lb
1699–1701	0.29	1698–1702	2.30	1693–1700	0.04	1698–9	4.01		
		1713–17	1.80	1711–19	0.12	1710–19	8.23		
1722–4	0.31	1718–22	2.62	1725–9	0.10	1720–9	12.02		
		1733–37	2.00	1735–9	0.14	1730–9	14.90	1730–9	0.50
		1748–52	1.94					1740–9	1.00
1751–5	0.42					1750–9	16.94	1750–9	1.10
						1770–9	23.02	1770–9	1.40
						1790–9	24.16	1790–9	2.10

Sources: Berg, 'Consumption in Britain', 367; Smith, *Consumption*, 302, 304.

as little as 4–5*s*. per pound.[45] Yet supplies were vulnerable to the exigencies of weather and war, and prices could fluctuate dramatically as a result, as Burnett demonstrates for early nineteenth-century Manchester.[46] By this time, colonial and other groceries were widely available and widely consumed. The diversity of supply and especially the commercial exploitation of colonial products undoubtedly brought a range of new groceries to a much broader set of consumers, helping to transform diet, social practices, and household economies. But where did consumers acquire what were initially new and unfamiliar goods, and how did growing demand link to supply from shops?

Table 2.2. Prices of selected groceries appearing in bills and advertisements, 1668–1806 (per lb)

Commodity	Julius Billiers (1668) / John Carter (1680)	George Murray (1712) / William Armstrong (1724)	Lily Smith (1764)	Tucker & Son (1806)
Souchong tea	—	16*s*.	10*s*.	8*s*.
Hyson tea	—	24*s*.	16*s*.	12*s*.
Coffee	—	5*s*. 6*d*.	6*s*. 4*d*.	7*s*.
Loaf sugar	7*d*.	9*d*.	1*s*.	1*s*. 1*d*.
Currants	5*d*.	6.5*d*.	6*d*.	9.5*d*.
Raisins	4*d*.	6*d*.	6*d*.	9*d*.
Pepper	3*s*.	3*s*. 6*d*.	3*s*.	3*s*.

Sources: SCLA, DR18/5/259, 643, 1837, 4177; *Newcastle Courant*, 25 July 1724; Rees, *Grocery Trade*, ii. 155.

[45] *Adams Weekly Courant*, 27 June 1780; *Liverpool Mercury*, 17 Oct. 1820.
[46] Burnett, *Plenty and Want*, 52–3.

SELLING THE NEW WORLD OF GOODS:
GROCERS' STOCK

The proportion of provincial towns with grocer's shops remained relatively low through the 1730s and 1740s, mercers and drapers being far more widespread.[47] While this might relate in part to regional variations in the title given to non-specialized shopkeepers, it also reflects more fundamental questions about which retailers were best placed to serve the rising demand for new groceries, especially tea and coffee. From a modern perspective, it seems inevitable that these should be sold by grocers: they were similar in character and required the same kind of retailing skills as established parts of the grocer's stock. However, contemporary perceptions linked them more closely to other retailers. Coffee houses quickly appeared as a specialist venue for consuming coffee and tea, and often sold beans and leaves for home consumption. When Pepys started drinking tea and coffee at home, he went to a coffee house, but their earlier associations with medicinal benefits meant that they could also be bought at the apothecary's shop.[48] Even as demand grew around the turn of the eighteenth century, the grocer was not the only or even the most obvious place from which to buy these goods.[49] Tea sat just as comfortably with chinaware, books, and toys as it did with raisins and pepper. Equally, milliners, china dealers, booksellers and even drapers attracted the sort of consumer who was increasingly engaged in the consumption of tea and coffee. What is most striking, perhaps, is the limited development of dealers who specialized in these key commodities: tea dealers became common only later in the eighteenth century, while coffee houses were primarily places to go rather than to buy from.

The variety of provincial retailers selling tea and coffee in the first half of the eighteenth century can be judged by analysing the stock listed in probate inventories and tradesmen's lists. A sample of 133 provincial shops selling groceries reveals caffeine drinks in the stock of victuallers, booksellers, brewers, mercers, widows, and chandlers as well as grocers. Tea and coffee thus formed an important sideline for various shopkeepers, and continued to do through much of the eighteenth century. In 1771, Benjamin Johnson advertised that 'a large stock of all sorts of Tea' was available at his toy shop on Broad Capuchin Lane in Hereford. Ten years later, a chemist and druggist called William Marshall issued a stock list to advertise his Northampton business that included bohea and green teas, coffee, and chocolate.[50] In some cases, selling tea could become a significant aspect of the business. Fletcher and Fenton were mercers in the Staffordshire town of New-castle-under-Lyme who, in addition to textiles, haberdashery and gloves, also sold bohea, singlo, souchong, congou, and green teas, as well as coffee. These were

[47] Stobart, Hann, and Morgan, *Spaces of Consumption*, 34.
[48] Ellis, *Coffee House*, 25–41, 75–85; Rees, *Grocery Trade*, ii. 1, 5, 18; Cowan, *Social Life of Coffee*, 47, 51. For coffee houses retailing ground coffee, see the trade card for Manwaring's coffee house, which advertised the sale of coffee powder (Bodl., Douce adds 138 (84)).
[49] Cox, *Complete Tradesman*, 204.
[50] Quoted in Rees, *Grocery Trade*, ii. 97; NCL, uncatalogued trade ephemera.

generally sold in small quantities (one-ounce and quarter-pound packages being typical), but they made up nearly 15 per cent of the transactions recorded in their day book between January and August 1768.[51] Importantly, many of these sales were made to people who did not buy cloth or haberdashery, suggesting that Fletcher and Fenton had managed to attract additional custom to their shop by offering groceries as well as textiles.

What is most striking about the stock lists of the 133 shopkeepers is that such a small proportion sold tea and coffee: just 23 per cent of the total, the majority from the 1750s or later. The evidence is by no means perfect, but it raises doubts about the extent to which demand for these goods lay behind any growth in shop retailing—at least before the mid-eighteenth century. Demand for tea in the 1710s and 1720s was kept in check by relatively high prices and was met in part by London tradesmen dealing direct with wealthy customers in the provinces. Only after prices had fallen and demand broadened do we see clear evidence of a stimulus on the grocery trade, with grocers' shops appearing in a growing number of towns and villages.[52] Most obvious in this regard is the growing number of licences issued to those wishing to sell tea. By 1765, there were 32,234 licence-holders in England and Wales, which, according to the calculations of Mui and Mui, means that around 30 per cent of shops were licensed to sell tea. This figure clearly included a wide range of trades and equated with one dealer in tea for every 210 people.[53] Moreover, given that the smuggling of tea was endemic and that many sellers remained unlicensed, it is likely that tea (and other groceries) were even more widely available than official figures would allow.

Despite this slow spread, Rees argues that tea and coffee, along with sugar, had become the defining elements of the grocer's stock by the mid-eighteenth century—replacing the earlier emphasis on spices.[54] If we examine stock lists from the 1780s and 1790s, this certainly appears to be the case. For example, in early 1787, William Hall was setting himself up as a grocer in Lechdale and placed an order with a London dealer for three types of sugar, two types of raisins, currants, rice, fig blue, black and white pepper, ginger, caraways, six types of tea, coffee, and cocoa. The total bill came to just £13 18*s.* 5*d.*, over £9 of which was for tea. Around the same time, Ann Gomm sold a corresponding range of teas, three types of coffee, a variety of sugar and tobacco, chocolate, orange peel, confectionery, and various spices from her shop in Shipton-under-Wychwood.[55] From this it would appear that these new groceries had transformed the grocer's shop; but how profound and how widespread was this change, and exactly when did the grocer move from a traditional emphasis on spice and drugs to a 'modern' focus on tea and sugar?

Systematic analysis of shopkeepers' stock indicates some important changes in the type and range of groceries being sold. In the post-Restoration period, grocers

---

[51] WSL, DW, 1788/V/108–11. [52] Stobart, Hann, and Morgan, *Spaces of Consumption*, 34.
[53] Mui and Mui, *Shops and Shopkeeping*, 161–7. [54] Rees, *Grocery Trade*, ii. 42–4.
[55] Quoted in Rees, *Grocery Trade*, ii. 108–9; ORO, OA/B/118. See also Bickham, 'Eating the Empire', 198–9.

invariably carried spices, dyes and starch, soap and related goods, fruit and nuts, sugar, and tobacco (Table 2.3). Many also stocked seeds; a range of local provisions such as hops, cheese, and grain; oils, salt, and vinegars; imported and locally produced spirits, and, more occasionally, apothecary wares including bayberries and wormseed. The range of stock was thus considerable, even in relatively modest village shops; but it was almost invariably supplemented by other goods, generally haberdashery and textiles. At this time, then, grocers often resembled general stores, catering for a wide range of needs, although they appear to have been servicing more than just the lower orders' demand for everyday goods.[56] The presence of groceries among the stock of such a range of retailers suggests relatively modest entry requirements in terms of capital and skills, especially when groceries could be traded alongside other goods. However, the grocery stock held by mercers, chandlers, booksellers, and other non-specialists was distinctly narrower in range: the vast majority sold sugar, soap, and candles alongside their main line of goods; some also had spices, fruit and nuts, tobacco, and hops, cheese, and grain; but very few sold apothecary wares or spirits.

Grocers continued carrying a similar range of goods into the early decades of the eighteenth century, but appear to have tightened their grip on the grocery trade during this period—an impression that is confirmed by contemporary descriptions.[57]

Table 2.3. Specialization and stock of grocery retailers, 1660–1830 (%)

Commodity	1660–99 Grocers (N = 7)	1660–99 Other retailers (N = 30)	1700–29 Grocers (N = 16)	1700–29 Other retailers (N = 41)	1730–79 Grocers (N = 7)	1730–79 Other retailers (N = 23)	1780–1830 Combined (N = 9)
Caffeine drinks	0.0	0.0	18.8	7.3	100.0	31.8	100.0
Sugar	100.0	96.7	100.0	68.3	100.0	72.7	100.0
Tobacco	100.0	60.0	100.0	73.2	85.7	90.9	71.4
Spices	100.0	70.0	93.8	73.2	71.4	77.3	85.7
Apothecary wares	42.9	23.3	50.0	7.3	57.1	9.1	28.6
Seeds	57.1	46.7	68.8	41.5	100.0	36.4	100.0
Fruit and nuts	100.0	73.3	81.3	46.3	71.4	72.7	100.0
Spirits	57.1	33.3	68.8	43.9	14.3	22.7	14.3
Other culinary groceries	71.4	63.3	75.0	34.1	100.0	31.8	100.0
Hops, cheese, grain, etc.	57.1	70.0	81.3	51.2	85.7	59.1	100.0
Dyes, starch, etc.	100.0	56.7	87.5	53.7	100.0	68.2	71.4
Soap, candles, etc.	100.0	86.7	100.0	78.0	100.0	77.3	100.0
Other lines	100.0	90.0	100.0	82.9	85.7	63.6	71.4

Sources: probate inventories; WSL, D1798 HM 29/2–4; WSL, D (W) 1788/V/108–11; MCL, MS F942; Bailey, 'Maintaining Status', app. 1; NCL, uncatalogued trade ephemera; Bodl., JJC, Tradesmen's Lists.

[56] Cox, *Complete Tradesman*, 204.   [57] See, e.g., Campbell, *London Tradesman*, 188–9.

While traditional items such as spices and dried fruit were no longer ubiquitous, they were still a mainstay of the grocer's shop, where they were increasingly joined by provisions, seeds (rice, caraway, and aniseed being the most common), and spirits. Meanwhile, the proportion of other shopkeepers selling groceries fell in many categories of goods. A small minority added tea and coffee to their stock, but notably fewer sold soap and candles, provisions, apothecary wares, fruit and nuts, and sugar than had been the case in a generation or two earlier. By the mid-eighteenth century, grocers had further strengthened their position and were dominant in the provision of tea and coffee as well as the more established lines of goods. It is striking, then, that apothecary wares continued to form an important element in the stock of around half the grocer's shops sampled, although the traditional stores of bayberries, alloes, and galls were being joined by patent medicines, such as the twenty-three bottles of Daffy's Elixir (with a total value of 15s.) listed in the stock of Thomas Wright of Burton Latimer.[58] There was, however, some decline in traditional areas: spirits, dried fruit, and spices were less widespread. While the last of these might be in part explained by the corresponding growth in the stock of seeds, especially mustard, there does appear to be something of a reorientation of grocer's stock towards caffeine drinks, and more basic household and culinary supplies. That said, the combined figures for the late eighteenth and early nineteenth centuries indicate a stabilization in everything except drugs and spirits, which appear to have increasingly become the province of specialist chemists and wine merchants respectively.

From this, the rise of tea and coffee might be seen as eclipsing traditional cornerstones of the grocer's trade. However, any decline in the importance of spices and dried fruit was marginal—they continued to be stocked by the vast majority of grocers. Indeed, stability and continuity are perhaps the most striking features, with sugar and tobacco already central to the grocer's stock in the seventeenth century and apothecary wares disappearing from their shelves only in the closing decades of the eighteenth century.[59] Around 1800, groceries could still be bought from a range of shops whose principal line of trade lay in other merchandise, but grocers were well established as the main source for a range of goods that would characterize their trade for the next 150 years or so.[60]

If grocers were increasingly distinct from other retailers in terms of their specialization, they also stood out because of the much greater range and choice that they offered in almost every line of goods. Taken together, mercers, chandlers, chapmen, ironmongers, apothecaries, and shopkeepers offered a variety of wares to match those available from grocers; yet only by visiting a grocer's shop could people access such a wide range of goods in a single place (see Table 2.4). On average, grocers stocked about thirty-four distinct grocery products in the late seventeenth century, rising to forty-two by the mid-eighteenth century. In comparison, other

[58] NRO, Thomas Wright, 1756.
[59] The early and enduring importance of sugar is attested by Stone, whose analysis of the stock of nine Midlands grocers shows that sugar comprised around one-third of their stock by value. In comparison, dried fruit and tobacco about 10% each; spices, spirits, other food and paper 4–5%; while dyes and apothecary wares were just 1–3% (see Stone, 'Grocers and Groceries', 67).
[60] Alexander, *Retailing in England*, 112–16; Rees, *Grocery Trade*, ii. 158–73, 320–48.

retailers stocked a much smaller and declining variety of groceries, the range falling from twenty-one to seventeen over the same period.[61] Differences were narrowest with tea and coffee, partly because London dealers increasingly sold their goods via local agents, many of whom were not grocers (see Chapter 3).[62] With goods such as spices, seeds, dried fruit, dyestuffs, and other culinary groceries, non-specialists held a comparable range to grocers in the late seventeenth century. For example, customers visiting the shop of the grocer William Rumfield of Wye in Kent could buy thirteen kinds of spices and seeds, while those buying from the Coventry mercer Julius Billers would have found sixteen different types.[63] However, both the relative and absolute provision in non-grocers declined in subsequent decades, so that, by the middle of the eighteenth century, grocers could offer customers a far greater choice.

Table 2.4. Range of grocery stock held, *c.*1660–1830 (mean number of varieties per shopkeeper)

Commodity (no. of varieties)	1660–99 Grocers	1660–99 Other retailers	1700–29 Grocers	1700–29 Other retailers	1730–79 Grocers	1730–79 Other retailers	1780–1830 Combined
Caffeine drinks (N = 5)	—	—	2.0	1.7	3.7	3.1	3.1
Sugar (N = 11)	3.4	2.0	3.6	2.3	4.1	1.9	3.3
Tobacco (N = 4)	1.7	1.5	1.4	1.4	2.7	1.6	1.8
Spices (N = 19)	5.6	5.1	6.1	3.1	7.8	3.4	7.2
Apothecary wares (N = 8)	2.3	1.7	2.8	1.3	2.0	1.0	4.0
Seeds (N = 7)	3.0	2.4	2.8	1.4	4.7	2.4	3.6
Fruit and nuts (N = 12)	2.9	2.9	3.3	1.8	4.2	1.8	3.8
Spirits (N = 5)	2.0	1.3	2.5	1.3	2.0	1.0	1.0
Other culinary groceries (N = 10)	2.8	2.9	2.8	1.4	4.7	2.4	3.6
Hops, cheese, grain, etc. (N = 13)	3.0	1.5	1.8	1.3	2.2	1.9	3.7
Dyes, starch, etc. (N = 15)	4.0	3.2	4.5	2.4	4.5	1.8	4.4
Soap, candles, etc. (N = 14)	5.6	3.7	6.9	3.7	7.6	3.9	5.1
Total groceries (N = 123)	33.9	20.6	35.8	14.7	42.3	16.8	37.6

Sources: probate inventories; WSL, D1798 HM 29/2–4; WSL, D (W) 1788/V/108–11; MCL, MS F942; Bailey, 'Maintaining Status', app. 1; NCL, uncatalogued trade ephemera; Bodl. JJC, Tradesmen's Lists.

[61] This does not include other lines sold by grocers and other shopkeepers. The overall range of goods stocked by mercers, for example, could be enormous; but their stock of groceries was more limited.
[62] Mui and Mui, *Shops and Shopkeeping*, 270–83.
[63] KAS, 11.58.121, William Rumfield (1694); LiRO, B/C/11 Julius Billers (1676).

These contrasts come out most sharply when looking at the stock held by individual retailers (Table 2.5). The village ironmonger Ralph Edge of Tarporley in Cheshire could offer his customers a choice of four grades of tobacco and three types of pepper, along with a choice of dried fruits, sugar products, and dyes. His small-town counterpart John Atkins of Kenilworth in Warwickshire had two types of sugar, a range of spices, and a choice of dried fruits. Such shops may have serviced day-to-day needs for groceries, but it was the specialist grocer, such as Alexander Chorley of Manchester, who provided by far the largest and most varied stock. He had ten different types of sugar—even distinguishing between Liverpool and Bristol loaf sugar—as well as considerable choice of tobacco, spices, spirits, dried fruit, and oils. Significantly, while Chorley sold tea and coffee, these do not appear to have been important elements in his stock. His inventory is meticulously ordered into different product types, opening with sugar and moving on through fruits, spices, seeds, oils, liquors, tobacco, and finally hops. Coffee and tea appear under this last heading, right at the end of the shop goods, and together worth just £3 7*s.* 9*d.*—less than his stock of wormseed (£4 19*s.*) and much less than his black pepper (£13 8*s.* 10*d.*), zante currants (£18 4*s.*), or Seville oil (£10 10*s.* 10*d.*).

Overall, there is limited evidence that tea and coffee revolutionized the grocery trade in the eighteenth century, at least in terms of the emergence of specialist shops and the stock held by retailers. A range of tradesmen and women sold tea, coffee, sugar, and the like; but grocers were numerically the most important retailers of these new goods. They slowly tightened their grip on the grocery trade, offering the widest choice of new and more traditional lines of stock. Indeed, there was marked continuity in the goods they sold. Tea and sugar, and to a lesser extent coffee, chocolate, and tobacco, were increasingly important, but they stood alongside goods that had for centuries been the mainstay of the grocer's trade: spices, fruits, dyes, provisions, and a range of hardware such as soap. It was this mix of goods that made the grocer's shop distinctive and that placed it at the epicentre of changing consumer practices and shifting patterns of world trade. Both of these domains were reflected descriptions of goods that told consumers about their provenance, quality, and character.

THE LANGUAGE OF SELLING: PRODUCE, PLACE AND PROVENANCE

Place names have long played an important role in the 'terminology of commodities', communicating something about the character of the goods and their relative attractions. They promoted demand and shaped the cultural context in which goods were consumed.[64] In this context, Bickham argues that 'imperial foods' were significant, not just in quantity, but also in their meaning. They carried with them something of the place in which they were grown and the system of political economy

[64] Cox and Dannehl, *Perceptions of Retailing*, 97. Their analysis focuses mostly on manufactured goods, as does that of Wilhelmsen, *English Textile Nomenclature*.

Table 2.5. Groceries stocked by specialist and non-specialist retailers

Commodity	Ralph Edge of Tarporley, ironmonger (1683)	John Atkins of Kenilworth, mercer (1730)	Alexander Chorley of Manchester, grocer (1723)
Caffeine drinks	—	—	Coffee, bohea tea
Sugar	Coarse brown sugar, molasses	Powder sugar, coarse sugar	Jamaica sugar, fine powder sugar, fine bastard sugar, coarse bastard sugar, loaf sugar, Bristol loaf, Liverpool loaf, white candy, brown candy, molasses
Tobacco	Brown tobacco, cut tobacco, coarse tobacco, roll tobacco	Tobacco	Best-cut tobacco, second sort tobacco, stripped tobacco, roll tobacco, tobacco dust
Spices	Jamaica pepper, long pepper, white pepper, aniseed, fenugreek, mace, coriander, nutmeg, cloves, cinnamon	Jamaica pepper, black pepper, raw ginger, powder ginger, mace, cinnamon, cloves, rice, nutmeg	Nutmeg, cloves, mace, cinnamon, clove Pepper, black pepper, long pepper, liquorice, ground ginger, white ginger, raw ginger, saffron, senna, bay berries, gauls, diapente, wormseed, aloes, aniseed, caraway, fennel, fenugreek, rice
Dried fruit	Prunes, raisins	Currants, malligoes	Currants, raisins, malligoes, figs, prunes
Spirits	—	Brandy	Brandy, cherry brandy, cinnamon water, aniseed water, caraway water, wormwood water, clove water, rum
Hops, cheese, grains, etc.	Hops	Peas, oatmeal	Capers, anchovies, hops
Dyes, starch, etc.	Starch, alum, logwood, indigo	Brimstone, sulphur, starch, powder blue	Sulphur, vitriol, saltpetre, alum, stone blue, starch, logwood, brimstone, copperas, vitriol
Soap, candles, etc.	Turpentine, linseed oil, vinegar, rosin, pitch, candles, soap	Gunpowder, candles, brushes, corks, paper	Turpentine, linseed, lamb black, Seville oil, Rape oil, vinegar oil, wax, rosin, glue, gunpowder, soap, wash balls, paper

Sources: CALS, WS 1683, Ralph Edge; LiRO, B/C/11, John Atkins (1730); LRO, WCW 1723, Alexander Chorley.

that framed their production and supply. These labels, Bickham suggests, carried 'nationally shared meanings' that transcended variables such as class, gender, and geography.[65] This was possible because they were comparatively new goods that were imported through relatively few ports and marketed nationally. The result was that commodities such as tea and tobacco had no particular regional associations—

[65] Bickham, 'Eating the Empire', 80–1, 86–92; quotation taken from p. 80. He notes sugar as an exception to this, with labels such as Jamaican, Barbados, and Antiguan rarely being deployed, since there was little to distinguish the product of the different islands. See also Walvin, *Fruits of Empire, passim*.

quality tobacco was 'Virginia's Best' not 'Glasgow's Best'—and thus tied consumers to colonies and imperialism. This argument is compelling, yet problematic: by focusing on imperial connections, it ignores other associations carried by and communicated through groceries. As we have already seen, much of the grocer's stock came from closer to home: sometimes Britain, but also Europe and especially the Mediterranean. To what extent did the places associated with groceries through nominal linkages reflect the provenance of groceries? Was there a shift to more exotic and imperial place names and what weight did such names carry in the broader lexicon of the grocery trade? Such questions are important in the context of Bickham's argument, but also, more widely, in the ways in which groceries were understood as consumer goods that varied in their quality, characteristics, and relative attraction.

By examining the use of particular place names in the description of groceries in inventories and stock lists, we can get a good impression of the changing world of the grocery trade.[66] As Table 2.6 makes clear, European place names were most numerous throughout the eighteenth century, with Mediterranean countries particularly well represented. We see, for example, Valencia almonds, Malaga raisins, and Portuguese grapes—products that could not be easily produced in Britain and that had long been associated with these places.[67] However, alongside these came a wide variety of other goods: Florence oil, Italian vermicelli, Castile soap, Spanish snuff, Lisbon sugar, and so on. What is striking is the range of places and products associated through these descriptions, some fourteen different Mediterranean locations being named in all. Cox and Dannehl argue that retailers in general preferred to use specific town names rather than general terms such as 'Italian' or 'Spanish'.[68] It is clear that Italian and Iberian towns clearly carried considerable meaning for British consumers of groceries, but more generic national labels were more common: Italian was applied to three different products and Spanish to five, whereas most towns were linked to one or two groceries at most. Much the same was true of the use of place names from elsewhere in Europe, although in this case it was regions that appeared rather than towns. Alongside goods described as Prussian (blue), Dutch (twine and coffee), and French (salt, olives, barley, and prunes), we see Flemish ashes, Burgundy pitch, and Savoy biscuits. Again, a striking number of names appear, linking the British grocer with places across northwest Europe. Closer to home, British counties and towns accounted for around one-quarter of the place names mentioned. These included Kent and Worcester (hops), Cheshire, Suffolk, and Essex (cheese), Scotland (snuff and barley), Liverpool and Bristol (sugar), Pontefract (cakes), and London (treacle and thread). The growing frequency with which these appeared in the early eighteenth century may reflect the emerging national market for certain commodities that struck Defoe so forcibly. He noted among many other things the huge trade in Kentish hops and Cheshire cheese. With this interchange came a growing awareness of the difference

---

[66] These are descriptive labels. The use of place names in promotional material is considered in Ch. 7.

[67] Roberts, *Merchant's Mappe.*   [68] Cox and Dannehl, *Perceptions of Retailing*, 122–4.

between places and the products with which they were associated, encouraging the use of regional and local labels for a wide range of products.[69]

European names would have been familiar to British consumers, as they defined the nexus of traditional patterns of trade and political engagement. Also long established in the European consciousness, if a little further removed geographically, were regions and countries in the Middle East. With groceries, Turkey was the dominant geographical association, being linked to cotton, coffee, figs, and rhubarb; but Smyrna (raisins), Mocha (coffee), and Levant (coffee) also appeared. The deployment of names from this area, as for Europe and Britain, was broadly stable over the eighteenth century—another indication of continuity in the grocery trade. The range of geographical associations gradually expanded as new places were added to those already well established in the lexicon. However, the most striking area of growth was in the use of transatlantic and Far Eastern place names. Early references to the latter come in the form of specific islands, Sumatra pepper and bark being listed amongst the extensive stock of Thomas Wotton.[70] In contrast, the terms deployed in the later eighteenth and early nineteenth centuries were usually either generic (East Indian ginger, rhubarb, and rice) or linked directly to India (soy, arrowroot, and tea). East Indian sugar was being promoted at this time as 'not made by slaves',[71] and it is possible that the same associations were being suggested for other products. That said, rice from the east was of a different strain from that produced in the New World, so descriptions probably communicated the eating qualities rather than the moral integrity of the produce. The growing use of India as a point of geographical reference is unsurprising, given the expansion of British interests in the subcontinent during this period and its importance as a

Table 2.6. First appearance of place names in lists of groceries, *c*.1670–1820

Geographical region	Before 1700	1700–39	1740–79	1780–1824	Total
America/West Indies	3	3	3	8	17
Far East	2	0	2	5	9
Levant/Africa	0	3	3	2	8
Europe, Mediterranean	4	6	5	6	21
Europe, other	2	3	5	4	14
Britain	2	7	7	5	21
Total	13	22	25	30	90

Note: Many other place names associated with groceries appear in the *Dictionary of Traded Goods and Commodities*. Those listed here link directly to the stock analysed for Tables 2.3 and 2.4 and form a good cross-section of goods and places. They also reflect stock actually held by retailers.

Sources: probate inventories; WSL, D1798 HM 29/2–4; WSL, D (W) 1788/V/108–11; MCL, MS F942; Bailey, 'Maintaining Status', app. 1; NCL, uncatalogued trade ephemera; Bodl., JJC, Tradesmen's Lists.

[69] Defoe, *Tour of Britain*, 131, 394–5; King and Timmins, *Industrial Revolution*, 33–66; Cox and Dannehl, *Perceptions of Retailing*, 100–9.
[70] TNA: PRO C5/582/120.   [71] Midgely, *Feminism and Empire*, 50.

source for many eastern products.[72] Colonial references also incorporated West Indian and North American place names, but here the trends were rather more complex, in part because of the sometimes dramatic changes in colonial power in the region. American colonies were only sparingly deployed. Virginia was used from the late seventeenth century (linked to tobacco and pepper) and retained its importance through much of the eighteenth century, but other references are restricted to Carolina (rice) and America (powder—that is, snuff). Caribbean islands appeared with increasing frequency: Jamaica from the seventeenth century, then Barbados and later Martinique and Cuba. Along with Brazil, these were linked to sugar, questioning Bickham's assertion that this was categorized by refinement rather than origin.[73] While the former was the dominant concern among people buying and selling sugar, those drawing up inventories and trade lists clearly ascribed some significance to place names. That said, sugar accounted for only a minority of the groceries that were linked to Caribbean islands: there was also Jamaica pepper, coffee, and ginger; Barbados tar and alloes, Martinique coffee, and Havana snuff.

References to empire were clearly growing more important to the grocery trade in the course of the eighteenth century. Taken in the context of all place names deployed, however, they did not dominate numerically, at most comprising about 40 per cent of new place names linked to groceries. It is all but impossible to judge the qualitative importance of different place names: as labels, did Cheshire cheese, French salt, or Malaga raisins carry more or less significance for consumers than Jamaican sugar, Virginian tobacco, or Indian soy? What we can do, though, is explore more fully the meaning of the place names with which groceries were associated. Manufacturing towns were often closely linked with the goods produced, be they Kidderminster carpets, Sheffield knives, or Norwich stuffs. Indeed, such was the strength of association that some labels became attached to goods produced in the broader hinterland as well as in the town itself. Manchester was sufficiently powerful as a name that it not only became ascribed to a range of textiles produced across south-east Lancashire, but was also capable of shifting its meaning, as the production of Manchester and its environs moved from cheap woollen fabrics in the sixteenth century to cotton textiles by the mid-eighteenth century.[74] This example is instructive, as it highlights many of the ways in which place names were used to describe the kinds of goods sold by grocers—communicating the provenance of goods, their wider cultural associations, and something of their intrinsic qualities.

Some place names appear to have been relatively uncomplicated indications of the location where groceries were produced. We know from his account books that the Bristol shot sold by the Worcester grocer Thomas Dickenson came up-river from the port.[75] Worcester and Kent hops, along with French salt, Sicily almonds,

---

[72] Chaudhuri, *English East India Company*, 79–130. It is notable that China was never explicitly linked to groceries, perhaps because it was understood that all tea at this time came from China.

[73] Bickham, 'Eating the Empire', 92.

[74] See Cox and Dannehl, *Perceptions of Retailing*, 100–9.   [75] WSL, D1798 HM 29/2–5.

and Valencia raisins might be read in a similar way, although the last of these (like the manufacturing towns discussed above) was clearly shorthand for goods produced across a wider hinterland. Whether the Japan and Indian soy listed in inventories was actually produced in those places is impossible to know, although William Jones emphasized that he stocked 'real' Japan soy as well as 'Real West India Cayenne Pepper'.[76] Turkey and Mocha coffee present similar problems. Both were places where coffee was produced for the British market and enjoyed a virtual monopoly before Jamaican and Javanese coffee began to reach London in the 1730s. Even in the middle decades of the eighteenth century, any 'Turkey coffee' sold by English grocers was probably from the Middle East; but, as West Indian imports grew in the mid-eighteenth century, Turkey and Mocha increasingly became labels used to connote quality rather than origin.[77] Grocers stocking coffee from Jamaica or Martinique were thus signalling provenance, quality, and cost. Sometimes this was made explicit, the Birmingham tea dealer Samuel Brook advertising Martinico Coffee at 4s. 9d. to 6s. per pound and Fine Turkey Coffee at 7s. 6d. to 8s. per pound; but the distinction was complicated by descriptions such as 'superfine Dutch and Jamaica coffee'.[78]

Provenance became most complex with tobacco and sugar. We have already seen that both products were linked to Caribbean or American colonies, but place names could also signal the quality of goods: Brazilian tobacco and Jamaica sugar were cheaper, but of poorer quality, than some of their rivals. The latter appears in a number of grocers' inventories from the 1720s, but is absent from promotional materials, suggesting that it was not held in great esteem.[79] Place names also communicated the form and flavour of these goods, since particular places were associated with different production regimes or plant varieties. The shortage of timber on Barbados limited the local production of refined sugar, so that much of the output of the island took the form of muscovado. Entries for Barbados sugar should be read in this light, retailers and consumers alike sharing an understanding of what this label meant. Similarly, John Houghton argued that Virginia tobacco was qualitatively different, being more strongly flavoured than Spanish tobacco. Only by 'treading it hard in earthen pots', and keeping it there for two or three years, would it be rendered 'very mild like Spanish'.[80]

Labels such as Spanish tobacco and Portuguese snuff also complicate notions of provenance. The crops were grown in transatlantic colonies, but the processing took place in European cities, and the products were associated with European states. The same is true of Scotch snuff, which was widely deployed as a descriptor throughout the eighteenth century for snuff made from the stem rather than the

---

[76] *Liverpool Mercury*, 11 Feb. 1820.   [77] Ellis, *Coffee House*, 208–9.

[78] *Aris's Birmingham Gazette*, 30 Sept. 1782; *Liverpool Mercury*, 15 Sept. 1820. Similar distinctions of quality were made between Carolina indigo and that of eastern origin (see Edelson, 'Characters of Commodities', 351–2).

[79] *Dictionary of Traded Goods and Commodities* <http://www.british-history.ac.uk/report.aspx?compid=58801> (accessed 11 Mar. 2011). Conversely, Jamaica ginger and rum were seen as being particularly high quality and featured in numerous newspaper advertisements.

[80] Houghton, *Husbandry and Trade*, 467. See also Goodman, *Tobacco*, 149–50.

leaves of the plant. It linked the tobacco trade to Scotland (though not specifically Glasgow) rather than the colonies, even when 'Scotch' was being manufactured elsewhere in Britain.[81] Sugar was also processed in European ports, which then became associated with the commodity. In 1723, the Manchester grocer Alexander Chorley stocked both Liverpool and Bristol loaf as well as Jamaica and other types of sugar. It is unclear whether there were qualitative differences between the products of these rival ports, but the labels presumably held significance to those appraising Chorley's stock. Lisbon sugar was a different matter, being clayed and therefore somewhat cheaper than refined products. In terms of geographical association, the effect was the same: sugar was tied to Europe rather than the colonies, despite its ultimate point of origin.

Associations with empire were thus complex. Consumers knew where sugar and tobacco were grown and they were aware of the production systems that operated in the colonies; but other intervening places and processes layered additional meanings onto goods. While sugar, tobacco, and increasingly coffee and spices were products of empire, and should be understood as such, they were also products of European refineries and mills. Moreover, the imperial associations of groceries are complicated by the fact that China and Turkey were powerful empires in their own right and fiercely resistant to attempts at colonial intervention. To be sure, these were exotic places that had long fascinated western commentators; but they were not straightforwardly imperial spaces, despite the EIC's monopoly over much of the oriental trade.[82]

The problem here is the elision of the exotic with empire—the two were related, but were not the same. Exoticism was something that could be conjured up through place names and, for that matter, the names given to particular goods. For centuries spices had been associated with ideas of paradise—a tangible place somewhere in the orient.[83] If the direct link imagined in the Middle Ages had been washed away in the wake of a growing sea trade with the east, it remained in the names given to certain commodities, most notably grains of paradise (Guinea pepper). Sometimes abbreviated to grains, these were listed among the inventoried stock of grocers from the sixteenth to the eighteenth centuries, and reflected wider associations with the exotic that still attached themselves to spices in the eighteenth century.[84] A similar association can be seen in attempts to deploy Indian names for certain pickles and sauces, even when they were being domestically produced in the later eighteenth century. Both piccalilli and the gloriously named 'zoobditty match'—a rich sauce made from or to be served with fish—appear to be western corruptions of Indian words. The link with the orient helped to underline the exotic nature of these commodities in much the same way as happened with a range of Indian textiles.[85] Turkey was also seen as exotic and mysterious, an image

[81] *Dictionary of Traded Goods and Commodities* <http://www.british-history.ac.uk/report.aspx?compid=58864> (accessed 11 Mar. 2011).
[82] See e.g. Cowman, *Social Life of Coffee*, 6, 113–45; Walvin, *Fruits of Empire*, 9–10.
[83] Schivelbusch, *Tastes of Paradise*, 3–14.
[84] LiRO, B/C/11, Thomas Finnies (1598); LRO, WCW 1732, Alexander Chorley.
[85] See Wilhelmsen, *English Textile Nomenclature*.

that was deployed in the promotion of coffee in the seventeenth century (see Chapter 7).[86] In this regard, it benefited not only from travellers' tales and the subsequent western adoption of certain goods and products, but also from its position as a staging post on the traditional trade routes to the orient. This meant that other oriental goods—for example, Turkey rhubarb—became nominally associated with the country.

As a point of cultural reference, the exotic should, therefore, be laid alongside empire. So too should cultural contexts closer to home, in particular the ancient and renaissance civilizations celebrated across Europe, not least through the Grand Tour.[87] Cox and Dannehl note how several Italian cities, prominent on the tourist circuit, were associated with a range of luxury goods, including silks and glass from Venice, and velvets and citrus fruit from Genoa.[88] Groceries were perhaps less obvious in their cosmopolitan associations, but Rome, Florence, and Naples were all linked to specific products, and there was a growing taste for Italian groceries more generally—a phenomenon marked by the rise of the Italian Warehouse, especially in London. One such retailer was Mrs Holt, whose shop stood opposite the Exeter Exchange on the Strand. The illustration on her trade card included Rome in the main scene and vignettes of Florence, Venice, Genoa, Naples, and Leghorn arranged around this. The text beneath listed Venice treacle, Florence cordials, Bologna sausages, parmesan cheese, and Naples soap.[89] Again, though, a simple geographical or cultural reading of these associations is misleading: Florence oil may have come from or been associated with the great renaissance city, but Roman vitriol and Naples biscuits were also descriptions of the *type* of product being sold. The former was shorthand for a particular kind of sulphate, distinguishing it (and its properties and uses) from Danzig, Hungarian, and Polish vitriol, among others. The latter were certainly made and served in Italy, but were also a distinct form of biscuit, recipes for which appeared in many eighteenth-century cookbooks.[90]

Some associations became so strong that the place name effectively became the product: Naples biscuits, Scotch snuff, Durham mustard, Prussian Blue, and Castile soap. The names might conjure up a range of images and associations; more fundamentally, though, they told the consumer about the intrinsic characteristics of the product. For example, Castile soap was made from a combination of soda and olive oil and boiled twice to make it fine and hard. It was very different from Windsor soap, which was brown and usually scented. Distinctions between the large range of soaps and wash balls stocked by London retailers are less clear cut, but it is likely that the differences were of type, rather than provenance, not least because British soap boilers were producing a range of products, including Castile soap, by the turn of the eighteenth century.[91] With produce, as opposed to processed or manufactured goods, geographical labels could identify specific varieties

---

[86] Cowan, *Social Life of Coffee*, 115–20.   [87] Black, *British Abroad*.
[88] Cox and Dannehl, *Perceptions of Retailing*, 123–4.
[89] BM, Heal Collection, 126.10.
[90] Cox and Dannehl, *Perceptions of Retailing*, 98; Cleland, *Memoirs of a Woman of Pleasure*, 66.
[91] Houghton, *Husbandry and Trade*, 352–3; Cox and Dannehl, *Perceptions of Retailing*, 121.

or species. Malaga raisins were certainly grown in southern Spain, but the name communicated more about the type of grape (muscatel) and the method of viniculture, the grapes being ripened on the vine and therefore sweeter. Knowledge of this also justified their arrival later in the year and their higher price. Similarly, while Jamaica pepper came only from that island, the label signified a very different product from its oriental namesake and it was used in a very different way from black or white pepper.[92] Its physical appearance perhaps explains why it was so widely known as Jamaica pepper, but its association with a place that was, in many ways, the centrepiece of British colonialism in the Caribbean is surely no coincidence. If its name was, indeed, an imperial statement, then it was an uncertain one; allspice and later pimenta were favoured as descriptions of the same product.

CONCLUSIONS

The reorientation of the British economy away from Europe and towards the colonies is widely accepted as one of the defining strands of the so-called commercial revolution. Central to this was an increase in the range and quantity of tropical groceries being brought into the country from imperial possessions and through imperialistic trading companies. It is difficult to imagine that the retail sector could have remained unchanged in the face of this influx of new goods and their uptake by an ever broader section of society. However, Shammas's suggestion that colonial goods stimulated a flowering of British retailing, with shops growing hugely in number and spreading out into the countryside, certainly overplays the point. In part, this arises from an underestimation of early modern shop retailing (see Chapter 1), but it also reflects the ability of retailers to accommodate new goods within established lines of stock. Grocers were by no means the only ones to respond to the opportunities afforded by this new set of goods, but they benefited most: growing more numerous, offering the widest range and choice of groceries, and becoming increasingly specialized. That said, the presence of new and old groceries in a variety of other shops indicates both the widespread demand for such goods and the attractions of diversified stock. Selling groceries in small quantities to customers who returned on a regular basis may well have underpinned the provision of other goods and allowed shops to survive in more marginal places. However, the causal direction was the reverse of that posited by Shammas: sugar, tobacco, and especially caffeine drinks were added to an established stock rather than being the initial stimulus to see a wider range of groceries. Moreover, as we move through the eighteenth century, groceries became more marginal to the stock of mercers, ironmongers, apothecaries, and the like, and increasingly the domain of the grocer's shop. The retailing of groceries through this period was marked by continuity as much as change, the system being able to accommodate new products within existing specialisms and shops. Once established in the later eighteenth century,

---

[92] *OED*. The terms 'Jamaica pepper' and 'allspice' were both widely used by grocers through the first half of the eighteenth century to refer to this spice. Thereafter, it was increasingly labelled as 'pimenta'.

however, the mix of goods sold by grocers held remarkably constant for the next 150 years.

The diversity that characterized retailing of groceries was also seen in the nomenclature used to describe the products themselves. Empire was an increasingly important point of reference—a reflection of the provenance of commodities such as sugar and tobacco, their centrality to the imperial project, and a growing public interest in empire. However, the association was complex, not least because colonial goods were often linked to European centres of processing. Moreover, other place names were used to describe goods, linking them to the exotic, European cosmopolitanism, and even British regional identity. In part, this reflected an increasingly complex geography of supply in which Europe remained important as a source of supply and a point of reference for retailers and consumers. Empire was just one part of a conceptual and linguistic map of the expanding world of goods that provided a matrix for assessing the quality, characteristics, and desirability of particular commodities. Seeing and perhaps purchasing Barbados sugar linked the individual consumer to empire, but it also told them about the physical qualities of the product and thus its use in the kitchen; labels such as Spanish, Cuban, or Virginian tobacco had similarly layered meanings, as did Mocha and Jamaican coffee. Imperial and other place names were clearly significant both to retailers and to their customers, but perhaps mostly in communicating diversity in the world of goods found in the grocer's shop.

Overall, then, it is clear that the shifts in international trade that characterized the commercial revolution had a profound impact on English retailing as well as English consumers. Yet the effect of this influx of new goods was complex and nuanced. Empire was important, but was only one point of reference for consumers, who were perhaps more concerned with quality and price than with engaging in some grand imperial project. At the same time, more goods and greater demand undoubtedly offered a stimulus to retailing and probably helped shopkeepers to prosper in greater numbers and in more marginal locations, but it did not bring about any fundamental transformation in the retail sector. In terms of stock and specialism, then, it appears that commercial and consumer transformation could occur without retail revolution.

3

From Colony to Counter: Networks of Supply

INTRODUCTION

The huge variety of goods sold by grocers was drawn from a wide range of sources. Some could be acquired directly from producers, but many were available only via an intermediary. Through the Middle Ages, the great fairs had played a vital role in supplying shopkeepers of all sorts, but the early modern period saw the rise of a new breed of tradesman, the wholesaler. This might be seen as part of a general shift in trading infrastructure from the periodic to the permanent or even a fundamental precondition for a supply system capable of supplying a range of imported foodstuffs to the mass market. The exact character and functions of these dealers changed over time: in the sixteenth century, definitions revolved around dealing in bulk, whereas eighteenth-century understandings were centred much more on their role as middlemen.[1] It is the latter function that Defoe highlighted when he wrote that

others who are called wholesalesmen...bring and take off from the merchants all the foreign goods which they import; these, by their corresponding with a like sort of tradesmen in the country, convey and hand forward these goods, and our own also, among the country tradesmen, into every corner of the kingdom, however remote, and then to the retailer, and by the retailer to the last consumer.[2]

It is telling that Defoe saw this as a system that incorporated both domestic and imported goods, and that was centred on London. Metropolitan dealers collected goods from merchants and producers and distributed these across the country via a series of 'country' tradesmen. This picture corresponds well with evidence that Cox has drawn from trade cards and advertisements, which, despite difficulties in disentangling wholesale from retail activities, suggests a higher concentration of self-styled wholesalers in London.[3] Such a concentration is unsurprising, since many foreign goods came in through the port of London, some of them part of the trading monopoly of the chartered companies, including the East India Company (EIC). For all their importance, there is a danger in overemphasizing the significance of London to many aspects of the grocery trade and thus of simplifying the

---

[1] Cox, *Complete Tradesman*, 188. As noted in the Introduction, grocers were part of this process of definition.

[2] Defoe, *Compleat English Tradesman*, i. 3.

[3] Cox, *Complete Tradesman*, 189.

networks of supply through which grocers' shops were stocked. Indeed, Defoe's metropolitan viewpoint obscures the fact that many goods were imported through provincial ports, which thus became major entrepôts in the distribution of imported groceries. Tobacco came through many west-coast ports, with Glasgow becoming increasingly dominant, while sugar came into Bristol and Liverpool in ever greater quantities, prompting the emergence of local refining industries.[4] Such provision, along with the growing number of ships coming to provincial ports from southern Europe and around the Mediterranean, meant that groceries were available from a large number of different sources.

All this is familiar. Less well understood are the routes by which retailers acquired these goods and the ways in which these changed during a period that saw growing demand for imported groceries, especially those from the colonies. The importance of these systems of supply to our understanding of eighteenth-century consumption and retailing makes their relative neglect in the historiography all the more surprising.[5] To address this lacuna, we must examine both the structure and the operation of supply systems and assess the various drivers of change. In structural terms it is possible to identify three key intermediaries in the groceries trade: the auctions of the EIC, which (in theory at least) formed the only place at which tradesmen could acquire stocks of tea; the illicit trade in tea, which arose as a means of circumventing and profiting from the ever-higher excise duties imposed to offset the growing costs of war; and provincial merchants, who supplied perhaps a narrower range but still significant quantities of goods. Shifts in the relative importance of these three can tell us much about the changing supply options open to grocery retailers, but much more can be learned from a fuller understanding of the business networks through which individual shopkeepers connected into these wider systems of supply. Here, the most fruitful approach is to focus on a small number of case studies and link these to ideas drawn from network theory and neo-institutional economics. This provides theoretically robust analysis of the form, operation, and durability of these networks and systems, and allows us to assess the nature and durability of business relationships, and the role played by reputation and trust in establishing and maintaining such links. Through this, we can gain a clearer insight into the ways in which shopkeepers accessed their stock-in-trade and, more fundamentally, assess the ability of established systems of supply to match growing demand with increasingly global networks of trade.

SOURCES OF SUPPLY: LONDON AUCTIONS, PROVINCIAL MERCHANTS, AND WHOLESALE GROCERS

The EIC was vital in supplying a wide range of durable goods and foodstuffs over which it held a monopoly. In the early years of the company, pepper had been sold

---

[4] Gore's *Liverpool Directory*, 1766; Langton, 'Liverpool', 15; Minchinton, 'Bristol', 77.
[5] But see Willan, *Inland Trade*, 107–48; Haggerty, *British–Atlantic Trading*, 183–210; Stone, 'Grocers and Groceries', 86–7.

in bulk to wealthy merchants or syndicates, who were then responsible for its distribution to retailers. By the late seventeenth century, however, it was being auctioned by candle at the quarterly sales, the put-up price (effectively a reserve) being determined by the EIC. In most cases, it preferred to keep this price fairly constant, varying the quantity offered according to market conditions and thus maintaining its profit margin.[6] Much the same was true of coffee, although here private sales continued alongside the auctions well into the 1680s, partly because the company remained nervous about its ability to shift all of its stock. This put considerable power into the hands a handful of wealthy London traders and caused considerable disquiet among lesser merchants, who were often left bidding for poorer-quality lots at the coffee auctions. In response to this, and the regularization of the Mocha and later the China trade, the EIC resolved to sell both coffee and tea by the same system it deployed for pepper: putting up lots at a set price and allowing competitive bidding by candle.[7] For tea in particular, the system evolved so that all lots being offered for sale were exposed for inspection by brokers and buyers, and a catalogue was issued describing its quality and put-up price. Coupled with the small number of brokers who were licensed to bid for lots on behalf of the buyers, this meant that most sales ran quickly, with little variation in price for a particular quality of tea, either within auctions or over the years. Whether or not the buyers were actively engaged in price fixing, they formed a powerful oligarchy, in terms of both their purchasing power and their role in splitting lots and blending teas for distribution to provincial dealers.[8]

This was a system based on trust, reputation, and stable relationships between provincial retailers and the London tea houses, but it was swept away by the price reductions and controversy caused by the Commutation Act of 1784.[9] Dealers began to advertise in the press, promoting the sale of tea at much reduced prices and offering to ship directly from the EIC sales in the original chests—a practice that had previously been frowned upon because it was felt that tea improved for being kept in canisters, and that quality and uniformity of taste were improved by expert blending.[10] Moreover, a new breed of dealer began to emerge: one that emphasized cheap prices and insisted on ready money. Leading the way were Edward Eagleton (described by Mui and Mui as a 'pushing entrepreneur'[11]) and G. Winter; but they were quickly followed by others whose expertise lay in marketing rather than the tea trade. Frederick Gye further developed the 'new' techniques of advertising and selling prepackaged tea through a network of agents spread across the country (see Chapter 7), while John Nicholson not only engaged in direct selling, but also set about publishing the prices obtaining at the EIC auctions, further

---

[6] Chaudhuri, *Trading World*, 317–18.

[7] Cowan, *Social Life of Coffee*, 69–71.

[8] See Mui and Mui, *Shops and Shopkeeping*, 253–86.

[9] This might be seen as an example of the bonding social capital lauded by Putnam; but it also links to Bourdieu's critique of social capital as exclusively benefiting those who were well connected. See Putnam, *Bowling Alone*; Bourdieu, 'Forms of Capital'.

[10] *Morning Post*, 7 Feb. 1785; Twining, *An Answer*, 3–4.

[11] Mui and Mui, *Shops and Shopkeeping*, 272.

fuelling demand for cheap tea. Such individuals were in the vanguard of commercial modernization associated with growing demand and a broadening of the market for exotic consumables.

By the 1820s, tea could pass from the auction to the shopkeeper's shelf by a great variety of routes: through traditional London dealers such as Twinings; via direct sales from one of the 'new' breed of London dealers, or by the shopkeepers themselves acting as agents for one of these dealers. In each case, the ultimate source of the tea was the EIC auction, yet it is clear that the company rarely managed to maintain a tight rein on supplies, even for goods where it theoretically held a monopoly. In the seventeenth century, it struggled to control the supply of pepper, as considerable quantities were periodically brought over from Holland under special licence. Turkish coffee was available from the Levant Company sales, and plantation coffee later came in from Jamaica and Holland. And, of course, huge quantities of illicit tea found their way into English shops and homes.

It is beyond the scope of this study to assess the illicit trade in any detail, but it is clear that smuggling represented an important mechanism of supply for provincial shops.[12] A steady flow of illicit tea had come onto the English market through the late seventeenth and early eighteenth centuries. However, with the end of the Seven Years War, tea began to pour into continental Europe, much of it aimed at supplying England. At its peak in the 1770s, smuggling accounted for as much as two-thirds of the tea consumed in Britain, and it was reportedly impossible to sell legal tea within 30 miles of the coast.[13] Wathal Fenton, a shopkeeper in Woodhouse near Cheadle in Staffordshire, reduced the amount of tea ordered from a London dealer from between 200 and 400 pounds to just a few pounds each year.[14] Such actions had a huge impact on the trade in legal tea: the amount sold at the EIC auctions dropped from an average of 7.5 million pounds in 1768–70 to just 3.6 million pounds in 1781–3, while the 'fair-trade' dealers were forced to reduce their margins to a minimum.[15] Despite increasingly stringent regulations on the movement of large quantities of tea and close records of its sale in retail shops, smuggling continued to be a major source of tea until the Commutation Act slashed the excise duties to just 12.5 per cent. Almost at a stroke, the trade in illicit tea was ended; retailers such as Fenton returned to their previous suppliers, and the EIC sales regained their virtual monopoly as a point of supply for tea.

Many groceries were not covered by the monopoly of the EIC and so passed through a variety of other channels on their way from global to local networks of supply. Sugar and tobacco could be obtained direct from merchants or brokers, as could a wide range of Mediterranean goods. Sometimes, the importing merchant himself was involved in distributing goods across the country.[16] Richard Houghton of Liverpool had shares in several ships to the York and Potomac rivers, and

---

[12] For detailed studies, see Mui and Mui, 'Smuggling'; Ashworth, *Customs and Excise*, 165–83.
[13] Mui and Mui, 'Smuggling', 65–6.
[14] BL, Add. MS 36,666. See also Mui, 'Commutation Act', 246.
[15] Mui and Mui, 'Smuggling', 67–70.
[16] Haggerty, *British–Atlantic Trading*, 192–200.

another to Nevis, together worth £389 10*s*. In addition, he was owed a total of £531 5*s*. 10½*d*. by two individuals in Antigua, three in St Christopher, and one each in Jamaica, Barbados, and Montserrat, and a further £50 9*s*. 5½*d*. by six people in the American colonies.[17] Matching these are debts recorded with over 140 individuals in a wide range of towns across England, Wales, and Ireland. In total, these amounted to about £5,834, with individuals owing anything from £1418 5*s*. (Thomas Thorne of Dublin) to 4*s*. (George Whittaker of Liverpool). The precise nature of these debts is rarely made explicit, but the widely varying amounts owed and their precise calculation (sometimes down to the last quarter penny) strongly suggests that they were book debts for goods supplied. This point is made explicit with Thorne, whose debt is accompanied by a note indicating the supply of sugar and tobacco, which probably accounts for most of the other debts as well. If this is the case, then we can see a single Liverpool merchant supplying groceries and extending credit to dealers and perhaps individual consumers in thirty-nine separate places, mostly in the north and Midlands (Table 3.1). The limited penetration of his business network into the south of England probably reflects a similar supply of these commodities by merchants in London and Bristol. Indeed, the London tobacconists were aggressive in their attempts to defend and extend their domination of the inland trade. In 1751, they proposed that no tobacco and snuff should be removed from the premises of provincial shopkeepers unless it had been properly certificated to guarantee that all duties had been paid. Such restrictions were opposed on practical grounds, but also because the certificate, in naming the supplier and the buyer, would 'discover the names of his customers and the extent of his trade to the Officer who by communicating the same to others may detriment him in his business'.[18] Judging from the debts he was owed, Houghton appears to have been willing to supply his sugar and tobacco in large or small quantities. In Liverpool itself, the sums owed were generally modest, the median being just £1 19*s*. 10*d*., suggesting that his customers were either small-scale traders or private individuals—a practice that echoes Haggerty's findings for the later eighteenth century.[19] Elsewhere, the larger size of individual debts indicates sales to more substantial tradesmen, perhaps engaged in wholesale as well as retail trade.

Houghton was engaged in both overseas trade and the distribution of goods to retailers and consumers across the country, but this dual role was difficult to sustain, and it was more usual for importing merchants to operate through brokers who might dispatch goods to dealers in the port's hinterland or dispose of them via public auctions. The newspapers in Liverpool and Chester carried large numbers of advertisements for such sales, the frequency of announcements growing significantly in the early nineteenth century.[20] A large proportion of these were for goods central to the Atlantic trade and to the commercial activities of the west-coast

---

[17] LRO, WCW 1712, Richard Houghton.
[18] *Leeds Mercury*, 28 May 1751.
[19] Haggerty, *British–Atlantic Trading*, 199–200.
[20] A survey of the Liverpool press suggests that the number of auctions increased by 50% (see Gore's *Liverpool Advertiser*, 1770; *Liverpool Mercury*, 1820; see also Haggerty, *British–Atlantic Trading*, 200–2).

Table 3.1. British debts owing to Richard Houghton of Liverpool, merchant (d. 1712)

Geographical location	No.		Value	
	No.	%	£	%
Lancashire	*93*	*65.5*	*2,202*	*37.7*
Liverpool	66	46.5	375	6.4
Manchester	11	7.7	1533	26.3
Warrington	3	2.1	152	2.6
Other	13	9.2	142	2.4
Cheshire	*9*	*6.3*	*68*	*1.2*
Cumberland/Westmorland	*3*	*2.1*	*30*	*0.5*
Yorkshire/Lincolnshire	*10*	*7.0*	*642*	*11.0*
Gainsborough	2	1.4	412	7.1
Other	8	5.6	230	3.9
Denbighshire	*3*	*2.1*	*458*	*7.9*
Ruthin	1	0.7	382	6.5
Other	2	1.4	76	1.3
Shropshire/Staffordshire	*4*	*2.8*	*194*	*3.3*
Derbyshire/Nottinghamshire	*5*	*3.5*	*350*	*6.0*
Ashbourne	1	0.7	294	5.0
Other	4	2.8	56	1.0
Other counties	*4*	*2.8*	*26*	*0.4*
London	*4*	*2.8*	*69*	*1.2*
Newcastle	*1*	*0.7*	*270*	*4.6*
Ireland	*6*	*4.2*	*1,525*	*26.1*
Dublin	3	2.1	1469	25.2
Other	3	2.1	56	1.0
Total	*142*		*5,834*	

Note: value of debt given to nearest pound sterling.

Source: LRO, WCW 1712, Richard Houghton.

ports: sugar, tobacco, and rum together accounted for over half of the advertise-ments; dried fruit for around one quarter, and tea and coffee for about one-eighth. In a practice that echoed the labels given to groceries listed in probate inventories, many advertisements noted the provenance of these goods. Over one quarter referred to West Indian produce, most notably Jamaican rum, which was the single most common point of reference (Table 3.2). Such was its prominence as a 'brand' that it was frequently named in a mixture of other goods. For example, in February 1770, Benson and Postlethwaite advertised the sale of 'Irish butter in full bound Firkins, Hides, Tallow, Beef, Pork, Kelp, and very good Jamaica Rum'.[21] Other notices highlighted Jamaica, Barbados, and Antigua sugar; Jamaica and St Domingo coffee, and Jamaica tobacco. The frequency with which Jamaica appears in

---

[21] *Gore's Liverpool Advertiser*, 9 Feb. 1770.

Table 3.2. Provenance of goods in a sample of auctions of ships' cargoes advertised in the Chester and Liverpool press, 1770–1820 (%)

Geographical location	Fruit (N = 17)	Sugar (N = 10)	Nuts (N = 6)	Tobacco (N = 5)	Rum (N = 5)	Rice (N = 3)	Other (N = 5)	Total (N = 51)
Mediterranean	27.5		11.8	2.0				41.2
Turkey	11.8			2.0				13.7
Barcelona			5.9					5.9
Jordan			5.9					5.9
Malaga	5.9							5.9
Other	9.8							9.8
West Indies		11.8		2.0	9.8		3.9	27.5
Jamaica		5.9		2.0	9.8			17.6
Barbados		3.9						3.9
Other		2.0					3.9	5.9
East Indies		7.8		2.0		3.9	2.0	15.7
North America				2.0		2.0		3.9
Other	5.9			2.0			3.9	11.8
France	5.9						2.0	7.8
Other				2.0			2.0	3.9

Sources: *Gore's Liverpool Advertiser* (1770); *Adams Weekly Courant* (1777–9); *Liverpool Mercury* (1820).

advertisements underlines its significance to British trade and British imperial interests during this period—easily overshadowing its Caribbean neighbours. It also outshone North American interests, with only occasional references made to Carolina rice or American leaf tobacco.[22]

As noted earlier, it is hard to judge the significance of these place names. They can be read as a gazetteer of Britain's expanding empire. Associating each colony with the particular products that it supplied to the mother country made empire into something real and tangible: a series of products to be sold, bought, and consumed.[23] However, as with the nomenclature of inventories, it is far from clear that this is how merchants and shopkeepers understood these labels. Jamaica rum and Barbados sugar were markers of quality and provenance rather than simply symbols of empire; they paralleled similar descriptors of non-imperial goods by communicating reputation.[24] Again echoing probate inventories, the Mediterranean provided by far the most common points of reference, although Turkey figs, Malaga and Zante raisins, Barcelona nuts, or French indigo were generic labels rather than necessarily being an indication of particular provenance. By the 1820s, the auctions also included goods from the East Indies—a reflection of the 1813

---

[22] *Liverpool Mercury*, 14 Apr. 1820, 17 Nov. 1820.
[23] See Bickham, 'Eating the Empire'; Walvin, *Fruits of Empire*.
[24] Cox and Dannehl, *Perceptions of Retailing*, 97–126; Edelson, 'Characters of Commodities'; Hancock, 'Self-Organized Complexity', 54–9.

Charter Act, which had effectively liberalized the trade with India.[25] Fairly typical was the announcement made by Duff, Finlay & Co. of Liverpool that they would shortly be offering: 280 bags and 126 boxes of 'Fine white East India Sugar'; 1,050 bags of 'Patna and Patcherry Rice'; 886 packets and 751 bags of ginger, and 11 casks of molasses, which were 'Now landing, ex Mary Kneale, from Calcutta'.[26] This indicates an important expansion of the routes by which East Indian goods could arrive with provincial dealers and reflected the growing liberalization of trade necessary to facilitate mass consumption. As Mui and Mui argue, the era of free trade was accompanied by a 'network of dealers prepared to adopt the aggressive policies of the new men of business'.[27] That said, this apparent modernization was accompanied by other, more haphazard forms of supply, including the sale of cargoes seized by customs officials, salvaged from wrecks or taken from captured French ships.[28]

It is difficult to know who bought commodities at these sales, but grocers were clearly an important market at least for John Brown, who advertised in the Liverpool press in May 1770 that he had 'A Cargo of New SUGARS, Of a very fine quantity, to be sold in lots suitable to the Grocers'.[29] The buyers would also have included specialist wholesale grocers, the largest of which were found in Liverpool, Bristol, and London, from where they dispatched goods across broadly defined regions.[30] From their order books and invoices, it appears that they were willing to send varying and sometimes quite modest consignments to their retail customers, who placed frequent but irregular-sized orders, presumably reflecting the level of their own sales. For example, between April and August 1813, John Smith of Faversham ordered goods from the wholesalers Toms and Hicks of Southwark on no fewer than eleven occasions. On 10 June he placed his largest order, worth £99 14*s*. 1*d*.; his next order, two weeks later, was the smallest at just £5 18*s*. 7*d*.[31] Orders could be placed by letter or sometimes via commercial travellers, but they were rarely accepted from small shopkeepers, who had to rely instead on more general wholesale/retail grocers. One such trader was Thomas Wootton of Bewdley. His inventory of 1667 includes a shop that was well stocked with a range of groceries and other goods, but there were also many goods in storerooms and a long list of debts owing to him.[32] The size and geographical spread of these suggest an extensive wholesale business that spread across six counties.[33] While the bulk of his sales were in towns and villages within a 20-mile radius of Bewdley, there was also a significant number of links with people over 30 miles distant (Table 3.3). The latter included some surprisingly distant places—Burton-on-Trent, Newcastle-under-Lyme, and Coventry—and indicate that Wootton was able to supply goods at a price

---

[25] Webster, 'Strategies and Limits', 745–6.
[26] *Liverpool Mercury*, 17 Mar. 1820.
[27] Mui and Mui, *Shops and Shopkeeping*, 286.
[28] See, e.g., *Adams Weekly Courant*, 24 Dec. 1776; *Adams Weekly Courant*, 9 Nov. 1779.
[29] *Gore's Liverpool Advertiser*, 11 May 1770 and repeated 18 May 1770 and 1 June 1770.
[30] Alexander, *Retailing in England*, 116–17.
[31] Quoted in Alexander, *Retailing in England*, 118.
[32] TNA: PRO C5/582/120.
[33] Wootton's inventory contains a separate heading for 'several sums of money all which stand due upon the Shopbooks of the said Thomas Wotton'. These appear to be retail customers.

Table 3.3. Debts owing to Thomas Wootton of Bewdley, grocer (d. 1667)

Geographical location	Distance from Bewdley (miles)	Debts owing	
		No.	%
Worcestershire		*73*	*41.7*
Kidderminster	3	29	16.6
Stourbridge	3	20	11.4
Bewdley	0	10	5.7
Tenbury	13	6	3.4
Other		8	4.6
Staffordshire		*48*	*27.4*
Wolverhampton	17	17	9.7
Burton-on-Trent	42	5	2.9
Newcastle-under-Lyme	46	5	2.9
Stafford	32	5	2.9
Other		16	9.0
Shropshire		*39*	*22.3*
Ludlow	18	20	11.4
Bridgnorth	12	5	2.9
Other		14	8.0
Warwickshire		*12*	*6.9*
Coventry	36	6	3.4
Birmingham	20	5	2.9
Other		1	0.6
Herefordshire		*2*	*1.1*
Gloucestershire		*1*	*0.6*
Total		*175*	

Source: LiRO, B/M/1667 Thomas Wootton.

or quality that could override the friction of distance. The inventory does not indicate the goods supplied, but a glance into his shop and storerooms suggests that it was most likely to have been sugar and tobacco, although there were also large quantities of raisins, alum, and oil. These goods were probably brought in through Bristol and transported up the River Severn to Bewdley.[34]

This dual wholesale/retail role might be seen as reflecting an underdeveloped commercial system, but it persisted through the eighteenth and well into the nineteenth centuries. During the 1840s, Jonathan Pedlar of St Austell had accounts with several shopkeepers whom he supplied with a wide range of goods, including lard, flour, bran, meal, and tobacco. His customers typically placed orders worth between £2 and £6 at fortnightly intervals, for which they received

[34] Wanklyn, 'Impact of Water Transport'.

a variable discount of up to 16.6 per cent. Around the same time, James Bowles, who kept shop in Balsham in Cambridgeshire, bought all his supplies from three grocers in Saffron Walden.[35] It is impossible to know what motivations and commercial imperatives underpinned these relationships. What is clear, however, is that many grocers from the late seventeenth to the early nineteenth centuries had a variety of options available to them when they wanted to restock their shops, from the EIC sales in London through provincial merchants, auctions, or wholesalers, to the illicit trade, especially in tea. This was a system of supply that offered options and was able to bring together overseas supplies and local shopkeepers. It was a system that worked, perhaps because it was so varied and flexible. To what extent, though, did individual grocers draw on the range of options available; is it possible to see a process of 'modernization' in the practices and mechanisms through which shopkeepers were supplied?

GROCERS AND THEIR SUPPLIERS

Shammas suggests that the systems of supply drawn upon by provincial shopkeepers were shaped by the nature of the town in which the shop was located, the type of stock held, and the distance from London. To this, Mui and Mui add two extra elements: first was the shift from a system dominated by London to one with multiple points of supply, and second was the move from the grocers having to seek out stock as best they could to one where suppliers were chasing custom.[36] They mark the two extremes of this transformation by the practices of William Stout in the late seventeenth century and the activities of a new breed of London tea dealers in the late eighteenth and early nineteenth centuries. The former was part of a system based on face-to-face contact and individual reputation and knowledge; the latter was characterized by market structures and a much freer flow of information about price and products—often in printed form.[37] Less clear from their analysis are the intermediate stages between these extremes and the extent to which individual grocers moved from one system of supply to another.

At the start of his business career in 1688, William Stout travelled to London with fellow Lancaster shopkeepers to acquire supplies for his shop. He took with him £120 borrowed from family and friends and visited various tradesmen to whom he had been recommended. From them he bought goods to the 'value of two hundred pounds or upwards, and payed each of them about halfe ready money, as was then usual to do by any young man beginning trade'. Sending his goods back to Lancaster by sea, Stout travelled home via Sheffield, buying £20 of metal wares, apparently direct from the manufacturers.[38] This routine remained in place for the next twenty years or so, but it was not as immutable as Mui and Mui suggest. By 1692 he had made arrangements with Obadiah Barlow in Sheffield 'to buy

---

[35] Quoted in Alexander, *Retailing in England*, 119.
[36] Shammas, *Pre-Industrial Consumer*, 242–3; Mui and Mui, *Shops and Shopkeeping*, 10–11.
[37] Mui and Mui, *Shops and Shopkeeping*, 8–9, 270, 281–6.
[38] Stout, *Autobiography*, 89. See also Alexander, *Retailing in England*, 117.

goods for me in my absence' and three years later returned via Bristol, where he 'bought sevrall parcels of goods'. In addition to these distant points of supply, Stout also acquired tobacco and sugar in Liverpool, Poulton-le-Fylde, and Lancaster; cheese from the fairs at Preston and Garstang, and 'nails and other things of this country's manufactories'.[39] Many of these transactions were carried out in person, but whether this was through necessity or choice is not easy to judge. Stout felt that the route to success was through close attention to business, yet he was also conscious of the trouble and expense of making such long journeys, and perhaps also of the advantages of being able to spread his network beyond individuals with whom he could do business face to face. In 1704, he began to draw on what Ben-Porath terms the 'implicit contract of family', arranging for his cousin's son, Peter Willson, to be apprenticed to a London dry salter.[40] Upon completion of his apprenticeship in 1711, Stout began buying goods directly from him and arranged for Willson to purchase and dispatch others on his behalf.[41] Five years after establishing his relation in London, Stout sought to redefine his relationship with his network of Sheffield suppliers. He took 'the names of the makers' so that he could place orders directly, arranging with a local ironmaster and factor to 'take them in and pack them and send them to me, allowing him a small sum on commission'. The correspondence that this inevitably involved strengthened his links to these men through regular interaction and the exchange of information.[42] At the same time, he sought to expand his business network, using a visit to Bristol to establish contacts with suppliers of sugar and tobacco. Here, the importance of trust and the ability to trade on the reputation of others is readily apparent; Stout followed common practice in taking with him letters of recommendation, 'we being altogether strangers'. Such introductions were necessary to include an unknown contact into a merchant's 'radius of trust'.[43] In Stout's case, it was clearly effective, since he was 'civilly entertained and recommended', and successfully settled a correspondence with Bristol merchants. In this way, he extended his own business network, adding so-called weak ties, which acted as bridges to other, wider networks of supply and thus to new supplies, information, and business opportunities.[44]

This growing web of contacts did not constitute a dramatic transformation of his trading practices, but it did mean that Stout had a choice of suppliers for each of the goods in which he traded. Tobacco was usually purchased at Lancaster. He took the opportunity to buy small quantities from the crews of the Virginia ships that came to the port, but got most of his supplies from the customs house, where

---

[39] Stout, *Autobiography*, 106, 114, 89. This reflects the punishing schedule followed by later commercial travelers (Popp, 'Building the Market').

[40] Ben-Porath, 'The F-Connection', 1. See also Stobart, 'Information, Trust and Reputation', 299–300.

[41] Stout, *Autobiography*, 166.

[42] Stout, *Autobiography*, 160. On the importance of correspondence in articulating business networks, see Stobart, 'Personal and Commercial Networks', 285–7; Haggerty, *British–Atlantic Trading*, 122–7.

[43] Stout, *Autobiography*, 114; Fukuyama, *Trust*, 155–7. See also Stobart, 'Information, Trust and Reputation', 300; Haggerty, *British–Atlantic Trading*, 128–41.

[44] Stout, *Autobiography*, 114; Granovetter, 'Strength of Weak Ties', 1364; Haggerty and Haggerty, 'Visual Analytics'.

he often benefited from an allowance that further raised his profit margin. He also had tobacco from London, Liverpool, and Bristol, from where he acquired sugar as well, although again there were alternatives, including the refinery in Lancaster operated by his neighbour John Hodgson.[45] Stout is rarely explicit about his motives in seeking out different suppliers, but they probably reflected a desire not to be reliant upon a single source. For much of his career, England was at war, which made the supply of many of his staples uncertain and unreliable. Added to this were the vicissitudes of the weather, illness at sea, and the variable quality of ships and sailors. As Stout found to his cost, these made overseas ventures a risky business; they also meant that it was advisable to secure a number of potential suppliers should one be unable to deliver.[46] At the same time, Stout was knowledgeable about the price and availability of commodities, and may have exercised choice in relation to the former. In this sense, Stout's contacts were important sources of information as well as goods—a common feature of networks during a period when more formal means of acquiring business intelligence were often absent.[47] Indeed, new institutional perspectives have stressed this role, the regular exchange of information helping to reduce transaction costs incurred because of the absence of information or where its reliability remained uncertain. For Burt, this was the 'information benefit' of networks.[48] Above all, though, Stout's knowledge came from his own experience. Although modest by Liverpool standards, his investments in overseas ventures gave him first-hand knowledge of the cost of the goods in which he traded in Lancaster and brought him into contact with a wider system of supply and exchange.[49]

If Stout's business networks were increasingly complex and diverse, his use of financial instruments remained straightforward. Many goods were paid for in cash: sometimes in person when they were acquired and sometimes via an agent. Only on very rare occasions do we see him using bills of exchange.[50] This might reflect customary practice, a lack of trusted connections, or limited development of other instruments of money transfer. However, paying with ready money afforded Stout some significant advantages, not least in terms of discounted prices. This is most explicit in his purchases of tobacco from the customs house in Lancaster, where 'as we endeavoured to pay most of the duty ready money we had halfe a penny a pound allowed for that, which reduced the price'.[51] Overall, Stout's network of suppliers remained constrained by personal contacts. His own expertise and experience were crucial to his success, while personal knowledge of individual business partners was central to his attempts to extend his web of contacts. In network

---

[45] Stout, *Autobiography*, 95, 106.

[46] In 1699, Stout lost nearly £40 on a £110 investment in a voyage to Virginia and just about broke even on a venture to Barbados. Later in the same year, he reckoned to have lost £70 on another venture, having waited four years for the ship finally to return from Philadelphia (Stout, *Autobiography*, 92–130).

[47] Haggerty, *British–Atlantic Trading*, 114–35.

[48] Burt, 'Network Entrepreneur', 156–8. See also North, 'Transaction Costs'; Pearson and Richardson, 'Business Networking', 658, 674; Hancock, *Citizens of the World*, 81–2.

[49] Stout, *Autobiography*, 138.   [50] Stout, *Autobiography*, 296.

[51] Stout, *Autobiography*, 161.

terms, he built strong ties with similar tradesmen, placed reliance on friendship and kinship ties, and valued long-established links, especially within the Lancaster trading community. His attempts to extend his network to include weak ties that acted as bridges to wider systems of supply—most notably via Bristol merchants— were relatively unimportant in his overall network of supply, which remained essentially regional and London centred.

A generation later, the supply network of Thomas Dickenson, a Worcester grocer, was rather different in character. While the nature of the sources means that we have less information on his attitudes and motivations, Dickenson's account books provide detailed insight into the operation of his supply network. He had a much larger network than Stout, drawing on a total of sixty-three suppliers between 1740 and 1749.[52] Shammas's analysis emphasizes the importance of London, but in reality it was Bristol that formed the key source of goods, especially imported groceries (Table 3.4).[53] About one-third of Dickenson's suppliers

Table 3.4. Location of suppliers to Thomas Dickenson of Worcester, grocer, 1740–1749

Geographical location	Suppliers		Where total values are known		Value		Suppliers of imported groceries	
	No.	%	No.	%	£	%	No.	%
Bristol	22	34.9	18	42.9	3,099	65.1	11	50.0
London	13	20.6	12	28.6	1,144.5	24.1	3	13.6
Worcester	13	20.6	6	14.3	444	9.3	4	18.2
Gloucester	1	1.6					1	4.5
Other Midland towns								
Bewdley	2	3.2					0	0.0
Cleobury	1	1.6	1	2.4	8	0.2	0	0.0
Bridgnorth	1	1.6	1	2.4	3.5	0.1	0	0.0
Broseley	1	1.6					0	0.0
Ludlow	1	1.6					0	0.0
NW England								
Chester	1	1.6	1	2.4	8.5	0.2	1	4.5
Preston	1	1.6					1	4.5
Unknown	6	9.5	3	7.1	50	1.1	1	4.5
	63		42		4,757.5		22	

Source: WSL, D1798 HM 27/5.

---

[52] WSL, D1798 HM29/5. Dickenson's near contemporary Thomas Turner drew supplies from seventy-one individuals (Vaisey, *Thomas Turner*, 344–6).

[53] Shammas, *Pre-Industrial Consumer*, 240–1. Thomas Turner, who lived in the Sussex village of East Hoathly, was more dependent upon London, around 40% of his suppliers being based in the metropolis, which could be reached in half a day (Vaisey, *Thomas Turner*, 22 Mar. 1759).

were Bristol wholesalers and manufacturers, who together provided nearly two-thirds of his stock, mostly sent up the River Severn. Foremost were sugar bakers, three of whom supplied nearly £1,400 of stock between 1740 and 1749; but he also received tobacco, soap, spices, dried fruit, tea, coffee, and a variety of other goods, often in mixed consignments.

As with Stout, some goods were sourced locally. Occasionally he bought from specialist producers, acquiring paper in Cleobury, corks and starch in Bewdley, pipes in Broseley, shot in Bridgnorth, and hops in Worcester.[54] He also obtained stock from or through other retailers in Worcester, including fellow grocers, tobacconists, and even a bookseller. Sometimes this involved goods being dispatched to neighbours—for example, when George Farr of London sent Dickenson 3 lb of sugar 'in a parcel to Mr Edwards'. This was Timothy Edwards, a fellow grocer with whom he had close and frequent dealings. Between December 1740 and March 1742 Edwards made 121 separate purchases from Dickenson's shop. Very occasionally these involved small quantities of goods that might be consumed by Edwards himself, but more often they comprised substantial quantities of particular items. Thus, on 20 March 1741, he bought: 1 treble sugar loaf, 1 lump loaf, 7 lb Jamaica pepper and 7 lb ordinary fig blue; returning the next day for 56 lb second powder sugar and three days later for 7 lb Spanish tobacco. The following month, he bought: 5 lb Jamaica pepper; ¾ cwt white lead; 4 lb Jamaica pepper, 2 lb best bohea tea, 1 lb hyson tea, ½ lb finest hyson tea, 56 lb middling bastard and 28 lb second powder sugar; 28 lb rice and 11 lb 6 oz treacle, and 28 lb rice, 28 lb white lead, a rundlet of treacle—all within the space of a week.[55] We know less about the goods supplied to Dickenson by Edwards, but they included some of the same items that he was buying in Dickenson's shop: rice, tobacco, tea, coffee, shot, spices, capers, and blue. These two grocers clearly enjoyed a particularly close relationship, regularly drawing on each other's stock to meet the needs of their own customers. Dickenson also drew on a wider network of fellow shopkeepers, his purchasing book being peppered with entries recording short-term loans of stock: ½ lb cloves from Mr Hope, 14 lb saltpetre from Henry Spencer, and 7 lb Jamaica pepper from Mr Forrest.[56] Placing emergency orders with local tradesmen was common and, as Alexander demonstrates, persisted well into the nineteenth century, the substantial grocer Thomas Bumpus maintaining accounts with three fellow Northampton grocers in the 1840s to ensure a good supply of stock.[57]

Reflecting the diverse nature of his contacts and network, Dickenson's relationship with his suppliers was far more varied than that which Stout tried to achieve. Whereas Stout generally attempted to establish long-term relations with his suppliers, Dickenson's network included a number of contacts who supplied goods only once during the period 1740–9 and over half sent goods on fewer than six

---

[54] Thomas Turner made more use of local suppliers, drawing on tradesmen in Lewes and buying from producers in at least thirteen towns and villages in Sussex and Kent.

[55] WSL, D1798 HM 27/5.

[56] WSL, D1798 HM 27/5, 19 Dec. 1745, 25 Jan. 1746. The loans were repaid in kind, usually within a few weeks.

[57] Alexander, *Retailing in England*, 120.

Table 3.5. Frequency of purchases from selected suppliers of Thomas Dickenson of Worcester, grocer, 1740–1749

No. of purchases	No. of suppliers	Value of business transacted (£)	Mean value of business (£)	Median contact period (months)
1	9	38	4.2	1
2–5	13	333	25.6	13
6–10	5	539	107.6	43
11–15	8	2,084	260.5	44.5
16 and over	6	1,760	293.2	66.5

Source: WSL, D1798 HM 27/5.

occasions (Table 3.5). This suggests a broad network with multiple, but relatively weak links. Contacts were infrequent and often short-lived: nearly one-quarter appear to have lasted for less than a year. However, this picture is complicated by Dickenson's links with men like Robert Makraire of Bristol, who appears in the accounts as supplying him with tobacco on five occasions over four and a half years.[58] Purchases amounting to a total of £41 11*s.* 2*d.* are not insignificant, but formed a tiny fraction of Dickenson's business (and presumably that of Makraire as well), yet it was clearly worth the two men staying in contact and maintaining a business relationship that included the granting of credit by Makraire. Such links underline the importance of weak links to the vitality of a business network: they offered diversity of supply, multiple sources information and ideas, and opportunities for developing new areas of business.[59] Nonetheless, Dickenson's network was centred on a core of strong links to between ten and fifteen suppliers with whom he did regular business and from whom he acquired over 85 per cent of his goods. This core group included local men, but most of them were from London or Bristol. Some of them supplied very large orders relatively infrequently, whereas others dispatched goods more frequently, but in smaller quantities. For example, William Miller of Bristol sent fourteen orders worth an average of about £41, while the London grocer Philip Cooke dispatched forty-three orders typically worth a little less than £5. Yet these average figures conceal a huge variation in the nature of consignments from particular suppliers. Both the range of goods supplied and the variation in the size of orders is apparent from Dickenson's dealings with Charles Davie of Bristol (Table 3.6). This variety was by no means unusual. Most of the consignments from the London haberdasher Thomas Spicer were for relatively modest amounts (£5 11*s.* for a parcel of coffee and £1 18*s.* for 12 lb of chocolate); but in November 1745 he sent two chests of tea, charging Dickenson £69 1*s.* 6*d.*, and a month later sent another chest of 'B B tea' worth £74 6*s.* 9*d.*[60]

[58] WSL, D1798 HM 27/5.

[59] See Granovetter, 'Strength of Weak Ties', 1362; Stobart, 'Information, Trust and Reputation', 301; Haggerty and Haggerty, 'Visual Analytics'; Hancock, 'Trouble with Networks', 478–88.

[60] WSL, D1798 M 27/5 and 29/1–4. It is interesting that the consignment was sent in chests rather than the canisters usually favoured by London dealers (see Mui and Mui, *Shops and Shopkeeping*, 259).

Table 3.6. Debit from Thomas Dickenson of Worcester to Mr Charles Davie of Bristol, 1741–1745

Date	Goods	£	s.	d.
1 November 1741	Goods received	43	14	2½
1 April 1742	Nutts & pepper	7	6	8
1 June 1742	Nutts & pepper	4	1	7
1 October 1742	Goods received	93	3	2
1 October 1742	a barrel of sugar	6	5	0
1 February 1743	Figs, prunes & belvidores	26	5	10
1 August 1743	Pimento, nutts & mace	5	17	5
1 November 1743	Jones' note returned	7	7	0
1 October 1743	Sugar & raisins	67	11	9
1 March 1744	Sugar	26	0	0
1 November 1744	Sugar	49	3	0
1 August 1745	Black & white pepper	2	12	8
1 October 1745	Rule twine	1	1	6
1 November 1745	2 of Bristol chocolate	0	8	6
	A parcel of seeds	1	1	0
	Total	341	19	3½

Source: WSL, D1798 HM 27/5.

Dickenson's ties with his core suppliers were also characterized by their longevity (Table 3.5). Those from whom he made fifteen or more purchases were in business with him for an average of five and a half years. Such intense and stable relations brought many advantages. First and foremost, they were a reliable source of goods, allowing Dickenson to maintain a wide range of stock in his shop and perhaps to supplement the stock of his neighbours' shops also. In addition, these men were known and trusted: they had supplied goods over a number of years, presumably at a price and quality to satisfy Dickenson and his customers. The trust thus established meant that transaction costs associated with uncertain supply, quality, or price would be reduced. It is also likely that these strong links were a route to other merchants. The goods dispatched via Timothy Edwards suggest that Dickenson may have been using his core contacts effectively to spread his business network much more widely—beyond what he could reasonably coordinate himself.[61] At the same time, stable long-term relations facilitated the provision of credit and the organization of secure and convenient modes of payment (Table 3.7). Dickenson was clearly trustworthy, over 80 per cent of his suppliers granting him credit over periods varying from a few weeks to several months. The London grocer Philip Cooke, for instance, received forty-three orders over a period of five and a half years worth a total of £209 12s. 1d. This account was settled on twenty occasions,

---

[61] See Pearson and Richardson, 'Business Networking'; Stobart, 'Information, Trust and Reputation', 301; Burt, 'Network Entrepreneur', 289.

Table 3.7. Payment arrangements of selected suppliers of Thomas Dickenson of
Worcester, 1740–1749

No. of purchases	Cash on order		Credit Cash		Cash and bills		Bills		Unknown		Total
	No.	% of total	No.	% of total	No.	% of total	No.	% of total	No.	% of total	
1	2	4.9	4	9.8					3	7.3	9
2–5	5	12.2	5	12.2	1	2.4			2	4.9	13
6–10					3	7.3	2	4.9			5
11–15			2	4.9	2	4.9	4	9.8			8
16 and over			2	4.9			3	7.3	1	2.4	6
Total	7	17.1	13	31.7	6	14.6	9	22.0	6	14.6	41

Source: WSL, D1798 HM 27/5.

with average payments of about £10 being made every fifteen weeks or so. By contrast, Dickenson's account with the Bristol sugar bakers Barnes, Hunt and Smith,
who supplied £959 5s. 12d. of sugar across a period of five years, was settled on
thirty-seven occasions, payments being made every seven weeks on average.[62]

Where credit arrangements were not in place, it was invariably with tradesmen
with whom he had limited contact—men like William Jenkins, the Bristol grocer.
Paying in cash, especially up front, may reflect a lack of established mutual trust,
yet Dickenson also paid cash to other tradesmen, even when he received a period
of credit. In such instances cash might be favoured because of the cheaper prices
offered for ready money, but it was sometimes used because relatively small payments needed to be made. Bills of exchange were usually for larger denominations
(in Dickenson's case, mostly for sums of £10) and were not easily split, making
cash the most convenient form of payment.[63] For larger transactions, bills were
generally employed, sometimes in conjunction with cash. This means of payment
was well established for overseas trade; its growing use in domestic transactions
reflected the development of both sophisticated systems of monetary circulation
and extensive business networks—part of the modernization of business that underpinned the growing volume of internal and overseas trade.[64] Bills of exchange
had been widely used by Stout's mercantile contemporaries, but they required the
presence of an individual against whom the bill could be drawn. Stout may have
lacked such contacts, in general preferring to use agents with whom he lodged
monies to pay for orders placed locally. Dickenson, by contrast, had a range of

[62] WSL, D1798 HM 27/5. Such variable periods of credit were quite common. See Haggerty,
British–Atlantic Trading, 145–50.
[63] Thomas Turner paid many of his smaller London accounts in cash, carefully recording the
amounts in his diary (Vaisey, *Thomas Turner*, 19–22 Mar. 1759).
[64] Mui and Mui, *Shops and Shopkeeping*, 202; Willan, *Inland Trade*, 112–15, 123–5.

Table 3.8. Location of suppliers of Abraham Dent of Kirby Stephen, 1756–1777

Location	Suppliers	
	No.	%
Kendal	34	17.9
Other Westmorland	8	4.2
Cumberland	20	10.5
Lancaster	10	5.3
Other Lancashire	27	14.2
Newcastle	20	10.5
County Durham	21	11.1
Yorkshire	14	7.4
London	12	6.3
Elsewhere/unknown	24	12.6
Total	190	

Source: Willan, *Abraham Dent*, 29.

trusted business contacts in both Bristol and London against whom his bills were to be drawn. In this way, his financial network reinforced his supply network, particularly in these two important points of supply.

The supply network established by Dickenson was extensive, with lines of heavy interaction and a range of other more lightly used contacts. Some of the latter resulted from opportunism or unsuccessful attempts to establish long-term relationships, but others, while sporadic, were sustained over a number of years. Social scientific models of business networks would identity such arrangements as inefficient, but they clearly worked, not least because of the flexibility of supply they afforded.[65] A generation later, Abraham Dent of Kirkby Stephen in Westmorland represented a different scale and in some ways a different era of shopkeeper. Dent stocked a rather wider variety of goods than did Dickenson, including textiles, ironware, and hardware; even so, his network of suppliers was significantly wider, incorporating, between 1756 and 1777, a total of 190 individuals in 49 locations (Table 3.8).[66] Given his remoteness from London, it is perhaps unsurprising that Dent drew on metropolitan tradesmen comparatively little, although we should recall that, a century or so earlier, Stout had been both willing and able to travel south to secure stock. London's relative unimportance is probably better explained in terms of the expanding range of alternative supply lines available to Dent and, more arguably, the different approaches taken by the two men. Stout travelled in person, whereas Dent operated through a dense network of contacts, accessing London goods via what were effectively wholesalers operating in provincial towns. Some of the sugar and tobacco that he purchased from suppliers in Lancaster was

[65] See Granovetter, 'Strength of Weak Ties'; Haggerty and Haggerty, 'Visual Analytics'.
[66] Willan, *Abraham Dent*, 28.

no doubt imported through the town; but a large proportion of the goods arriving via Kendal and especially Newcastle—his other two main sources of groceries— were probably carried from London. Much the same was true for some smaller ports, including Stockton-on-Tees and Milnthorpe.[67]

An integrated urban system, wherein towns were linked by efficient transport and commercial infrastructure, was a characteristic of industrializing economies and provided Dent with a greater range of possibilities than had been available to Stout.[68] Combined with the inland location of Kirkby Stephen, it also meant that no single entrepôt dominated the supply of imported goods—as had been the case with Dickenson. Lancaster was the most important source of supply for sugar and tobacco, with Lawson Rawlinson & Co. sending regular consignments through the 1760s; but tobacco also came via Kendal, Newcastle, and even Sheffield, while sugar was obtained in London, Kendal, and Newcastle—often as part of more general parcels of goods. Much the same was true of tea, coffee, and spices, which arrived through suppliers in London, Newcastle, Kendal, Lancaster, Darlington, and elsewhere.[69] The task of maintaining such a widespread and diverse network of supply was mitigated by the fact that not all suppliers were actively engaged at any one time. Willan notes that there were forty-seven recorded in the peak year of 1763, new ones being recruited as others disappeared from the records. Typical of this kind of arrangement were the Ashburners, who operated as papermakers, printers, and booksellers in Kendal. Thomas Ashburner supplied paper, magazines, books, and patent medicines between 1759 and 1762, while James Ashburner did the same from 1762 to 1772.[70] More fundamentally, Dent's network, like that of Dickenson, included a relatively small number of key suppliers with whom he did a considerable amount of business on a regular basis, and a much larger set of small-scale or intermittent suppliers. For the year 1763, Dent bought about £677 worth of goods, 65 per cent of them from eight suppliers.[71] Central to his network were men such as John Whitwell, a Kendal tradesman who supplied over £300 of groceries between 1759 and 1769; Lawson Rawlinson & Co., who supplied £170 in 1764–65, and Atkinson and Hall of Newcastle, who presented bills totalling £587 in 1763, 1766, and 1770.[72]

What marked out these suppliers was the amount of business being conducted and the long-term nature of their relationship with Dent. As with Dickenson, continuity of supply was clearly important, allowing trust to be built between trading partners and easing the flow of information and credit.[73] John Whitwell, for

---

[67] Willan, *Abraham Dent*, 40. London wholesalers were, of course, still active in supplying provincial grocers (Rees, *Grocery Trade*, ii. 108–13).

[68] Stobart, *First Industrial Region*, 175–218; Wilson and Popp, 'Introduction'.

[69] Willan, *Abraham Dent*, 31–41. In contrast with Dickenson, Dent does not seem to have stocked his shop from local supplies. This appears to reflect the relatively small range of goods produced locally—chiefly knitted stockings.

[70] He spent as little as 11s. 6d. with one supplier, but £98 4s. 8½d. with another (Willan, *Abraham Dent*, 32).

[71] Willan, *Abraham Dent*, 28.   [72] Willan, *Abraham Dent*, 31, 35, 39.

[73] See Stobart, 'Information, Trust and Reputation'; Casson, 'Institutional Economics'; North, 'Transaction Costs'.

example, appears in the first accounts that survive for Dent in 1756, and he continued to trade with him until 1769, when he was replaced by his kinsmen, Thomas and Anthony Whitwell, who supplied Dent at least through to 1777. This suggests a strong element of allegiance between tradesmen, a sentiment explicitly drawn upon by Mathias Strickland, who supplied Dent with flour and wrote to him on 8 December 1764 thus:

I have Sent you 2 Load of fine flower But I am Surprice that you Didd Nott Send soner. I think you will forsack mee Sone and I Do Nott Now your Reason for allwase use you well and you Now I Denied Several peple In Kerby of flower when you and I Began trading, So I Desire you Will Lett me Have your Costom . . .

Strickland's plea appears to have been answered in the positive, with further orders coming from Dent, at least until 1769, when he disappears from the accounts.[74] Yet long-established trade did not mean that the relationship was necessarily an easy one. Dent frequently recorded his complaints about goods that he was sent: they were of poor quality, too costly, or underweight. His business with Edward Clark of Gateshead, for example, was marked by: 'sope a pound short' (1756); 'powder charged more than agreed for' (1757); 'sope overcharged 6*d.* a firkin' (1760), and 'sand not worth carriage' (1762).[75] What is remarkable is less the serial complaining and more the fact that Dent continued to place orders with Clark over this period. This does not appear to have reflected a lack of choice—indeed, Dent's network was characterized by the kind of weak links that made shifting orders between different suppliers relatively straightforward. Dent's commentaries should be read as an essential form of communication between supplier and customer. Rather than indicating malpractice or a lack of trust, they demonstrated attention to the detail of stock and business, and kept open a flow of information that served to integrate the network. Certainly they indicate an absence of information asymmetries: Dent had clear expectations about the price and quality of goods built on his previous trading experience and his wide network of suppliers.[76]

Trust and loyalty were clearly important elements within this network, yet the diversity of suppliers upon which Dent could draw gave him the opportunity to respond actively to poor quality or high prices and to switch suppliers. His comments make it abundantly clear that Dent was aware of the price normally paid for different goods, from either the same supplier or elsewhere. Importantly, his suppliers were themselves aware that Dent had this level of knowledge (not least because he kept telling them that their goods were overpriced). Thus we see the agent of Lawson Rawlinson & Co. writing to Dent on 10 October 1765 about a consignment of sugar dispatched from Lancaster: 'You'll, no doubt, think the prices high, but are the lowest we are selling at and I do think they'll go a deal higher, that if you can at Newcastle do better you'd do well to lay in a stock.'[77] Three things are important here. First, it is recognized that Dent has options for buying sugar in at

[74] Willan, *Abraham Dent*, 30–1.
[75] Willan, *Abraham Dent*, 39.
[76] See North, 'Transaction Costs'; Stobart, 'Personal and Commercial Networks', 285–7.
[77] Willan, *Abraham Dent*, 35.

least two places, although one detects a certain confidence on the part of Rawlinson that his price will not be bettered. Second, it assumes a good level of prior knowledge about prices and about their volatility. Third, like much correspondence between merchants and other tradesmen, it contains important information about prices and supplies. In this way, it acts as a forerunner or perhaps an informal and personalized version of the circulars that appeared in growing numbers from the 1770s.[78]

Whether Dent had access to such formal announcements is uncertain, though Mui and Mui insist that he did. If this is correct, then they would have complemented his personal knowledge and that obtained through his dealings with a wide range of suppliers. Indeed, as Burt notes, one key advantage accruing from a large network was a wealth of business information of the sort Dent deployed when registering complaints to his suppliers.[79] Another advantage of being well connected, especially to suppliers with whom he had a long-term relationship, was the provision of credit. While there was no standard period of credit, it is apparent that most suppliers gave him several months grace: Atkinson and Hall offered four to six months, as did Lawson Rawlinson & Co., while John Whitwell allowed seven months to a year.[80] The mutuality of such arrangements not only lubricated trade; it also reflected and bolstered trust between supplier and retailer.[81] Like many retailers, Dent made some payments in kind: Matthew Birkbeck in Barnard Castle, for example, supplied Dent with cloth in exchange for tea and coffee of various different types—an arrangement that appears to have suited both parties for at least two or three years.[82] However, most accounts were settled with cash, bills, or a combination of the two.

As with Dickenson, the precise means of payment reflected the size of the account: small bills were settled in cash—occasionally including bank notes from Newcastle or Leeds—and larger ones with bills, drawn against a variety of individuals. In this, Dent's business practices differed little from those of his predecessors. One significant distinction was the way in which he ensured that his ledger was signed off by the supplier once the account had been settled. Willan's analysis of this suggests that Dent sometimes went on trips to see his suppliers in London, Newcastle, and probably elsewhere. Yet on other occasions he appears to have been visited by suppliers or at least their agents. This is important, as it indicates a shift in the balance of activity of the kind suggested by Mui and Mui: away from the shopkeeper travelling widely to secure stock and towards the supplier having to work much harder to secure orders from provincial shopkeepers.[83] There is evidence that such practices were established by the mid-eighteenth century, Thomas Turner being

---

[78] Stobart, 'Personal and Commercial Networks'; Haggerty, *British–Atlantic Trading*, 114–28; Mui and Mui, *Shops and Shopkeeping*, 14–15. These circulars are discussed in more detail in Ch. 6.

[79] Burt, 'Network Entrepreneur', 268–88. See also Hancock, *Citizens of the World*, 81–2.

[80] Willan, *Abraham Dent*, 45.

[81] Muldrew, *Economy of Obligation*, 186–9.

[82] Willan, *Abraham Dent*, 38.

[83] Willan, *Abraham Dent*, 44; Mui and Mui, *Shops and Shopkeeping*, 10–11. See Popp, 'Building the Market', for an example of manufacturers engaged in similar activities.

visited by merchants' agents travelling from Manchester and elsewhere.[84] However, there is an important difference between Dent's business network—marked by the circulation of detailed business and market information, and the use of a formalized system of agents—and those of Dickenson and especially Stout, which relied much more on close personal links. That said, Dent also drew on his personal contacts and previous business dealings when gathering market information. His network was thus essential to shaping both his business transactions and his conception of business more generally.

From the later years of the eighteenth century, established business networks were augmented by a growing array of printed and published business and market information. Newspapers frequently carried commodity prices pertaining in London or provincial towns, and many dealers issued circulars that detailed goods, prices, and more general market information. This growing reliance on formal published information in some ways took business from the private into the public realm and made it more 'modern'. It was most pronounced in the tea trade, where the emergence of a new breed of London dealers in the 1780s was linked to a growing use of newspaper advertisements that listed provincial agents and the retail prices of a variety of teas as well as coffee and chocolate (see Chapter 7).[85] Shopkeepers were sent circulars that provided a similar set of information, but that also served as a prompt for orders to be placed. The Staffordshire draper Walthal Fenton received such a circular from the London tea dealer Charles Brewster in May 1781, returning an order in June that detailed the type, quality, and price of the goods that he required.[86] Wholesaling grocers issued similar circulars containing appraisals of the current and future price and availability of various goods. In 1779, the London firm of Smith, Nash, Kemble, and Travers advised that the loss of Grenada 'has caused an advance in Raw Sugar...Refined Sugars are very scarce and dear, but will be more Plenty in a Month or six Weeks, and hope cheaper.'[87] Similarly, if less bullish, Wells, Sayer, and Co. wrote on 9 September 1814 that, 'as we have too much Reason to believe the Crop has fallen short in several of the Islands, the future Imports will be, comparatively, very trifling that we think you would do wisely to lay in a Stock for the Season, before there is a further Advance'.[88] There followed a list of commodities and current prices, which, it would appear from the dates of previous circulars, would pertain for around two weeks only.

This established mechanism for providing limited market information was dramatically superseded in 1823 when John Nicholson issued his *Tea Book* and *Sale List*. The former was essentially a reproduction of the EIC's *Sale Catalogue*, and thus contained information on the quantity, quality, and put-up price for each break of tea at the auctions. The latter listed the bid-up price for each break. While both sets of information were already publicly available to those attending

---

[84] Vaisey, *Thomas Turner*, 11 May 1756, 23 Feb. 1762, 5 Mar. 1764.
[85] Mui and Mui, *Shops and Shopkeeping*, 281–3.
[86] BL, Add. MS 36,666, fos 29, 41. Similar circulars were produced by provincial tea dealers, including William Tuke and Son of York (see Mui and Mui, *Shops and Shopkeeping*, 15).
[87] Quoted in Mui and Mui, *Shops and Shopkeeping*, 15.   [88] NRO, O (N) 30.

the sales, Nicholson made them much more widely accessible. Together with his aggressive marketing campaigns, very low commissions charges, and at times libellous denunciation of the practices of established London tea dealers, this had a dramatic impact on the tea trade. In particular, it altered the relationship between London dealers and the provincial retailers who formed the bulk of their customers. Increasingly, shopkeepers knew what teas were available and at what price, and they would pay only a small commission on this, albeit with the condition that payments were made when the order was placed.[89] As one London dealer reported, the country trader would ask for specific teas and then, 'instead of your fixing the price, says, it cost so much at the Company's Sale and I will give you so much for it'.[90]

Faced with evidence for a proliferation of printed information available to provincial grocers, it would be easy to conclude that their personal networks were no longer important in gaining market information. This would tie grocers' experiences into the general shift towards formal business institutions and contractual relationships, and thus link them to the 'institutionalization' of commerce and, more arguably, to the commercialization of society. Moreover, it appears that suppliers were so anxious to court business that stocking a shop was an easy matter. However, some things had not changed that much: many payments were made in advance; London retained its importance as a source of goods, and personal contacts and judgement remained vital in judging what to buy and from whom. On the back of the circular from Wells, Sayer, and Co. there is a handwritten letter discussing the merits of buying various goods. Regarding sugar, it notes: 'I think you may buy a few for on Friday a friend of Mr Laund's, a West India Mercht called with Mr I——, and he has sugars to sell but says he does not intend selling till Decr as he thinks they will be higher then.'[91] Clearly this buyer was still willing to obtain, trust, and utilize commercial information from both formal and informal sources.

CONCLUSIONS

The supply networks discussed in this chapter tell us much about the ways in which grocers obtained stock in the long eighteenth century, the operation of business during this period, and the emergence of consumer society. The first point of access to certain groceries were the EIC sales, attended by an exclusive group of London dealers who bought supplies that they then sold on to metropolitan and provincial tradesmen. While apparently stable and hierarchical, this system was under strain long before the Commutation and Charter Acts liberalized the trade in eastern goods. The EIC monopoly was rarely complete; smuggling (especially of

---

[89] Nicholson insisted on payment in advance since this provided his capital to buy at the EIC auctions (see Mui and Mui, *Shops and Shopkeeping*, 283).

[90] Parliamentary Papers, 1st Report, Royal Commission on Excise Establishment (Tea Permits), 1833: 21 (417), 174.

[91] NRO, O (N) 30.

tea) was a growing problem, and many goods lay outside the purview of chartered companies. This meant that grocers could draw supplies from a wide variety of sources, including provincial ports and inland entrepôts. The flexibility and capacity of this system allowed retailers to meet growth in demand for groceries, especially those imported from the colonies, and were thus vital in underpinning changes in consumption practices in this period. Indeed, it could be argued that such a supply system was a necessary precondition to any consumer revolution. Yet it was a system marked by strong continuities and the enduring importance of personal relationships.

At the start of the eighteenth century, personal contacts and face-to-face meetings were paramount. Stout's network was characterized by strong ties with similar tradesmen, transaction costs being reduced and risk mitigated by focusing on suppliers with whom he had a personal relationship and could therefore trust. By the middle of the century, Dickenson enjoyed more extensive networks in which he successfully mixed opportunistic and short-term supply chains with a substantial core of long-term and trusted suppliers, reducing his transaction costs by drawing on known and trusted suppliers with whom he had good credit. Two decades later, Dent's supply network was more extensive and formalized. He sometimes dealt with agents and may have drawn upon published information to shape his business decisions, but it was through personal knowledge and his regular and frank exchanges with suppliers that he was able to acquire his stock. This combination of public and personal continued through into the nineteenth century: published commercial information became increasingly important (especially in the highly competitive tea trade), but many business decisions were still mediated and risk averted through the deployment of information gained through personal contacts.

Theorizations of eighteenth-century consumption are remarkably silent about this aspect of the supply of goods to the consumer. This makes it difficult to generalize about the role of wholesaling in the emergence of a consumer society during this period. There is little evidence that either changes in the goods stocked by grocers or shifts in the pattern of demand resulted in any fundamental transformation in the systems of supply that serviced the grocer's shop. The tea trade was marked by more overtly competitive behaviour, aggressive publicity and a large volume of printed material; but this was not typical of the supply of other commodities. Growing demand was largely accommodated within existing structures, not least because the networks of supply established and maintained by shopkeepers was dynamic and responsive. There were few large wholesale companies, no comprehensive switch to printed market information or institutionalized systems of exchange, and few attempts at vertical integration of the type later developed by Co-Operative Societies and multiple retailers.[92] Above all else, what emerges is the importance of the individual in creating, sustaining, and operating systems of supply. There was no single model of success, for either business contacts or busi-

---

[92] See Jefferys, *Retailing in Britain*, 16–18, 21–9.

ness networks. Rather, it was down to the skill, judgement, and hard work of the shopkeeper. His job may have become a little easier as dealers increasingly chased after his business—especially apparent in the tea trade—and as published prices and market information levelled the playing field. Yet it was still the shopkeepers who ensured that they had well-stocked shelves, good credit, and prices appropriate to their customer base.

4

Geographies of Selling: The Grocery Trades in Provincial Towns

INTRODUCTION

A key feature of our understanding of both consumer and retail evolution in the eighteenth century is the growing importance of the retail shop. It formed a permanent point of supply and transformed the ways in which goods were bought and sold. Research on English retailing presents us with a pretty clear picture of shops growing rapidly in number and becoming increasingly widespread, both across the country and down the settlement hierarchy.[1] Moreover, as interest in retail history spreads to other parts of Europe, it is becoming apparent that these developments were not peculiar to Britain.[2] Indeed, it might be argued that the long eighteenth century experienced not only a Europe-wide revolution in domestic consumption, but also a revolution in retailing, at least in terms of the spread of shops and their penetration into the lives of ordinary people. Yet the expansion of the retail sector and its distribution across space was uneven at every scale, from the international to the intra-urban. These differences resulted from uneven growth in consumer demand and the differential interplay between various systems of supply (fairs, markets, itinerants, and shops). As de Vries notes, consumer demand was strongest in the burgeoning economies of north-west Europe, which were also characterized by increasingly shop-based retail systems. Demand was less broad-based in central Europe and Scandinavia, for instance, and supply systems were accordingly more dependent upon itinerants and periodic markets or sales.[3] Within England, Mui and Mui have argued for a marked north–south divide in the number and size of shops. They see London as a strong stimulus to commercial development and contrast a well-developed retail system in the south and east with one that was, 'relatively speaking, in a primitive stage' in the 'upland zone'.[4] The validity of this contrast is questionable; it ignores the evident sophistication of much retailing in the north and west of the country, and the strong intra-regional

---

[1] Alexander, *Retailing in England*, 89–109; Mui and Mui, *Shops and Shopkeeping*, 29–45; Shammas, *Pre-Industrial Consumer*, 225–65; Mitchell, 'Urban Retailing'; Cox, *Complete Tradesman*, 38–75; Hann, 'Industrialisation'; Stobart, Hann, and Morgan, *Spaces of Consumption*, 33–8.

[2] See, e.g., the contributions in Angiolini and Roche (eds), *Cultures et formations négociantes*; Blondé et al. (eds), *Buyers and Sellers*; Blondé et al. (eds), *Retailers and Consumer Changes*.

[3] De Vries, *Industrious Revolution*, 46–58, 169–71; Lilja, Murhem, and Ulväng, 'Indispensible Market'.

[4] Mui and Mui, *Shops and Shopkeeping*, 42.

variations revealed in the analysis they present. Shammas and Cox have, therefore, sought explanations for this variegated retail geography in terms of population density, local socio-economic conditions, and competition from other centres— London casting a shadow over neighbouring counties.[5] It is important to understand how groceries were situated within these general trends: how developed was retailing in different parts of the country and what implications does this have for access to new groceries and to shifting consumption practices more generally?

Within towns, the eighteenth century witnessed a shift away from the market and the marketplace, and onto shops and what might be termed the high street. Attempts to delineate this emerging locus of retailing are surprisingly rare, in part because of the problems of precisely mapping the location of retailers in the period before trade directories. In their study of York, Mui and Mui applied a broad brush, including half of the city's parishes within the 'central shopping district'.[6] Others have sought a narrower definition, based on the clustering of high-order shops—a process that invariably identifies a few central streets as the core of the retail district.[7] The causal factors are largely implied, but centre on notions of access to potential customers. In retail location theory, there is a tension between accessibility and cost, usually seen as being resolved through bid-rents, with more accessible and desirable locations commanding higher rents.[8] That such forces were important in Georgian England is apparent from a contemporary guide to Chester, which noted that the corner of Eastgate Street and Bridge Street had a 'decided preference...shops let here at high rents and are in never-failing request'.[9] Yet there is also evidence of a different set of priorities shaping the location decisions of some grocery retailers. In their study of eighteenth-century Antwerp, Van Aert and Van Damme note that tea houses and tobacco sellers were highly dispersed, locating towards consumers and thus in residential areas.[10] These different interpretations also link to questions about how the urban retail landscape was conceived by retailers and perceived by customers: where did the key locations lie and what made them important?

To address these questions, it is necessary to explore in detail the geography of grocery retailing. At the national scale, such analysis has generally drawn on taxation records, largely because these form unified and seemingly comprehensive sources. However, additional insights can be gained from the consciously commercial listings found in trade directories and the straightforward occupational data contained in parish registers.[11] Of particular importance here is the way in which the geography of grocery retailing responded to shifts in the number and

---

[5] Mui and Mui, *Shops and Shopkeeping*, 29–45, 191–200, 295–9; Shammas, *Pre-Industrial Consumer*, 248–58; Cox, *Complete Tradesman*, 51–8, 72–4.

[6] Mui and Mui, *Shops and Shopkeeping*, 124–6.

[7] Stobart and Hann, 'Retailing Revolution', 177–81; Van Aert and Van Damme, 'Retail Dynamics'; Bennett, *Shops, Shambles and the Street Market*; Barnett, 'Shops, Retailing and Consumption', 111–42; Lesger, 'Patterns of Retail'.

[8] See Brown, 'City Centre Retailing'; Young and Allen, 'Retail Patterns'.

[9] Roberts, *Chester Guide*, 65.

[10] Van Aert and Van Damme, 'Retail Dynamics', 159–65.

[11] Acknowledgement of Leigh Shaw Taylor.

socio-economic circumstances of consumers. For consumption practices to be reformed around a new set of imported foods in the way posited by de Vries, Smith, McKendrick, and others, these goods needed to be readily available to consumers—supplied by local shopkeepers. Within towns, the distribution of grocers can tell us much about the ways in which they fitted into broader systems of supply. Locating alongside drapers, mercers, and toy shops in the principal shopping areas implied very different associations to being found in the back streets: it would place both grocers and their wares in the vanguard of changing consumption practices. In this context, the position of the shop within consumers' mental landscapes was just as important as its physical location within the town. Prominence within real and imagined space would make the grocer's shop more influential in shaping consumer behaviour, in terms of both visiting particular premises and promoting the consumption of groceries more generally. These geographical issues are thus critical to our understanding of consumer practices.

NORTH AND SOUTH: THE GEOGRAPHY OF GROCERY RETAILING

The early modern period saw a widening distribution of shopkeepers in general and grocers in particular as shops appeared in a greater number and variety of places. Patterns varied from region to region, sometimes reflecting local socio-economic conditions, but also resulting from the deployment of different occupational titles. Thus, while grocers were recorded in 76 per cent of East Anglian towns in the late seventeenth century, they were found in only 41 per cent of towns in north-west England and the west Midlands, and were completely absent from Gloucestershire, where their function appears to have been carried out by mercers.[12] It is clear, however, that groceries could be bought in a broad range of settlements by the early eighteenth century, including a number of villages. In Cheshire, for example, probate records show specialist grocers in four villages and other retailers selling groceries in at least another ten.[13] Along with tailors, shoemakers, mercers, and chandlers, grocers thus formed part of the bedrock of service provision. Indeed, they were important in distinguishing and defining towns as central places, their absence calling into question a settlement's urban status. Thus, with just a single grocer listed in the probate records in the period 1700–50, Abbots Bromley was damned by Blome as a 'very poor town' with a market described as 'very mean'.[14]

Provision extended and deepened during the course of the eighteenth and early nineteenth centuries: 32,234 tea dealers were licensed in 1764–5, rising to 52,292 by 1793—an increase that is partly explained by the changing tax system and the

---

[12] Patten, *English Towns*, 283; Stobart, Hann, and Morgan, *Spaces of Consumption*, 34; Smith, *Men and Armour*.
[13] See Stobart, 'Food Retailers'.   [14] Blome, *Britannia*, 205.

resulting decline in the illicit trade, but that also reflected buoyant demand.[15] Certainly, the number of towns with grocers, tea dealers, or tobacconists had grown by the time the *Universal British Directory* (*UBD*) was published in the 1790s. This records a total of 4,823 such retailers in provincial England and Wales, spread across 490, or 76 per cent, of the towns listed in the directory. They were, of course, most numerous in the larger centres, a clear urban hierarchy shaping their presence in smaller towns.[16] However, numbers were not simply a reflection of urban population. Many emerging industrial towns were poorly provided with shops in relation to their more established neighbours. Thus, places like Dudley and Kidderminster in Worcestershire, Hanley and Wednesbury in Staffordshire, and even Stockport and Macclesfield in Cheshire had far fewer shops per head of population than did their less industrial or older established neighbours—town such as Bromsgrove, Newcastle-under-Lyme, and Chester. These often remained the focus of retail trading, even when population shifts meant that they were demographically overshadowed by their industrial neighbours. In the new industrial centres, population growth appears to have outstripped the expansion of local shop-based retailing, at least until the second quarter of the nineteenth century, although many workers undoubtedly patronized petty shopkeepers, who were rarely included in early trade directories.[17] Indeed, from the mid-eighteenth century, there is good evidence that industrial workers were buying a greater range of shop goods, especially imported groceries, and thus encouraging the appearance of such shops at a local level. For instance, the Lancashire cotton dealer Samuel Finney reported that the number of shopkeepers in the industrializing parishes of north-east Cheshire had 'increased amazingly' in the third quarter of the eighteenth century, with some of them dealing in 'a great variety of articles' including tea, coffee, sugar, and spices.[18] This growth of rural provision was by no means unique. Data derived from baptism records in the period 1813–20 indicate 9,950 grocers, tea dealers, and tobacconists spread across 1,774 English parishes (excluding London and Middlesex). Included in this number were many 'country shops', which Shammas associated so closely with growing demand for imported groceries.[19] They were found in places as small as Berkswell and Priors Hardwick in Warwickshire, and Dickleborough and Winfarthing in Norfolk. These grocers were hardly the upmarket retailers of the urban high street, but were important in serving the day-to-day demand for small luxuries of the kind highlighted by Finney.

---

[15] Mui and Mui, *Shops and Shopkeeping*, 161.

[16] See, e.g., Stobart, Hann, and Morgan, *Spaces of Consumption*, 38–49; Patten, *English Towns*. The omission of grocers from places such as Auckland in County Durham, Ilminster in Somerset, and Aldborough in Suffolk reflects the ways in which information for the *UBD* was collated, which effectively excluded the numerous petty shopkeepers, many of whom sold groceries and no doubt were numbered among the retailers licensed to sell tea. See Fowler, 'Changes in Provincial Retail Practice'; Shaw and Alexander, 'Directories'.

[17] Hann, 'Industrialisation', 50–2; Stobart and Hann, 'Retailing Revolution', 183–4; Mitchell, 'Supplying the Masses', 271–3.

[18] Quoted in Ashton, *Economic History*, 216.

[19] Shammas, *Pre-Industrial Consumer*, 225–6.

Reading the growth of grocery retailing in this way equates supply, in terms of the number of shops, directly with demand from consumers. This connection is made by de Vries and parallels Weatherill's linking of innovative urban demand and the supply of goods from urban shops and factories.[20] However, it needs to be examined more closely in the light of pronounced variations in the distribution of grocers across the country. Mui and Mui account for their distinct north–south divide in terms of agricultural systems (a contrast being drawn between the mixed farming of a predominantly lowland south and the pastoral farming of the upland north and west); settlement patterns (nucleated as opposed to isolated farmsteads and hamlets), and the provision of market towns (the south and east possessing a dense network of such settlements).[21] But these are generalizations, which overlook the details of local socio-economic conditions and the reality of retail provision and shopping behaviours. Many of the counties in Mui and Mui's northern sector were industrializing during the second half of the eighteenth century. As Finney observed, and de Vries has theorized, this process often helped to orient consumers more strongly onto market provision and widened the range of goods that they saw as necessary to their daily lives.[22] Also, while the resulting demographic growth served to create a 'thickening of the population over the countryside',[23] it took place within the structure of a well-defined and dynamic urban system. Newer urban centres were certainly not awash with shops, but retailers in Ashton-under-Lyne and Oldham paid more shop tax than their counterparts in established towns such as Middlewich, Sandbach, and Burnley. Moreover, existing towns grew as central places, providing goods and services to their own burgeoning populations as well as those of their hinterlands.[24]

The lack of alternative nationally available data sources make it difficult to test directly the validity of the Muis' north–south divide in the early eighteenth century. That said, their characterization of shopkeeping outside the lowland zone as 'primitive' is certainly mistaken and gives a misleading picture of suppressed demand and provision in these areas. More recent research has revealed the sophistication of early eighteenth-century retailing in north-west England and the west Midlands, while Weatherill demonstrates that consumers in these regions were by no means laggards in their uptake of novel domestic goods.[25] Moreover, the suggestion that this divide persisted into the 1790s stands in stark contrast with the

---

[20] De Vries, *Industrious Revolution*, 169–74; Weatherill, *Consumer Behaviour*, 84–7.

[21] The distinction was especially marked in the mid-1700s, but persisted to the end of the century. Mui and Mui, *Shops and Shopkeeping*, 193, 37–41. Shammas, *Pre-Industrial Consumer*, 248–58, highlights similar factors, but places particular emphasis on the density of population.

[22] See Ashton, *Economic History*, 216; de Vries, *Industrious Revolution*, 44–58.

[23] Wadsworth and Mann, *Cotton Trade*, 311.

[24] See Stobart, *First Industrial Region*, 146–74; TNA: PRO E182—shop tax for Lancashire, 1785.

[25] Mui and Mui, *Shops and Shopkeeping*, 42. On the sophistication of shopping in north-west England and the west Midlands, see Stobart and Hann, 'Retailing Revolution'; Hann and Stobart, 'Sites of Consumption'; Mitchell, 'Supplying the Masses'; Fowler, 'Changes in Provincial Retail Practice'; Weatherill, *Consumer Behaviour*, 43–6.

picture painted by data from the *UBD* (Table 4.1).[26] These show considerable variations in the distribution of grocers, tea dealers, and tobacconists across the country, but indicate an overall pattern almost entirely the reverse of that suggested by Mui and Mui: counties north of their line had more grocery retailers per town and per head of population.

Of the northern counties, Lancashire, Cheshire, Northumberland, Cumberland, and Staffordshire were particularly well served, as were Hampshire, Somerset, Buckinghamshire, and Kent in the south. Most of these were highly urbanized, and many contained particularly large or rapidly growing towns: Liverpool and Manchester, Stockport and Macclesfield, Newcastle-upon-Tyne, Whitehaven, and Workington, the Potteries and Black Country towns, Portsmouth and Southampton, and Bristol. In these same counties, provision was also strong in traditional

Table 4.1. Distribution of tea licences and grocers, tea dealers, and tobacconists in England, 1790s and 1813–1820

Region	Population per tea licence	Grocers, tea dealers, and tobacconists per town (*UBD*)	Population per grocer (*UBD*)	Population per grocer (parish registers)
South of line				
Region II	148	5.7	1,549	1,001
Region III	159	5.9	1,754	879
Region IV	167	4.8	2,482	1,240
Region V	127	6.7	1,669	1,274
Region VI	158	10.4		1,002
Total	154	6.2	1715	991
North of line				
Region I	158	4.6	2,,093	1,984
Region VII	186	9.3	1,564	1,026
Region VIII	182	17.2	958	1,006
Region IX	170	8.7	1,675	927
Region X	208	14.1	1,170	1,012
Total	177	10.1	1,389	1,045

Notes: Regions are taken from Mui and Mui, *Shops and Shopkeeping*, table 37: I: Cornwall, Devon; II: Berkshire, Dorset, Gloucestershire, Hampshire, Somerset, Sussex, Wiltshire; III: Bedfordshire, Buckinghamshire, Essex, Hertfordshire, Kent, Surrey; IV: Norfolk, Suffolk; V: Cambridgeshire, Huntingdonshire; VI: Leicestershire, Northamptonshire, Rutland, Warwickshire, Worcestershire; VII: Herefordshire, Shropshire, Staffordshire; VIII: Cheshire, Cumberland, Lancashire, Westmorland; IX: Derbyshire, Lincolnshire, Nottinghamshire, Yorkshire; X: Durham, Northumberland.

Sources: Mui and Mui, *Shops and Shopkeeping*, table 37; *Universal British Directory*; parish registers; Wrigley, 'English Counties', table 5.

[26] The coverage of the *UBD* is far from perfect, with certain towns being particularly poorly covered: see Shaw and Alexander, 'Directories'. However, there is little evidence that coverage was systematically better or worse in particular counties. While total numbers are undoubtedly underestimated, there is little reason to suppose that the distribution of grocers is anything other than broadly accurate.

centres (Chester was the largest retail centre in Cheshire, and the same was true of Canterbury in Kent and Carlisle in Cumberland), underlining the importance of the established urban hierarchy in shaping access to goods and services. This becomes clearer still in the case of Lancashire. Here, provision was dominated by Liverpool and Manchester, with Bolton, Lancaster, and Warrington forming important secondary centres. Below this, industrial centres such as Wigan and Bury ranked alongside much smaller, but more established market centres such as Ulverstone and Ormskirk—a structure that closely resembles that seen in the early decades of the eighteenth century.[27] Counties with relatively few grocers listed in the *UBD* were scattered across the southern zone, from Norfolk and Suffolk in the east, to Hereford and Gloucestershire in the west. Essex and Surrey appear to have had particularly low numbers of grocers, perhaps because of the shadow cast by London. However, any metropolitan impact appears to have been quite specific, as other neighbouring counties were much better served, notably Kent but also Berkshire.[28]

To an extent, these patterns are a product of the source, which omits rural retailers. This can be addressed by taking parish register data for a large sample of urban and rural parishes (Table 4.1). These also show a considerable degree of variation between counties and regions in terms of the distribution of grocers, but a far more even density of grocers in the north and south of the country. Significantly, industrializing and urbanizing counties still appeared among those that were better served, but they were joined by a range of agricultural counties including Leicestershire, Huntingdonshire, and Berkshire. In regional terms, Cornwall and Devon were notably lacking in grocers, but Dorset and Wiltshire were also poorly served, as were Bedfordshire and Essex. The last is of particular interest, as it appears to underline the geographically specific London shadow noted from the *UBD* data.

How are we best to understand this distribution of grocers? The density and growth of population are not especially useful measures when considering per capita levels of provision. The latter might indicate general dynamism of an area, but real growth would need to be reflected in a declining ratio of persons per shopkeeper. In reality, there was often a lag between demographic and retail growth, seen most obviously in the relatively low number of shops—even grocers' shops—in newly industrializing towns.[29] Moreover, it is clear from individual cases that even quite sparsely populated counties (for example, Cumberland and Northumberland) or those with modest rates of demographic growth (Berkshire and Hertfordshire) could have a relatively high proportion of grocers per head of population.

Demand was not simply a reflection of population levels. As de Vries argues, what was important was the growing market orientation of consumers and their increasing willingness to reorient their demand towards the market and towards specific bundles of goods. In particular he emphasizes a switch to new luxuries—a mode of consumption characteristic of urban and middle-class consumers.[30] This

---

[27] Stobart, *First Industrial Region*, 159–68.
[28] See Shammas, *Pre-Industrial Consumer*, 254.
[29] Hann, 'Industrialisation', 50–2; Mitchell, 'Urban Retailing', 271–3.
[30] De Vries, *Industrious Revolution*, 44–56.

is borne out here in the level of urbanization and urban growth correlating closely with provision. Importantly, it was not simply the density of the urban network that mattered—after all, counties such as Essex, Bedfordshire, and Wiltshire had plenty of small market towns, but were lightly populated with grocers. Far more significant was the presence of large towns or dynamic commercial centres. These tend to loom large in trade directories such as the *UBD* because they were the places most likely to be visited by those compiling directories. They also contained the greatest number of commercial-minded shopkeepers most inclined to advertise themselves in such listings.[31] But their retail strength was not merely a construct of the source: commercial centres contained large numbers of prosperous middling sorts—precisely the people who lay at the heart of burgeoning demand for new goods. Moreover, many of the grocers in these towns also served not just the town's own population, but also those visiting from the surrounding countryside and smaller neighbouring towns. The shopkeepers in Newcastle-under-Lyme, for example, were important in servicing the needs of the burgeoning populations of neighbouring Potteries towns, while the established and perceived hierarchy is reinforced by the *UBD*'s listing of Burslem, Hanley, Lane End (Longton), Shelton, Stoke, and Tunstall under the Newcastle heading.[32]

Perhaps most telling in shaping demand for grocers, and shops more generally, were local socio-economic conditions.[33] Weatherill identifies tradesmen as among the most innovative consumers in the early decades of the eighteenth century and de Vries has argued that divisions of labour, proto-industrialization, and wage labour all encouraged increased demand for goods provided through markets and shops, and specifically those goods sold by grocers.[34] These were the kind of changes being felt in the textile-producing districts of Lancashire, Cheshire, and Yorkshire; the metalworking settlements of the west Midlands, and the coal-mining towns and villages in north-east England and the Cumberland coast. They were also important in the dockyard and port towns of Devon, Kent, and Hampshire, north-east England, and, most strikingly, in places such as Liverpool and Bristol, which, in the 1790s, formed the two biggest concentrations of grocers outside London.[35] Moreover, towns were also key points in the importation and wholesaling of groceries (see Chapter 3), which again placed greater emphasis on the larger commercial centres, but also on the hierarchical structure of the local and regional urban system. Even with everyday goods such as groceries, higher-order centres contained much greater numbers of retailers, who also tended to operate at a larger scale, both spatially and in terms of turnover. From the shop tax, it is possible to trace the proportion of shops paying at each of the various

---

[31] See Barker, *Business of Women*, 48–52. They were also more likely to have existing directories that could be drawn upon or plagiarized.

[32] HRL, D4842/14/4/7—receipts of John Wood of Burslem, 1797–8.

[33] Cox, *Complete Tradesman*, 51–8. See also Dean and Cole, *British Economic Growth*, 103.

[34] Weatherill, *Consumer Behaviour*, 166–89; de Vries, *Industrious Revolution*, 73–121, 154–69.

[35] *UBD*. Liverpool had 158 grocers, tea dealers and tobacconists, and Bristol had 109. Next came Plymouth (98), Manchester (92), Hull (75), Birmingham (70), Newcastle-upon-Tyne (62), and Portsea–Portsmouth (55).

assessment categories at which the tax was levied. In a group of large towns (Bath, Bristol, Liverpool, Nottingham, Salisbury, Southampton, and Worcester) only half the shopkeepers paid in the bottom two categories (that is, under £15), whereas nearly three-quarters of retailers fell into these categories in other smaller towns.[36] It would be wrong, of course, to see these larger towns as monolithic, in terms of either the composition of their grocery trade or the ways in which it was internally structured. Indeed, the intra-urban geography of retailing was as varied as the regional patterns described above.

THE INTRA-URBAN DISTRIBUTION
OF GROCERY DEALERS

The fragmentary nature of the evidence makes it very difficult to establish with any certainty the detailed distribution of grocery dealers in the early eighteenth century. Where sources do exist, they suggest a spread of grocers across town, but with a strong concentration into central areas. In Norwich, for example, the 1714 poll book indicates that grocers were resident in twenty-four of the city's thirty-five parishes, with only the thinly populated western parishes being without any shopkeepers of this type. However, ten of the forty-five grocers listed lived in the large central parish of St Peter Mancroft (which also contained the main marketplace) and a further eight were found in the neighbouring parishes of St Stephen and St John Timberhill.[37] While this picture is broad brush, it suggests a distribution shaped by the twin forces of dispersal among residential areas (including the largely industrial parishes north of the River Wensum) and concentration, mostly around the market.[38] From these parish-level data, it is unclear whether grocers were found on the most prestigious streets, but a detailed map of Eastgate Street, Chester, drawn up in 1754, confirms their presence in small numbers on the foremost shopping street in the city.[39] Among the 102 retailers identified on the map were 4 grocers and a tea dealer, scattered across street and first-floor, row level shops on both sides of the street.

The spread of provincial town directories after the 1760s allows detailed comparative analysis, albeit with the caveat that these early directories usually list only the principal traders. This tends to exaggerate the concentration of retailing, but comparisons with later directories are valid, since these differentiate between grocers and a generally larger number of 'shopkeepers and dealers in groceries and sundries'.[40] Taking the distribution of high-status retailers as a whole, it is possible to identify the principal retail districts for each of eight sample towns (Table 4.2). In Liverpool, over half of the listed retailers were located on five streets: Dale Street

---

[36] Mui and Mui, *Shops and Shopkeeping*, 90.
[37] Norwich Poll Book, 1714.
[38] See Barnett, 'Shops, Retailing and Consumption', 102–4.
[39] CALS, CR/63/2/133/17.
[40] Pigot, *National Commercial Directory* (1828–9), 323.

and Water Street running down to George's Dock, and High Street, Castle Street, Derby Square, and Pool Lane, which ran on a perpendicular axis towards the Old Dock; one-quarter were concentrated into the stretch between the town hall in Derby Square and the exchange on the corner of High Street and Water Street.[41] If we repeat this analysis for each town and take the streets with the largest number of retailers as the 'core', it is possible to define 'connecting' streets as any that joined directly to these central streets, the remainder being designated as back streets or 'outer' locations. Mapping the distribution of those listed as grocers, tea dealers, and tobacconists onto this typology gives us a framework for assessing the comparative and changing location of the grocery trade through the late eighteenth and early nineteenth centuries.

The core retail area accounted for the largest share of grocery dealers in the 1760s–80s (Table 4.2). This was true of all the sampled towns, but the extent of clustering varied considerably. It was highest in the smaller towns—in part an inevitable consequence of the more restricted options in terms of retail locations and the ease with which those living in any part of town could access shops in the centre. Indeed, size appears to have been more significant than the socio-economic character of the town: in county towns (Chester and Northampton), market towns (Nantwich), and growing industrial centres (Walsall), over 70 per cent of grocery dealers were found on the central streets. In Chester, they were predominantly ranged along the four streets meeting at the Cross and on the main road leading out of the city towards London, although a significant minority (and especially female retailers) were found on connecting streets. In Northampton, Nantwich, and Walsall, it was the Market Square and/or the High Street that formed the main focus, as it did in

Table 4.2. Distribution of grocers, tea dealers, and tobacconists in selected towns, *c.*1770s

Town	Core streets		Connecting streets		Other areas		Total
	No.	%	No.	%	No.	%	No.
Nantwich	6	85.7	1	14.3	0	0.0	7
Northampton	9	90.0	1	10.0	0	0.0	10
Walsall	5	83.3	1	16.7	0	0.0	6
Chester	23	71.9	8	25.0	1	3.1	32
Liverpool	17	37.8	17	37.8	11	24.4	45
Birmingham	17	37.8	14	31.1	14	31.1	45
Manchester	15	53.6	11	39.3	2	7.1	28
Norwich	15	32.6	5	10.9	26	56.5	46
Total	107	48.9	58	26.5	54	24.7	219

Sources: Cowdroy, *Directory and Guide for Chester* (1787); Northampton Poll Books (1774); Broster, *Chester Directory* (1782); Gore, *Liverpool Directory* (1766); Pearson and Rollason, *Birmingham Directory* (1777); Raffald, *Manchester Directory* (1772); *Norwich Directory* (1783).

[41] See Stobart and Hann, 'Retail Revolution', 177–81.

many smaller towns. The limited geographical extent of the built-up area meant that there was little opportunity for significant suburban retailing to develop, although it is likely that there were also less prosperous back-street retailers not listed in the trade directories.[42] What is certain is that large numbers of grocers, tea dealers, and tobacconists chose to locate in the prime retail areas of these towns.

The situation in larger towns was rather different. All had a much smaller proportion of grocery dealers trading on the principal retail streets, but the overall distribution was highly variable. The degree of concentration was greatest in Manchester, where over 50 per cent were in the core area and only 10 per cent in outer or back-street locations. This may simply reflect the relatively low number of grocers listed in the 1773 directory, although it is telling that Elizabeth Raffald herself had relocated her business in August 1766 from a shop on Fennel Street to new premises at 12 Market Place.[43] Liverpool and Birmingham had broadly similar proportions in the three areas, which suggests a more dispersed pattern of grocery retailing. In Birmingham, grocers were spread across a range of streets only slightly removed from the central streets, but also along Digbeth/Deritend—the road to Coventry and Warwick. For Liverpool, clustering was slightly stronger, but there were also the beginnings of a much wider dispersal of retailing. A small number of grocery dealers appeared some distance from the core area: in the streets south of the Old Dock and further up the hill near to the recently formed Ranelagh Gardens. Both of these were, at the time, up and coming residential areas and represented a new locational attraction for retailers. That said, any shift was modest, and the central axis of retail streets remained a strong attraction for the town's shopkeepers, both male and female. Indeed, women seem to have been more prominent in Liverpool retailing (or at least in its early directories) than they were in other towns. There were female grocers on three of the main shopping streets in 1766, and a number remained in business for a considerable period: Elizabeth Hankey, for example, ran a grocery shop on Mersey Street for at least ten years around the turn of the nineteenth century.[44] Dispersal was still more pronounced in Norwich, where over half the grocery dealers were in the outer streets or backstreet locations. This reflects the dispersed pattern already apparent in the city in the early eighteenth century and shows a retail system that might be seen as mature: a central cluster of shops being balanced by diffusion to residential areas and along major thoroughfares.[45]

These more dispersed patterns indicate a number of processes at play. Setting up shop on streets outside but connecting with the core retail areas might suggest an unwillingness or inability to pay the high rents that these locations generally demanded. In Chester, this involved grocers being located primarily along Northgate Street and Bridge Street, while the premier shopping area of Eastgate Street was

---

[42] See Mui and Mui, *Shops and Shopkeeping*, 160–72.

[43] Barker, *Business of Women*, 76. Raffald's shop was listed under her husband's name, although a small number of other women were listed, including Mrs Priestnall, who ran a grocer's shop on Deansgate.

[44] Gore, *Liverpool Directory*; Haggerty, 'Women, Work and the Consumer Revolution', 116.

[45] Barnett, 'Shops, Retailing and Consumption', 125–36.

dominated by mercers, drapers, toy dealers, and the like.[46] In Liverpool, it meant locating on one of the many streets leading off Castle Street or Dale Street—places that were central and accessible, but less prestigious and costly. Such explanations accord well with modern bid-rent theories and imply a rational economic ordering of urban space.[47] However, there were other reasons for dispersal, especially when this involved locating on streets away from the core retail area and connecting streets. As Van Aert and Van Damme argue, it might reflect a decision to locate towards the consumer, especially among those selling new consumables and more particularly female shopkeepers.[48] This would allow customers easy access to goods and perhaps encourage the adoption of new groceries as part of everyday living. Such location patterns are most apparent in Norwich, where grocery dealers were spread across the city, albeit principally on the main rather than the back streets, and Liverpool with the nascent drift of retailing to the south and west of the established centre.[49] However, as the number of recorded grocers, tea dealers, and tobacconists grew over the following forty or fifty years, it became a feature of most towns, large and small.

By the end of the 1820s, grocers had become more dispersed, with just one-quarter being found on the main retail streets (Table 4.3). Smaller towns retained the highest levels of concentration, but only in Chester was the degree of clustering apparently undiminished. In Northampton, Walsall, and Nantwich grocers, both male and female, had spread into the adjoining streets and beyond, arguably helping to extend the central retail district. Dispersal was most marked in Walsall, while women grocers were more widespread than their male counterparts in Nantwich; but in both towns the overall numbers were small. Even in Chester, there is some suggestion of a gradual displacement of grocers from the most central locations. Bridge Street and Northgate Street gained additional grocers as Eastgate Street consolidated its position as a high-class shopping street. Indeed, a detailed set of engravings of the city's main streets, made about this time, confirms the presence of grocers all along these streets, but especially the north–south axis of Northgate Street and Bridge Street. Thus, walking down the west side of Bridge Street from the Cross to Bridge Gate, a shopper would have encountered two grocers, a grocer and tea dealer, a tea and coffee dealer, two tobacconists, and a tobacco and snuff dealer, as well as three wine vaults, two flour warehouses, and a cheese dealer.[50] While some way from the specialist clusters that characterized shopping streets in many nineteenth- and twentieth-century towns, this represented an important concentration of shops selling groceries. In contrast, there is little sign that grocers were spreading onto Chester's more peripheral streets, although again it is likely that back-street shops were to be found in such locations.[51]

[46] Stobart and Hann, 'Retailing Revolution', 179; Stobart, 'Shopping Streets', 13–14.
[47] Carter, *Urban Geography*, 136–9.
[48] Van Aert and Van Damme, 'Retail Dynamics'. See also Wild and Shaw, 'Locational Behaviour'; Barnett, 'Shops, Retailing and Consumption', 117–36.
[49] See Lawton, 'Great Cities', 206–7.
[50] Hughes, *Ancient Chester*.
[51] The listings in Pigot, *National Commercial Directory* (1828–9) for Chester do not include shop-keepers or provisions dealers, so it is difficult to test this during the 1820s.

Table 4.3. Distribution of grocers, tea dealers, and tobacconists in selected towns, *c.*1828–1829

Town	Core streets		Connecting streets		Other areas		Total
	No.	%	No.	%	No.	%	No.
Nantwich	17	54.8	9	29.0	5	16.1	31
Northampton	13	59.1	8	36.4	1	4.5	22
Walsall	9	64.3	2	14.3	3	21.4	14
Chester	28	71.8	8	20.5	3	7.7	39
Liverpool	17	7.1	24	10.0	199	82.9	240
Birmingham	37	30.6	30	24.8	54	44.6	121
Manchester	54	37.0	8	5.5	84	57.5	146
Norwich	18	20.7	11	12.6	58	66.7	87
Total	193	27.6	100	14.3	407	58.1	700

Sources: Pigot, *National Commercial Directory* (1828–9); Pigot, *National Commercial Directory* (1839) (Norwich).

Sharply different was the situation in larger towns, where the selling of groceries became more evenly spread across the urban landscape. In Manchester, the central streets remained significant, mostly by virtue of the spreading of grocers further south along the length of Deansgate. Streets adjoining this core retail area declined in their relative importance as newer clusters of grocery retailing emerged to the north and east of the established centre, most notably on Swan Street, Shudehill, and Oldham Street. A similar process can be seen in Birmingham, where a growing density of grocers on the principal shopping streets was matched by an expansion of the central retail district. This growth took place primarily along the main arterial routes: Digbeth to the south-west, Snow Hill to the north-east, and, to a lesser extent, Aston Street to the north. However, the expanding residential areas between St Philip's and St Paul's were also served by a number of grocers and tobacconists in a pattern that resembles that seen in Norwich a generation earlier. In Norwich itself, there was also a growing number of grocery dealers in both the central area, around the marketplace, and on outlying streets. Given that the population of the city did not change much between the late eighteenth and early nineteenth centuries, this was less a reflection of shifting residential patterns and more to do with growing demand from residents and visitors to the city.[52] The latter is evidenced by the tendency for clusters of grocers to emerge along routes into the city, most notably on Stephen's Street and Ber Street—the main roads out to London.

The most profound spatial changes were seen in Liverpool. Quite apart from the dramatic increase in the number of grocery dealers, they became much more evenly spread across the town. This was not a gradual expansion of the core retail area (as seen in Birmingham and, to a lesser extent, Manchester); rather, it was a reorientation towards the better residential areas to the south-east of the town. Bold Street

---

[52] The better coverage of the early nineteenth-century directories was also an important factor, both here and elsewhere (see Shaw, *British Directories*, 25–8).

became the focus of high-status retailing, earning the epithet 'Bond Street of the North'.[53] Grocers, tobacconists, and tea dealers were increasingly spread along arterial routes: Pitt Street and St James' Street to the south; Ranelegh Street and Brownlow Hill to the south-east; London Road and Islington to the east, and Byrom Street and Scotland Road to the north. This distinction appears to have been particularly true of female grocers and especially tea dealers. For most towns, the number of women listed under these trades is insufficient to establish a definite distribution, but they broadly followed the general trends outlined above. The Liverpool directory, however, lists forty-two female dealers—eight grocers, eight tobacconists, and twenty-six tea dealers—located on over thirty different streets. While being widely dispersed, they were found most often in the new residential areas and seldom on either the core shopping streets or the main arterial routes. This might reflect a lower economic position, although this is doubtful, as they were listed under named occupations rather than being grouped with the lower-status shopkeepers. More likely, it suggests a different style of shop—one that catered for the everyday needs of a respectable and local clientele. That said, the distribution of female tea dealers was not profoundly different from that of their male counterparts, indicating that there was probably little to distinguish the two in terms of the character of their shops and businesses.

At one level, the general processes behind the redistribution of grocery dealers in Liverpool and other growing commercial towns were straightforward: they were following their customers towards, if not into, new suburban residential areas. Central place theory suggests that the distance over which consumers are willing to travel to acquire everyday goods such as tea, tobacco, sugar, spices, and dried fruits is quite low, leading to their presence in small settlements and low-order intra-urban shopping centres.[54] In practical terms, this would mean that few people would travel into the centre of town to make such purchases. At the same time, bid-rent models indicate that retailers of lower-order goods, such as groceries, would be forced out of prime retail locations, because they were unable or unwilling to afford the increasingly high rents charged in such places. There is undoubtedly much truth in both of these arguments. Young and Allen, for example, demonstrate how grocers in Chester spread into streets with lower rateable values during the course of the nineteenth century. However, neither the distribution of grocers nor the explanations for their location within the urban retail landscape are this simple. For one thing, the absolute number of 'high-street' grocers appearing in the directories grew significantly in most towns (Tables 4.2 and 4.3). While some of this growth was due to the better coverage afforded by the later directories, it is far from apparent that grocers were being forced from the high street into secondary retail locations. Indeed, Young and Allen show that they remained a strong presence on the most costly streets; it was shopkeepers who were more thoroughly dispersed, perhaps suggesting the kind of growing divide observed by Mui and Mui.[55]

[53] Lawton, 'Great Cities', 206.
[54] For a fuller discussion of Christaller's central place theory, see Stobart, *First Industrial Region*, 22–6, 159–70.
[55] Young and Allen, 'Retail Patterns', 9–12; Mui and Mui, *Shops and Shopkeeping*, 160–73.

Many grocers chose (and could afford) to locate in the central retail district. To exemplify, when George Heywood was looking to establish himself in business after a lengthy period working as a journeyman for the Manchester grocers Roylance and Jones, he considered a number of premises, all of which were centrally situated, on or near to the town's core shopping streets. His comments on the first shop that he viewed (on 19 February 1815) are particularly revealing. It was located on 'a very public road over Old Bridge from Smythy Door—there is no Grocer nearer than Littlewoods or Brudens'.[56] Three things stand out from this description. First is the central location near to the market and to high-status shops, which would have drawn in consumers from the surrounding area. Second, and running slightly counter to this, is the position of the shop relative to other grocers. Clustering might bring certain advantages in terms of creating a critical mass of provision, but Heywood was clearly concerned that his shop should not lie in the business shadow of competitors. Third is the busy nature of the street itself—an attraction that also features in many newspaper advertisements for shop premises. Thus, for example, in April 1822, the *Bristol Mercury* carried an advertisement for an 'old established business in the tea and grocery lines, centrally situated in this City, commanding a good connection both in town and country'.[57] The importance of the country trade to grocers situated in the heart of towns and cities is also apparent from William Stout's comments on his activity in preparation for market day and from grocers' account books, which suggest a mixed customer base, including many from the town's hinterland and others from a resident middling sort (see Chapter 6). The Worcester grocer Thomas Dickenson drew the majority of his customers from within the city, but 25 per cent came from the surrounding villages and small towns, and a further 17 per cent from places more than 10 miles distant.[58] This distribution would make a central location extremely advantageous. Others found it better to situate themselves elsewhere, mostly on arterial routes. These would have afforded a high level of visibility and, in modern terms, a good footfall from people moving between new residential areas and the centre of town, where many of the middling sorts would have been employed.[59]

While the category 'grocer' undoubtedly included retailers with widely different levels of wealth, customer base, and selling practices, Mui and Mui suggest that the real social divide lay between the respectable grocer and the ubiquitous 'shopkeeper'—a category that the directory compilers saw as being linked to, but distinct from, grocers.[60] The social distinction that they drew was made all the more emphatic by a profound spatial differentiation. The grocers, tea dealers, and tobacconists who appeared in the directories were only occasionally found on back streets. Dealers in these streets were largely omitted from the directories published

---

[56] JRL, Eng. MS 703.   [57] *Bristol Mercury*, 27 Apr. 1822.
[58] WSL, D1798 HM 27/5.
[59] This point has been noted in analyses of retail location from the Middle Ages to the present day. See, e.g., Stabel, 'Market to the Shop'; Harding, 'Shops, Markets and Retailers'; Stobart, 'City Centre Retailing'.
[60] Mui and Mui, *Shops and Shopkeeping*, 160–72.

Table **4.4.** Distribution of 'shopkeepers' in selected larger towns, *c.*1828–1829

Town	Core streets		Connecting streets		Other areas		Total
	No.	%	No.	%	No.	%	No.
Liverpool	0	0.0	5	3.8	126	96.2	131
Birmingham	2	1.3	13	8.7	134	89.9	149
Manchester	10	3.1	1	0.3	308	96.5	319
Norwich	0	0.0	4	3.1	128	96.9	132
Total	12	1.6	23	3.1	696	95.2	731

Sources: Pigot, *National Commercial Directory* (1828–9); Pigot, *National Commercial Directory* (1839) (Norwich).

in the 1770s and 1780s, rarely forming part of the principal tradesmen who were the object and subject of these volumes. By the 1820s and 1830s, however, these places were the domain of the shopkeeper (Table 4.4). In the four large towns contained in the present sample, they were largely absent from the central retail districts: only 12 shopkeepers were recorded in core areas, compared with 126 grocers, tea dealers, and tobacconists. They were slightly more numerous in the streets connecting to the centre and in the arterials roads that formed the locus around which much grocery dealing was reorienting in the early nineteenth century. Yet even these streets housed less than 5 per cent of shopkeepers. They were overwhelmingly found in other places: more distant arterials, link roads between these main routes, and, above all, back streets. These were generally the resort of a poorer local clientele, but they also picked up trade when other, more respectable shops were closed.[61] What is striking is the consistency of this distribution across four towns with such different economies, histories, and geographical constraints. Shopkeepers were thus both spatially and functionally distinct from grocers. While they were oriented towards the everyday provisioning poorer consumers, grocers were set more firmly on the main streets of the town and in the mainstream of new consumer cultures.

GROCERS AND THE VIRTUAL LANDSCAPE OF CONSUMPTION

The distribution of shops across the urban space formed a matrix of opportunities for the consumer. With good credit, they could patronize a number of shops, choosing between suppliers on the basis of a range of factors, including availability, price, quality, convenience, service, and loyalty. All these things were played on by retailers when they advertised their shops and their wares, and attempted to attract new customers and retain their existing clientele. As well as offering crucial information about the world of goods and a rhetoric of persuasion,

---

[61] Alexander, *Retailing in England*, 174–5.

advertisements also helped to produce virtual landscapes of consumption.[62] These comprised an image in the consumer's mind of the presence and location of certain shops and certain goods, and an overall framework of locations, routes, and nodes by which they might negotiate and navigate their way through the town's retail space.

These virtual landscapes were constituted by a wide range of media and experiences. Of fundamental importance was the shopper's established knowledge and experience based on earlier visits to shops and shopping streets. Shopping was and is an iterative process, characterized by regular and often subconscious acts: walking the streets, visiting shops, browsing goods, making purchases.[63] Such processes involved movements through space of the type pictorialized by Hägerstrand in his diagrams showing the intersecting and overlapping paths of individual journeys.[64] These activities not only built identity as a shopper; they also helped to construct a mental image of the town as a consumption space. Layered onto this were other influences, such as conversations or correspondence with friends. Indeed, such influences were practically unavoidable, as many shopping trips were undertaken with or on the behest of others.[65] However, printed media were also influential. Trade directories formed an important representation of the retail landscape. As we have seen, their listings highlighted certain shops and streets, while obscuring others, and thus formed a powerful mechanism for shaping perceptions of urban space. As Corfield argues, they rendered a town 'intelligible, decipherable and finite, however mysterious, inchoate and vast it might appear'.[66] Perusing the pages of the directory provided the visitor or shopper with a particular representation of the consumption landscape—one that directed his or her movement through a mental image of the town.

Newspaper advertisements could have a similar impact, but they were much more selective in the places that they highlighted and thus brought the virtual landscapes of consumption into sharper relief. This selectivity was born of the small if variable proportion of shopkeepers who chose to advertise in this way (see Chapter 7). Chester appears to have been characterized by an unusually high level of activity, with a ratio of advertisements per grocer of around one in three, although this figure was inflated by the relatively large number of notices placed by London tea warehouses and their local agents. In Liverpool, Birmingham, and Norwich, only 9–13 per cent of grocers and tea dealers placed advertisements in the 1770s and 1780s—a figure that, in Liverpool at least, had risen to about 16 per

---

[62] See, e.g., Barker, *Business of Women*, 27–34, 72–89; Stobart 'Selling (through) Politeness'; Stobart, Hann, and Morgan, *Spaces of Consumption*, 171–89; Barnett, 'Shops, Retailing and Consumption', 137–40.

[63] See Glennie and Thrift, 'Consumers, Identities and Consumption Spaces', 28–31; Miller et al., *Shopping, Place and Identity*, 10, 20–1; Shields, 'Spaces for Consumption', 11–17.

[64] Hägerstrand, 'What about People?'. See also Pred, 'Choreography of Existence'.

[65] Walsh, 'Shops, Shopping and the Art of Decision Making', 169–72; Walsh, 'Social Relations'; Miller, *Theory of Shopping*, esp. 5–9.

[66] Corfield and Kelly, 'Giving Directions to the Town'. See also Barker, *Business of Women*, 47–54.

cent by the 1820s.[67] Whether these advertisers were typical retailers is unimportant here; what matters is the way in which they shaped consumer perceptions of the retail geography of the town.

This was done, first and foremost, by highlighting the address of the retailer—a crucial element of most advertisements.[68] Although the sample is quite small, the patterns revealed in the four study towns are telling, the vast majority of advertisers in the 1770s and 1780s being located in the core retail areas (Table 4.5). Indeed, only Liverpool departs from this model, with the streets leading off the central districts being more prominent. This suggests that it was higher-status grocers who chose to advertise in this manner—clearly, they were not troubled by the same concerns that made newspaper advertising so abhorrent to Josiah Wedgwood.[69] More important to the present discussion, the consumer landscape constructed through these notices was focused on the main retail streets. Appearing in the local press heightened both the visibility of these places and their prominence in the mind of (potential) consumers; the 'real' geography of retailing was thus reinforced by the virtual geography created on the pages of the newspapers. This close relationship is particularly important, given the changing distribution of grocery dealers noted earlier. What is striking, in Liverpool at least, is that the geography of newspaper advertisers closely reflected the dispersal of grocery retailing to new areas away from the established retail districts. By 1820, only 12 per cent of advertising grocers were located in the core area, while half had shops on one of the arterial roads that were at the heart of Liverpool's new retail geography, most notably Byrom Street and St James Street. At one level, this suggests that it was the more dynamic rather than simply the high-status grocers who chose to advertise; at another, it is clear that virtual landscapes of consumption were quickly remoulded around the shifting geography of retailing.

Advertisements, though, did not simply form a (pale) reflection of the reality on the ground; they helped to shape this reality. While the precise ways in which advertising works to encourage consumption and direct consumer choices remain unclear, even to advertising professionals, it is apparent that there exists some kind of positive relationship between the two.[70] Newspaper advertisements served to promote the advertiser's business and the place in which that business took place. The close link between the shopkeeper and the location of the shop was important for practical reasons: it allowed consumers to find the right premises among the

---

[67] Total numbers are taken from: Gore, *Liverpool Directory* (1766); Pearson and Rollason, *Birmingham Directory* (1777); *Norwich Directory* (1783); Pigot, *National Commercial Directory* (1828/9); Pigot, *National Commercial Directory* (1839) (Norwich). The number of advertisers is ascertained from: *Aris's Birmingham Gazette* (1782); *Bristol Mercury* (1820–4); *Gore's Liverpool Advertiser* (1770); *Liverpool Mercury* (1820); *Norwich Gazette* (1782). Growth in the number of retail advertisements is discussed in Ferdinand, 'Selling it to the Provinces', 399–402.

[68] The only advertisements that failed to mention a local address were those placed by London tea warehouses. Most of these named local agents, but they sometimes offered goods direct to the consumer and thus included only their London address (see Ch. 3).

[69] See Berg, *Luxury and Pleasure*, 147–8; Stobart, 'Selling (through) Politeness', 310–11.

[70] For a brief discussion, see Wischermann, 'Placing Advertising', 15–25. More detailed analysis can be found in Richards, *Commodity Culture*.

Table 4.5. Distribution of grocers and tea dealers advertising in newspapers in selected towns, 1770s and 1780s

Town	Core streets		Connecting streets		Other areas		Total
	No.	%	No.	%	No.	%	No.
Chester	10	100.0	0	0.0	0	0.0	10
Liverpool	2	40.0	3	60.0	0	0.0	5
Birmingham	4	80.0	1	20.0	0	0.0	5
Norwich	3	75.0	1	25.0	0	0.0	4
Total	19	79.0	5	21.0	0	0.0	24

Sources: Adams Weekly Courant (1784–5); *Gore's Liverpool Advertiser* (1770); *Aris's Birmingham Gazette* (1780); *Norwich Gazette* (1782).

network of urban streets and lanes. It also projected that location into the mind of the consumer and thus made the grocer's shop more prominent in terms of consumer behaviour. It is significant, therefore, that the shop address frequently appeared in the opening lines of the advertisement or even formed part of the heading. However, grocers' shops did not stand apart from each other or from the rest of the street; they were situated in a web of spatial interactions and interrelations. Moving from one space to another—from shop to shop, or from inn to shop to market—was part of the everyday life of most people. Indeed, for Pred, the bundling of these routes and interactions can tell us much about the ways in which people experienced the city.[71] Many newspaper advertisements drew on and reinforced these routines and the ways in which they linked together different spaces.

This spatial linkaging drew on three set of reference points (Table 4.6). First were nodes within the network of streets. In the 1770s, these were used comparatively rarely—the only instance in my sample being Joseph Farror's announcement that he had just moved to 'a commodious shop [on] the corner of Moor Street'.[72] By the 1820s, though, such references were quite common, advertisers stressing that their shop was 'near the bottom of Bold Street', 'opposite Marsh Street', or 'nearly opposite Circus Street'.[73] This reflects a combination of factors: the growing complexity of the street network, the increasing length of certain streets (especially arterial routes), and the rising density of shops along these streets. Together, these made it ever more difficult to find particular shops, even when properties were numbered. The need for more precise descriptions meant that advertisements drew on and heightened the importance of junctions as prime retail locations, not only because of their advantages in terms of passing traffic, but also because they were more easily imagined and more prominent within consumers' mental maps.

The second set of reference points were prominent buildings or urban institutions. Inns were the most important landmarks in eighteenth-century advertise-

[71] These ideas form the focus of analysis in Pred, *Lost Words*.
[72] *Aris's Birmingham Gazette*, 25 Nov. 1782.
[73] *Liverpool Mercury*, 3 Mar. 1820; *Bristol Mercury*, 9 Sept. 1822; *Liverpool Mercury*, 8 Sept. 1820.

Table 4.6. Spatial references within provincial newspaper advertisements, *c.*1770s and *c.*1820

Date	Street layout No.	Street layout %	Landmarks No.	Landmarks %	Late owner No.	Late owner %	Total No.
1770s	2	10.5	7	31.6	11	57.9	20
1820s	5	38.5	3	23.1	5	38.5	13
Total	7	21.2	10	30.3	16	48.5	33

Sources: *Adams Weekly Courant* (1784–5); *Aris's Birmingham Gazette* (1780); *Bristol Mercury* (1820–4); *Gore's Liverpool Advertiser* (1770); *Liverpool Mercury* (1820).

ments: Samuel Brooks, for instance, advertised his shop as being opposite the Hen and Chickens on the High Street in Birmingham, while that of S. Swann was opposite the White Lion on Northgate Street, Chester.[74] Churches, theatres, and markets were also used to situate shops more firmly in space—a reflection of their physical prominence within the landscape of many towns. Thus, Samuel Parry's newly opened shop on Northgate Street, Chester, was 'next Door to the Royal Theatre'.[75] By the early nineteenth century, these had been joined by civic buildings, both the Council House and the Exchange being used in this way in Bristol. This linking of civic, religious, and commercial space is very similar to the effect produced by the walking itineraries offered in a growing number of town guides, although in these the interlinking was far more sustained. For example, in his *History of Warwickshire*, William West details a number of walks through the streets of Birmingham. The second of these centres on New Street, 'which evinces from its name and modern growth, and improvement, what it evidently is, the most attractive on in the town. The consequence and elegance of the well stocked shops, in articles of taste, of luxury, and of general consumption, arrest attention.'[76] Although he does not mention grocers specifically, West affords shops a central position within his construction of the modern town. They are linked to art, craftsmanship, and taste, both in terms of the goods that they contained, through their architectural merits, and by association with the neighbouring buildings. On the one hand, this served to make these shops respectable, even fashionable sites of consumption; on the other, it defined the culture of New Street (and, by association, Birmingham as a whole) in commercial as well as aesthetic terms. Similarly, advertisements that linked shops to churches, exchanges, and town halls reflected the daily routines of many urban dwellers and helped to construct a mental landscape in which commercial, civic, and cultural space were tied together.

In addition to these overtly spatial references, grocers' advertisements also sought to situate them in a landscape of consumption that was defined by an established matrix of retailers. This was sometimes done by locating the shop in

[74] *Aris's Birmingham Gazette*, 30 Sept. 1782; *Adams Weekly Courant*, 7 Nov. 1775.
[75] *Adams Weekly Courant*, 5 Jan. 1779. [76] West, *History of Warwickshire*, 210.

relation to that of another more prominent retailer. Much more common, especially in the 1770s and 1780s, was for new grocers or tea dealers to name the previous owner of the shop. In doing so, they drew on the reputation of the late owner and often made an implicit plea to their customers to remain loyal to the new proprietor—John D. Ellis, for example, advertising in 1820 that his tea and grocery warehouse on Gloucester Road in Bristol was an 'old-established shop', previously owned by a Mr Saunders.[77] They also benefited from the prominence of the previous owner within consumers' mental maps. Two examples serve to illustrate this point. The grocers, seedsmen, and tea dealers Bancroft and Lorimer advertised their Liverpool shop as being 'near the Top of Dale-Street, No. 8, late occupied by Miss Edwardson's'.[78] We know from the trade directories that this shop was occupied by the grocer William Edwardson before passing to what was presumably his daughter or sister, and then on to Bancroft and Lorimer. It thus had an established identity as a grocer's shop that transcended changes in ownership. Similarly, in Bristol, Samuel Bryant proudly announced that he would shortly be opening his tea warehouse in the premises formerly occupied by Gye & Co., proprietors of the London Genuine Tea Company.[79] With its long association with this London company, 23 Clare Street must have been a prime site: it was a place that Bristolians associated with tea, to which they were accustomed to going, and that was therefore prominent in their imagining of the town's commercial landscape.

CONCLUSIONS

The distribution of grocers across the country was shaped by demand and supply factors. On the supply side, the routes through which groceries were distributed across the country were important. They were structured in large part by the existing urban hierarchy, but big, dynamic commercial centres appear to have been particularly well supplied with grocers. This reflected not just internal demand and their ability to draw in customers from a broad hinterland, but perhaps also a particularly enterprising spirit that made them keen to appear in directory listings and allowed them to operate at a larger scale than their small-town counterparts. On the demand side, the number of potential consumers was important in shaping patterns of retailing, but so too was the character of those consumers. As de Vries argues, they needed to be willing and able to purchase a widening range of goods (including groceries) from shops—a process that developed earliest and most fully in commercialized economies. To properly understand what was going on here, it is useful to recall what grocers, tea dealers, and tobacconists were offering their customers and how this linked into wider changes in consumer demand. The goods they sold included everyday items, but also a range of small luxuries that were increasingly important in the lives of consumers, both the middling sorts and

---

[77] *Bristol Mercury*, 7 Feb. 1820. For more discussion of the importance of reputation, see Ch. 7.
[78] *Adams Weekly Courant*, 7 Nov. 1775.   [79] *Bristol Mercury*, 20 Jan. 1823.

the lower orders. Tobacco, sugar, and tea are prominent here, but so too were spices, dried fruits, and even fine white flour and oil-based soaps.[80] To be readily adopted by consumers, these goods needed to be supplied locally. Rapid development of grocery trade in a particular area was thus crucial in facilitating the broader uptake of the new groceries that were central to the emergence of a consumer society. Given this, it is significant that grocers appear to have colonized new industrial towns and districts more quickly than did other retailers. In doing so, they encouraged a partial reorientation of the retail hierarchy away from small market towns and onto newer industrial centres. Regional patterns of supply were thus shaped by as well as helping to structure the shopping practices and mental landscapes of consumers.

The intra-urban geography of grocery dealing is important because it tells us a lot about the ways in which groceries fitted into broader processes of retailing and consumption. Locating on the main streets made groceries more visible and desirable; it also placed them alongside other consumer goods, helping to link them together, both spatially and conceptually, into consumption bundles. Central locations might thus be seen as pivotal both to the status and business of the individual grocer and to the perception of groceries as objects of desire—especially when they were still novel items. But this might be stretching the symbolism of the high street a little too far: keeping a shop on the high street (or, more particularly, near to the market) made good business sense in terms of drawing in customers. Also attractive were locations on arterial routes and increasingly those in better residential areas. Locating towards customers in this way made it easier for people to access goods—a growing consideration as new groceries became familiar and everyday goods, stripped of some of their earlier symbolism as exotic novelties. It also reduced rental costs. The dispersal of grocers into the suburbs thus reflected a combination of demographic, cultural, and economic changes.

Crucially, grocers remained spatially and socially distinct from the 'back-street' shopkeepers who were a growing feature of nineteenth-century directories and towns. They were more firmly tied into polite lifestyles and consumption practices, their shops as well as their wares being set alongside other markers of polite domestic sociability: the china dealer, toy shop, draper, and upholsterer. In this way, the setting of the grocer's shops was important in linking groceries into Smith's notion of respectability.[81] This association was reinforced by the position of grocer's shops within virtual landscapes of consumption that were created through newspaper advertisements and trade directories. These drew on and privileged key markers in the urban landscape and gave consumers a mental map by which to negotiate the retail geography of the town. In direct terms, they helped to shape choices about which shop to visit to buy particular commodities; more generally, they served to place grocers' shops centrally within polite consumption landscapes and practices.

---

[80] De Vries, *Industrious Revolution*, 149–54. [81] See Smith, *Consumption*.

5

Selling Spaces: Display and Storage of Groceries

INTRODUCTION

Shops were not only growing in number through the eighteenth and early nineteenth centuries; they were also becoming increasingly sophisticated spaces. Recent work by Walsh, Cox, Berry, and Stobart has recognized them as complex social and economic environments in tune with the changing cultures of consumption that characterized the period.[1] These analyses offer an important historical contextualization for nineteenth-century development, Walsh in particular revealing how department stores had their roots deep in the eighteenth century.[2] More importantly, perhaps, they also serve to emphasize the role of shops in broader processes of economic, social, and cultural change in eighteenth-century society. Shops gave access to a wide range of goods—important for urban populations who increasingly looked to retailers to provide not just luxury but also a growing number of more mundane items. Indeed, they were the principal point of access to the burgeoning world of goods that underpinned nascent consumerism and, Berg argues, helped to shape fashion by contextualizing or individualizing goods, and by bringing them together in new or recognizable combinations.[3] The ways in which they were arranged and presented to consumers can thus reveal much about how goods were conceived and about the cultural contexts in which they were consumed. Societal values, such as politeness and respectability, were therefore important in shops as well as homes and arenas of commercialized leisure. They gave access to the material trappings of politeness and thus constituted an important part of polite urban space; but they also formed settings within which Addisonian conceptions of commercially oriented politeness could be defined and refined.[4] Improvements made to the physical fabric of shops and shopping streets in many towns thus formed an integral part of a more general renaissance of urban culture and environments.[5] In the most fashionable areas, this created an urban shopping experience where retailing and leisure came

---

[1] Walsh, 'Shop Design'; Cox, *Complete Tradesman*; Berry, 'Polite Consumption'; Hann and Stobart, 'Sites of Consumption'; Stobart, Hann, and Morgan, *Spaces of Consumption*, 123–32.

[2] Walsh, 'Newness of the Department Store'. See also Stobart and Hann, 'Retailing Revolution'.

[3] Berg, *Luxury and Pleasure*, 255.

[4] See Sweet, 'Topographies of Politeness', 356; Klein, 'Politeness for Plebes'.

[5] Borsay, *English Urban Renaissance*, 41–113; Stobart, 'Shopping Streets'.

together in space, time, and purpose, creating arenas of polite consumption. These were places where the social imperatives of politeness and, more arguably, imitative emulation acquired material form both through the goods purchased and the retail spaces created to satisfy these needs.

Walsh reminds us that shops in the seventeenth and eighteenth centuries encompassed a wide variety of formats, including small wooden lock-ups or sheds, wooden booths constructed up against another building (so-called bulk shops, which often had pentices over their fronts to guard against the weather), and retail spaces contained within the structure of the building itself, almost always occupying the front room and opening directly onto the street. These various different formats remained viable alternatives for retailers and shoppers throughout the period, but the shop within the house gradually came to dominate. This signalled the emergence of new forms of consumption, changing expectations on the part of consumers, and the growing respectability of the retail shop. Within such spaces, Walsh demonstrates that shopkeepers went to considerable trouble and expense when furbishing their premises.[6] Of central importance here was the notion of display, a retail strategy that had four main purposes. First, display was a marketing device, which promoted the sale of goods by making them more visible, appealing, or fashionable, often by framing them in an orderly setting. Second, it enhanced the reputation of the shopkeeper, projecting important messages about his or her status, skill, and trustworthiness. Third, and closely related to this, a well-organized display allowed the shopkeeper to serve customers in an efficient manner—knowing where goods were placed on shelves or drawers, or in boxes, barrels, or canisters, showed the shopkeeper to be businesslike.[7] Finally, shop display linked closely to shopping as a polite and pleasurable activity, politeness and status often being judged by physical appearance as well as civilized behaviour.[8] Creating the appropriate visual impression was also important in determining the position of a shop and shopkeeper in local retail and social hierarchies: the shop display would match the status of the target customers. Providing for the comfort of (potential) shoppers—creating a pleasant physical environment and offering attentive service—enhanced the pleasure of shopping and locked fashionable shops into the polite social round.[9]

I have explored these ideas elsewhere, arguing that Walsh's model holds good for provincial as well as metropolitan shops.[10] Yet many questions remain about the changing character of grocery shops and how this linked into broader processes of consumer and retail transformation. One important issue is the extent to which those selling groceries deployed the strategies revealed in these broader surveys. Was display as important when the goods were visually less striking and not amenable to the same tactile interaction seen with textiles, for instance?

[6] Walsh, 'Shop Design', 167–8.
[7] Walsh, 'Stalls, Bulks, Shops'.
[8] Sweet, 'Topographies of Politeness', 361.
[9] Walsh, 'Shop Design', 168; Berry, 'Polite Consumption', 380–1.
[10] Hann and Stobart, 'Sites of Consumption'.

Leading from this are questions concerning the timing and spread of any changes in the shop environment: when and where can we identify the advent of the 'modern' grocer's shop? Third, if those selling groceries were concerned with the presentation of their goods, what was their motivation for doing so? In Berry's browse-bargain model of polite shopping, groceries might be seen as the kind of mundane item that was bought in a perfunctory manner, perhaps by servants. Were grocers therefore more concerned with retail efficiency and business reputation? Most fundamentally, how does the changing character of the grocer's shop tie in with attitudes to and consumption of the goods it sold: were these retail spaces innovative, respectable, or even exotic in the same way as the goods themselves are seen to be? In addressing these various questions, the focus inevitably falls onto the higher-end shops, for which we have most information, but the shopkeepers analysed here include a wide range of retailers from specialist grocers to general chandlers, who were often seen as selling groceries to the poor.

MAKING THE 'MODERN' GROCER'S SHOP

Inventories and trade cards of London shopkeepers reveal opulent settings within which goods were often displayed in glass-fronted cases, or framed by plaster moulding and gilded cornices.[11] The fittings of provincial grocers were generally more modest, but their basic structures were essentially the same. Some shopkeepers still kept their stock in a chest or coffer, to be produced at the customer's request, much as their predecessors had done in earlier centuries, but it was increasingly the exception (Table 5.1). Already in the third quarter of the seventeenth century, counters, shelves, and drawers were nearly as common as boxes and chests. Over the following one hundred years or so, such fittings characterized ever greater numbers of shops selling groceries: counters became ubiquitous, shelves and nests of drawers appeared in the majority of shops, and a growing minority of appraisers even noted window grates or goods in the window.[12] By contrast, chests became less common and were found in less than one grocer's shop in twelve by the second quarter of the eighteenth century. Always present, but infrequently noted by appraisers, were the bags in which a wide variety of goods might be stored and the smaller paper packets in which they were often sold. We get a glimpse of this in the 'small parcel of penny sugars' listed in the 1725 inventory of the Kentish tallow chandler Richard Johnson; the wrappers found in the shop of Thomas Wright, a Birmingham grocer (d. 1788), and the 'sundry packages' listed among the shop fixtures advertised for sale in the *Bristol Mercury* in 1822.[13] They also appear

---

[11] See Walsh, 'Shop Design'.

[12] The listing of shelves in shop inventories is somewhat erratic, as it appears that some appraisers viewed them as fixtures and therefore as part of the real estate, not to be included in an inventory of personal property.

[13] KAS, 11.77.190, Richard Johnson (1725); LiRO, B/C/5, Thomas Wright (1788); *Bristol Mercury*, 6 July 1822.

Table 5.1. Changes in the fittings in shops selling groceries, c.1650–1750 (%)

Date	No. of inventories	Counter (%)	Shelves (%)	Boxes (%)	Cupboard (%)	Nest of drawers (%)	Chest (%)	Window/ grate (%)	Scales (%)	Average no. of items
Before 1675	11	36.4	45.5	54.5	0.0	36.4	45.5	9.1	72.7	3
1675–99	15	53.3	53.3	53.3	20.0	60.0	20.0	6.7	86.7	3.6
1700–25	31	77.4	51.6	61.3	19.4	67.7	19.4	16.1	71.0	3.8
After 1725	15	100.0	66.7	53.3	6.7	80.0	6.7	13.3	80.0	4.1
Total	72	70.8	54.2	56.9	13.9	63.9	20.8	12.5	76.4	

Source: probate inventories.

occasionally in witness statements from trials for shoplifting, but in such a way as to suggest that they were the norm. Thus we see three separate thefts of a bag containing 17 lb of tea, another with 14 lb of ginger, and a sack with 56 lb of rice. Also stolen were 'a paper of nutmeg' and a 'parcel of almonds'.[14]

Changes in the type of fittings listed in inventories point towards a growing sophistication in the way in which shops were furnished, with a grouping of counter, shelves, and drawers increasingly defining the shop. Before 1675, only one shop contained all three of these items: that belonging to John Dyer, a yeoman-shopkeeper of Minster in Kent (d. 1671). Dyer had two counters, three nests of boxes, ten empty casks, and three shelves, together rather modestly valued at £1.[15] In addition, there were a number of other barrels and casks containing soap and sugar. More typical of their age were John Knowler, a grocer from Milton, also in Kent (d. 1668), and William Bramstone, a weaver and shopkeeper from Tregony in Cornwall (d. 1673).[16] Knowler's shop contained counters, boxes, scales, and weights, plus unspecified 'lumber'. The boxes may have been arranged on shelves not itemized by the appraisers, but the extent of furnishing seems less sophisticated than that seen in Dyer's premises, despite being valued at £5 13s. 4d. The shop fittings listed in Bramstone's inventory were even more modest: his stock of textiles, haberdashery, spices, sugar, fruit, and ironware is summarized, but just one box of drawers and an unspecified number of 'shop chests' and 'other old boxes' are listed. This suggests that storage rather than display was critical to Bramstone, although it also highlights the dilemma facing any shopkeeper selling groceries: to keep them fresh, they had to be stored in airtight containers, so any display was of the containers, not the groceries themselves.

By the turn of the eighteenth century, one-fifth to one-quarter of shops selling groceries contained a counter, shelves, and drawers; a further third had two of the three. A generation later, all the grocery shops surveyed had a counter combined with either shelves or drawers; half of them had all three. Fairly typical was the grocer William Claridge of Great Brington in Northamptonshire, who died in 1755 leaving a shop containing a range of groceries (including tea and coffee) and fitted out with 'counters, shelves, boxes, cupboard and draws'.[17] Although they were valued at just 5s. 6d.—a remarkably small amount, which suggests that they were poor quality, old, or of very modest proportions—these fitments offered Claridge a range of options for storing and presenting goods to his customers. His inventory provides few clues about how these were arranged, but contemporary illustrations of shop interiors suggest a standard arrangement whereby the counter would be set at right angles to the front of the shop, sometimes with a perpendicular return and sometimes with a second counter running parallel down the other side of the shop. Behind the counter were ranged the shelves and nests of drawers

[14] OBP: 9 Sept. 1742, Christopher Peterson (t17420909-1); 8 Apr. 1812, William Rogers (t18120408-55); 3 Dec. 1817, Thomas Jones (t18171203-23); 26 Feb. 1735, John Dwyer and Will Bentley (t17350226-33); 2 July 1817, Edward Young (t18170702-70).

[15] KAS, 11.33.86, John Dyer (1671).

[16] KAS, 11.30.141, John Knowler (1668); CRO, B1698, William Bramstone (1673).

[17] NRO, William Claridge, 1755.

(an arrangement that discouraged theft and facilitated service), while boxes, chests, and barrels might be set in various locations around the shop. At the back of the shop there was often a door leading into more private space, typically the shop-keeper's parlour.

One context in which these changes to the structure and fixtures of the shop took place was the gradual shift in terms of stock. It is difficult to be certain about the impact that this change might have had, since counters, shelves, and drawers were suitable for a wide variety of goods, while only a handful of containers were specific to the preparation or storage of particular commodities. Most obvious in the inventories are coffee mills, which spread slowly in the early eighteenth century, but newspaper advertisements and trade cards indicate that tea canisters were also coming into use around the same time. Perhaps more telling were two broader sets of socio-cultural changes. The first, outlined above, was the shifting priorities of buying and selling inherent in the growing consumerism of the age, coupled with the strictures of polite and respectable living. The availability of and desire for new consumer goods had important implications for the means through which shopkeepers sought to present their wares and engage their customers. So too did the polite cultural contexts in which these goods were consumed. The systems of meaning enmeshing the consumption of coffee, tea, sugar, and tobacco can be overplayed, but they undoubtedly reflected back onto the place in which these goods were acquired.[18] Second, and reinforcing this, was the dramatic change in domestic material culture that occurred between the mid-seventeenth and mid-eighteenth centuries. Certain aspects of this were closely related to the advent of new groceries, including the desire for tea tables and boards; tea, coffee, and chocolate pots; china tableware, and so on.[19] But others were more general: most notably the move to cheaper and less durable types of furniture, a shift that seems to have been accompanied by a reduction in real terms of the cost of many inventoried goods.[20]

Grocers' shops were, therefore, changing in character and structure at precisely the time when the nature of groceries and the tastes of consumers were being transformed, and when many durable goods were apparently steady or coming down in price. It would be wrong to draw any simple lines of causality, but choices about how to furnish shops were clearly being made in these broader contexts: a shift to more modern forms of and attitudes to material culture affected the shop as well as the home. It is, therefore, significant that this grouping of counter, shelves, and nests of drawers became the standard fittings in grocers' shops for the following two hundred years. In his late-eighteenth-century shop, Thomas Wright had three counters (all containing drawers); various shelves (including one set with 'sugar holes', presumably for holding sugar loaves); 'four nests with 82 drawers'; twenty-three canisters and a 'frame of shelves' for them to sit on; coffee,

---

[18] Smith, *Consumption*, esp. 9–24, 226–32. See also Blonde and Van Damme, 'Retail Growth'.
[19] See Weatherill, *Consumer Behaviour*, 25–42; Overton et al., *Production and Consumption*, 87–120; de Vries, *Industrious Revolution*, 144–9. These are discussed in detail in Ch. 10.
[20] Overton, 'Prices from Probate Inventories'.

pepper, and rice mills, and a wide range of barrels, cans, measures, scales, and weights. He also had a counting house separated from the shop by a partition, door, and sash.[21] A generation later, the fittings from a grocer's shop in Castle Street, Bristol, were being auctioned; they comprised: one mahogany-topped counter and two deal counters, a nest of drawers with mahogany fronts, shelves, copper scales, a beam and scales, weights, a counting-house desk with mahogany top, sample drawers for sugar, an iron chest, canisters for tea and coffee, and a variety of barrels and casks.[22] There are some interesting developments here: the prominence of tea canisters, the sugar drawers, and increasingly the abundance of mahogany—a feature that became synonymous with solid and respectable retailing, especially in department stores.

Beyond these few innovations, many of the fittings in these shops would have been familiar to grocers from one hundred years earlier. Moreover, they changed little through to the 1920s and beyond. A photograph of George Mason's grocery shop in Leamington Spa (*c.*1929) shows the counter running along the length of the wall, mirrored by another on the opposite side of the shop.[23] Behind it were shelves and drawers stacked with tea canisters, packets, bottles, and tins, while similar displays punctuated the length of the counter itself. In front were chairs, for use by the customers, and larger crates of goods. Still more remarkable in its continuity with the past is a photograph taken in the 1970s of the interior of a small shop on Fore Street in the village of Hartland in Devon.[24] This illustrates the continued centrality of the counter, with its scales, weights, and string for wrapping parcels, while shelves and nests of drawers are ranged behind. Although somewhat anachronistic by this date, the persistence of such arrangements underlines their durability and fitness for purpose; it also indicates the prevalence of these essential fittings, even in shops at the lower end of the market.

As the inside of the eighteenth-century shop was slowly reoriented around fitments augmenting the presentation as well as the storage of goods, the shop window became increasingly significant. Many retailers had traditionally sold goods through the window, displaying their wares on boards let down in front of the shop that effectively served as counters.[25] This mode of selling encouraged a particular composition of the shop space: the interior was a place of storage, while exchange took place over the threshold of the shop. Such practices and arrangements were seen in the shops along medieval Cheapside, and they persisted through the eighteenth century and beyond, especially for those selling fresh foods.[26] Combining stall and shop trading in this way made sense: it allowed the shopkeeper to compete with the immediacy of the market and presented the shop as familiar and trustworthy. Increasingly, however, the shop window was used as an enclosed space

---

[21] LiRO, B/C/5, Thomas Wright (1788).
[22] *Bristol Mercury*, 6 July 1822. See also *Liverpool Mercury*, 27 Apr. 1820, 23 June 1820.
[23] Available at <www.windowsonwarwickshire.org.uk/> (accessed 15 July 2011).
[24] Evans and Lawson, *Nation of Shopkeepers*, 21.
[25] Cox, *Complete Tradesman*, 130–1. This mode of selling is discussed in detail in Ch. 6.
[26] Keene, 'Sites of Desire', 129–32; Cox and Dannehl, *Perceptions of Retailing*, 39.

in which to display goods rather than to sell them—a practice reflected in the growing appearance in inventories of lattices and sashes (Table 5.1).[27]

Glazing was a rarity in the early eighteenth century, even in London, but it became more widespread as the manufacture of glass improved. Larger panes and narrow glazing bars created the impression of a wall of glass, while bow windows enhanced both display space and the amount of light falling on the goods contained therein. Unsurprisingly, they became synonymous with shops, even after building regulations restricted their encroachment onto the thoroughfare, with the archetypal 'modern' shop of late Georgian England comprising a double front of bow windows and a central door, which was also often glazed.[28] Such arrangements were typical of most branches of retailing, so that the basic appearance of a draper's shop differed little from that of a grocer or an ironmonger.[29] This made the display of goods in the window still more important in communicating the nature of the retail business and the kind of stock being carried. As the cost decreased, glazed windows became ever more widespread, especially after the introduction of plate glass in the early nineteenth century. Around the same time, some towns saw the construction of rows of shops built in a uniform style, thus enhancing the integrity and unity of the streetscape. One of the best surviving examples of this trend is in the small Staffordshire town of Cheadle, where a row of shops was built on the market square, each comprising a double front with central door all set within a single enlarged bow.[30]

Shopping streets in 1800 thus looked very different from those of 1700, although a mix of shop fronts characterized most provincial towns. Something of this can be seen in a series of engravings made of the main shopping streets in early nineteenth-century Chester.[31] There is limited coverage of some streets, most notably Eastgate Street, but the engravings cover much of the length of Bridge Street, Lower Bridge Street, and Northgate Street. Only eight of the seventy-nine street-level shops illustrated on these three thoroughfares were open fronted, although it is likely that this format was more common on back streets. Most of these were clustered on the east side of Bridge Street and appear to be butchers' shops with meat hung over the window and trestle tables laid out in front. Elsewhere, glazing predominated, but there was a wide variety of window types. Harrison, a grocer on Bridge Street, had a classic double-fronted shop, although the front was flat. A few doors down, Jones's shop had two windows that curved in towards a recessed door, while on the opposite side of the street a druggist named Titley had a double-fronted shop and a large bow window, but the door and windows were set into the original walls rather than being a single integrated unit. By far the most common arrangement, especially among grocers, tea dealers, and tobacconists, was the single-fronted shop: a door (often illustrated open—see Figure 5.1) set to the side of a

[27] Hann and Stobart, 'Sites of Consumption', 171; Cox, *Complete Tradesman*, 96–7.
[28] The London Building Act of 1774 restricted them to a projection of just 10 inches or less on narrower streets. Similar regulations were enforced, albeit less vigorously, in many provincial towns. See Powers, *Shop Fronts*, 3; Stobart, 'Shopping Streets', 18–19.
[29] Powers, *Shop Fronts*, 9.
[30] Powers, *Shop Fronts*, 51.   [31] They were published as Hughes, *Ancient Chester*.

large window glazed with panes measuring perhaps 18 inches by 12 inches, much the same size as those in the houses above.

It is difficult to see any details of the goods displayed in the windows of these Chester shops, but many were drawn with items visible, usually arranged so that each pane framed a separate object. These displays were clearly important in projecting the shop onto the street, an imperative that remained, even if the nature of the window and display changed in subsequent years. A trade card for Banks' Norfolk and Norwich Tea Warehouse (probably dating from the 1830s or 1840s) shows an elegant and substantial shop situated opposite the Guildhall on the Market Place, its corner entrance flanked by columns.[32] Large glazed windows occupy much of its two frontages and are filled with a range of groceries, including tea canisters and sugar loaves. A well-dressed couple have paused to peer into the window. The same emphasis on display is still seen in the 1860s, in the trade card of the Wimbledon grocer T. E. Smart, again showing windows filled with goods.[33] However, two key differences are also apparent. One is the appearance of tinned goods, which are illustrated in neat pyramids and occupy much of the lower window space. The other is the inclusion of posters and what appear to be price labels

Fig. 5.1. West side of Bridge Street, Chester, early nineteenth century (© Cheshire Archives and Local Studies)

---

[32] Bodl., JJC, Trade Cards 11 (90). Similarly, Whittock's image of an early Victorian confectioner's shop shows table centrepieces, swan blancmange moulds, syllabub glasses, and so on, arranged across the height and breadth of the window (see Whittock, *Shop Fronts of London*, plate 14).
[33] Bodl., JJC, Trade Cards 11 (53).

within the window display. The former are placed along the top of the window, proclaiming the availability and price of goods within, while the latter are propped against the stacks of tins and packets. As with interiors, this basic arrangement remained in place in many grocers' shops into the twentieth century, although there were pressures to modernize. One ideal type dating from 1919 had large panes of plate glass, separate windows for different stock lines, and light sliding sashes that facilitated regular (even daily) redressing of the window. The displays would comprise more staging and less stock: 'art-coloured majolica pedestals, flower-pots, figures and other pottery, combined with ferns, palms, etc.'[34] Although taken up by some multiple retailers, this was either an unnecessary expense or an unrealizable dream for most grocers. Into the 1920s and beyond, many shops retained small glazing panes and window displays that comprised stock piled high and posters trumpeting particular brands.[35]

SPATIAL AND SOCIAL ASPECTS OF MODERNIZATION

The 'modern' grocer's shop did not arrive everywhere at the same time. Its distribution reflected the spread of new goods and the social practices that surrounded their consumption, but also polite forms of shopping, especially among a metropolitan elite. London inevitably led the way, with famous grocers such as Fortnum and Mason, established on Jermyn Street in 1707, furnishing their shop in an opulent manner from the outset. By the early nineteenth century it occupied an elegant four-bay building on Piccadilly, each bay being separated by ornate pillars enclosed by low-level delicate iron railings. In the windows were arranged a variety of goods, apparently set out on sloping shelves designed to produce coherence in the display rather than simply present a mass of stock.[36] This was a response, in part, to the demands of a discerning clientele (including royalty), but also a reflection of the intense competition among retailers in the capital. Similar imperatives operated, albeit less intensively, outside the capital. If they were faced with local competition, it would make sense for provincial shopkeepers to spend money on enhancing the quality of their premises. Unsurprisingly, then, it is easy to find examples of elaborate shop fittings in a number of Chester shops; but there was little to distinguish them from shops in smaller towns and even villages where the level of local competition was extremely limited.[37] We have already noted the varied fittings in the mid-eighteenth-century village shop of William Claridge. Some seventy years earlier, Ralph Edge of Tarporley in Cheshire (d. 1683) had 'scales and weights, 2 counters, shelves, ranges and boards pinned to the wall'—a very similar range of fittings to those found in the shops of urban retailers.[38] Edge was identi-

[34] Maund, *The Modern Grocer* (London, 1919), quoted in Powers, *Shop Fronts*, 24.
[35] Morrison, *English Shops*, 80–6; Evans and Lawson, *Nation of Shopkeepers*, 16–17.
[36] Whittock, *Shop Fronts of London*, plate 11.
[37] See, e.g., CALS, WS 1724 Thomas Moreton; LRO WCW 1724, Ambrose Pierpoint; LiRO, B/C/11, Thomas Clarke (1717).
[38] CALS, WS 1683, Ralph Edge.

fied as an ironmonger, but sold a huge variety of goods, including textiles and groceries. Any of these goods could have been arranged on the shelves or boards, including his extensive stock of spices, fruits, and seeds—no doubt contained in boxes, packets, bags, or other containers not thought noteworthy by his appraisers. They would have been taken from these places and presented to the customer on one of his counters, before being weighed out into smaller quantities for purchase. Subsequent developments stretched the difference between urban and rural shops, with the former growing larger and grander in their architectural schemes and internal opulence. However, the same essential arrangement was in place in both town and country from around the turn of the eighteenth century.

Regional differences in the diffusion of 'new' shop fittings were similarly muted. Here, it might be expected that proximity to London would encourage the early adoption of more modern shop fittings. True, shopkeepers selling groceries in Cornwall had far fewer counters, shelves, and drawers than their counterparts in the other regions (Table 5.2). They also possessed a much narrower range of the shop fittings: averaging just 2.7 items per shop. William Bramstone's simple and in some ways rather old-fashioned means of storing goods (chests, boxes, and drawers) was almost a standard feature of Cornish grocers, whereas it was noted in just one Kentish shop. Elsewhere, however, distinctions were less pronounced. Shops in Kent, Oxfordshire, and Northamptonshire had more elaborate and a wider range of shop fittings, especially in terms of those oriented towards the display of goods. For example, the 1720 inventory of Nathaniel Jorden of New-ington in Kent lists four nests of drawers, two counters, four shelves, racks, boxes, tubs, and a further pair of drawers; there were two grates, most likely for the win-dows, and also a mortar and pestle, a mill, weights and measures, scales, sieves, and the shopkeeper's apron. Such a shop would have provided a wide range of possibilities for storing and displaying goods, and surely created a striking visual impression, perhaps like that seen in the trade card of Henry Lilwall (Figure 5.2).[39] But this image of greater sophistication masks a large degree of variation: none of the inventories of shops in Northamptonshire and Oxfordshire mentions window grates or goods in the window, while the chest in Elizabeth Wiles's Len-ham shop would appear to have contained her entire stock of 'candles, cheese, butter and grocery goods' since no other shop fittings are listed in her inventory of 1732.[40] Moreover, there is not much to distinguish shops in these three coun-ties from those in the west Midlands and north-west England. The range of fit-tings is somewhat broader, but there is little difference in the frequency with which key items such as counters, shelves, and nests of drawers appear. At one end of the scale, Thomas Moreton's Chester shop appears very similar to that of Nath-aniel Jorden; at the other, John Malham of Colne in Lancashire (d. 1708) made do with 'shop boxes' and chests.[41]

---

[39] KAS 11.75.92, Nathaniel Jorden (1720); Bodl., JJC, Trade Cards 11 (30).
[40] KAS, 11.80.80, Elizabeth Wiles (1732).
[41] CALS, WS 1724, Thomas Moreton; KAS, 11.75.92, Nathaniel Jorden (1720); LRO, WCW 1708, John Malham.

Fig. 5.2. Trade card of Henry Lilwall of London, tea dealer and grocer, late eighteenth century (© Bodleian Library, University of Oxford: John Johnson Collection: Trade Cards 11 (30))

The implications of the widespread use of a common set of 'modern' shop furnishings are significant. It is tempting to see any change in retailing as imitative of London shops, perhaps even part of the emulative consumption suggested by McKendrick.[42] However, while the writers of guidebooks and town directories were keen to draw parallels between the local high street and Cheapside, Regent Street, or Bond Street, there is little evidence that provincial shopkeepers were trying to emulate their metropolitan counterparts. If anything, they looked to their

---

[42] McKendrick, 'Consumer Revolution'. See Davis, *History of Shopping*, for this broad view of retail change.

Table 5.2. Regional variations in the fittings in shops selling groceries, c.1650–1750 (%)

Region	No. of inventories	Counter (%)	Shelves (%)	Boxes (%)	Cupboard (%)	Nest of drawers (%)	Chest (%)	Window/grate (%)	Scales (%)	Average no. of items
Kent	22	77.3	63.6	36.4	9.1	68.2	4.5	18.2	90.9	4
Northants & Oxon	11	72.7	81.8	72.7	9.1	72.7	18.2	0.0	90.9	4.2
Staffs, Warks, & Worcs	15	80.0	40.0	60.0	13.3	60.0	13.3	20.0	60.0	3.5
Lancashire & Cheshire	17	76.5	52.9	41.2	23.5	64.7	29.4	11.8	64.7	3.6
Cornwall	7	14.3	14.3	42.9	14.3	42.9	71.4	0.0	71.4	2.7
Total	72	70.8	54.2	48.6	13.9	63.9	20.8	12.5	76.4	

Source: probate inventories.

neighbours and direct competitors. A more likely explanation is that the same socio-economic imperatives were at play across the country, shopkeepers and their customers having common expectations about how a shop should operate and how goods should be displayed.

If geography made little difference to the nature of shops fittings, then wealth certainly did (Table 5.3). This was clearest in the case of window sashes and grates, which appeared more than twice as often in inventories over £200 in value. With counters and nests of drawers, the relationship was more complex, but the general trend was the same. Conversely, boxes and chests were most common in lower-value inventories. The former might be arranged along shelves, on the counter or underneath it; the latter could be stacked against the wall or be central to the shop, as they appear to have been in the premises of Elizabeth Wiles.[43] These broad quantitative trends were reinforced by differences in the quality and value of the fittings themselves: wealthier shopkeepers tended to have more expensive furniture in their shops. The shelves, drawers, counters, boxes, measures, barrels, and mortars belonging to John Read of Lenham (d. 1692) were together worth £8; Thomas Clarke's elaborate set of fittings was valued at £5 8*s*. 6*d*., and Thomas Moreton's was worth a total of £6 6*s*.[44] Although their wealth varied from £1,230 1*s*. 11*d*. down to about £270, these were all relatively wealthy shopkeepers. At the other end of the scale were men such as John Key of Ringstead in Northamptonshire (d. 1775) and John Questead of Milton in Kent (d. 1704).[45] Key's entire estate was worth just £80 19*s*. While he possessed an impressive range of shop fittings, including scales and weights, a grist mill, boxes, drawers, cannisters, counter, shelves, and a brass mortar and pestle, these were worth only £1 13*s*. in total. Similarly, Questead's entire stock of Cheshire cheeses, sugar, plums, soap, candles, worsteds, yarns, tapes, threads, pins, and smallwares, along with his scales and weights, mortar and pestle, pewter and wooden measures, counter, nest of drawers, shelves, boxes, pots, and crocks was worth just £5 10*s*., and his whole estate amounted to £74 11*s*. 10*d*. While the shop fittings formed a similar or larger proportion of the overall estate of these men, their lower absolute value suggests that either the condition or the quality of the fittings must have been inferior to those of their wealthier counterparts.

The spatial and economic relationship between wealthier and more impecunious grocers is hard to judge. Mui and Mui argue that village and 'back-street' shops served the needs of agricultural labourers and the urban poor, whereas specialist shopkeepers catered to the needs of the more affluent consumer.[46] Much of their analysis focuses on the consumption practices of the poor, but there is some evi-

---

[43] In his deposition against Thomas Smith, the London grocer Thomas Crofts stated that the stolen chest containing 12 lb of tea was one of four 'placed by the door, one on the top of the other'; there was another set of chests' by the stairs (Old Bailey Online, Thomas Smith, 12 Apr. 1809).

[44] KAS, 11.56.159, John Read (1692); LiRO, B/C/11, Thomas Clarke (1717); CALS, WS 1724, Thomas Moreton.

[45] NRO, John Key, 1775; KAS, 11.65.113, John Questead (1704).

[46] Mui and Mui, *Shops and Shopkeeping*, 148–59. They offer a swingeing critique of the assertion made by Jefferys, *Retailing in Britain*, 3–5, that, before the mid-nineteenth century, poorer consumers were dependent upon markets and fairs for most of their needs.

Table 5.3. Wealth levels and the fittings in shops selling groceries, *c*.1650–1750 (%)

Total value of inventories	No. of inventories	Counter (%)	Shelves (%)	Boxes (%)	Cupboard (%)	Nest of drawers (%)	Chest (%)	Window (%)	Scales (%)	Average no. of items
<£100	15	73.3	66.7	80.0	6.7	60.0	20.0	6.7	86.7	4
£100–199	16	43.8	43.8	68.8	12.5	68.8	18.8	6.3	81.3	3.4
£200–349	16	81.3	56.3	50.0	6.3	56.3	12.5	12.5	68.8	3.4
£350	19	84.2	57.9	52.6	26.3	84.2	15.8	15.8	78.9	4.2
Total	66	71.2	56.1	62.1	13.6	68.2	16.7	10.6	78.8	

Note: Six inventories had no overall value.
Source: probate inventories.

dence that the basic distinction that they draw is accurate. In 1711, the Lancaster grocer William Stout set up a shop in Cheaney Lane for Elin Godsalve, providing 'about £10 value of grocery goods and other small ware'. He was pleased to record that 'she had quickly good custom…and sould by retail as much as any shop in the town'.[47] Clearly, he was not setting up someone to compete with his own business or that of his neighbours on Market Street; nor was he comparing her sales with his own. Yet the extent to which Stout's shop differed in structure and practice from that of Godsalve is difficult to judge. Her capitalization is comparable to that of Key and Questead, and probably her shop fittings would have been broadly similar as well. This suggests that the divide between shops on the high street and those on the back street or the village green was perhaps not profound—at least in terms of the essential infrastructure of selling. This supports the idea that there were common requirements for the retailing of groceries that were understood by retailers and customers from all social groups. Moreover, while it is clear that petty shopkeepers drew their customers largely from the poorer sections of society, distinctions should not to be drawn too firmly. Contemporary critics berated the poor for buying on account from shops, rather than at the market; and they railed against petty shopkeepers: 'the next class of oppressors' who sought to cheat the poor with inflated prices and false weights.[48]

It is difficult to get a clear view of the retail premises of these petty shopkeepers. Mui and Mui dedicate considerable space to discussing their relative wealth and status, and their role in serving the needs of workers. They also note that 'shopkeepers' were both numerous and widespread, drawing on tax records to identify a huge disparity between the number of tradesmen licensed to sell tea and the number of grocers and tea dealers listed in contemporary directories.[49] What they fail to do, however, is explore the physical nature of their 'back-street' shops. It is often assumed that these were, at best, the front room of the retailer's house and therefore contained little by way of specialist equipment. Certainly Rowlandson's 1784 cartoon, *The Last Stake*, which depicts back-street shops during election time, shows premises that were very basic. Indeed, it appears that the clientele (like the man canvassing support) did not even enter the shop, but would instead be served through the window.[50] Cox and Dannehl suggest that such arrangements may also have characterized the East Hoathly shop of Thomas Turner. Since 'nobody smart shopped there', Turner probably had little need to ornament his shop, which was probably stuffed so full that there 'was barely room to turn'.[51] However, it is clear from their inventories that even the more marginal shopkeepers had appropriate fitments for storing, selling, and displaying their wares. For example, Elizabeth Kennett (d. 1741) sold a small range of groceries from the 'fore-room' of her Folkestone home, which was ostensibly furnished as a parlour, but she still managed to

[47] Stout, *Autobiography*, 165.
[48] Clayton, *Friendly Advice to the Poor*, quoted in Mui and Mui, *Shops and Shopkeeping*, 149; *Leeds Mercury*, 17 Aug. 1773.
[49] See Mui and Mui, *Shops and Shopkeeping*, 160–72.
[50] For further discussion of this image, see Cox and Dannehl, *Perceptions of Retailing*, 33.
[51] Cox and Dannehl, *Perceptions of Retailing*, 36.

squeeze in a counter, three shelves, and four 'little drawers', two pairs of brass scales with lead weights, and boxes, bottles, and tubs. A similar arrangement is pictured in *The Chandler's Shop Gossips*, an undated mezzotint, but clearly depicting an eighteenth-century shop.[52] The counter is central to the image and the shop; a nest of drawers occupies the space behind, with shelves being visible through a window to the left. Into the later eighteenth and early nineteenth centuries, this same basic structure appears to have remained: the premises were small and the amount of stock limited, but the counter, drawers, and shelves were ubiquitous.

By this period, higher-end provincial retailers were following a metropolitan lead in creating large and elaborate shops: architecturally striking and ornately decorated within. Two notable examples in London were Twining's Tea Warehouse on the Strand and Sparrow's Tea Warehouse on Ludgate Hill. Twining's included, over the imposing door, a lion supported by two seated Chinese figures, symbolizing the imperial and oriental connections of the company and its stock. There are hints here at Whittock's rather later suggestion that decorative styles should match the goods being sold. He argued:

If a grocer requires a front that will distinguish his shop from the draper or ironmonger, any person but an architect would direct his attention to producing a design something in the Chinese or Indian style of decoration; but the very mention of the terms would distress a regular architect—to him sugar and tea would lose their flavour if they were not sold beneath a Grecian entablature, copied with great minuteness from a temple at Athens.[53]

Quite apart from the not so gentle dig at the architectural profession, Whittock's choice of design has strong echoes of the imagery used on grocers' trade cards, with its allusions to the orient and perhaps to empire (see Chapter 7). Sparrow's, meanwhile, was an interesting case of the whole frontage of the building being incorporated into the design of the shop—the ornamentation of columns, cornicing, and statuary rising in a series of tiers above the large double front of the shop itself.[54] Such architect-designed shops were being built across the country by the 1830s. In Liverpool, for example, Harvey Lonsdale Elmes, the architect of St George's Hall, drew up plans for a group of houses in Lime Street, which incorporated three alternative designs for shop fronts in their ground floors, the whole being set within a flowing neoclassical frontage.[55] Around the same time, *West's Directory of Warwickshire* describes a whole series of large shops on New Street in Birmingham, aligning them with the cultural infrastructure of the town.[56]

Early nineteenth-century grocers' shops look rather modest in comparison. Yet, in the crucial years of the early eighteenth century, which marked the emergence of the 'modern' shop, grocers were innovative in furnishing their shops. Indeed, what is striking from the sample of shopkeepers studied here is that it was grocers,

[52] KAS, 11.82.18, Elizabeth Kennett (1741); The Colonial Williamsburg Foundation, 1973–262.
[53] Whittock, *Shop Fronts of London*, 4.
[54] Powers, *Shop Fronts*, 47, 60.
[55] Powers, *Shop Fronts*, 16, 63.
[56] West, *History of Warwickshire*, 188–9, 220; Morrison, *English Shops*, 125–8.

Table 5.4. Trade specialism and the fittings in shops selling groceries, c.1650–1750 (%)

Occupation	No. of inventories	Counter (%)	Shelves (%)	Boxes (%)	Cupboard (%)	Nest of drawers (%)	Chest (%)	Window (%)	Scales (%)	Average no. of items
Grocer	23	87.0	65.2	60.9	17.4	73.9	8.7	26.1	78.3	4.2
Other	41	65.9	48.8	53.7	14.6	61.0	26.8	7.3	73.2	3.5
Unspecified	8	50.0	50.0	75.0	0.0	50.0	25.0	0.0	87.5	3.4
Total	72	70.8	54.2	58.3	13.9	63.9	20.8	12.5	76.4	

Source: probate inventories.

rather than other traders engaged in selling groceries, that possessed the most elaborate shop fittings (Table 5.4). They had the largest number of items on average and were significantly more likely to possess those fittings that allowed for the orderly storage and display of their goods: counters, shelves, nests of drawers, and window fitments. The contrast was greatest between grocers and retailers whose trade was not specified on their inventory. For example, the inventory of David Gradwell, a Bolton grocer who died in 1723 leaving a total estate of £376 3s. 6¾d., lists two small counters, drawers, three further counters, a press, drawers, and boxes worth a total of £4. In contrast, John Hopkin of Liverpool (d. 1700) sold a similar range of goods, but was styled 'gentleman' on his inventory. His only shop fittings were a counter and boxes worth just 15s., despite his overall estate being valued at £236 19s. 11d. Similarly, the Congleton mercer Zachariah Shelley (d. 1728) had a range of groceries as well as large quantities of cloth and haberdashery in a shop that was apparently equipped with nothing more than counters, drawers, weights, and scales, and a mortar and pestle worth just £1 10s.[57] My point here is not that grocers' shops were necessarily the most elaborately furnished in the late seventeenth and early eighteenth centuries. Indeed, I have argued elsewhere that it was generally mercers and drapers who appear to have taken most trouble when fitting up their shops.[58] However, the data presented here make it clear that grocers increasingly furnished their shops to augment the storage and display of their wares. This begs the question of what they hoped to gain by organizing their shops and presenting their goods in these ways.

DISPLAYING WARES: SALES, REPUTATION, AND RESPECTABILITY

Display has always formed an important element of retail strategy, with stalls at markets and fairs piled high with goods available for the purchaser to inspect. In part, the visibility of the stock was seen as a safeguard against malpractice, but displaying goods openly also made them more familiar and appealing. This was particularly true for retailers of textiles and other durable goods that had important visual qualities, but was also important in selling the array of new and often unfamiliar commodities that had to be marketed by the retailer to an often conservative public.[59] In this context, the situation with groceries is intriguing. They were, at least initially, unfamiliar and might thus have benefited from being promoted in this way. However, most were not visually appealing in themselves, and they usually needed to be kept in sealed containers to retain their flavour and contain their aroma. Contemporary illustrations show that they were, in some senses, visible in

---

[57] LRO, WCW 1723, David Gradwell, WCW 1701, John Hopkin; CALS, WS 1728, Zachariah Shelley. None of these shops includes shelves, which were sometimes omitted by appraisers, but the contrast between them remains.

[58] Hann and Stobart, 'Sites of Consumption'; Walsh, 'Shop Design'.

[59] Cox, *Complete Tradesman*, 210–12; Styles, 'Product Innovation'; Blondé and Van Damme, 'Retail Growth'.

the shop: candles were hung from hooks on the wall or stacked on shelves along-side tea canisters and loaves of sugar, and baskets and boxes were arranged on counters—open to public view. This visibility is confirmed by accounts of theft from shops. For example, in 1717 Nicholas Corbett appeared at the Old Bailey, accused of stealing sugar from a London grocer called Susannah Miler. She claimed that he 'took the loaves off from a shelf', dropping them when she cried out. Simi-larly, in 1735, John Dwyer and Will Bentley appeared for stealing 3 lb of nutmegs, valued at 16s.; their accomplice gave evidence against them, claiming that, 'seeing no body in the Prosecutor's Shop, Dwyer stept in and took a Paper of Nutmegs and a Sugar Loaf off the Counter'.[60] These items were clearly visible and knowable, despite being enclosed in boxes, tins, and packets. Sometimes goods were recogniz-able from their packaging. This was true in a generic sense for sugar loaves and for some teas, which were increasingly presented in tin canisters. Indeed, by the early nineteenth century, some teas were being marketed on the basis of their packaging (see Chapter 7). The sealed and branded canisters used by the London tea dealers Long & Co., for example, would have been clearly visible and, for some consumers at least, instantly recognizable on the shelf of the grocer's shop.[61]

Placing goods (or perhaps more likely empty containers) in the window fur-thered the role of display as an advertisement for the goods available. Glazed win-dows symbolized both wealth and modernity: they also helped to illuminate the shop interior, allowing the stock to be displayed more effectively. Indeed, petitions from Chester tradesmen wishing to enlarge their windows repeatedly stressed the desire to 'lighten [the] shop and ornament it to public view'.[62] The ambition here was to open up the shop to the gaze of the passer-by and transcend the divide between interior and exterior space. Yet there was an inherent contradiction between this desire for illumination and the use of the window to display goods. A full window inevitably meant that less light entered the shop and it obscured views of the interior space. Shopkeepers nonetheless made full use of their win-dows to display goods, thus projecting information about their wares onto the street. Combined with printed advertisements, this helped to reduce the transac-tions costs of buying groceries by providing consumers with information about the nature and perhaps quality of goods to be found in different shops.[63]

When laying out their premises, eighteenth-century shopkeepers were con-cerned not only that their wares were displayed to the best possible effect, but also that the visual appearance of their shop fostered and projected an appropriate image for the business. Here, Benjamin's emphasis of the visual image ties in with Lefebvre's notion of the conscious manipulation and projection of space. Through careful attention to the facade and interior decor, the astute tradesman could con-sciously construct a shopping environment designed to appeal to a discerning and

---

[60] OBP, 1 May 1717, Nicholas Corbett (t17170501-12); 26 Feb. 1735, John Dwyer and William Bentley (t17350226-33).

[61] See *Bristol Mercury*, 7 July 1823.

[62] CALS, A/B/4/259v.

[63] On transactions costs, see North, 'Transaction Costs'; Stobart, 'Information, Trust and Reputation'.

polite clientele. The spaces thus produced were symbolic as well as practical: they linked ideology with everyday practices.[64] An elaborate window display and well-furnished interior conveyed an image of opulence and sophistication, and by association suggested that a business was successful. Cultivating such an image was particularly important for those involved in the luxury trades, especially in London. This trend was noted by Defoe, who commented disapprovingly on such developments in 1726, noting that, 'in painting and gilding, in fine shelves, shutters, pediments, columns of several orders of architecture, and the like; in which, they tell us now, 'tis a small matter to lay out two or three, nay five-hundred pounds, to fit up what we might call the outside of a shop'.[65] What dismayed Defoe was the growing tendency for the high-class shopkeeper to build his reputation on the basis of the luxuriant imagery of his shop rather than his retailing expertise. The shop had become a space of representation, a receptacle for coded messages, projected by the tradesman and interpreted by the discerning customer.

Important here is the idea of luxury, the opulence of the shop reflecting the character of the goods within and helping to construct them as luxuries. But groceries were quickly brought within the realm of what de Vries terms 'new luxuries': their consumption was democratized, at least to an extent.[66] As a result, provincial grocers eschewed London grandeur and constructed modest and respectable displays. These are illustrated nicely in the furnishing and ornamentation of a small number of Norwich shops.[67] Elizabeth Neale (d. 1706) had the usual nests of drawers, counters, shelves, pots and storage jars, weights and scales, and so on.[68] She also had a wire lattice (presumably for the window) and a 'black boy'—the traditional symbol of the tobacconist, but here deployed in a grocer's shop. It forms a rare example of the direct association between the products of plantation economies being sold by grocers and the slaves upon whom that production depended.[69] Later in the eighteenth century, the *Norwich Mercury* carried a number of advertisements from confectioners who announced the special efforts they were making for Twelfth Night. Widow Cockey informed the public that her shop would be 'handsomely illuminated and decorated after the London taste with Plumb Cakes', while her near neighbour Francis Horne announced that 'his Shop will be illuminated in a most elegant Manner, and decorated in the Pastry Way, with all the Ornaments that Art and Fancy can invent'.[70]

In general, provincial shopkeepers were more focused on the practicalities of storing and presenting goods than on emulating the premises and practices of high-status London retailers.[71] As with printed advertisements, part of the message carried by goods stacked on shelves and counters—and ranged around the shop

[64] Lefebvre, *Production of Space*, 40–6.   [65] Defoe, *Compleat English Tradesman*, i. 269.
[66] De Vries, *Industrious Revolution*, 44–5.
[67] For fuller discussion of these, see Barnett, 'Shops, Retailing and Consumption'.
[68] NoRO, ANW23/3/209.
[69] Walvin, *Fruits of Empire*, 132–54; Bickham, 'Eating the Empire', 86–7.
[70] *Norwich Mercury*, 27 Dec. 1783.
[71] Stobart, 'Accommodating the Shop'. See also Blondé and Van Damme, 'Retail Growth'; Walsh, 'Stalls, Bulks, Shops'.

floor in boxes, barrels, and chests—was one of variety and choice. The huge amounts of stock listed in inventories give substance to the images in trade cards and descriptions in trial depositions of shops filled with goods. In some cases, stock spilled out into domestic space. The Liverpool grocer Robert Rownson had boxes of oranges, lemons, and almonds, and a parcel of sweetmeats in a first-floor parlour, and the Leek cheesemonger John Finney had hops and yarn in a bedchamber.[72] Yet most goods were stored in an orderly manner—if not in the shop, then in cellars or warehouses. Rownson's inventory lists 200 lb of rice, 1.5 cwt of starch, 70 lb of tobacco, 40 lb of caraway seeds, 12 lb of coriander seeds, 24 lb of raisins, and 8 gross of tobacco pipes in his warehouse, and Finney had a cellar containing £10 6s. of hops, £13 of cider, £12 1s. 6d. of malt and £5 17s. 4d. of bacon as well as large quantities of cheese.

What of the shops themselves? The long lists of inventoried goods suggest that few took Defoe's advice that the tradesman should 'take an especial care to have his shop not so much crowded with a large bulk of goods, as well as with a well sorted and well chosen quantity, proper for his business'.[73] However, the format of inventories indicates that they were often arranged in a systematic manner. The 1723 inventory of the Lenham mercer Richard Reade is typical.[74] It starts with his cloth, which is meticulously itemized and valued separately. This is followed by a series of entries for haberdashery, hardware, and other miscellaneous items such as writing paper and brushes. The listing then moves on to earthenware and glass, candles, wool, and finally an assortment of groceries. Clearly such a methodical description of the shopkeeper's wares owed much to the diligence of the appraisers, but it does suggest that different types of goods were stored separately within the shop, a point made more forcefully by the 1736 inventory of Samuel Gibbard. This Coventry mercer had a large stock of cloth and haberdashery listed as 'shop goods'. His groceries, however, appear under a separate heading of 'grocery ware' further down the page.[75] The appraisers of a fellow Coventry mercer, Julius Billers, who died sixty years earlier, referred specifically to his '5 double chests on the grocery side'.[76] This seems to indicate that cloth and groceries were sold from different parts of the shop—a very modern demarcation of space, creating specialized areas and encouraging an orderly conception of goods and shopping practices. A natural extension of this careful arrangement of merchandise within the shop was the placement of different types of stock in different rooms. The Kentish tradesman William Rumfield had extensive premises comprising: 'a shop' filled with haberdashery wares and groceries; a 'little shop' containing clothing, earthenware, and drinking glasses; a 'pottery chamber' with some further earthenware; several 'back chambers' holding large quantities of cheese, hops, and candles; and a 'shop over the way', which appears empty apart from the shelves, counters, and racks.[77]

---

[72] LRO, WCW 1709, Robert Rownson.   [73] Defoe, *Compleat English Tradesman*, i. 76.
[74] KAS, 11.75.115, Richard Reade (1723).   [75] TNA: PRO PROB 3 35/26.
[76] TNA: PRO PROB 4 4125.   [77] KAS, 11.58.121, William Rumfield (1694).

There were pragmatic reasons for such orderly arrangements of shop space. Delicate fabrics could quite easily have been damaged by accidental spillages, and they were stored and displayed in rather different ways from spices, currants, oil, and sugar. Yet all goods needed to be kept in an orderly manner that allowed the shopkeeper to locate and access them quickly and easily. As Walsh argues, 'speedy and efficient service was dependent on the sound organisation of goods behind the counter and around the shop'.[78] Such efficiency cut the amount of time required to serve the customer and thus helped to reduce transaction costs, regardless of the mode of selling in which the shopkeeper was engaged. If we assume that it is a reasonably faithful representation of the shop, Henry Lilwall's trade card conforms with this model of the orderly shop, with its neat rows of canisters, nests of drawers, and stacks of sugar cones. Going one stage further and organizing goods into different parts of the premises helped to create distinct retail spaces, perhaps constructed around different selling techniques.

Spatial order was also important to the image that a retailer wished to project through his shop; the practical necessities of storage and display were symbolic of an effective retail business.[79] If we think of Lilwall's trade card more as a representation of the ideal shop, then we can draw out those elements that were most important in constructing and bolstering the reputation of the grocer as a respectable man of business.[80] There are goods spread across the floor and shelves, but the overall image is one of restraint and order: everything is in its rightful place, including the shopkeeper and his customers. They are placed either side of the counter, which thus demarcates the retail space. Many wares were displayed on shelves, in boxes and nests of drawers positioned behind the counter, from where they could be brought down for inspection on request. This separation of shopkeeper and customer helped to maintain a certain distance, an otherness that bolstered the authority of the tradesman without necessarily undermining the close and friendly relationship they might share with their customers (see Chapter 6).[81] The shopkeeper was the guardian of specialist knowledge and the gatekeeper—both literally and metaphorically—to a world of goods. Such conventions connoted that things were as they should be: the stock was of high quality, legitimately acquired, and with taxes paid. The neat organization symbolized good supply networks and sound knowledge of the stock. Particularly telling is the account book, set open on a small alcove in the shelving behind the counter. There is a pen in the inkwell, ready for Lilwall carefully to enter the goods bought and the amount owed. The message is clear: his shop is in order and so too are his accounts and, by extension, his business. Importantly, these meanings would have been readily understood by Lilwall's customers. Here was a man of substance who would be trusted to provide good-quality groceries and to deal in an open and honest manner—important considerations in an age when food quality was highly variable and adulteration

[78] Walsh, 'Stalls, Bulks, Shops'.   [79] Walsh, 'Shop Design', 171.
[80] On the representation of shops, see Cox and Dannehl, *Perceptions of Retailing*, 32–6.
[81] Walsh, 'Advertising', 88; Wallis, 'Consumption, Retailing and Medicine', 33.

widespread.[82] In this way, the image reinforces the very process of producing and distributing trade cards, linking both to financial security and the importance placed upon cementing close and long-term relationships with valued customers.[83] In short, both image and display showed the shopkeeper to be virtuous and respectable—embodiments of the sobriety and respectability that Schivelbusch and Smith read into the consumption of colonial groceries.[84]

Of course, shops were much more than projected images of the shopkeeper's business acumen; they were also places of sociability. This might be interpreted in terms of a polite social round and elite shopping practices, with shops being places where customers could linger: talking with friends, taking refreshments, inspecting goods at their leisure, and perhaps being served by the shopkeeper.[85] Such imperatives informed the furbishing of many respectable London shops and spilled over into the smart shops of resort towns such as Bath. However, the extent to which it went further than this appears to have been limited. Blondé and Van Damme, in their study of eighteenth-century Antwerp, suggest that selling was about the personal service, not about furnishing the premises for leisure shopping. This argument rests on the fact that few shops contained the kind of furnishings that would produce this leisurely environment. There is much in this, with studies of provincial English towns revealing few shops with paintings, mirrors, sconces, and so on.[86] What is less clear, however, is whether this lack of decorative items meant a similar lack of emphasis on sociability within the shop.

Groceries would not appear, at first glance, to lend themselves to such retail and shopping practices. They do not obviously fall into Berry's browse–bargain mode of shopping, and there is little to suggest that grocers ever sought to furnish their shops in the same opulent manner as drapers, glass and china warehouses, or even confectioners. There was no slavish adherence to fashions in shop design. However, the inventories of around one-quarter of grocers do list stools or chairs in the shop, suggesting either that there was a need to provide some comfort for customers who might spend a considerable amount of time in the shop or that they were being treated with deference—sitting while the grocer stood and served them. Both of these explanations are probably true, although there is a telling distinction between the standing figures in the small plebeian shop illustrated in *The Chandler's Shop Gossips* and those sitting, comfortable but erect, in Lilwall's trade card. Their dress and deportment confirm their respective social standing, while the seating provided (or at least imagined) by Lilwall signals his desire and ability to cater for well-to-do customers. The implication is that respectability was a product of where and how goods were acquired, as well as what was consumed. That said, it is clear that the chandler's shop is a welcoming place. The easy interchange between the

[82] Burnett, *Plenty and Want*, 99–120. For examples of customers complaining about the quality of food purchased, see Ch. 8.
[83] Barker, *Business of Women*, 74–5; Blondé and Van Damme, 'Retail Growth'.
[84] Schivelbusch, *Tastes of Paradise*, 15–79; Smith, *Consumption*, esp. 223–37.
[85] Berry, 'Polite Consumption', 386; Walsh, 'Shops, Shopping, and the Art of Decision Making'.
[86] Blondé and Van Damme, 'Retail Growth'; Stobart, 'Accommodating the Shop'.

two women is underlined by a portrait on the chimney, a roaring fire in the hearth, and a teapot with two cups and saucers on the mantelpiece. These were common features in the parlours and chambers of many shopkeepers,[87] and blur the distinction between shop and home. Indeed, one explanation for the apparently rather sparse decoration of the shop is that attention was focused instead on key spaces within the home—most particularly the parlour. Although the relative location of different rooms is difficult to judge from probate inventories, it is clear that the parlour often opened onto the shop. This is implied in the trade card of the London mercer Benjamin Cole, which shows a room beyond the shop: its fashionably framed door is ajar, revealing a welcoming fire.[88] It becomes more explicit in the depositions made at trials for shoplifting. In the trial of Thomas Gentry for stealing 28 lb of butter, the shop assistant stated that 'I was in the parlour with Mr Tapperell's daughters; Miss Tapperell saw the prisoner go out of the shop; I looked and saw the prisoner go off the steps of the door'. Similarly, in his evidence against Edward Young, the grocer Robert Lawrence declared that 'I was coming out of the parlour into the shop, and I saw him go out'.[89]

If we peer more closely into grocers' parlours, many emerge as suitable places in which to entertain selected customers. Perhaps most obviously equipped for entertaining was that of the Daventry grocer John Battin, which contained: two mahogany tables and six chairs; twelve pictures and a looking glass; a well-furnished fireplace; over £15 worth of silver (including a tankard, sugar tongs, teaspoons and a punch ladle); a china basin and six cups and saucers, and a delft punch bowl and four cups. Yet there were many others that offered comfortable and fashionable living/commercial spaces. The parlour of Robert Rownson of Liverpool, for example, was furnished with a clock and case, twelve carved-back chairs, one large square table and one small oval table, a small spinet, a looking glass and five pictures, two Oxford almanacs, two tall child's chairs, a bookcase and books, a writing desk, six patchwork cushions, and the fire grate. Even in remote Tregony, the shopkeeper Stephen Lawrence had a parlour furnished with a round table, twelve cane chairs, a tea table, and five china dishes. On the walls were hung a number of maps.[90] These rooms conform to the picture painted by Defoe of a typical grocer's home: well furnished and comfortable, but hardly luxurious.[91] This underscored the respectability of the shopkeeper and reflected back onto the goods being sold in the shop. Moreover, it linked closely to the domestic cultures of consumption that encouraged the widespread uptake of new groceries. Shop and home, buying and consuming, business and pleasure were thus closely bound in spatial, conceptual, and functional terms.[92]

---

[87] See, e.g., CRO, William Bastard, 1720; NRO, James Hollis, 1723.
[88] BM, Heal Collection, no. 70.39.
[89] OBP, 2 July 1812, Thomas Gentry (t18120701-61); 2 July 1817, Edward Young (t18170702-70).
[90] NRO, John Battin, 1751; LRO, WCW 1709, Robert Rownson; CRO, L1249, Stephen Lawrence, 1721.
[91] Defoe, *Compleat English Tradesman*, i. 348–9.
[92] For fuller discussion of this, see Stobart, 'Accommodating the Shop'.

CONCLUSIONS

In this chapter, I have explored how provincial grocers used display to promote their businesses, to shape public attitudes to them as businessmen, and to tap into new cultural practices of leisure and consumption. The conscious display of shop wares was well established as a specific if multifaceted marketing technique by the early decades of the eighteenth century. It drew on and promoted a particular set of shop fittings and arrangements of interior and exterior space. Once the 'modern' shop was established, there was a strong degree of continuity, which lasted through to the early twentieth century. Writing in 1919, Edward Maund complained about grocers' shops that were characterized by 'small panes of glass, the heavy wood-work…the ugly fittings with candle lockers, the square canisters, the old tea-pot shaped treacle cisterns, the tee-shaped iron hangers for hand scales (often screwed down with a nut to the counter), sugar mills and old signs'.[93] All these things he considered old fashioned, yet they were a product of changes that had taken place around the turn of the eighteenth century. Significantly, there is little evidence for a London-based or hierarchical diffusion of innovatory practices: shop displays were present in small remote villages as well as fashionable county towns. That said, the quality and sophistication, and especially the combined impact of shop displays, were undoubtedly greater in larger centres. Here the clustering of fashion-able shops matched the emergence of shopping as a polite leisure activity to create a new urban shopping experience.

Display was thus linked to new forms of consumption in both the use of goods and the processes whereby they were acquired. In this way, retail space was part of broader consumer culture, not merely as a place where groceries were bought, but also as an arena for social and cultural interaction centred on particular sets of goods and practices. A growing number of shopkeepers, especially those operating at a larger scale and serving a better-off clientele, clearly recognized the value of their premises as a promotional tool rather than simply a receptacle for the wares being sold. They manipulated the shop space to project key messages about them-selves: specialized and ordered space spoke of knowledge and expertise. The shop thus held meanings as well as material goods. But it also linked into emerging cultural practices of browsing and window shopping. Outside, this emphasized the importance of window displays; inside, it encouraged the use of shelves, nests of drawers, and counters to create an image of abundance and choice, but also efficiency and quality.

Above all, we can see the shop as an increasingly ordered and respectable space: there were careful displays of canisters, boxes, and jars; chairs set out for custom-ers; a fire burning in the grate, and the account book open and ready to record transactions. All these spoke of the shopkeeper's honesty, integrity, and respecta-bility. But I would go further and argue that, just as fashion was made by retailers and consumers as well as designers,[94] so it is possible to see shopkeepers playing a

---

[93] Maund, *Modern Grocer*, quoted in Powers, *Shop Fronts*, 24.
[94] Berg, *Luxury and Pleasure*, 255.

role in spreading a culture of politeness and respectability. Defoe saw tradesmen as models of moderation, probity, diligence, and industry from whom others (specifically the gentry) could learn much. His broader agenda, like Addison's, was the marrying of genteel and mercantile cultures to produce a civil and virtuous, yet commercial society.[95] Smith makes much of the role of colonial groceries in this marriage process, arguing that their consumption in a variety of cultural contexts was central to the making of respectability. For him, the key player in these processes was the consumer. What we have seen here is that virtue and respectability could also be a product of where and how goods were acquired. This places greater emphasis on the shopkeeper and on the shop where the bundling of spaces, goods, and practices produced another cultural context for the consumption of groceries. In this chapter, we have seen the importance to this process of shop space and shop fittings; next we must turn to the practices through which groceries were bought and sold.

[95] Smith, *Consumption*, 228–9.

6

Selling Groceries: Service, Credit, and Price

INTRODUCTION

In essence, the shop can be seen as a space for selling goods. As such, any continuities or changes in its structure and use were informed by broader developments in retail practices. For Jefferys, Matthias, and others, space and practice were revolutionized by the emergence of multiple retailers and department stores in the second half of the nineteenth century.[1] Their widespread use of cash sales, fixed prices, ticketing, and branded goods was linked to new shopping environments, which swept away established practices based on service, customer loyalty, and credit. We have already seen that these ideas have been challenged by revisionist work, much of which links earlier changes in retailing to notions of politeness and sociability. While it would be wrong to equate politeness entirely and unproblematically with the pursuit of fashionable goods and leisure activities, such practices were an important constituent of polite identity.[2] Selling politeness was thus important to many eighteenth-century shopkeepers. Linked to this is McKendrick's notion that shifting consumption practices were causally linked to changes in the ways in which these goods were promoted and sold. He used the examples of Wedgwood and Packard, arguing that such entrepreneurs revolutionized retail practices as part of a broader consumer revolution. These ideas have been reworked most recently by Berg as part of her analysis of the market for and retailing of the semi-luxuries produced in ever-larger quantities by the likes of Wedgwood and Boulton. They also appear in Peck's work on luxury consumption in the seventeenth century.[3] For all these historians, retail change was a necessary part of consumer change: retailers not only responded to shifting demand, but also helped to shape that demand through their promotional and retail practices, not least in terms of making certain goods and sets of goods more desirable. However, this link between consumer and retail change has been challenged by Blondé and Van Damme, who argue that dramatic changes in consumption and material culture pre-date any significant transformation in retail practice. Further, they suggest that the successful

---

[1] Jefferys, *Retailing in Britain*; Mathias, *Retailing Revolution*.
[2] Campbell, *Romantic Ethic*, 288. See also Berry, 'Polite Consumption'; Stobart, Hann, and Morgan, *Spaces of Consumption*, 12–13, 148–9; Walsh, 'Shops, Shopping and the Art of Decision Making'.
[3] McKendrick, 'Josiah Wedgwood'; McKendrick, 'George Packwood'; Berg, *Luxury and Pleasure*, 247–78; Peck, *Consuming Splendor*, 25–72.

introduction and sale of a large quantity and range of novel goods was dependent upon traditional service-oriented retailing.[4] If they are right, then we must rethink both the timing and the significance of retail change and its relationship with consumer evolution.

The exact position of groceries within these broader debates remains unclear, not least because attention has focused primarily on the retailing of durable goods. Yet their importance to wider consumption processes makes the grocery trade a useful lens through which to examine these different theories. Within this, three sets of questions are important. The first relates to the character of 'traditional' forms of service-based retailing and the way in which it related to ideas of sociability and politeness. To what extent was this form of selling possible with products such as groceries and how did it vary between different venues and customers? The second centres on the skills and attributes required of the shopkeeper who sold in this way. Of particular interest here are the ways in which knowledge and reputation structured the interaction between shopkeepers and their customers. So too is the use of credit, both as a retail instrument and as a means of defining the relationship between shopkeeper and customer. Contemporary critics often saw credit as restrictive and costly, but it could also be flexible and liberating—allowing consumers to buy goods and exercise choice. The final set of questions focuses squarely on the emergence of 'new' retail practices, including cash sales and fixed prices. Groceries would appear to lend themselves to such practices, but were they deployed as a result of active business strategies or was it merely a reflection of the standardization of goods? More fundamental to debates over retail and consumer revolution, we need to know the extent to which these 'new' forms of retailing were associated with novel goods such as tea, coffee, and chocolate.

SELLING IN AND OUT OF THE SHOP

Today it is difficult to imagine buying from a shop without entering it. However, as we saw in the previous chapter, sales through the window were an important part of many shopkeepers' business throughout the eighteenth century. In the late seventeenth century, Stout described how he 'attended the shop in winter with the window open, without sash or screen till nine in the evening'. While we do not know for certain, it is likely that the things being sold through the window comprised the parcels of sugar, tobacco, nails, and prunes that he describes making up in preparation for market day, when sales were at their most brisk.[5] Selling smaller items to customers waiting outside made it possible to capture some of the traffic passing by the shop—something that was much harder if the customer had to be enticed inside. It also had the advantage of speed and was particularly well suited to the sale of basic groceries, where customers needed to spend relatively little time

[4] Blondé and Van Damme, 'Retail Growth'.
[5] Stout, *Autobiography*, 80, 79.

selecting goods, particularly if they regularly bought the same goods from the same shopkeeper. Given this, it is almost certain that these would be cash transactions, especially as Cox argues that most of the customers served in this way would be too poor to be given credit and perhaps not sufficiently respectable to be allowed into the shop.[6] The logic of such sales is clear enough, but the evidence remains tantalizingly elusive. As cash sales, such transactions would not normally be entered in account books, and grocers' day books rarely make any comment on the process or location of the transaction. One exception is William Wood of Didsbury. His account book begins with detailed entries of the goods sold to each account customer, but in the last year of his life he summarized many transactions as 'bill in shop', 'bill out of shop', or, very occasionally, 'goods out of window'.[7]

If the customers came inside the shop to buy groceries, they experienced a rather different mode of selling. Naturally, there were a number of common elements, not least the sale of goods in small, manageable amounts. Oil, vinegar, spirits, and treacle were measured into bottles, jars, or tubs. Sometimes these were provided by the customer, 'the buyer finding his own hogshead' for the wines supplied by John Fell and Isaac Murray in 1735. On other occasions the retailer supplied them, but made a charge. Joseph Taylor's trade card noted: 'Casks, bottles, jars and hampers charged and allowed for when returned', while Frances Field's 1789 bill to Mary Leigh included a total of £1 7s. for hampers, bottles, and casks.[8] Similarly, spices, seeds, tobacco, sugar, tea, and coffee all had to be taken from drawers, canisters, or boxes and weighed out into paper packages. Small containers and especially paper were thus important, but often underestimated, parts of the grocer's trade.[9] Occasionally, manufacturers offered packaging alongside their products. The Virginia Factory, for example, advertised that they would provide, *gratis*, 'Penny Papers' in which to package tobacco bought from the company, along with a mould to assist in the process of packing, and Wills also offered to supply papers to its customers.[10] More usually, though, paper was anonymous, as with the '2 Ream of Tobacco papers, & some Shop paper' itemized in the 1702 inventory of Henry Bolt, a Bromsgrove mercer; the 'brown papers' in the shop of Elizabeth Wells of Bridge in Kent (d. 1743), and the range of paper and wrappers listed in Thomas Wright's Birmingham shop in 1773.[11] By the early nineteenth century, packaging increasingly took the form of bags. The sale of John Champion's shop goods in 1816 included various grades of paper (including blue paper, generally used for wrapping sugar), but also 109 lb of paper bags, sold in seven separate lots.[12] Similar

---

[6] Cox, *Complete Tradesman*, 77–83.

[7] MCL, MS F942.

[8] SA, 112/6/Box 34/36; BM, Banks Collection, 89.41.3. (I am grateful to Nancy Cox for supplying these references.) SCLA, DR18/5/5865. Many grocers' bills presented to the Leighs contain no charge for and no mention of containers, but it is unclear who supplied containers in these cases.

[9] The use of paper to wrap tobacco and sugar is briefly discussed in Cox, *Complete Tradesman*, 218; Welford, 'Functional Goods and Fancies', 141; Alexander, *Retailing in England*, 114.

[10] *London Morning Advertiser*, 4 Sept. 1741; Cox, *Complete Tradesman*, 218.

[11] LiRO, B/C/11, Henry Bolt (1702); LiRO B/C/5, Thomas Wright (1773); KAS, 11.82.116, Elizabeth Wells (1743).

[12] NCL, M0000533NL, John Champion of Kettering, 5, 27.

packaging was deployed throughout the nineteenth century and beyond, sometimes being used to advertise the shop as well as package goods (Figure 6.1). A rare survival from mid-century Northampton carries the name of the shopkeeper, R. T. Gudgeon, and outlines some of his stock lines and terms of business ('All Orders promptly attended to and delivered Carriage Paid').[13]

Splitting large quantities and packing them into papers and bags were central parts of the service that grocers provided to their customers.[14] This sometimes meant that goods sold in the shop were pre-packaged. Thomas Turner, for example, spent many hours splitting large consignments of tobacco into scores of 4 oz papers, which he could then sell over the following days and weeks. Such packages were also found in the 1720 inventory of the Cornish merchant William Bastard, which included 3 lb of 'papered tobacco'.[15] However, it was common for goods sold in the shop to be weighed and packed while the customer waited.[16] This service held obvious advantages to customers, not least in terms of allowing them to purchase the specific type and quantity required. Shopkeepers' account books reveal a degree of standardization of the quantities in which groceries were bought. William Woods's customers, for example, often bought tea by the ounce or half-ounce and sugar by the half-pound, although amounts varied considerably.[17] This was more evident in Thomas Dickenson's accounts, which show that, while most of his customers purchased tea in quantities of ¼ lb, the amount varied from ¼ oz to 6 lb. Very small amounts were comparatively rare, but indicate that customers were able to specify precisely the amount and quality of the tea that they wanted. For example, on 20 March 1741, Stephen Langstone purchased ¾ oz of plain green tea and ¼ oz of bohea, as well as 1 lb of sugar.[18]

Having goods weighed out also provided an opportunity to inspect them before they were purchased. Appearance, smell, and taste could be tested to assess the quality, freshness, and appeal of particular consignments or types. Some shopkeepers made a virtue of this, John Gibson advertising in the Newcastle press that 'The Kettle will be always boiling. Gentlemen and Ladies may try the Teas'—a service that was made available by a growing number of tea dealers in the closing decades of the eighteenth century.[19] Waiting for goods to be weighed and packed also meant that customers spent a good amount of time in the shop. They might be seated in front of the counter while the shopkeeper brought goods from the shelves and drawers behind to place on the counter for inspection or to wrap in paper ready for carrying home. Such arrangements are shown in several trade cards illustrating shop interiors and suggest that shopping for groceries—at least in high-end establishments—may not have been so very different from shopping for the durable goods that lie at the heart of Berry's model of polite consumption. This

---

[13] NCL, uncatalogued trade ephemera.
[14] Alexander, *Retailing in England*, 112–15.
[15] CRO, William Bastard (1720).
[16] See, e.g., OBP, 12 Apr. 1809, Thomas Smith (t18090412-35).
[17] MCL, MS F942. See also Mui and Mui, *Shops and Shopkeeping*, 213.
[18] WSL, D1798 HM 29/2–4.
[19] *Newcastle Courant*, 15 Aug. 1752.

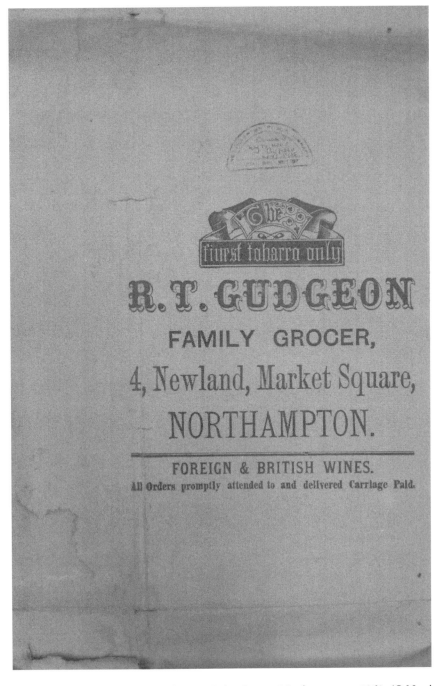

Fig. 6.1. Sugar paper of R. T. Gudgeon, Market Square, Northampton, *c.*1860s (© Northamptonshire Library and Information Services)

reinforces the idea that respectability came through processes of acquisition as well as of consumption; that rituals of buying as well as consuming were important in constructing a self-image of politeness and virtue.[20] Yet the sociability of shopping did not have to be framed by the cultural context of politeness. Whether seen as a critique of the social practices of the lower orders or a parody of the polite pretensions of shops, the interchange between the women in *The Chandler's Shop Gossips* reflects the reality of shopping as a sociable activity. The fact that the teapot and cups remain untouched on the mantelpiece might suggest that the gossiping women are beneath such dignities, but their presence is significant and reflected everyday activity in lower-order shops. In regularly sitting and drinking tea with his customers, Thomas Turner engaged in sociable interaction that helped to pass the time, but that also constituted a form of self-regulation that cemented his respectability and that of his shop and customers.[21]

Turner's impromptu meals and tea-drinking confirm the easy sociability between shopkeeper and customer, even when the goods being sold were relatively mundane. It also underlines Smith's point about the importance of such virtuous behaviour in constructing self as respectable.[22] This was facilitated by the lack of distinction between his shop and home; indeed, Turner appears to have sold goods from what was, in effect, his front room. Much the same arrangement can be seen in the inventory of Elizabeth Kennett (d. 1741), a widow who kept shop in Folkestone. Her house was modest, with two bedchambers, a kitchen, cellar, 'little room', and 'fore room'.[23] The last of these was comfortably, even fashionably, furnished, with one large and one small oval table, three rush-bottomed chairs, a fireplace, six pictures, and a small pair of window curtains. Alongside these was the equipage for respectable entertaining: a tea kettle, two china bowls, four delftware bowls, ten plates, two glass tumblers, two salts, two glasses, fourteen blue and white cups, and six saucers. Yet, as we have already seen, this room was also her shop and contained a range of shop furniture. Her stock was modest and, at best, could not have supplied more than the immediate needs of a small number of customers. There was 1.5 lb of Scotch snuff and 0.5 lb of Spanish snuff; a small parcel of raisins and another of currants; rice, soap, spices, and powder blue; tape and binding; mops, candles, and brushes, and 2 lb of lump sugar. In this room, Kennett would have been able to entertain her customers—treating them to tea in much the same manner as Thomas Turner.

Similar experiences of socializing with shopkeepers were recorded by Henry Blundell and Parson Woodforde.[24] However, while Turner's enjoyment came from the harmless pleasures of drinking tea and playing cards, it is more difficult to

[20] Berry, 'Polite Consumption'; Smith, *Consumption*, 189–222.

[21] Vaisey, *Thomas Turner*, 11 July 1764, 14 Jan. 1763. This respectable behaviour contrasts with bouts of drunkenness that are noted with some remorse in Turner's diary.

[22] Smith, *Consumption*, 196–7.

[23] KAS, 11.82.18, Elizabeth Kennett (1741).

[24] *Diurnal of Nicholas Blundell*, ed. Tyrer, 16 May 1718, 15 Oct. 1710; Beresford (ed.), *Diary*, 26 Aug. 1778, 7 Oct. 1794.

judge the motivations of the shopkeepers who treated Blundell and Woodforde. It is doubtful that they were entirely altruistic, since both men were valuable customers and reliable payers, and shopkeepers often sought to bind such consumers to them with ties of loyalty and friendship. Close personal bonds were important in providing the shopkeeper with continued business (it is telling that Blundell bought sugar from Mrs Lancaster after being treated to dinner), but perhaps also in bolstering their reputation and standing. Turner worked hard to cultivate business at Halland House, the Sussex residence of the Duke of Newcastle. He notes one occasion when the duke's steward, Christopher Coates, came for dinner with his wife and at least four other couples.[25] More often, though, Turner met Coates at the homes of other customers or at Halland House itself. The monetary returns for his efforts were not great—the Duke's bill in 1762 amounted to 18*s*. 2*d*.—but he probably gained other, less tangible benefits.[26]

Such direct interaction was possible only when the customer lived relatively close at hand. As distance increased, the immediacy and intimacy of face-to-face contact were replaced with an emphasis on the efficiency and efficacy of service. Something of this can be gleaned from the account books of the Worcester grocer Thomas Dickenson, who supplied goods via carriers on at least fifteen occasions in 1741–2. For example, Sarah Harrison of Droitwich bought and delivered goods for three customers in her home town: single consignments of tea for Mrs Philpott and Mrs Smith, and tea, nuts, raisins, sugar, treacle, pepper, and tobacco on nine separate occasions for Frank Webb. Dickenson was content to consign goods in this manner, even though it was not a regular arrangement. Webb was a good customer, buying a wide range of groceries on a total of eighty occasions in 1741–2; but Smith and Philpott each made just one other purchase from Dickenson during this period. Despite this infrequency, there was clearly a reasonable level of trust between shopkeeper, customer, and carrier—each being relied upon to fulfil his or her part in this form of distance shopping. Such arrangements were by no means unusual, especially for London grocers and tea dealers, some of whom enjoyed considerable trade with customers in the provinces. For example, Blakiston, Myles, & Co. were patronized by a wide range of gentry families from as far away as Durham, while the tea dealer Charles Brewster supplied retail and private customers in the Midlands and elsewhere.[27] That the gentry sent to London for a range of luxury goods is well established. Analysis of the bills and receipts of the Leigh family of Stoneleigh in Warwickshire indicates that over half of their supplies came from the capital, a figure that increases to two-thirds for groceries.[28] London tradesmen were especially important in supplying high-quality tea, coffee, and chocolate, but only occasionally did they provide specialist lines that were apparently less easily available in local towns.

[25] Vaisey, *Thomas Turner*, 14 Mar. 1758.
[26] Vaisey, *Thomas Turner*, 4–5 Apr. 1761; 23 Aug. 1762.
[27] Berry, 'Prudent Luxury', 148; Stobart, 'Gentlemen and Shopkeepers'; Mui and Mui, *Shops and Shopkeeping*, 15, 48.
[28] Stobart, 'Gentlemen and Shopkeepers', table 1.

The precise relationship between high-end London grocers and their provincial customers is difficult to discern, but it appears that most responded to specific orders placed by consumers. However, this did not necessarily mean that they were passive partners in the relationship. When Joshua Long, the London grocer and tea dealer, sent his bill to a wealthy Norfolk landowner named Sir Martin Folkes, he took the opportunity not only to include his current list of goods, but also to inform Foulkes about particular goods that he felt might be of interest.[29] Similarly, Charles Hancock, a London tea dealer who supplied the Gibbards in the 1820s, occasionally sent much larger quantities than had been ordered.[30] He must have felt secure in this relationship with the family and confident that a bigger consignment would be welcomed and paid for. Part of this might have come from the long-standing relationship he had with the Gibbards—a common feature in the supply of groceries to elite consumers. Many of the London grocers selling to the Leighs did so over a number of years: Matthew Blakiston sent his first consignment in 1755, and he continued to do business with the inhabitants of Stoneleigh Abbey for the next eighteen years; Thomas Thompson sold them tea, coffee, and chocolate over a twelve-year period, and Thomas Ballard did the same for much of the 1790s, during which time he sent seventeen bills.[31] Such long-term relationships built bonds of trust that helped to minimize the risk of buying goods unseen. These bonds reflected well on the customers and especially on the shopkeepers, as they demonstrated their ability to meet the demands of elite consumers in terms of both the goods and the service provided.

'TRADITIONAL' SHOPKEEPING: SERVICE, REPUTATION, AND CREDIT

Selling in and beyond the shop relied heavily on the service provided by the retailer. Indeed, for Defoe, it was central to the shopkeeper's art and to his or her business success.[32] Importantly, though, service was not simply about persuasion: the shopkeeper's knowledge, skills, and expertise assured the quality of goods and provided reassurance about the experience of buying them. These were part of the implicit contract between the reputable retailer and the consumer, but they only occasionally become visible above the surface of day-to-day buying and selling. Edward Robinson's advertisement in the Birmingham press is therefore particularly revealing. He announced a rather eclectic stock of Seville and China oranges and lemons; herrings and white fish; Spanish nuts, figs, pomegranates, and chestnuts, and 'all sorts of Worcestershire fruit', and ended by noting: 'All Persons that are not Judges in the above Goods may depend on being used well, and without

---

[29] NoRO, MC50/23/5.

[30] e.g. BLA, GA5, bill from Charles Hancock, undated. On this occasion, he sent 30 lb rather than the 12 lb that had been ordered.

[31] See the index for Leigh bills and vouchers (SCLA, DR18/5).

[32] Defoe, *Compleat English Tradesman*, 64–71.

Extortion.'[33] The ways in which Robinson actually dealt with his less well-informed customers are unknown. As with much of the wisdom and advice imparted in the shop, they have left no trace in the records; but they were surely important in shaping the experience of shopping. They probably resembled the kind of advice written to those buying at a distance, attempting to steer the consumer gently through the choices available. In the note appended to his bill to Sir Foulkes, Joshua Long suggested that 'teas are a great deal dearer' and chocolate 'much better' than they had previously been. Similarly, William Coplin wrote to Sir Roger Newdigate in 1803, advising him that a very abundant and good crop of hops was selling 'exceeding quick and at advancing prices'. Striking a more perfunctory tone, someone from the London partnership of Wilson, Thornhill and Wilson added a note to a 1792 bill for muscadella raisins and Jordan almonds, explaining that, as 'the season for Prunellas and Gamaroons is now over, we have none that we can recommend & have therefore omitted them'.[34] Such advice was impersonal in nature, reflecting a businesslike relationship. This stood in marked contrast to Mary Gibbard's regular and friendly correspondence with her London tea dealer. Yet Hancock's letters, while striking a personal tone, were also about business. He wrote in the mid-1820s to commend certain teas that were 'such as I use myself' and 'so cheap and good, and we are not likely to have any more of the kind'.[35]

Service did not stop at offering advice: many groceries needed careful storage, and some had to be processed before they could be sold. This required a further set of skills and a range of specialist equipment. Dried fruit had to be sorted, cleaned, and packaged, a Kent grocer noting in his diary in 1809 that he had 'picked 2 Baskets Raisins of 112 lbs in 2 Hours and a half'.[36] Hard soap might be supplied in moulded bars, but many customers required smaller quantities, which had to be cut. Soft soap was stored in large bins, often in the darkest and coolest part of the cellar; it had to be scooped out into the customer's own container. Spices were generally bought from the wholesaler unprocessed and sometimes needed grinding and mixing before they were ready for sale. For example, pepper might be sold whole or ground, the latter requiring a mill of the sort listed in a number of mid-eighteenth-century shops. These were often of modest pieces—John Sterndale's was valued at just 1*s*. 6*d*., compared with 7*s*. 6*d*. for his weights and scales and 5*s*. for a brass mortar—but they were important to the service provided by the grocer.[37] New commodities brought the need for new skills and equipment. Sugar came in a wide range of different forms, depending on the degree to which it had been refined. Loaf sugar had to be cut, pounded into granules, and packaged in sugar paper, whereas treacle needed to be carefully tapped from barrels or crocks into pots.[38] Coffee required more preparation, as the beans had to be roasted and

[33] *Aris's Birmingham Gazette*, 12 Jan. 1756.
[34] NoRO, MC50/23/5; WRO, CR136/8/2625a; SCLA, DR18/5/5992.
[35] BLA, GA5, undated bill.
[36] Quoted in Alexander, *Retailing in England*, 115.
[37] LiRO, B/C/11, John Sterndale (1747). Pepper and coffee mills are also found in early nineteenth-century inventories (LiRO, B/C/5, Benjamin Gilbert (1825); LiRO, B/C/5, James Coxon (1821)).
[38] Alexander, *Retailing in England*, 114.

ground—a deceptively simple process that needed considerable skill.[39] As a consequence, many London coffee houses were buying in roasted beans by the end of the seventeenth century. Initially offered by specialist coffee men, this service spread gradually, so that, by the early nineteenth century, provincial dealers were advertising 'Coffee roasted on reasonable terms' or the opening of a 'Public Roasting-House for Coffee', where dealers could be served at prices equal to those in London.[40] Whoever roasted the beans, the coffee still needed grinding—another service generally offered by grocers, whose inventories often included coffee mills alongside canisters and weights and scales.[41]

Tobacco required a greater investment in equipment in order to prepare it for sale. It needed drying, cutting, rolling, and milling—processes that increasingly took place in centralized mills, but that continued to be undertaken by retailers well into the nineteenth century. An advertisement in the Liverpool press in 1820 announced to 'Tobacconists and others. On sale, three tobacco cutting engines complete.' They were clearly suitable for use in a domestic workshop, since they were 'calculated to work by hand or machinery'.[42] One hundred years earlier, such equipment was found in several grocers' shops: from a total of eighty-seven shopkeepers selling tobacco, fourteen owned tobacco knives, blocks, or presses, and ten had engines or mills. These engines were costly and bulky—that of Isaac Heath of Birmingham, for example, was valued at £3 10s. and was situated in the cellar under the shop, where the processing could take place out of view of the customer.[43] Yet there was some acknowledgement of the benefit of having a skilled supplier who processed the tobacco to a high standard. This is apparent from the trade card of Benjamin Pearkes of Worcester, which illustrated tobacco leaves being dried, packed, and milled.[44] The message can be read in a number of ways, but it is apparent that Pearkes wished to communicate his skills as a tobacconist as well as a retailer.

The importance of the grocer's skill and knowledge was also apparent in the sale of tea and particularly in the ability to offer a range of different qualities and blends. Critical here were links with London dealers, in whose hands traditionally lay the art of blending. Reputation was all important, not least because of perennial concerns about adulteration of tea, which prompted many dealers to take to the press, most often to stress the purity of their teas, often guaranteed by a particular form of packaging or seal (see Chapter 7).[45] Many of these very public battles over reputation and probity concerned London dealers rather than provincial

---

[39] Quoted in Ellis, *Coffee House*, 119.
[40] *Liverpool Mercury*, 15 Sept. 1820; *Leeds Mercury*, 6 July 1784.
[41] See, e.g., KAS, 11.75.92, Nathaniel Jorden (1720); KAS 11.82.221, Edward Gilbart (1748); LiRO, B/C/5, Frances Nutt (1793), LiRO, B/C/5, James Coxon (1821). Even when they were situated in the home (e.g. with John Sterndale—see n. 37), they might still be used for commercial purposes.
[42] *Liverpool Mercury*, 21 Apr. 1820.
[43] LiRO, B/C/11, Isaac Heath (1701). See also LiRO, B/C/11, Walter Storey (1695).
[44] Bodl., JJC, Trade Cards 11 (21); Bodl., JJC, Trade Cards 28 (26).
[45] Mui and Mui, *Shops and Shopkeeping*, 254–5, 281–4. See also Rappaport, 'Packaging China'.

shopkeepers.[46] However, the latter were sometimes implicated, not least in their capacity as agents for one or other of the London warehouses. It is difficult to judge the relative importance of the two in the public's reading of reputation and their choice of tea. Most advertisements were placed by the London dealer, a list of local agents being appended to the bottom of what were often long lists of goods and prices. However, the local agent sometimes took the initiative, his or her name accordingly being more prominent, even if the basic structure of the advertisement remained the same. This suggests that reputation was not reduced to a particular name or brand and that the standing of individual shopkeepers remained important.

Concerns over tea were part of a more general and long-running debate about the reputation of those selling groceries. Respectability was extremely important. It was intimately tied up with personal virtues of honesty and integrity, and with the quality and purity of the goods being sold. Doubts about the trustworthiness of lower-class shopkeepers were especially deep-seated and were still being subjected to satirical treatment into the nineteenth century and beyond. This is seen in a ballad entitled 'Chandler's Shop', which sours the dream of a courting couple with the man's professed intention of dishonesty:

SHE: To give good weight, Sam, we'll not fail—
HE: Barring a penny under the scale.
SHE: We'll sell the very best bohea.
HE: And I'll chop some birch broom up, d'ye see.
SHE: We'll sell the best sugar in the land,
HE: I'd improve it with a little sand.[47]

With popular caricatures such as this, it is unsurprising that those selling groceries should be concerned with their reputation and with cementing strong and trusting relationships with their customers. Credit played a key part in this process and was central to traditional modes of buying and selling. It lubricated trade, circumvented the problem of scarcity of small coinage, and shaped the relationship between shopkeepers and their customers. Cox has traced evidence of credit sales from the sixteenth century, but suggests that the practice was much older.[48] By the early eighteenth century, it was impossible to conceive of a shopkeeper selling only for ready money, Defoe arguing that 'the tradesman that trades wholly thus, is not yet born'.[49] Yet selling on credit was not straightforward. Most fundamentally, it required a proper system for recording who owed how much and for what. This task was especially onerous for grocers, whose customers frequently bought a range of goods in small quantities—a practice that necessitated the careful recording of numerous items, weights, and costs. These details would be noted in the shop book, which then became an important record of individual debt. As such, it was

[46] An interesting variant on the London formula is found in *Adams Weekly Courant*, 15 Dec. 1778.
[47] Bodl., JJC, Trades and Professions 6 (54a).
[48] Cox, *Complete Tradesman*, 146.
[49] Defoe, *Compleat English Tradesman*, ii. 28.

open to error and deliberate fraud, a concern that prompted a 1609 Parliamentary 'Act to avoid the double Payment of Debts'.[50] In restricting to one year the time that a shop book could be used as evidence of a debt, the Act aimed to protect the customer from being charged twice for the same bill. However, it also had the effect of establishing the legitimacy of the shop book as a record of debt.

At their most straightforward, shop books recorded sales for which payment had yet to be made. Some were chaotic in their structure, but the standard of account books improved through the eighteenth century with the spread of double-entry or the Italian method of book-keeping.[51] Whatever their form, shop books attest to the importance of credit to shopkeepers. They created a bond of mutual obligation between the shopkeepers and their customers—part of Muldrew's broader 'economy of obligation'.[52] The number of customers to whom grocers extended credit varied considerably, often reflecting the location and scale of the business, with rural grocers tending to have rather fewer account customers than did their urban counterparts. The probate inventory of William Claridge, a grocer in the Northamptonshire village of Great Brington, lists a total of 39 people who owed book debts at the time of his death in 1755. A generation later, an unknown grocer trading in Greens Norton, also in Northamptonshire, had 29 people listed in his account book. His contemporary, William Wood, had 107 names in his ledger, but only one-third of these appear to have purchased goods in his shop—the rest were supplied with coal or with drinks at the inn.[53] In contrast, the Bewdley mercer and grocer Thomas Wootton (d. 1667) had 198 retail customers in addition to those that he appears to have supplied wholesale.[54] Henry Snow, trading in Wolverhampton some sixty years later, had debts owing from 154 people, while the Warrington grocer Ralph Bates was owed book debts by a total of 311 people, drawn mostly from the neighbouring towns and villages.[55]

Despite its obvious benefits, credit exposed shopkeepers to the risk of default on payments and potentially the failure of their business. Upon analysing the accounts after his first year in business, William Stout found that he had 'sould goods for ready money about £450 and upon credit about £150'. He clearly felt that this balance was not right and that he had been 'too forward in trusting and too backward in calling, as is too frequent in young tradesmen'.[56] While direct comparisons are problematic, in that they record total assets rather than sales, analysis of grocers'

---

[50]   7 JAC1 c. 12 (1609).

[51]   Cox, *Complete Tradesman*, 148–53.

[52]   Muldrew, *Economy of Obligation*, esp. 173–96.

[53]   NRO, 1755 William Claridge; NRO, Y.Z.4040; Mui and Mui, *Shops and Shopkeeping*, 212, 340.

[54]   The distinction is marked in his probate inventory. Retail customers are listed under the heading: 'Unsatisfied...these several sums of money all which stand due upon the Shopbooks of the said Thomas Wootton'; most lived in towns and villages around Bewdley. Wholesale customers were spread far more widely (see Ch. 3) and were headed: 'Debts owing unto the s'd Thomas Wootton att his decease'. Both are distinct from a 'Schedule of bonds specialities & other securities belonging to the estate of Thos Wotton'. See TNA: PRO C5/582/120.

[55]   LiRO, B/C/11, Henry Snow (1731); LRO, WCW 1756, Ralph Bates.

[56]   Stout, *Autobiography*, 96.

Table 6.1. Grocers' book debts, 1668–1775

Date	Shopkeeper's name	Occupation	Total estate (£)	Total debts (£)	% debts	Good debts (£)	Bad debts (£)	% bad debts
1668	John Knowler of Milton	Grocer	270.8	105.8	39.2			
1670	William Richmond of Penrith	Grocer	236	23	9.7			
1675	John Burden of Canterbury	Grocer	369.1	22.6	6.1			
1676	John Ladd of Canterbury	Shopkeeper	102	34.7	34.0	26.6	8.1	7.9
1687	Hester Aldworth of Charlbury	Widow	69.8	12.4	17.8			
1708	John Malham of Colne	Gentleman	127.3	10.7	8.4			
1709	Henry Jolly of St Columb major	Mercer	145.2	7	4.8			
1709	Robert Rownson of Liverpool	Grocer	319.1	216.9	68.0	83.3	134	41.9
1710	John Clarke of Biddenden	Shopkeeper	392.6	62.5	15.9	50	12.5	3.2
1720	Henry Davis of Towcester	Grocer	155	10	6.5			
1720	Nathaniel Jorden of Newington	Grocer	1048.6	125	11.9			
1720	Thomas Taylor of Rochdale	Grocer	108.2	16	14.8			
1723	David Gradwell of Bolton	Grocer	376.2	182.8	48.6	100	82.8	22.0

(continued)

Table 6.1. (*Continued*)

Date	Shopkeeper's name	Occupation	Total estate (£)	Total debts (£)	% debts	Good debts (£)	Bad debts (£)	% bad debts
1723	James Hollis of Thrapston	Grocer	143.9	59.4	41.3			
1724	Thomas Moreton of Chester	Grocer	268.2	12.1	4.5	10.4	1.7	0.6
1728	Henry Faulkner of Chorley	Shopkeeper	158.9	20	12.6			
1732	Wiliam Hockenhall of Newcastle	Grocer	1128	733	65.0			
1735	Peter Lorain of Canterbury	Shopkeeper	20.3	0.4	2.0			
1741	Elizabeth Kennett of Folkestone	Widow	42.9	3.1	7.2			
1755	William Claridge of Great Brington	Grocer	141.6	88.5	62.5	80.6	7.9	5.6
1775	John Key of Ringstead	Grocer	80.9	33	40.8			
			271.6	84.7	24.8			

Source: probate inventories.

probate inventories confirms Stout's misgivings. Looking at a broad range of shop-keepers, Cox found that the ratio of shop debts to total inventory value varied considerably, from just 1 per cent up to 78 per cent, but that 10–20 per cent was most typical.[57] Grocers' exposure to credit appears to be rather higher, book debts accounting for 26 per cent of the total inventory value on average (Table 6.1). While some had very small amounts owing, 40 per cent had over one-third of their estate tied up in debts resulting from their credit arrangements with customers, with Robert Rownson, William Hockenhall, and William Claridge being particu-larly noteworthy.

For most retailers, these totals reflected the accumulation of a large number of small debts. Thomas Moreton, for example, was owed £1 11s. 9d. by an apothecary called Croughton, but almost half of his debtors owed less than 2s., the lowest debt being 2d., owing from Humphrey Oldfield. More occasionally, the figures could be skewed by a single large account. Most of William Claridge's thirty-nine book debts were for a few shillings, but the account of the 'late Mr Spencer of Althorp Hall' amounted to a massive £58 5s. 10¾d.—over two-fifths of Claridge's total estate.[58] Fortunately, his executors were able to recover this debt, as they were the majority of outstanding accounts. Indeed, the exposure of Claridge—or rather his executors—to bad or desperate debts was fairly modest. Not so lucky were the executors of David Gradwell and especially Robert Rownson, whose inventory included over £80 'in debts oweing that are thought to be desperate'.[59] Quite apart from the problems of interpreting what might be poorly constructed account books, executors were faced with the task of tracing debtors who may have run up their accounts over a number of years. On 22 August 1756, the appraisers who drew up Ralph Bates's inventory carefully noted 'a list of outstanding Debts', which included names, amounts owed, and the year in which the debt had been incurred. These were probably taken from his account book and so reflect credit granted to customers and the last date at which accounts had been settled (Table 6.2). They reveal that the majority of unsettled accounts dated from the previous two or three

Table 6.2. Debts owed to Ralph Bates of Warrington, grocer (d. 1756)

Year of debt	No.	%
1756	90	28.9
1754–5	66	21.2
1751–3	43	13.8
1747–50	56	18.0
1737–46	43	13.8
1729–36	13	4.2
	311	

Source: LRO, WCW 1756, Ralph Bates.

[57] Cox, *Complete Tradesman*, 154–5.
[58] CALS, WS 1724, Thomas Moreton; NRO, William Claridge, 1755.
[59] LRO, WCW 1709, Robert Rownson.

years, with many being less than eight months old. However, there are also a considerable number of customers whose accounts had not been settled for several years. There are various explanations for this, the most obvious being that they had died before paying Bates; but what these figures reveal is the fine line that shopkeepers needed to tread between granting credit to facilitate sales and limiting their exposure to unpaid debts.

Managing credit was one of the most problematic areas for shopkeepers—one that reflected on their standing as well as their business. As Defoe noted, 'he that takes credit may give credit, but he must be exceedingly watchful, for it is the most dangerous state of life that a man can live in'.[60] This watchfulness involved two aspects: assessing whether to grant credit to a customer, and managing the level and duration of the credit offered. The first of these was shaped by social as much as by economic factors. In financial terms, the shopkeeper needed to assess whether the customer was likely to be able to pay for goods received on credit. Knowledge of the individual and his or her personal circumstances was clearly useful in making such assessments and served to limit the geographical bounds of credit. But the issue was complicated by the way in which credit was a mark of honour and worth as well as a means of acquiring goods. To refuse credit was effectively to dishonour and, in an age where appearances increasingly stood for social and economic worth, shopkeepers were often willing to oblige anyone who looked the part.[61] One advantage that grocers had over many others was that many of the goods that they sold would generally be bought in small amounts, and, while regular purchases could soon build up sizeable bills, it was more difficult for acts of deliberate fraud to be perpetrated. The real problem was that of customers who either could not or would not settle their accounts in a timely manner.

Stout berated himself for being 'too backward in calling', but there is evidence that many grocers carefully managed the credit accorded to their various customers. Those buying from William Wood made regular payments against their accounts, although this rarely meant paying off their debt in full. Mui and Mui quote the example of Ann Hadkinson as being fairly typical. On 1 April 1786, she paid £1 1s. against her account of £1 8s. 6½d.; by 5 May additional purchases had inflated her bill to £1 7s. 4d. and she again paid off £1 1s. This pattern of roughly monthly payments of 1 guinea continued through to September, when she cleared her bill with a payment of 16s.[62] However, not all customers were granted the same period of credit, nor were they allowed the same terms of payment. In 1797, William Menchell made between three and five purchases each week from the anonymous Greens Norton grocer, mostly butter and bread, but also sugar, oil, flour, and meat. Although these usually amounted to no more than a few pence and never more than one or two shillings, the account was totalled and crossed through each week, indicating that full payment had been made. Other customers were allowed

---

[60] Defoe, *Compleat English Tradesman*, i. 51.
[61] See Corfield, 'The Rivals', 14–16; Borsay, *English Urban Renaissance*, 225–56; Klein, 'Politeness for Plebes', 364–5.
[62] Mui and Mui, *Shops and Shopkeeping*, 215.

more credit over a longer period, but still paid in full. Mary Pinder, for example, settled bills of £1 6s. 11¼d. on 11 October 1797, £2 3s. on 28 December, and £3 10s. 1½d. on 19 February 1798. Edward Williams, by contrast, made payments towards his bill rather than clearing it. These were not a set amount, ranging from £1 1s. to £1 8s.; but they were made each time his account was totalled—an event that happened every month or so.[63] In Westmorland, Abraham Dent was similarly flexible. Some of his customers paid their bills within a few weeks of buying the goods. John Barnett, for instance, had groceries worth £4 6s. over sixteen days before paying for them with his final purchase on 9 November 1762. For others, the time between purchase and payment was much longer. At the extreme was Thomas Hutchinson, who bought goods worth 12s. 10d. in the summer of 1762, but only paid for them five years later.[64] It is impossible to know the precise reasons for these different arrangements, but they clearly reflect shopkeepers' perceptions of the ability to pay and the respectability of the customer.

Most payments were made in cash, but it is clear that Wood and Dent also accepted payments in kind. John Thompson, for example, was credited for plastering work that he had carried out for Dent, and the carriers Anthony Cleasby and John Brunskill for transporting treacle, sugar, hops, and flour. Andrew Whitfield, a cobbler, presented a bill in November 1765 for mending Dent's shoes, as well as those of his wife and daughter. This work, which had been carried out over the previous six months or so and amounted to 5s. 8½d., was set against his grocery bill of 7s. 9½d. Other tradesmen were credited for goods supplied: Robert Nickolson for coal and Alexander Simpson for a range of seeds, plants, and herbs. Again, these credits were set against the sums they owed Dent for groceries and cloth.[65] Similarly, Ann Brancroft paid off some of her bill with Wood by 'spreading mole hills', and the account of Robert Blomily was credited at a rate of 1s. 6d. per day for work done in Wood's garden.[66] Rather more complex were the arrangements made with William Birch. His wife (Mary) and daughter carried out mowing in July 1787 to help pay off an old bill carried over from an earlier account book; Mary did the same in July and August 1791, and was credited with a total of 19s. 5d. against an account of £1 19s. 11¾d. All the while, William was receiving regular credit for his work in supplying or mending shoes for Wood and his family.[67]

Such arrangements might suggest the weak development of a market economy or that these shopkeepers were operating in a premodern form of exchange. However, if it allowed people to acquire more goods, then it might be seen as an effective means of expanding the business and its turnover. Moreover, to see these transactions as primitive ignores the careful book-keeping that allowed Dent, Wood, and the Greens Norton grocer to keep track of their credit customers and the various ways in which they settled their accounts. All three men took positive

[63] NRO, Y.Z.4040, fos 13–14, 43–5.
[64] Willan, *Abraham Dent*, 26.
[65] Willan, *Abraham Dent*, 24–5.
[66] Mui and Mui, *Shops and Shopkeeping*, 212.
[67] MCL, MS F942, fos 589–90.

action when customers stopped at least servicing their debts. Dent 'sent a note' to remind customers of old or outstanding debts, while the other two restricted the amount of credit offered to those who proved to be poor payers. For example, James Cash had accumulated a debt of £3 2s. 1½d. when Wood drew up his account on 12 February 1787. He paid £1 1s. of this and continued to buy on credit over the next month, purchasing over £1 worth of goods and raising his total bill to £3 4s. 10½d. by 13 March. No payment was made against this bill, and for the next two months spending was limited to a total of just 12s. 1¼d.—about one-quarter of the previous level. On 15 May, he paid £2 12s. 6d. and from June returned to the earlier pattern of spending and payments.[68] Either Cash's require-ment for groceries had dramatically fallen in April and May, or the credit extended to him had been limited by Wood. Similarly, William Rogers, a regular customer of the Greens Norton grocer, appears to have been allowed £5 to £6 of credit.[69] Most of his payments were of one guinea, but the precise amount and especially their frequency varied according to the rate at which he spent. While he normally paid on a monthly basis, as little as three weeks or as much as two months could elapse between payments. Importantly, the frequency of payments appears to have been driven by the shopkeeper not his customer: a payment is recorded on each occasion that the account is totalled and presumably, therefore, the bill presented.

Despite such attempts to manage carefully the amount of credit allowed to par-ticular customers, it was inevitable that some would default on their debts. When he inspected his books in 1697 (after about ten years of trading), Stout found that he had 248 insolvent debtors owing a total of about £220. Like Dent, he had sent reminder notes to these customers, but to no avail. His autobiography notes with a tinge of regret that he had 'seldom made use of attorney', perhaps because he was worried about the consequences for his own reputation or for the fate of the debtor thus charged.[70] Turner certainly agonized over this. On the morning of 22 May 1758 he went to Lewes to commit to his attorney 'the management of the debt due from Master Darby', which he estimated to be at least £18. Finding that his own attorney was not at home, and worried that delay might further damage his chances of recovering the debt, he went to another attorney, who proposed issuing a writ for Darby's arrest. Turner then records his worries:

To think what a terrible thing it is to arrest a person, for by this means he may be entirely torn to pieces, who might otherwise recover himself and pay everyone their own. But then on the other hand let me consider some of this debt hath been standing above four years, and the greatest part of it above three years. I have tried very hard to get it these two years and cannot get one farthing. They have almost quite forsaken my shop, buying nothing of me that amounts to any value, but every time they want anything of value, they go to Lewes.[71]

[68] MCL, MS F942, fos 17–18.
[69] NRO, Y.Z.4040, fos 18–20.
[70] Stout, *Autobiography*, 119–20.
[71] Vaisey, *Thomas Turner*, 22 May 1758.

As Cox argues, this shows that Turner expected his customers to be creditworthy, to pay off at least some of their debts, and to continue to patronize his shop.[72] In short, they needed to respect the mutuality of the bond between shopkeeper and customer. This is exactly what the majority of the people appearing in the account books of Dent, Wood, and the Greens Norton grocer managed to do. Selling goods on credit allowed these shopkeepers to expand their businesses by tying customers to them with bonds of mutual dependence and trust. The limits of that trust are clear from the various strategies for managing credit and, ultimately, in a willing-ness to recover debts from the worst offenders. But credit came at a cost. For the shopkeeper it brought the risk of default and potential ruin; for the customer it meant higher prices—or at least that was the rhetoric of the growing number of retailers who advertised their wares for ready money only.

'NEW' MODES OF SELLING: FIXED PRICES AND READY MONEY

Cash sales and fixed prices lie at the heart of established notions of retail revolution, being seen as central to transparent and efficient selling, and to the fostering of competition—all of which were to the ultimate benefit of the consumer. The extent and timing of any changes in these practices is, therefore, important to more general questions of retail and consumer evolution. In the tea trade, both cash sales and fixed prices rose to prominence around the time of the Commutation Act of 1784 as the key selling points of a new breed of dealer.[73] Leading the way was Edward Eagleton, who advertised his tea in a wide range of provincial newspapers from the late 1770s. For example, on 18 August 1778 he placed a notice in the Chester press, which listed a wide variety of teas: from 'Good Common Bohea tea', at 3s. 10d. per pound, to Superfine Hyson at 14s. 6d.[74] Similar notices also appeared in newspapers in Gloucester, Bristol, Leeds, Manchester, and elsewhere. They listed not just tea, but also coffee and chocolate, again with prices specified for particular types and qualities. Significantly, with chocolate, there was a premium for recognized brands: whereas 'Good and fine plain Chocolate' cost as little as 3s. 8d. per pound and superfine was 4s. 8d., 'The finest Vanilla, Sir Hans Sloan's Milk, and Churchman's Patent Chocolate' each cost 5s. 6d. Those ordering from Eagleton, therefore, knew exactly the price and quality of the goods before they bought them. Moreover, as a growing number of dealers advertised their prices, consumers could compare the cost of particular teas and choose their supplier accordingly.[75] Most, like Eagleton, were confident that their tea was offered at the best price, though few chose to match his offer to potential customers that, if the goods 'did not match their utmost

[72] Cox, *Complete Tradesman*, 160.
[73] See Mui and Mui, *Shops and Shopkeeping*, 250–87.
[74] *Adams Weekly Courant*, 18 Aug. 1778. For details of this advertisement, see Ch. 7.
[75] See, e.g., the advertisements placed by G. Winter in the *Manchester Mercury*, 30 June 1795, and Long & Co. in the *Bristol Mercury*, 3 Jan. 1820.

Expectations, the money will be returned and the goods sent for again; Free of Trouble or Expense'.[76] This 'expectation' referred partly to the quality of the goods, but also to the saving of between 10 and 20 per cent that Eagleton claimed his customers would make. The discount was spelled out in specific comparisons made clearest in a lengthy advertisement placed in 1779 that gave his prices along with what he claimed was the standard price.[77] While many of these appear to be suspiciously rounded, they correspond closely with his broader estimates: around a median of 12.5 per cent, savings on tea ranged from 6.7 per cent on bohea to 20 per cent on very fine souchong, while roasted coffee was offered at an apparent saving of 21.4 per cent. The real significance of this is that goods were being sold on price, and more particularly on their price relative to that charged by others. Eagleton went further, announcing that his teas 'are delivered with every parcel, the price marked on each'.[78] These were not quite the ticketed prices lauded by Alexander as emblematic of modern retailing, but they formed a close approximation in that they made transparent the price of each individual purchase.[79]

The low prices offered by London tea warehouses were possible because they insisted on ready money. Eagleton announced that 'all goods must be paid for on or before delivery. Good bills at a short date inclosed with orders taken in payment.'[80] Only in this way could he and his competitors offer low prices and low rates of commission for those buying crates direct from the East India Company's auctions.[81] Their profit margin was small, but they made up for this by selling large quantities—a classic ploy of the 'modern' retailer. Credit was portrayed as a costly undertaking that inflated prices, a sentiment echoed by those provincial dealers who moved to adopt Eagleton's practices. William Shackleton of Wakefield made his position clear, announcing that he accepted 'Ready Money only, thereby avoiding bad debts, omission of putting down parcels, and the saving of interest on book debts'. He was, therefore, able to 'sell lower than credit terms can possibly admit of'.[82] James Rich of Bradford took a similar approach, emphasizing his ability to provide 'cheap' and 'useful' teas. However, not all dealers looked down market. H. Doubleday & Co. of Castle Street in Liverpool, for example, itemized the (low) prices of their common and breakfast teas, but they also offered 'finer kinds', which were available at the 'very lowest terms'.[83] Similarly, some tradesmen advertised high-quality groceries at fixed prices. William Jones, also of Liverpool, listed the price of his cranberries, Indian arrowroot, vermicelli and macaroni, real West Indian cayenne, French olives, Real Japan soy, and superfine mustard. He also offered 'Spices, Pickles & c. much reduced in Price'.[84]

[76] *Adams Weekly Courant*, 18 Aug. 1778.
[77] *Adams Weekly Courant*, 3 Aug. 1779.
[78] *Leeds Mercury*, 7 Nov. 1786.
[79] See Alexander, *Retailing in England*, 136.
[80] *Adams Weekly Courant*, 3 Aug. 1779. The wording was repeated in *Felix Farley's Bristol Journal*, 5 Jan. 1782 and elsewhere.
[81] Mui and Mui, *Shops and Shopkeeping*, 269–71.
[82] *Leeds Mercury*, 19 Apr. 1785.
[83] *Leeds Mercury*, 4 May 1793; *Liverpool Mercury*, 27 Oct. 1820.
[84] *Liverpool Mercury*, 11 Feb. 1820.

There is little doubting that fixed prices and ready money were important in the retailing of tea and other groceries by the late eighteenth century, but to what extent were they a genuinely new phenomenon in the grocery trade? That prices for most goods were known if not fixed is apparent from the fact that appraisers could evaluate shop goods when drawing up inventories. In many cases, they gave the quantity of goods and a price per unit—be it length of cloth, number of nails, or weight of sugar—calculating the value down to the halfpenny. The broad consistency with which the value of particular goods was estimated suggests that knowledge of their price was widespread and consistent. Any fluctuations reflected seasonal changes in availability or structural changes in the market, rather than individual negotiation. William Wood, for example, charged the same price to all his customers, suggesting that there was little place for haggling in his shop. Prices rose and fell over the years, but the only variation was a discount of 1*d*. per pound to those buying treacle in larger quantities.[85] Further evidence that prices were effectively fixed comes from contemporary cookery books, which sometimes indicated the amount of a particular ingredient by price. For example, in Henry Howard's 1708 book, the recipe for rice pudding calls for 'one penny-worth of mace', and to 'pot beef like venison' the cook needed 'two penny-worth of Saltpetre; the same of Sal prunellae'. There is also an indication that the quality of the commodity could be judged from its price, 'an extraordinarily good sack-posset' requiring three-quarters of a pound of six-penny sugar.[86] Equally, contemporaries were clear that many sales of groceries would be for cash. In arguing that the tradesman who deals *only* in ready money 'is not yet born', Defoe clearly acknowledged that an important part of any shopkeeper's business would be cash sales.[87] This is evident from Stout's assessment of his first year in trade. For all his concern about extending too much credit, his sales for ready money were worth three times those made on account.[88]

Cash sales and standardized prices as an everyday part of retailing are rather different from their being central to the retailer's promotional strategy. That said, there is evidence that fixed prices at least were an important part of shopkeepers' marketing from the start of the eighteenth century.[89] Almost from its inception, the *Norwich Gazette* carried advertisements. One of the earliest announced a one-off sale of tea and coffee at fixed prices, to be held at the shop of a reputable retailer, John Pegnott.[90] This turned out to be a hoax and caused the publishers some trouble, but it suggests that fixed prices were nothing unusual, even at this time. By 1711, there were at least ten advertisements mentioning fixed prices, most of them for groceries. Fairly typical were those of John Hoyle, who advertised 'Good Cheshire Cheese at Three Pence Half-Penny a Pound, Warwickshire at Three pence Farthing', and Mr Beever, who offered, among other things, 'Virginia Tobacco both

---

[85] Mui and Mui, *Shops and Shopkeeping* 215.
[86] Howard, *England's Newest Way*, 3, 80, 127.
[87] Defoe, *Compleat English Tradesman*, ii. 28.
[88] Stout, *Autobiography*, 96.
[89] The following draws on Barnett, 'Shops, Retailing and Consumption'.
[90] *Norwich Gazette*, 4–11 Mar. 1707.

ROBERT BARET, at the Sun and Golden
Still, right over against St Andrew's Steps in
Norwich, has just now come Home a large
Quanti-ty of TEA, drawn fresh out the India
House, which he will sell as follows, viz.
Superfine Hyson, Eighteenth Shillings per Pound
Second Ditto, Fourteen Shillings per Pound
Third Ditto, Twelve Shillings per Pound
Caper Hyson, Sixteen Shillings per Pound
Congo and Pekeo, Twelve Shillings per Pound
Singlio Green, Eight Shillings per Pound
Bohea, Eight Shillings per Pound
Common Ditto, Seven Shill. Six-Pence per Pound
N.B. He has a large Quantity of Capers to dispose of, which will be sold
at Forty-Four Shillings per Hundred, Five Pence per Pound, or Four
Pence per Pint; likewise, the best Brunswick Mum, neat as imported, and
Anchovies, One Shilling per Pound.

Fig. 6.2. Advertisement by Robert Baret of Norwich, grocer (Source: *Norwich Mercury*, 8 May 1742)

large Cut and small Cut at 16 pence a pound'.[91] Price was clearly seen as a selling point, even if those prices being advertised were for just one or two commodities. This practice continued into the 1730s, with the number of goods advertised by price increasing steadily. Indeed, the regular notices placed from about 1737 by the grocer Robert Baret closely resemble the later advertisements of Eagleton and others (see Figure 6.2). There was a range of qualities and prices, and the promise that other goods were sold 'at the very lowest prices'. Other retailers also emphasized their cut prices, William Livingstone advertising 'The best Old York River Tobacco at 20*d.* down to 16*d.* per pound. Neat and well manufactured.'[92] Both Baret and Livingstone appear to have been conventional retailers who chose to promote their business through competitive pricing. Rather different was the India Warehouse, for which advertisements appeared in the early 1780s. Originally a tea warehouse, the business had been expanded to include a wide range of groceries, textiles, and clothing, all of which had the very lowest prices fixed upon them—a practice that closely resembles those of the drapery warehouses seen by Alexander as leading the shift to fixed and ticketed prices.[93]

It is difficult to judge whether grocers were particularly innovative in their promotion of fixed prices. In Norwich, they formed a large proportion of those

[91] *Norwich Gazette*, 10–17 Mar. 1711, 5–12 Jan. 1712.
[92] *Norwich Mercury*, 23 May 1761.
[93] *Norwich Mercury*, 5 Apr. 1783; Alexander, *Retailing in England*, 136.

advertising in this way, but were by no means alone. As early as 1711, two hosiers were engaged in a somewhat acrimonious campaign of competitive pricing.[94] A generation later, William Steel advertised a long list of drapery 'at the lowest Prices; for Ready Money only', and the range of goods advertised by price expanded thereafter to include, among other things, wallpaper and stays.[95] Yet there is evidence that groceries were especially amenable to fixed pricing. William Chase, a bookseller and stationer by trade, sold a wide range of goods, from beauty products to musical instruments. Many of these were mentioned in his advertisements, but only Indian ink, Spanish snuff, and a range of teas, coffees, and chocolates were listed with fixed prices.[96] The motivations behind selling at fixed prices are also hard to discern. For the London tea warehouses, it was a deliberate sales strategy: initially they sought to attract trade away from the established dealers who sold on the basis of service rather than price; later they tried to keep ahead of their rivals.[97] Something similar was probably true for Norwich shopkeepers, especially those selling groceries. Even when prices were not specified, many advertisers insisted that their goods were sold at the best or lowest price.

In some ways, it is possible to see a link between novel goods and new forms of consumption, on the one hand, and new retail practices, on the other. The innovative and increasingly aggressive strategies of tea dealers were closely linked to the growing demand for cheaper teas. It is unlikely that traditional forms of supply could have serviced the massive expansion in consumption seen in the late eighteenth century. The quantity of tea delivered out of the EIC warehouses grew from 4.9 million lb per annum in 1781–3, to 21 million in 1800–1 and 30 million in 1834. Over the same period, the number of licensed retailers went from 33,788 to 91,701.[98] Yet there are problems in equating too closely these two processes. Tea was hardly a novelty and was widely consumed before 'new' systems of selling became widespread in the 1780s. The evidence from Norwich, meanwhile, shows that price-based selling of tea and other groceries was practised from the 1730s. Equally, tea was by no means the only commodity sold on price: so too were many well-established products (sugar, tobacco, spices) and a range of newer or newly popular goods (ready-made pickles and sauces, cayenne). Sales of such goods were no doubt increased by their promotion through competitive pricing, but were driven by changing consumer tastes. Knowledge of these shifts and the ability to provide for them relied on grocers retaining much of their traditional expertise. Indeed, it is telling that the spread of fixed prices does not appear to have been accompanied by a retreat from established practices of service-based selling.

Few grocers who promoted fixed prices insisted upon ready money, which suggests that credit sales remained important to the businesses of regular shopkeepers, if not the large-scale tea warehouses. Indeed, Alexander's analysis confirms that

[94] *Norwich Gazette*, 10–17 Mar. 1711, 5–12 May 1711.
[95] *Norwich Mercury*, 19 Nov. 1737, 1 Aug. 1761, 9 May 1761.
[96] *Norwich Mercury*, 26 Mar. 1737, 11 June 1737.
[97] Mui and Mui, *Shops and Shopkeeping*, 22–4, 269–72.
[98] Mui and Mui, *Shops and Shopkeeping*, 251.

credit was central to many retail businesses through the early decades of the nineteenth century.[99] The grocer and draper Joseph Gibbs of Ramsey had healthy sales of £34 per week in the 1830s; his contemporary, Peter Burdell of Sheerness, had a lower turnover, with weekly takings of about £12. For both, credit accounted for half of their sales—a figure that appears typical for grocers, but was substantially lower than that for many high-class drapers, hatters, and shoemakers. The account books of shopkeepers such as Gibbs and Burdell were full of small (unpaid) debts, just like those of their predecessors. Indeed, their position in relation to bad debts appears to have worsened. Analysis of grocers' accounts presented to the Court of Bankruptcy shows that doubtful debts comprised on average 47 per cent of credit sales, compared with 29 per cent in the late seventeenth and early eighteenth centuries. While the situation was not as bad as might appear—bad debt generally represented a more modest 3–5 per cent of turnover—there was clearly a problem with calling in a significant proportion of accounts.

Faced with these problems, nineteenth-century shopkeepers resorted to a variety of mechanisms for managing credit. The St Austell grocer Jonathan Pedlar had a large number of account customers, including a miner called John Bear, who purchased a variety of groceries on a weekly basis, paying between £1 1s. and £3 3s. each month towards his bill. Bear's spending gradually ran ahead of his payments and his debt grew from 6s. 6½d. in September 1839 to £5 16s. 9½d. in November 1844. Like William Wood before him, Pedlar restricted the credit of this indebted customer, eventually withdrawing further credit in 1845. But Pedlar also deployed other techniques, imposing differential charges on some of his overdue accounts. These varied not with the size of the debt, but apparently with Pedlar's perception of the debtor: in 1843 John Boyle was charged 1.5 per cent on a debt of £24 10s. 4½d. whereas Peter Merifield had to pay 5 per cent on £15 18s. 9d. Other retailers managed credit more actively. Giving evidence in a bankruptcy hearing, the Salisbury grocer William Hillier claimed that he always 'demanded ready money for the first two or three orders'.[100] That he then went on to offer credit illustrates its continued importance as part of the service that shopkeepers were expected to provide to their customers. As one witness to a parliamentary inquiry into debt put it:

There are many businesses in which it is absolutely impossible to avoid giving credit...we are obliged to live by the goodwill of our neighbours, and if we were not to accommodate them by giving credit, and very often we cannot do it with safety, we should get that ill-will, which would be very detrimental to our trade.[101]

In short, the logic behind credit remained unchanged: it was a service offered to customers in order to facilitate sales and by which shopkeeper and customer were bound together. The 'modernization' of grocery selling was thus patchy and contingent, and the importance of reputation remained paramount. Its points of

---

[99] Alexander, *Retailing in England*, 174–85.
[100] Alexander, *Retailing in England*, 182.
[101] Report on the Recovery of Small Debts, 43–4.

reference might have shifted away from sociability and towards efficiency and price; but questions of integrity, trust, and respectability remained central to the grocer's standing and business.

CONCLUSIONS

To what extent did the grocery trade witness structural change in its retail practices between the Restoration and the start of Victoria's reign? While standardized prices were probably commonplace at the start of this period, there was a growing tendency for these to be fixed and, more importantly, advertised. This not only meant that consumers could know what they might expect to pay for particular goods before going into the shop, but also that price emerged as a key selling point for certain retailers. The precise timing and spread of such practices were complex and probably related to local trading conditions, especially the level and nature of competition. This was certainly instrumental in shaping the strategies and advertising campaigns of the tea warehouses. Ready-money transactions had always formed part of any retailer's trade, although again they became more important through the eighteenth century, especially in terms of promoting the lower prices that they facilitated. Yet only a small number of retailers attempted to trade solely for cash, most continuing to offer credit facilities to those whom they judged worthy. It is more difficult to summarize the impact of these changes, along with others such as the introduction of new commodities or products, on the everyday retail practices of grocers. Fixed prices and an insistence on ready money would certainly have simplified accounting procedures, but it probably had less effect on the way in which shopkeepers interacted with their customers. Most groceries continued to require careful processing, weighing, and packaging, so that visits to the grocer could be time-consuming and involve a degree of homely sociability or more polite interaction. These practices continued through the nineteenth century and into the twentieth century, as did the need for shopkeepers to offer and manage credit.

Selling groceries is thus a story of change, but also marked continuities. What does this tell us about the link between retail and consumer change? Was development led by supply or demand? It seems doubtful that the enormous growth in the consumption of tea could have been accommodated within existing retail structures, but other products were sold in significantly larger quantities without such dramatic changes. Sugar, for example, continued to be traded in its myriad forms—each with its attendant demands for storage, processing, and packaging—in much the same way throughout the period. Moreover, service-based selling remained important as grocers continued to provide their customers with help in choosing goods by offering information about price, availability, and quality. While there was a move to provide more of this information in printed form, most consumers relied on their local grocer or, as with the Gibbards, retained a close relationship with a distant supplier. This reminds us of the continued importance of reputation and respectability to processes of buying and selling. Much as Blondé and Van Damme argue, bonds of trust were cemented rather than broken by the introduction of new goods and with them new concerns about the supply, quality, price, and integrity of products.[102] Such concerns were best addressed by focusing on service while embracing new forms of promoting and selling goods. Focusing on heroic figures such as Wedgwood has tended to exaggerate the speed and completeness of retail change. Looking instead at ordinary provincial shops reveals how 'modern' and traditional practices often went on hand-in-hand, procedures being moulded to the changing needs of consumers.[103] This suggests that changes in supply systems, including retailing, were driven by consumer demand, but does not mean retail innovations were unimportant in shaping that demand. Indeed, one of the key areas of change came in terms of the growing number and shifting character of published advertisements, to which we turn our attention next.

---

[102] Blondé and Van Damme, 'Retail Growth'.
[103] See Cox, *Complete Tradesman*, esp. 223–8.

7

Exotic, Empire, or Everyday? Advertising Groceries

INTRODUCTION

That eighteenth-century advertising was widespread and increasingly sophisticated is a commonplace. Early work by Walker, McKendrick, and Mui and Mui has hardly caused an avalanche of interest, but the basic parameters of printed advertising are well established.[1] Newspaper advertisements became more numerous through the eighteenth century, although there is some debate over whether this formed a sea change in the marketing strategies of retailers, as Mui and Mui have argued. Indeed, Cox has suggested that comparatively few tradesmen chose to advertise in either provincial or London newspapers, established and high-status shopkeepers being particularly reluctant to engage in what Wedgwood, among others, viewed as pushy sales techniques.[2] Yet this appears to have been a shrinking minority of opinion: by the mid-eighteenth century, the growing opportunities afforded by an expanding provincial press were coupled with a noticeable shift in attitudes among shopkeepers.[3] In 1757 Postlethwayt could argue that, 'however mean and disgraceful it was looked on a few years since ... to apply to the public by advertising in the papers, at present times it seems to be esteemed quite otherwise'.[4] This sentiment was underscored in the same year by an editorial in first issue of the *Liverpool Chronicle*, which reads as an apologia for the newspaper carrying advertisements—or, perhaps, an appeal for tradesmen to place notices in the newspaper. In particular, it notes that

it is become now fashionable for very eminent tradesmen to publish their business and the peculiar goods wherein they deal, in the News Papers, by way of Advertisement; nor can any one make appear what disgrace there can be in this, for do not the great trading corporations apprize the public of their sales in the public News Papers? In a word Advertisements in these papers form, on the general, to be of no less utility to the public in the concerns of real business, to the trading and busy World, than the Common news is to people of more leisure.[5]

---

[1] Walker, 'Advertising'; McKendrick, 'George Packwood'; Mui and Mui, *Shops and Shopkeeping*.
[2] Mui and Mui, *Shops and Shopkeeping*, 225–48; Cox, *Complete Tradesman*, 108–9.
[3] Ferdinand, 'Selling it to the Provinces', 398; Barker, *Business of Women*, 78–9; Cox and Dannehl, *Perceptions of Retailing*, 75.
[4] Postlethwayt, *Universal Directory*, 22.
[5] *Liverpool Chronicle*, 6 May 1757.

The pitch here was clearly towards the established tradesmen of the town, who were, perhaps, reluctant to see their names appearing alongside the patent medicines and books that formed the largest proportion of newspaper advertisements through the middle decades of the eighteenth century.[6] However, Ferdinand's analysis of the *Salisbury Journal* reveals that these declined in relative numbers through this period: from around 45 per cent in the 1740s to less than 30 per cent by the 1760s. At the same time, notices placed by local tradesmen and professionals offering goods, services, or leisure activities grew from 17 to 28 per cent.[7] Moreover, many shopkeepers in provincial towns began to adopt the practice, already established among London retailers, of issuing illustrated handbills and trade cards. The use to which these were put varied: they were mostly deployed to cement relationships with existing customers, but were sometimes distributed more widely in an attempt to expand customer networks.[8] At their height they were being issued by a wide range of provincial tradesmen, including many in small market towns. If illustrated by a well-known artist or engraver, trade cards could be very costly; but they could also be had more cheaply. Indeed, Bickham suggests that 15*s.* would buy between 500 and 1,000 illustrated cards in the second half of the eighteenth century—about the same as three medium-sized advertisements in a provincial newspaper.[9] This made them worth including in even quite modest orders or sending out to a wide range of customers with whom the shopkeeper had (or desired) some connection. Despite this, their use was in decline by the nineteenth century, partly because customer networks were growing too large to be reached in this manner. However, many of the same images were deployed on bill headings and in advertisements in trade directories.[10]

In the eighteenth century, both newspaper advertisements and trade cards were primarily linked to the individual, rather than the product, George Packwood being unusual in this regard.[11] However, Wischermann certainly overstates the case when he argues that it was only with the introduction of 'new and formerly unknown goods into the market' in the early nineteenth century that 'a need arose for advertising which provided the customer with information about the product, not just where it could be found'.[12] The personal nature of many eighteenth-century advertisements does not mean that products were irrelevant. Indeed, those for

---

[6] Public auctions were also commonly advertised (see Lyna and Van Damme, 'Strategy of Seduction?').

[7] Ferdinand, 'Selling it to the Provinces', 399–402.

[8] Barker, *Business of Women*, 74–5; Berg and Clifford, 'Commerce and the Commodity', 191–2; Berg and Clifford, 'Selling Consumption', 147, 162. See also Stobart, 'Selling (through) Politeness'.

[9] Bickham, 'Eating the Empire', 84–5.

[10] The images used on trade cards were often reproduced as headers on bills, and, more occasionally, the cards themselves were used for recording bills. For a useful overview of the development of such ephemera, see Lambert, *Nation of Shopkeepers*.

[11] Ferdinand, 'Selling it to the Provinces', 399–402; Barker, *Business of Women*, 80; McKendrick, 'George Packwood'.

[12] Wischermann, 'Placing Advertising', 8.

a range of groceries, and especially tea, were concerned with communicating key messages about the nature, provenance, quality, and price of goods. Fully to understand the importance of advertising to the grocery trade, it is necessary to explore in detail the subject, composition, language, and appearance of trade cards and newspaper advertisements.[13] In treating these two media in turn, I consciously juxtapose their form and content: the intensely visual imagery of trade cards with its emphasis of empire and the exotic contrasting with the more prosaic lists of goods and prices that characterize notices in newspapers. That said, the picture was more complex than this simple dichotomy would allow, with the exotic and the everyday placed alongside one another in both forms of advertising. The consumers were thus situated simultaneously in a global–imperial economy and in their own consumption milieu. Examining these two contexts and the links between them thus provides a fuller insight into how groceries were perceived by shopkeepers and consumers. More generally, it tells us much about the active role of shopkeepers in shaping demand for what began as 'new luxuries' but increasingly became everyday goods.

WHY ADVERTISE?

The purpose served by advertising is a knotty question that cannot be fully addressed here.[14] In essence, advertisements aim to generate business and reduce transaction costs by communicating to (potential) customers what is available and from where.[15] Such information was important to the success of any retail business and could be acquired from a variety of sources: previous experience, personal interaction, informal social networks, or browsing in the shop itself. But it also came through reading advertisements in newspapers and trade cards, both of which contained a wealth of information on the range, type, and quality of goods available. As with shop interiors, they informed consumers about the availability of goods and formed a carefully constructed representation of the retail business. Richards has argued that the development of a 'specific representational order of advertising' occurred in the second half of the nineteenth century, its origins in Britain lying in the Great Exhibition of 1851.[16] However, as Cox and Dannehl have shown, many eighteenth-century advertisements drew on broader cultural and political constructs rather than simply detailing the goods as goods. Similarly, studies by Barker, Berry, and Stobart have demonstrated the ways in which advertisements drew on and promoted notions of civility and politeness through their language, structure, and symbolism, while McClintock and Bickham, among others,

---

[13] See Gotti, 'Advertising Discourse', 23–38; Gieszinger, *History of Advertising Language*.

[14] For a brief discussion, see Wischermann, 'Placing Advertising', 15–25. More detailed analysis can be found in Richards, *Commodity Culture*.

[15] Berg and Clifford, 'Selling Consumption', 155; Cox and Dannehl, *Perceptions of Retailing*, 71–4; Lyna and Van Damme, 'Strategy of Seduction?'.

[16] Richards, *Commodity Culture*, 17–72.

have shown the sophistication with which empire was deployed as a marketing device.[17] Advertisements thus sought to attract trade by creating a 'positive impression on the minds of the consuming public'.[18] At the same time, they also carried messages about the cultural significance of goods—as polite, fashionable, exotic, imperial, healthy, and so on—and about some of the socio-economic processes of production and consumption. Trade cards were especially important in this regard: they were promotional representations of the goods being sold by the shopkeeper, but they also carried meanings in their own right. This symbolism needed to be interpreted by the consumer just as carefully as that of the goods themselves.

Within this general framework, the position of those selling groceries is especially intriguing. Many of the goods that they offered were imported, some of them from colonies or via chartered companies, and thus can be seen as foreign, exotic, or imperial. Their consumption has been closely linked with polite and rational social practices, from afternoon tea in the domestic realm to the public sphere of the coffee house. We might, therefore, expect that grocers, tea dealers, and the like would be enthusiastic advertisers, producing sophisticated advertisements rich with symbolism and playing on the imperial connections, exoticism, and polite credentials of their wares. Moreover, with such a wide range of reference points, they would have been able to deploy a number of tropes and selling points, drawing on symbolic imagery and playing on variety and choice. In reality, it appears that grocers were not among those retailers most inclined to advertise in newspapers, although Bickham certainly overstates their scarcity.[19] A survey of various provincial newspapers from the 1740s to the 1820s suggests that those selling durable goods were most numerous.[20] Drapers were especially prominent, perhaps because—as many of their advertisements highlighted—they needed to inform the public about the availability of new fashions. In contrast, grocers, tea dealers, and the like appear much less frequently. Between September 1741 and July 1742, the *Norwich Gazette* carried just four original advertisements for groceries; from April 1778 to March 1779, there were only eight such notices placed in the Chester newspaper *Adams Weekly Courant*, and the *Bristol Mercury* contained the same number in the calendar year 1820. Each of these newspapers had wide circulations, stretching well beyond city boundaries to incorporate surrounding towns and villages, and often carrying advertisements from these 'hinterland' tradesmen as well as those from the place in which the newspaper was produced. Taking Chester as an example, and assuming that the *Courant* drew advertisements only from retailers in Cheshire (and it is very clear that, in reality, its readership spread far into north Wales as well), there were at least 168 grocers, tea dealers, and tobacconists who could potentially place advertisements.[21] This means that less

---

[17] Cox and Dannehl, *Perceptions of Retailing*, 100–9; Barker, *Business of Women*, 72–89; Berry, 'Promoting Taste'; Stobart, 'Selling (through) Politeness'; McClintock, *Imperial Leather*; Bickham, 'Eating the Empire'.

[18] Barker, *Business of Women*, 72.

[19] Bickham, 'Eating the Empire', 82.

[20] For details of the sample, see Table 7.1.

[21] Barfoot and Wilkes, *Universal British Directory*, list 168 grocers, tea dealers, and tobacconists. Any growth in numbers between the 1770s and 1790s would easily be offset by the incomplete coverage of the directory.

than 5 per cent of retailers chose to advertise in the local press. Even though there was clearly some growth in advertising through the late eighteenth and early nineteenth centuries, numbers remained small. That said, these notices would have reached a broad readership in coffee houses and taverns as well as individual homes. Trade cards and handbills probably had a narrower circulation, but appear to have been more favoured by grocers than other retailers. The John Johnson Collection indexes 239 entries for grocers and 157 for groceries in comparison to just 98 for drapers and 148 for drapery.[22]

The relative lack of newspaper advertising may reflect the more muted influence of fashion on the grocery trade or perhaps a different level or operation of competition. Advertising is, after all, a competitive device, even if the objective is more to 'seduce' customers than to claim a larger market share.[23] Indeed, it is clear that at least some of those selling groceries were keenly aware of the competition. In 1820, Sparrow & Co.—one of a new breed of London tea dealers—were anxious to cement their reputation and distance themselves from those that they saw as inferior competitors. They warned against shopkeepers who, 'from their former avocations, can know but little of the real qualities and properties of Tea, but who are inundating both Town and Country with the most bombastic advertisements, letters, handbills, &c. in the true lottery style'. In contrast, Sparrow & Co. highlighted their 'judgement matured by upwards of twenty years experience'.[24] This invective gives us an idea both of the array of advertising techniques available and of the way in which some were still viewed, at least in polemic terms, in a disparaging manner. The widespread use of trade cards implies a similar concern for reputation and standing. Image construction could operate through the mechanism of distributing these cards, but also through the illustrations themselves: the associations and symbolism that they invoked.

SELLING EMPIRE AND THE EXOTIC

Bickham asserts that 'three products dominated the imagery of shops selling imperial foods: tobacco, tea and coffee'.[25] Yet this presents a narrow and rather static view of the trade cards and bill heads used by grocers. These, like the goods that they advertised, changed according to prevailing trends and fashions. Many of the earliest examples—especially those of London shopkeepers—reproduced the sign under which the retailer traded. Thus, the 1737 bill head of Thomas Arnold, a grocer trading at the Ship on the corner of Watery Lane and Fleet Street in London, included an image of a three-masted vessel, while that of Thomas Edwards

---

[22] See the index of the John Johnson Collection, available at <http://www.bodley.ox.ac.uk/johnson/johnson.htm> (accessed 9 Mar. 2012).

[23] Lyna and Van Damme, 'Strategy of Seduction?'.

[24] *Liverpool Mercury*, 21 Jan. 1820. See also Mui and Mui, *Shops and Shopkeeping*, 256–61, who argue that this kind of advertisement was a product of the shifting nature of the tea trade in the late eighteenth and early nineteenth centuries.

[25] Bickham, 'Eating the Empire', 85.

illustrated the fig tree that appeared on his shop sign in Brewer Street, London.[26] This explicit link between the card, the retailer, and its geographical location was important, given the personal nature of both trade cards and shopping experiences. However, some retailers sought to exploit the product-specific nature of their sign or to augment their card with images of the wares that they sold. The first of these approaches is illustrated by Elizabeth Hodnet, who sold 'all sort of Grocery, Oils & Pickles, Mould and Store Candles, Mops Brooms & Brushes &c.' from her shop at 3 Hanover Street. Appropriately, she traded under the sign of the Golden Sugar Loaves and Oil Jar, and illustrated her trade card accordingly with three sugar loaves arranged elegantly (if improbably) over a decorated jar set on a low table.[27] Those receiving her card would thus be reminded of her address and of the nature of the products available there. The hybridizing of shop signs and shop goods, meanwhile, is evident on the trade card of the china-man and glass seller John Cotterell, who also sold India fans, lacquered ware, tea, coffee, chocolate, and snuff. He traded near the Mansion House at the 'Indian Queen and Canister'—the latter perhaps being an element that he had added to the sign himself to underscore his tea-dealing business. His card, from about 1751, included a typical depiction of an Indian queen, complete with retinue, but also illustrates the range of his wares: china, a fan, and a canister labelled 'fine tea'.[28]

By the middle decades of the eighteenth century, trade cards increasingly illustrated the goods being offered for sale. Their style was also changing, images often being structured as elaborate cartouches, with the goods on offer arranged within and around rococo frames. Sometimes these appear to have been aimed at communicating the range of goods available, underscoring the lists often printed in the centre of the cartouche. Thus, the card of the London grocer George Farr includes not just his shop sign (the beehive and three sugar loaves), but also illustrations of tea canisters, barrels of rum and brandy, Scotch rappée, and snuff making. On other occasions, commodities were set alongside images of manufacturing or processing, as with the trade card of Benjamin Pearkes of Worcester, which illustrated tobacco leaves being dried, packed, and milled.[29] This reinforced messages about the quality and authenticity of the wares, as well as producing a fashionable and elegant picture. As an image, it stands in stark contrast with the figure of the native American (often pictured smoking a pipe), which was commonly deployed to symbolize tobacco—as in the *c*.1760 trade card of Turner, who traded at the two Black Boys on Tower Street in London. Even further removed from the elegant stylization of Pearkes was Archer's *c*.1770 trade card, which showed a West Indian plantation with black slaves packing and loading barrels of tobacco onto a waiting ship while a white overseer lounges against other barrels, calmly smoking his pipe.[30] Bickham argues that these two typify the imperial imagery deployed when promoting tobacco. In reality, they

---

[26] Bodl., JJC, Bill Headings 11 (67); SCLA, DR18/5/4711.
[27] Bodl., JJC, Trade Cards 11 (26c).
[28] Bodl., JJC, Trade Cards 6 (18).
[29] Bodl., JJC, Trade Cards 11 (21); Bodl., JJC, Trade Cards 28 (26).
[30] BM, Heal Collection, box 12, card 117.156; box 12, card 117.4; both reproduced in Bickham, 'Eating the Empire', 86–7.

were one, albeit important, genre adopted by tobacconists. Pearkes's trade card drew on allusions to European fashionable design rather than imperial production or racial stereotypes.[31] Importantly, though, it was the card and perhaps the retailer, rather than the products, that were contextualized in this way.

Trade cards promoting coffee also varied in the imagery used. Some of the very earliest illustrated interior scenes from coffee houses. That promoting Will's coffee powder, for example, shows four seated men engaged in a variety of activities and being served by a waiter pouring coffee. Here, the link is to the venue where the coffee can be purchased and consumed: Manwaring's Coffee House in Falcon Court off Fleet Street.[32] Other cards played on the strong association of coffee drinking with the Turkey and Arabia. Not only was this connection seen as a positive reason for drinking coffee; it was also used in the promotion of venues where it could be consumed. Numerous coffee houses in London and the provinces were named the 'Turk's Head' or the 'Sultan's Head' and many issued cards illustrating the same.[33] This broad notion of exoticism—of linking the English coffee house to those in the Middle East—was sustained even in the face of growing imports of plantation coffee, produced in the West Indies. As we saw earlier, Turkey remained associated with higher-grade coffees, so retaining the Turk as a symbol for coffee thus made a great deal of business sense. There were also later trade cards that made a positive virtue of the imperial connections of West India coffee. That of the London coffee merchant Anthony Schick (1812) shows Britannia receiving goods from her colonial subjects or 'lending a helping hand to her colonies', as the accompanying legend tells us.[34]

In contrast, trade cards promoting tea displayed a remarkable degree of consistency in the imagery deployed. They drew on the broader move in trade-card design to replace abstract designs with classical or romantic imagery, incorporating idealized landscapes and elegant human figures. Within this general movement, grocers' cards stand out in their depiction of Chinese people with tea chests, ginger jars, and pagodas—a formula that had become all but ubiquitous by the early nineteenth century, well before the mid-Victorian advertisements examined by Rappaport.[35] Again, Bickham reads these as depictions of empire—part of the growing public engagement in the British imperial experience—but their complexity and variety of detail resist any single interpretation. They also played upon the fascination with and admiration for China that pervaded until the mid-nineteenth century, linking into contemporary artistic representations of the country to produce idealized, pastoral images, while drawing allusions to polite European practices of tea drinking. This situates these promotional images in an interesting place with regard to McCracken's discussion of displaced meaning, China being cast as the 'other' into which Western cultural ideals were projected.[36]

[31] See Berg and Clifford, 'Selling Consumption', 149–54.
[32] Bodl., JJC, Douce adds. 138 (84).
[33] Cowan, *Social Life of Coffee*, 115.
[34] BM, Banks Collection, box 4, card 38.10, reproduced in Bickham, 'Eating the Empire'.
[35] Rappaport, 'Packaging China', 136.
[36] McCracken, *Culture and Consumption*, 104–17.

Within this overall genre, three broad groupings can be identified. The first focused on human figures and exotic commodities, often packaged up, as if for export. The card issued by William Dax of Welshpool shows a simple scene with two Chinese figures in conversation, one seated on a stack of tea chests, while a pagoda towers in the background.[37] These formed the stock elements of most 'exotic' images, connecting grocers and their wares to distant points of supply. They are developed much more fully on the card of Thomas Sheard of Oxford. This shows several figures in Chinese costume: some are picking tea and laying it out on sheets to dry, while others are packing the finished product into chests. The whole is set within an approximation to a Chinese landscape, complete with mountains and pagoda.[38] As a representation of the products being sold by Sheard, this image affirms their provenance and presents them as authentic and exotic. The bill head of Thomas Dainty of Northampton focuses more closely on the Chinese figures (Figure 7.1). One is depicted leaning against tea chests and barrels marked up with 'coffee' and 'tobacco and snuff'; the other holds a spice jar, and a sugar loaf stands in the foreground. Here we see a broader range of grocer's wares being linked to China, despite their origin in other disparate parts of the globe. In effect, China was being mobilized as shorthand for the exotic nature of these goods, despite their obvious and well-recognized provenance elsewhere.[39]

Dainty's card also includes a ship sailing along in the background—an allusion to trade with Europe. This element is clearer in the second grouping, which make the export trade more explicitly part of the image, strengthening the portrayal of these goods as exotic and of their consumers as part of an international and perhaps

Fig. 7.1. Bill head of Thomas Dainty of Northampton, grocer, tea dealer, hop & cheese factor, *c*.1835 (© Northamptonshire Library and Information Services)

[37] NCL, uncatalogued trade ephemera.
[38] Bodl., JJC, Oxford Trading 4.
[39] NCL, uncatalogued trade ephemera. The frequent portrayal of sugar in these images is overlooked by Bickham, 'Eating the Empire', 92.

imperial system of exchange. The trade card of Andrew William Lee—a tea dealer, grocer, and cheesemonger in Sunderland—shows the ubiquitous Chinese figure in the foreground holding a sprig of tea and being fanned by a black slave. He looks over to a stack of tea chests, sugar cones, and barrels, while in the background a European ship sails into the distance.[40] Both the figures and the commodities form an interesting cosmopolitan blend of east and west, linked by European trade. This notion of east meeting west is brought to the fore in the illustration used by G. Edwards, a grocer and cheesemonger in Gravesend. Here we have a Chinese figure and what is probably an English merchant, apparently negotiating the purchase of the commodities that surround them. Their cultural differences are emphasized by their dress and their deportment: the Englishman is standing and active while the Chinese figure is seated and passive—reinforcing notions of the west as the initiator of trade (and, more generally, the agent of historical change).[41] These differences in culture and modernity are reinforced by their respective backdrops: a junk and a fully rigged brig, although here there is at least a hint of Chinese involvement in the processes of supply.[42] The notion of exchange is also apparent in the nineteenth-century card of Robert Kitton of Norwich, which forms an intriguing variation on the oriental theme (Figure 7.2). On one side of the card is a Chinese man, a pagoda, and tea canisters, underneath which is written 'coffee, chocolate and spices'; in the middle is a trading vessel and Kitton's address, and on the other side

Fig. 7.2. Trade card of Robert Kitton of Norwich, tea dealer and tobacconist, early nineteenth century (© Norfolk Library and Information Services)

[40] Bodl., JJC, Trade Cards 11 (100). [41] Crang, *Cultural Geography*, 66–7.
[42] Bodl., JJC, Trade Cards 11 (83).

is a Scottish man, smoking a cigar and leaning against a barrel containing Virginia and Maryland tobacco.[43] Here we have certain imperial and exotic foods assembled under the catch-all Chinese label; but also a rare example of an imperial product being associated more directly with the place in which it was processed rather than produced—that is, Scotland and, more specifically, Glasgow.

This cultural and commercial interchange, and the notion of authenticity, is both carried a stage further and linked back to polite social practices in the trade cards of Joseph Ward of Coventry and John Smith of Northampton (Figure 7.3).[44] In both, a group of Chinese people are shown taking tea, sitting in upright chairs around distinctly European-looking tables. In Ward's, a black man smokes a long earthenware pipe—the standard symbol for tobacco, but here mixed with a Chinese scene to produce an imperial–exotic montage. Both tobacco smoking and tea ceremony are presented as 'authentic' practices to which polite consumers were connected, the latter through their own china tea services and rituals of tea drinking.[45] The link is made explicit in a smaller number of images that depict Chinese men taking tea with European women. The undated trade card of William Marshall of London has the woman in Chinese dress with her companion pouring tea (itself an interesting reversal of gender roles), while in the background a woman in European clothing carrying a parasol crosses a traditional Chinese bridge. A similar arrangement is found in the 1824 newspaper advertisement of the London and Yorkshire Tea Warehouse. Here, the Chinese man points skywards as he and his European female companion sit on tea chests drinking tea.[46] Setting Chinese and European figures alongside each other in such polite social rituals served to domesticate the exotic, the commodity acting as a bridge between western culture and its oriental 'other'—much as McCracken argues.[47] It also served to reinforce messages

Fig. 7.3. Bill head of John Smith of Northampton, grocer and tea dealer, *c*.1822 (© Northamptonshire Library and Information Services)

[43] NLIS, NP00012331.
[44] NCL, uncatalogued trade ephemera; BM, Banks Collection 68.143 (MY17-WRDJ).
[45] Smith, *Consumption*, 171–5.
[46] Bodl., JJC, Trade Cards 11 (33); *Bristol Mercury*, 6 Aug. 1824.
[47] McCracken, *Culture and Consumption*, 109–15.

about the authenticity of the product (the tea came directly from the Chinese 'producer' and was drunk by both characters) and the social practices. What is notable about all these images is the way in which the emphasis is always placed on tea and on the link to China, not merely as a source for this commodity, but as a shorthand for the exotic. The image of the orient is simple and stereotypical: in drawing on an unthinking racial typecasting, it forms an easily read message about authenticity and quality.[48] In doing so, it might even be seen as restating displaced meaning—an attempt to remake tea (the bridge between reality and an ideal of orientalism) into something exotic and special when, in reality, it had become familiar and everyday.

These powerful images form a remarkably consistent representation of commodities and behaviour—one that dominated the grocery trade from the late eighteenth to the mid-nineteenth century and beyond. Even images that were apparently far removed from this genre could be shaped by its norms and idioms. The best example of this—and one that I have discussed elsewhere[49]—is the card for Henry Waterfall's, Provision Warehouse in Coventry, which drew its strength from the allusions that it made to wider print culture and the assumed understanding of this by those receiving and reading the card.[50] In an interesting twist on the Chinese tea motif, a classical female figure is placed in the midst of a rural scene. The image cleverly draws on the growing fashion for the pastoral—the type of engraving or painting that would adorn the walls of polite customers to whom Waterfall's card was directed—but the specific point of reference is clear. A windmill appears in place of the pagoda, while sacks of grain, barrels of butter, and ham replace the tea chests and ginger jars. The allusion is clear and deliberate, yet its success relies upon the consumer being aware of both idioms. The illustration thus operates at a number of levels: an advertisement for the goods, a visual pun, and a fashionable image that drew on and reinforced notions of taste and polite discernment.

The relationship between imported groceries and consumer identity constructed through trade cards was clearly significant in how grocers saw their businesses and how they wished others to perceive them. Imperial associations were important, and retailers certainly did not hide them, but they formed only one trope within a wide array of symbolic and descriptive imagery that also placed considerable emphasis on the exotic and cosmopolitan. As advertisements, these trade cards were certainly intended to promote sales, suggesting that links with China formed a key touchstone in terms of making goods attractive—a point to which we return later. However, cards and bill heads were not the only form of printed advertisement deployed by grocers: newspapers were also used to communicate with potential customers. While they advertised a similar range of goods, their form and character were very different; so too was the image they constructed of the retailer.

---

[48] For a fuller discussion of the relationship between race and advertising, see McClintock, *Imperial Leather*.

[49] See Stobart, 'Selling (through) Politeness', 323.   [50] Bodl., JJC, Trade Cards 11 (76).

EVERYDAY GOODS? POLITENESS
AND PRACTICALITIES

As noted earlier, newspaper advertisements were a significant, if not defining, element of the grocer's array of marketing devices. They almost invariably highlighted the tradesman or woman as the source of particular goods, thus providing the consumer with essential market information and encouraging more business for the advertiser.[51] Given the diverse nature of their stock-in-trade, it is unsurprising that grocers' advertisements made mention of a wide range of goods, from coffee to capers to candles. Many of them were imported, with 'new' or imperial groceries featuring prominently (Table 7.1). In part, this was a reflection of the increasing tendency for London tea warehouses to advertise in the provincial press—a point discussed in more detail below. Certainly, the growing proportion of advertisements for tea contrasts with the steady or declining proportion of those for tobacco, which appeared in nearly half the advertisements for groceries in the 1740s and 1750s, but less than one in twenty by the early nineteenth century. Perhaps most surprising, though, is the limited reference to spices and sugar—arguably the old and new staples of the grocer's trade.

Table 7.1. Groceries advertised in provincial newspapers, 1740s–1820s

Commodity	1740s–50s		1770s–80s		1820s		Total	
	No. (N = 18)	%	No. (N = 34)	%	No. (N = 34)	%	No. (N = 86)	%
Tea	10	33.6	26	76.5	31	91.2	67	77.9
Coffee	7	38.9	15	44.1	15	44.1	37	43.0
Chocolate	6	33.3	14	41.2	12	35.3	32	37.2
Grocery	7	38.9	7	20.6	4	11.8	18	20.9
Tobacco/ snuff	8	44.4	5	14.7	1	2.9	14	16.3
Sugar	2	11.1	4	11.8	5	14.7	11	12.8
Wines/ spirits	5	27.8	2	5.9	4	11.8	11	12.8
Dried fruit	1	5.6	4	11.8	2	5.9	7	8.1
Spice	0	0.0	0	0.0	6	17.6	6	7.0
Paper	1	5.6	1	2.9	3	8.8	5	5.8
Cheese/ butter	0	0.0	2	5.9	2	5.9	4	4.7
Other	6	33.3	16	47.1	2	5.9	24	27.9

Note: Repeat advertisements are excluded from the analysis.

Sources: *Adams Weekly Courant* (1774–1780); *Aris's Birmingham Gazette* (1755–6, 1782); *Bristol Mercury* (1820–4); *Gore's Liverpool Advertiser* (1770); *Liverpool Mercury* (1820); *Northampton Mercury* (1743–4, 1780); *Norwich Gazette* (1741–2, 1757); *Worcester Journal* (1742–52).

[51] See Lyna and Van Damme, 'Strategy of Seduction?'.

It is not easy to make sense of the changing emphases within grocers' advertisements. The passing of the mid-eighteenth-century craze for snuff may partly explain the declining number mentioning tobacco, and the rise and fall of coffee and chocolate can be linked to the phenomenal growth in consumption of tea. Selling tea had become a much more overtly competitive business, especially after the Commutation Act of 1784, so it is understandable that tea dealers would be anxious to advertise their presence in town. Announcements from provincial retailers were supplemented by those placed by a new breed of London dealers who sold direct to the public or via local agents, rather than supplying provincial grocers. One of the first, Edward Eagleton, advertised his Grasshopper warehouse widely and heavily, placing notices throughout the provincial press (including Leeds, Chester, Birmingham, Norwich, Bristol, and Gloucester) and often repeating advertisements several times in quick succession.[52] Eagleton was followed in the early nineteenth century by several others, most notably Frederick Gye, Frederick Sparrow, and Henry Long, who all adopted a similar strategy, so that few provincial newspapers were without advertisements from London tea dealers by the 1820s.

A favoured style of both provincial grocers and London dealers was to present lists of the goods being offered for sale (Table 7.2). At first glance, such advertisements can appear to be rather pedestrian and prosaic. Yet, at a time when the availability of new stock was uncertain, and with the pressure to keep up with other businesses, it was vital that the potential customers knew what stock shopkeepers carried. By detailing the goods in the shop, such advertisements contributed to growing consumer knowledge and presented an image of plenty and choice: a cornucopia providing the consumer's every need. Moreover, they allowed shopkeepers to style themselves as helpful guides through the shifting landscape of goods, varieties, qualities, and prices. For example, one London dealer announced in 1820 that:[53]

The EAST INDIA COMPANY'S DECEMBER SALE now being ended, FREDERICK SPARROW and Co. take the earliest opportunity of informing their numerous friends the result:— Boheas and the inferior Congous are still lower—the middling and most useful kinds are also cheaper— Common Greens rather dearer, there being a great proportion of the finer sorts which have sold reasonable—Souchongs and Hysons remain much as before.

As Mui and Mui argue, presenting this kind of information served to open up the market in tea by making pricing more transparent—a process that had begun in a century earlier.[54] But Sparrow went on to 'particularly recommend' a range of good-quality teas as being especially 'desirable to purchase'. He thus attempted to position himself as a provider of disinterested consumer advice both on the overall market and on the types of tea that represented the best buys at the time.

Lists of advertised goods were rarely presented in neutral terms, most items being accompanied by some form of description. As Lyna and Van Damme note, using descriptive or persuasive language could 'make the difference between simply informing customers about available merchandise and convincing them of the

---

[52] Mui and Mui, *Shops and Shopkeeping*, 268–71.   [53] *Liverpool Mercury*, 21 Jan. 1820.
[54] Mui and Mui, *Shops and Shopkeeping*, 272–8.

Table 7.2. Principal focus of grocery advertisements in provincial newspapers, 1740s–1820s

Focus of advertisement	1740s–50s		1770s–80s		1820s		Total	
	No. (N = 18)	%	No. (N = 34)	%	No. (N = 34)	%	No. (N = 86)	%
List	7	38.9	16	47.1	12	35.3	35	40.7
Prices	4	22.2	10	29.4	9	26.5	23	26.7
New business	4	22.2	8	23.5	6	17.6	18	20.9
New premises	1	5.5	6	17.6	6	17.6	13	15.1
New stock	1	5.5	5	14.7	4	11.8	10	11.6
Cheap	3	16.7	3	8.8	2	5.9	8	9.3
Polemic	0	0.0	2	5.9	6	17.6	8	9.3
Other	3	16.7	1	2.9	2	5.9	6	7.0

Note: Repeat advertisements are excluded from the analysis.

Sources: *Adams Weekly Courant* (1774–80); *Aris's Birmingham Gazette* (1755–6, 1782); *Bristol Mercury* (1820–4); *Gore's Liverpool Advertiser* (1770); *Liverpool Mercury* (1820); *Northampton Mercury* (1743–4, 1780); *Norwich Gazette* (1741–2, 1757); *Worcester Journal* (1742–52).

merchandise's intrinsic value'.[55] Significantly, grocers and tea dealers displayed a wide lexicon. Many goods were described as 'fine' or 'best'—terms that helped to distinguish them from standard or inferior quality alternatives, and that were routinely used in bills presented to customers, suggesting that they formed categories that were well understood by consumers. Sparrow's recommended teas included good and finest Congou, and good, fine, and superfine Hyson; but he also emphasized the flavour and strength of some teas, including 'fine full flavoured Souchong' and 'finest strong Congou'.[56] Other groceries were also accorded richer descriptions, which often drew on geographical references in much the same way as occurred on the inventories and bills examined earlier. Commodities such as Valencia almonds, Lisbon sugar, and India soy were used to communicate information about the nature of the goods and helped to differentiate them from other types (respectively: bitter almonds, Bristol sugar, and Japan soy). Other geographical references were more clearly linked to the provenance of the goods—French olives, Turkey figs, and West Indian coffee—while others again were hybrids, where the place of origin was in the process of becoming a label for the intrinsic qualities of the goods: Pontefract cakes and Turkey coffee. These were persuasive semantics, creating a discourse of variety, choice, and exoticism that was intended to convince consumers to choose particular goods and buy from particular shops.

As discussed earlier, prices were often added to these lists, appearing in more than one-quarter of newspaper advertisements and characterizing notices placed by a wide variety of tradesmen. Those placed by tea dealers were particularly

[55] Lyna and Van Damme, 'Strategy of Seduction?', 110. See also Gieszinger, *History of Advertising Language*, 129–44.
[56] *Liverpool Mercury*, 21 Jan. 1820.

detailed. For example, in 1778 Eagleton's 'original Tea Warehouse, the Grasshopper' on Bishopsgate Street, London, advertised a range of teas and coffees, each
with the price clearly stated. There was:

> Good Common Bohea tea, at 3s. 10d. *per pound*
> Fine Bohea ditto Congou leaf, at 4s. 4d. to 4s. 8d.
> Good and Fine Congou or Souchong, at 5s. 8d. to 6s. 6d.
> Fine and very Fine Souchong, at 7s. 6d to 8s. 6d.
> Superfine Souchong, the best that is imported by the East India Company,
>   which is sold at 12s. per lb. at 9s. 6d.
> Good Common Green Tea, at 5s. 4d. to 5s. 8d.
> Fine and Superfine Singin, at 6s. 6d. to 7s. 6d.
> Very Fine Hyson or Plain Green, at 9s. 6d. to 12s.
> Superfine Hyson or Plain Green, best that is imported by the East
>   India Company, which many Persons pay from 16s. to 21s. per
>   lb at 14s. 6d.
> Good and fine roasted Coffee, at 3s. 8d. to 4s. 8d.
> Superfine Turkey ditto, neat as imported, which is sold at 6s. per lb. at
>   5s. 4d.
> Good and fine plain Chocolate, at 3s. 8d. to 4s. 4d.
> Superfine ditto, which is sold from 5s. to 5s. 6d. per lb at 4s. 8d.
> The finest Vanilla, Sir Hans Sloan's Milk, and Churchmans Patent
>   Chocolate, each at 5s. 6d.[57]

Including prices in this way had two key effects. First, it heightened the notion of
choice. Eagleton could provide teas to suit most pockets as well as most tastes—
although he did not offer the very best and most expensive Gunpowder tea—so
that all could enjoy the pleasures of tea drinking and the benefits of his money-
back guarantee. Second, it gave advertisements a competitive dimension: Eagleton
suggested that his superfine souchong, hyson and Turkey were all of the very best
quality, yet were being sold up to 25 per cent cheaper than elsewhere—although
the identity of these rival dealers remained unspecified (see Chapter 6). As Mui
and Mui make clear, this competitive price listing was a common feature of tea
advertisements in the late eighteenth and early nineteenth centuries, with low
prices sometimes being further discounted for bulk purchases.[58]

Scorned by traditional London dealers, such advertising has a modern feel and
works on the consumer being motivated by choice and price, rather than more
traditional concerns, such as the service offered by the retailer. It is also suggestive
of an increasingly competitive market. This impression is confirmed by the emergence of a new type of advertisement in the early nineteenth century—one that
used invective to undermine the claims of rival retailers. Attention frequently
focused on two related issues. First was the real or perceived quality of the tea being
sold; second was the claim, generally made by London dealers, that rivals were
passing off low-quality teas in imitation of their own, superior goods. Attention
here was frequently focused on the packaging in which tea was sold, with a clear

---

[57] *Adams Weekly Courant*, 18 Aug. 1778.   [58] Mui and Mui, *Shops and Shopkeeping*, 255–8.

link being drawn between the identity of the dealer, the packaging used, and the quality of the product. This practice was pioneered by Eagleton, who sold tea 'packed and marked with the sign of the Grasshopper', and with the price and quality clearly indicated.[59] It developed rapidly in the early nineteenth century as competition between London dealers increased. Many of the concerns and discourses are captured in an 1820 advertisement placed by Long & Co.[60]

CAUTION—It is *earnestly* requested the Public will *not confound this* ESTABLISHMENT with its numerous 'IMITATORS'. The *unexampled* Sale of these Teas has given rise to a host of *Speculators, styling themselves 'Companies'*, who, by their disgusting puffs and *false statements*, have justly excited a strong prejudice with the Public. For *Seven Months after this Establishment was formed and until these Teas were in universal demand*, there was *not a House* that *even pretended* to sell Tea *free from Mixture*.—This *system of adulterating* the *best Teas* with that *Trash* BOHEA, has *just* been *renewed* and *carried on in the last Two Months*, to a *vast extent*. These *Teas are secured in Tin Canisters*, the *only way possible* to *preserve* the *strength* and *flavour* of *the Tea*, and are thus *distinguished* from the *spurious Imitations* which are in *flimsy paper packages*.

The link between the assured quality of the product and its packaging is clear and explicit. This is not quite the branding of goods that characterized patent medicines and some chocolate products (including Sir Hans Sloan's Milk Chocolate and Churchman's Patent Chocolate), and that became widespread later in the nineteenth century. However, as with the later packaging of butter and other groceries, the act of pre-packing foods was closely linked with assurances of purity and quality. The public could be confident that Long & Co.'s teas were free from 'that trash' bohea *because* they were offered in sealed canisters. Moreover, the quality and strength of the packaging signified the characteristics of the goods that they contained: imitators are portrayed as offering their goods in flimsy paper packages.

A few years later, Long & Co. were advertising under the banner 'Canister Teas'—the name of the company being explicitly branded with its packaging.[61] However, despite the rhetoric, they were far from unique in their use of such packaging. Indeed, teas had been packed in tin canisters from the turn of the eighteenth century. As early as 1711, the Leigh family in Warwickshire were being sent imperial and fine green tea from a London dealer called George Dottin, who also billed them for two tin canisters.[62] Moreover, the claims made for Long & Co.'s mode of packaging did not go unchallenged. Readers of the *Bristol Mercury* in July 1823 were faced with the rival claims of the London Genuine Tea Company, which sought to undermine many of the claims made by their competitors—part of the increasingly fierce and often vitriolic rivalry between London tea dealers.[63]

These advertisements suggest an increasingly competitive market, but this polemical style characterized only a minority of advertisements—all of them placed by London tea warehouses. The most striking feature of grocers' advertisements through this period was

[59] *Manchester Mercury*, 13 Oct. 1795.   [60] *Bristol Mercury*, 10 Apr. 1820.
[61] *Bristol Mercury*, 7 July 1823.   [62] SCLA, DR18/5/1826.
[63] See Mui and Mui, *Shops and Shopkeeping*, 273–6.

the enduring importance of traditional styles and linguistic forms.[64] Over half took the form of notices, ostensibly advising the public of a new business being established, a change of address or fresh stock acquired. Significantly, this proportion was maintained through the late eighteenth and into the early nineteenth centuries, underlining the enduring importance of established trading practices and the continued need to remain within the bounds of respectability. This was important in maintaining the good name of the retailer, reputation being essential to creditworthiness and thus to business success.[65] This was true of the agents of London warehouses as much as independent tradesmen. Thus, even advertisements engaged in the mud-slinging of commercial rivalry could still be framed in terms of notices from a shopkeeper to his established customers. Thus, W. C. Hill—the Bristol agent of 'Canister Teas'—added a paragraph to the bottom of the company's advertisement, where he 'returned his sincere thanks to the Nobility, Gentry and the Public for the very kind patronage he has received…and most respectfully begs leave to inform them that he has received a large supply of real CHINA TEAS'.[66]

Such attempts to link tradesmen and women to the social elite were widespread. Some advertisers undoubtedly had ambitions to supply such prime consumers, but for most it is doubtful whether the gentry formed a large section of their clientele. Indeed, it is unlikely that they were even the intended target of advertisements apparently aiming to solicit their custom. As with the proliferating 'useful manuals' studied by Klein, the real audience was probably those members of the middling sorts with pretensions to upward social mobility.[67] In addressing notices to the gentry, the shopkeeper aligned both themselves and their customers with the local elite, thus enhancing their genteel credentials and ambitions. Given the increasing fluidity of status titles through the eighteenth century, they might even see themselves to be part of the burgeoning urban gentry.[68] Moreover, the salutation with which Hill concluded his advertisement formed part of the careful wording of advertisements, which were, as Barker observes, 'almost always couched in a particular form of polite, deferential language'.[69] Many advertisements expressed thanks for past 'favours' and the hope of further patronage, which would be warranted by their assiduous attention to the needs of the customer. In 1757, the Aylsham grocer James Drake announced his retirement in favour of his sons. He took the opportunity to return 'his most grateful thanks to all his Friends, who have favoured him with their custom', recommended his sons as being worthy of their continued custom, and closed by assuring 'all those who are pleas'd to favour them with their Commands may depend on their utmost Care in the execution thereof, and they will be gratefully acknowledged, by their most obedient humble servants'.[70] Significantly, this kind of formalized, polite language mirrored that of the circulars issued by traditional London tea dealers. Richard Twining, for example, wrote:

The sale of teas being now over, we take the liberty of troubling you with a list of our prices…Our teas in general are remarkably fresh and good and we cannot omit this opportunity of assuring our customers that, in return for the many favours which they

[64] See also Lyna and Van Damme, 'Strategy of Seduction?', 111–12.
[65] Muldrew, *Economy of Obligation*, 148–72.   [66] *Bristol Mercury*, 7 July 1823.
[67] Klein, 'Politeness for Plebes', 371–2.   [68] Corfield, 'The Rivals'; Stobart, 'Urban Gentry'.
[69] Barker, *Business of Women*, 81.   [70] *Norwich Gazette*, 9 July 1757.

have conferred upon us…they may depend upon every possible attention on our part to supply them with the best teas at the most reasonable prices. Your most obliged Humble Servant …[71]

In certain respects, this kind of polite linguistic convention was linked into traditional forms of retailing. Yet it continued to be deployed alongside commercial rhetoric well into the third quarter of the eighteenth century, declining only slightly with the emergence of more polemic forms of advertising in the early nineteenth century (Table 7.3).

It is difficult to assess the broader social and economic implications of such polite discourse. Barker has suggested that it conferred a 'degree of servility', but, as I have argued elsewhere, the use of courteous and flattering forms of address did not necessarily imply subservience.[72] Rather than fawning to the gentry, shopkeepers were making themselves part of the process whereby politeness and polite society were being reconfigured. As Defoe noted, the model shopkeeper was 'the most obliging, most gentleman-like, of a tradesman'.[73] Part of this meant adopting the language and 'patrician manners' of the elites; more fundamentally, it was central to the Addisonian marrying-up of polite and commercial worlds.[74] The same integration of politeness onto commerce can be seen in the practice of addressing advertisements to 'friends' and 'the public'. This had the effect of differentiating a set of privileged (and self-identifying) customers from the general reader. Friends were valued customers with whom personal bonds were strong—the sort of person who might receive a trade card or be invited into the back space of the shop.[75] In focusing on these people, shopkeepers looked to cultivate their key customers, but

Table 7.3. Language used in grocery advertisements in provincial newspapers, 1740s–1820s

Form of language	1740s–50s		1770s–80s		1820s		Total
	No. (N = 18)	%	No. (N = 34)	%	No. (N = 34)	%	
Polite	4	22.2	18	52.9	17	44.1	39
Commercial	1	5.5	10	29.4	11	32.3	22
Descriptive	13	72.2	5	14.7	4	11.8	22
Other	0	0.0	1	2.9	1	2.9	2

Note: Repeat advertisements are excluded from the analysis.

Sources: *Adams Weekly Courant* (1774–80); *Aris's Birmingham Gazette* (1755–6, 1782); *Bristol Mercury* (1820–4); *Gore's Liverpool Advertiser* (1770); *Liverpool Mercury* (1820); *Northampton Mercury* (1743–4, 1780); *Norwich Gazette* (1741–2, 1757); *Worcester Journal* (1742–52).

[71] Twining, *Two Hundred and Twenty-Five Years*, 22.
[72] Barker, *Business of Women*, 82–3; Stobart, 'Selling (through) Politeness'.
[73] Defoe, *Compleat English Tradesman*, quoted in Klein, 'Politeness for Plebes', 372.
[74] Berg, *Luxury and Pleasure*, 233; Klein, 'Politeness for Plebes'.
[75] Berg and Clifford, 'Selling Consumption', 149–51; Cox, *Complete Tradesman*, 127–39.

also to create an atmosphere of sociability and respectability.[76] Again, this combination of commercial and polite ambitions links these advertisements to traditional notions of service-oriented selling. Yet this formula remained important well into the nineteenth century, despite the spread of the more overtly commercial advertisements of London tea dealers. As with their retail practices, grocers' advertisements demonstrated strong continuities as well as innovatory and more overtly competitive aspects.

The image of groceries constructed through newspaper advertisements was generally much more mundane than the exoticism of many trade cards. There was a focus on practical issues of supply, quality, and price, and a growing commercialism that sometimes spilled over into open rivalry. Moreover, while the illustrations on trade cards and bill heads portrayed the grocer as part of a world economy, linking the consumer with distant production, most newspaper advertisements locked them more firmly into a local social milieu by emphasizing the centrality of the relationship between the shopkeeper and the customer. Empire and exoticism were replaced by politeness and respectability. In part, of course, this distinction was linked to the different rationale of the two media, but differences in form and function can too easily be overplayed. The exotic and the everyday were often placed alongside each other in advertisements that focused on the provenance and quality of the goods, and the everyday practices of consumption with which they were associated.

EXOTIC, EMPIRE, AND EVERYDAY: QUALITY AND CONSUMPTION

In presenting their lists of goods, some grocers and tea dealers also made mention of the distant locations from which these goods were brought (Table 7.4). The range of places mentioned closely resembles that found in inventories and bills, and covers a wide variety of places in Britain, Europe, and the colonies, reinforcing the varied geographical and cultural context in which groceries and consumers were situated. In stark contrast with the trade cards, China is mentioned very little: it is the implicit source of all tea, but the particular points of reference are the East India Company sales and the types and grades of tea being offered for sale. The names of these were, themselves, exotic: souchong, hyson, pekoe, congou. However, rather than linking the consumer to specific places, they communicated the flavour and quality of the tea. Other exotic-sounding references achieved much the same, despite their apparent geographical specificity. Of course, regardless of whether they were describing provenance or quality, long lists of place names, such as that appearing on the hand bill of John Watkinson, could situate the consumer in a nexus of global and colonial trade.[77]

Some grocers went further and made much of the genuine provenance of their wares. William Jones, advertising in the *Liverpool Mercury* in 1820, listed Indian

[76] See Borsay, *English Urban Renaissance*, 267–82.
[77] Bodl., JJC, Tradesmen's Lists.

Table 7.4. Places mentioned in grocery advertisements in provincial newspapers, 1740s–1820s

Country	1740s–50s		1770s–80s		1820s		Total
	No. (N = 18)	%	No. (N = 34)	%	No. (N = 34)	%	
Britain (regions)	2	11.1	4	11.8	0	0.0	6
Malaga/Seville	1	5.5	3	8.8	1	2.9	5
Turkey	2	11.1	2	5.9	1	2.9	5
Jamaica	1	5.5	0	0.0	2	5.9	3
China	1	5.5	0	0.0	1	2.9	2
France	0	0.0	0	0.0	2	5.9	2
Lisbon/Portugal	0	0.0	1	2.9	1	2.9	2
Holland	0	0.0	0	0.0	1	2.9	1
India	0	0.0	0	0.0	1	2.9	1
Italy	0	0.0	0	0.0	1	2.9	1
Japan	0	0.0	0	0.0	1	2.9	1
Levant	1	5.5	0	0.0	0	0.0	1

Note: Repeat advertisements are excluded from the analysis.

Sources: *Adams Weekly Courant* (1774–80); *Aris's Birmingham Gazette* (1755–6, 1782); *Bristol Mercury* (1820–4); *Gore's Liverpool Advertiser* (1770); *Liverpool Mercury* (1820); *Northampton Mercury* (1743–4, 1780); *Norwich Gazette* (1741–2, 1757); *Worcester Journal* (1742–52).

arrowroot, and Italian vermicelli and macaroni; but also 'Real West India Cayenne Pepper' and 'Real Japan Soy'.[78] Yet this advertisement is unusual in its emphasis of explicitly colonial goods. This is not to say that empire was unimportant but rather to emphasize again that it was just one point of reference for grocers and tea dealers, who were perhaps more interested in the exotic rather than the imperial. The former comes over in a particularly idiosyncratic advertisement placed by an un-named Bristol tobacconist (Figure 7.4). He drew on the public's familiarity with *Gulliver's Travels* and particularly the nature of Lilliput, presenting his shop as a magical world and his tobacco as a mysterious herb, indigenous to the place. Even the process of buying is presented as novel and unfamiliar, visitors bringing their silver and gold (the 'chief deficiencies' in Lilliput) so that they 'may have its productions in exchange'.[79] While highly unusual in its fanciful use of allegory and metaphor, this advertisement can be read as an idealization of colonial trade: the modern and sophisticated western consumer is linked with an idyllic foreign land where desirable commodities grow naturally and abundantly (no suggestion here of plantations and slave labour); goods flow in one direction and capital in the other, so that everyone benefits from a fair exchange. The style is totally different, but the message is perhaps not that distant from that of Britannia receiving tribute from the colonies—the image deployed in Schick's trade card discussed earlier.

---

[78] *Liverpool Mercury*, 11 Feb. 1820.   [79] *Bristol Mercury*, 23 Aug. 1824.

Gulliver's Lilliput Discovered.

STRANGE as it may appear, this opulent City positively has Lilliput in its very heart; it abounds with that most deliciously sedative Herb, TOBACCO, in all its varieties. As it is also presumed that the flavours are superior, its Amateurs are respectfully invited to visit Lilliput, and taste its productions; and those who have not as yet become Amateurs are respectfully informed, that the above Herb not only possesses the quality of sedativeness, but also of giving vigour of intellect, vivacity to the imagination, and dispelling the gloom which sometimes beclouds the minds of even the most sprightly of Adam's sons. The chief deficiencies in Lilliput are silver and gold; so that Visitors have only need to bring either, and they may have its productions in exchange—have a cordial welcome, and be remembered with gratitude. The above mentioned Lilliput is situated at the Top of *BROAD-STREET*, next to Christ-Church.

Fig. 7.4. Advertisement for tobacco (Source: *Bristol Mercury*, 23 August 1824)

Lists of places and magical constructions might help to create an image of the exotic, but they could also communicate something of the character and quality of the goods on offer. As Cox and Dannehl have demonstrated, such considerations had long been of concern to British consumers, and they featured in a growing number of grocers' advertisements and trade cards.[80] Indeed, a focus on the quality and purity of produce became a core feature of tea advertisements in the late eighteenth century. One manifestation of this that had begun much earlier was the marketing of proprietary brands of chocolate, often sold by tea warehouses but also stocked by provincial grocers such as Watkinson. These brand names reassured the public of the quality of the goods and were a guarantee, of sorts, against inferior or adulterated products. Such concerns grew in the early nineteenth century—part of a general anxiety about hygiene and the quality of food being sold in British shops.[81] Tea dealers fed into and exploited such concerns. For example, Sparrow & Co. advertised that 'the Public are not perhaps sufficiently aware of the shameful adulterations which have long been practised in the article of Chocolate and Cocoa'. They were pleased to announce that 'having erected suitable premises for the manufacture of those essential articles [we] are enabled to offer them to the public in their *pure* and *unadulterated* state'.[82] It may be that Sparrow was trying to extend concerns over food safety into new areas. Certainly, the main commodity causing public anxiety at this time was not chocolate, but tea.

In 1818 there was a series of legal cases brought against manufacturers and sellers of counterfeit and adulterated teas. One problem, noted earlier, was the use of

[80] Cox and Dannehl, *Perceptions of Retailing*, 97–126.
[81] See, e.g., Burnett, *Plenty and Want*, 99–120.   [82] *Liverpool Mercury*, 21 Jan. 1820.

cheap Bohea to bulk out higher grades of tea, thus compromising their quality and cheating the customer. The response of many tea dealers was to supply and advertise teas in sealed containers—a practice followed by many of the newer London dealers, including Gye, Sparrow, and Long.[83] More specifically, there was the question of the safety of tea—a consequence of the practice of 'reviving' tea or turning low-grade black tea into more expensive green tea by adding colouring agents.[84] An advertisement from Long & Co. makes the point explicit: 'This Establishment was formed in April 1818 in consequence of the discovery of that baneful traffic in POISONOUS verdigrease Tea, which was proved (by various convictions in the Court of Exchequer) to be carried on to a most alarming extent in almost every part of the Country.'[85] Their solution was simple: people should buy their tea packaged, thus ensuring that their drink was free from noxious substances. And yet the packaging of tea brought its own problems: the London Genuine Tea Company had to defend its practice of packing tea in lead. They advertised to refute the allegation that tea was 'injured' by such practices, asserting that those who made these claims 'never purchased Teas in their original packages, or they would know that Teas *are never* imported *but in lead*, which is the only way of preserving its fine flavour and strength'.[86]

At this time, the adulteration of tea was seen as a British problem, carried out by greedy and unprincipled dealers. Later, attention switched to China as the setting for malpractice as the image of the country was blackened in the press. Before the 1840s, however, advertisements portrayed China in a very positive light, making much of the purity of the tea being brought over. In the newspapers, readers were assured that tea was 'genuine, as imported by the East India Company', or 'pure as received from China', sealed canisters being a guarantee of purity.[87] As we have already seen, on trade cards and bill heads, a positive and pastoral image was constructed: China was a pre-industrial (even premodern) producer of pure and wholesome teas. More specifically, the pairing of a Chinese man pouring tea for his female European companion seen on William Marshall's trade card suggests tea passing directly and unmediated from producer to consumer; the fact that they share the drink further implies its unadulterated state.[88] In case these messages needed reinforcing, the images were frequently accompanied by the assurance that the teas were 'genuine as imported'. Sometimes, this would be written as an accompanying banner, as with Thomas Dainty and John Bull of Northampton; more occasionally, it was incorporated into the image itself: on the card of W. Brown, of the Strand, a Chinese man sits on a tea chest and holds a plaque on which is written 'Teas, Genuine as Imported'.[89]

These concerns over quality and purity were a reflection of the commercial rivalry within an increasingly important tea trade. They were closely linked to the need to persuade consumers to choose particular 'brands' and patronize certain

[83] Mui and Mui, *Shops and Shopkeeping*, 273–6.   [84] Rappaport, 'Packaging China', 131.
[85] *Bristol Mercury*, 7 July 1823.   [86] *Bristol Mercury*, 7 July 1823.
[87] *Bristol Mercury*, 20 Dec. 1822, 7 July 1823.   [88] See Bodl., JJC, Trade Cards 11 (33).
[89] NCL, uncatalogued trade ephemera; Bodl., JJC, Trade Cards 11 (8).

dealers, but they also promoted the consumption of tea more generally and com-municated broader notions of consumer culture: the desirability of imported goods, the attraction of those rituals involved in their consumption, and the ways in which these practices shaped the identity of the consumer as polite or respect-able. I have argued elsewhere that eighteenth-century advertisements were, in part, concerned with selling politeness.[90] They played on its competitive aspect, appeal-ing to the aspirations of consumers and offering guidance as to how to enter the world of polite consumption. They conveyed direct and powerful references to genteel taste; the rise of fashion; the emergence of new goods; social emulation, and the cultural cache of London—all important aspects of polite material culture. Such considerations were less apparent in advertisements for groceries than was the case for drapers, china dealers, or hairdressers, for example; but both newspapers and trade cards were employed to communicate something of the polite practices of everyday consumption.

Images of Chinese figures taking tea can be read as an allusion to the polite social practices of middling-sort households as well as being representations of authentic practices or signifiers of empire or the exotic. Very occasionally, there were trade cards that highlighted more directly the everyday practices of buying and consuming groceries, invariably presented as orderly, rational, and respectable. In a very early example, a *c.*1700 card for 'Will's Best Coffee Powder' (discussed earlier) includes an image of a London coffee house.[91] It shows four well-dressed men drinking coffee and smoking tobacco pipes, apparently engaged in earnest conversation. One man is reading a broadsheet and another has one laid on the table in front of him. Behind them, on an unoccupied table, rests a third broad-sheet, while a fifth man pours coffee in an elegant arc into a cup. The whole forms a perfect representation of the male public sociability of the coffee house: rational debate combining with manly consumption of coffee and tobacco.[92] As such, it conforms to the norms of many contemporary engravings of coffee houses. Yet this is a promotional image. Its significance lies partly in its depiction of the coffee house as a 'key venue for the promotion of coffee as a desirable new commodity',[93] and partly in what it tells the consumer about the practices and rituals of coffee consumption. In short, it promotes coffee and the social practices of polite and rational coffee drinking.

CONCLUSIONS

The advertising of groceries took many forms in eighteenth-century England, including entries in trade directories, notices in newspapers, handbills and trade cards, and illustrated bill heads. Although only a minority of grocers advertised in the printed media, these were widely available and had the potential to reach a

[90] Stobart, 'Selling (through) Politeness'.   [91] Bodl., JJC, Douce adds. 138 (84).
[92] Smith, *Consumption*, 139–70; Cowan, *Social Life of Coffee*, 89–112.
[93] Cowan, *Social Life of Coffee*, 51.

large and varied audience. The messages they carried about retailers and the groceries that they sold thus had the potential to influence the attitudes and practices of
a broad range of respectable consumers. Advertisements were therefore an important mechanism through which shopkeepers could shape demand, both for their
own goods and for groceries more generally. This made them central to McKendrick's conception of a nascent consumer society—one that was more commercially
oriented but also more acutely aware of the relative merits of different goods or
retailers.[94] It is very difficult to assess the actual impact of advertising on individual
consumers or on consumer behaviour in general—just as today, the link is rarely
simple or linear. In some respects, this impact is a secondary issue. The media and
form of advertising themselves tell us much about the marrying of polite and commercial worlds, and about the broadening of consumer horizons to encompass a
world of goods.

The analysis offered here has focused firmly on the advertisements themselves,
identifying a dualism between trade cards and bill heads, on the one hand, and
newspaper advertisements, on the other. The former drew on sometimes complex
symbolism to emphasize the exotic and imperial character of certain goods, while
the latter focused on more everyday concerns such as availability, quality, and price.
We might thus characterize the impact of trade cards as cultural, while that of
newspaper advertisements as commercial. However, it would be a mistake to see
the distinctions in such stark terms: both shared a common language of politeness
and played an important role in integrating polite and commercial values. Moreover, while retailers sometimes made a choice between these two forms of advertising, consumers often experienced them in combination. Read alongside one
another, their messages were complementary, linking the consumer both to a global economy and to their own consumption milieu. The extent to which any one
element dominated is hard to assess. Empire formed an important theme in many
trade cards and undoubtedly linked into public interest in imperialism. So too did
the exotic—a notion that is difficult to disentangle from the imperial, but that
forms a more appropriate lens through which to view images of Turkish and especially Chinese figures. The latter became a leitmotif for grocers in the early nineteenth century both in an attempt to re-emphasize the exotic nature of what was,
by then, a pretty mundane commodity, and to reassure the public of the purity of
the product and the trustworthy nature of its provider. More generally, they can be
seen as linking into ideas of displaced meaning, China being the repository of
cultural ideals of authenticity and simplicity, but also exoticism and luxury, while
groceries (especially tea) formed the bridge between western culture and this idealized 'other'.[95]

On a more practical level, much of the advertising discussed here was ultimately
about reputation, of both the goods and the retailer. This has several related aspects.
First, by presenting information on price, quality, and availability, the shopkeeper
was portrayed as an honest intermediary between global systems of production and

[94] McKendrick, 'Consumer Revolution'.
[95] See McCracken, *Culture and Consumption*, 104–17.

local supply networks. Second, in constructing an image of his or her wares as genuine and wholesome, the retailer was seen as virtuous and trustworthy—especially important when goods were unfamiliar or sourced from afar. Third, through emphasizing the exotic provenance and authenticity of groceries, the shopkeeper was cast as a gatekeeper to the expanding world of goods and, more arguably, a new set of experiences and practices. Fourth, by writing all these in the language of politeness, the exotic and novel were brought within the realm of respectability in ways that were rather different from those envisaged by Smith. The context was commercial rather than cultural, and the imperative was less social and more economic; but the impact on consumption was just as important.

8
Baskets of Goods: Customers and Shopping Practices

INTRODUCTION

Shopping forms the crucial link between shop and home, retailer and consumer. At its most basic, it defines the process of acquiring goods—a definition that is reflected in economic models that have long sought to explain shopping behaviour in rational terms and which thus links to rationalist explanations of consumption.[1] From this perspective, attention focuses on what is bought, in what combination and from where, and on the ways in which these choices were driven by quantifiable considerations such as price or journey times.[2] Yet such reductionist viewpoints ignore the wide range of skills and pleasures involved in shopping. Indeed, they obscure the significance of shopping as an important process in itself: an end as well as a means to an end. In the eighteenth century, as today, shopping was—for some at least—a leisurely or even a leisure activity. It involved the sociability of conversation, the pleasure of interacting with new and familiar objects, the frisson of the crowd, and the satisfaction of securing desired or necessary goods.[3] This places shopping more centrally in the evolution of consumer society—part of the broadening set of experiences that comprised commercialized leisure and the start of a longer process of ownership and consumption of material goods.[4]

More fundamentally, shopping is also constitutive of identity. From one perspective, it can be seen as a purposeful activity wherein consumers are active and knowing agents, often consciously constructing their identity through their shopping practices as well as the goods that they purchase and consume. In this light, shopping can be linked to conspicuous or emulative consumption, but also to rational and polite sociability.[5] As Berry argues, the rituals and performances of shopping can themselves become a pleasurable activity 'associated with sociability, display and the exercise of discerning taste—in sum, the performance of the

---

[1] Davis, 'English Foreign Trade'; de Vries, *Industrious Revolution*, 186–237.
[2] For a discussion of these, see Carter, *Urban Geography*, 61–98.
[3] In a modern context, see Miller et al., *Shopping, Place, Identity*; Miller, *Theory of Shopping*; Stobart, *Spend, Spend, Spend*, 193–210; Dennis, *Objects of Desire*. For the eighteenth century, see Berry, 'Polite Consumption'; Stobart, Hann, and Morgan, *Spaces of Consumption*, 149–60; Walsh, 'Shops, Shopping and the Art of Decision Making', 169–72; Walsh, 'Shopping Galleries'.
[4] Plumb, 'Commercialization of Leisure'; Stobart, Hann, and Morgan, *Spaces of Consumption*, 142–60; McKendrick, 'Consumer Revolution'.
[5] See Sweet, 'Topographies of Politeness', 356; Klein, 'Politeness for Plebes'.

Addisonian model of politeness'.[6] Alternatively, shopping can be seen as intuitive and habitual: identity being created performatively through repeated action; the everyday processes of consumption. This links closely to the notion that shopping was (and remains) an essentially female activity, or, in more nuanced terms, that women bore the brunt of everyday shopping while men restricted themselves to more costly and occasional purchases.[7] From this viewpoint, the routines of shopping and female identity become mutually reinforcing. While often set up in opposition to one another, these two positions can, in part, be reconciled through Miller's argument that the identity of consumers is a 'social process that shifts according to social context'.[8] In short, people might engage in shopping for some goods and in some places as an active process of identity construction, while other forms of shopping were more mundane and habitual. There is an obvious parallel here with Berry's 'browse–bargain' model of shopping in the eighteenth century, wherein certain goods were carefully viewed, compared, selected, and haggled over, while others were bought in a more peremptory fashion, perhaps on the basis of a (mental) shopping list.[9]

We know little about how groceries fitted into this model or more general processes of shopping. It is assumed that they formed part of the mundane and everyday goods that lay outside the browse–bargain process, but is this true? To address such questions we need to understand more fully the ways in which consumers engaged with retailers; how they selected goods for purchase, and what they chose to buy. More specifically, we need to examine in detail the changing patterns and practices of shopping for groceries, an undertaking that involves three related elements. The first is to explore the social and gender characteristics of those buying new and more traditional groceries, and examine the extent to which it is possible to identify a 'basket of goods' that typified the purchases of different groups. A key concern here is how far these might parallel the consumption bundles highlighted by de Vries.[10] The second is to uncover the timing and frequency of purchases and the extent to which consumers were reliant upon particular suppliers. Groceries might be seen as mundane, everyday goods; but to what extent do shopping practices support this view? Moreover, does it follow that everyday goods were purchased in a routinized manner, or is there evidence that customers shopped around on the basis of price, quality, or service? The third is to consider the actual modes of shopping through which groceries were acquired. Here, I take Berry's model as a starting point to examine how shopping for groceries was experienced as a social as well as an economic activity—one that involved browsing as well as buying. Together these different strands of analysis can tell us much about the

---

[6] Berry, 'Polite Consumption', 377.
[7] e.g. Vickery, *Behind Closed Doors*, 106–28; Walsh, 'Shops, Shopping and the Art of Decision Making', 162–8. But see Finn, 'Men's Things'.
[8] Miller et al., *Shopping, Place and Identity*, 20. See also Berry, 'Polite Consumption'; Vickery, *Gentleman's Daughter*, 250–2; Berg, *Luxury and Pleasure*, 247–78; Glennie and Thrift, 'Consumers, Identities and Consumptions', 39–40.
[9] Berry, 'Polite Consumption'.
[10] De Vries, *Industrious Revolution*, 31–7.

processes of shopping for groceries and the role these played in broader changes in consumption and consumer evolution.

SHOPPING PATTERNS: WHO BOUGHT WHAT?

Even a cursory examination of the account and day books of provincial shopkeepers confirms that a wide variety of people purchased groceries from fixed shops. In the fourteen-month period from December 1740 to February 1742, the Worcester grocer Thomas Dickenson had at least 186 account customers.[11] Of the 117 for whom occupations can be traced, around one-fifth were drawn from the urban or rural elite—9 per cent being gentry and 11 per cent professionals, mostly clergy and attorneys. A further 37 per cent were fellow shopkeepers or merchants, with a similar proportion being craftsmen retailers (tailors, shoemakers, bakers, and the like) or those engaged in production or building (maltsters, joiners, masons, and so on). While there is no mention of labourers, it is apparent that both wealthy and relatively poor consumers were patronizing his shop, and were being granted credit. Rather lower down the retail hierarchy was William Wood's shop in Didsbury. His account book lists a total of 108 customers, but not all of them bought shop goods: Wood also sold ale and liquors, supplied coal, and did ploughing, activities that formed his main source of income from the wealthier sections of the local community. Those with honorific titles such as 'Esq.' or 'Mr' eschewed buying groceries in his shop, perhaps preferring to travel to nearby Stockport or Manchester.[12] Wood's shop customers thus comprised the ordinary people of Didsbury, including shoemakers, gardeners, labourers, and domestic servants.

This kind of social differentiation is perhaps unsurprising, but how far did it extend to the purchases made in these different shops? Here, we know most about the purchasing patterns of the elite. The detailed bills and inventories of the Leigh family of Stoneleigh Abbey in Warwickshire afford an excellent insight into the quantity, range, and type of groceries being purchased over a 160-year period. They reveal that the Leighs bought a wide range of commodities, from saltpetre to souchong tea. In all, the 52 grocers' bills sampled for this analysis show a total of 129 different goods, if all the variants of teas, sugars, fruits, and so on are included.[13] The range of groceries purchased grew steadily from the seventeenth to the mid-eighteenth century, and very rapidly from the 1760s (Table 8.1). In the late seventeenth century, a typical basket of groceries comprised dried fruits, sugar, and perhaps some seeds or spices. By the early eighteenth century, tea, coffee, and chocolate were being bought alongside established products, a trend that continued into the next generation, when these formed the most commonly purchased items in an otherwise varied basket that also included sauces and ketchups. These collections of goods were loosely linked in their orientation towards the meal table

---

[11] WSL, D1798 HM 29/2–4.
[12] Mui and Mui, *Shops and Shopkeeping*, 212.
[13] SCLA, DR 18/5, Leigh bills and vouchers.

Table 8.1. Edible groceries purchased by the Leighs, by commodity type, 1630–1792

Product	1630–81 (N = 13)			1710–38 (N = 14)			1768–92 (N = 17)		
	No. of varieties	No. of bills		No. of varieties	No. of bills		No. of varieties	No. of bills	
		No.	%		No.	%		No.	%
Dried fruit	16	9	69.2	5	6	40.0	8	7	41.2
Spices and seeds	7	6	46.2	10	7	46.7	14	5	29.4
Sauces, ketchups, etc.	0	0	0.0	2	4	26.7	13	4	23.5
Sugars	5	9	69.2	6	7	46.7	8	6	35.3
Tea, coffee, chocolate	0	0	0.0	12	5	33.3	13	10	58.8
Miscellaneous	3	4	30.8	4	4	26.7	8	6	35.3
Total	31			39			64		

Note: 'No. of varieties' indicates the range of different goods purchased within each commodity type; percentages are calculated from the total number of bills for each period (N).

Source: SCLA, DR18/5, Leigh bills and vouchers.

rather than the closely linked bundles. Moreover, the variety of groceries also increased markedly; in all, at least ten different types of sugar and sixteen types or grades of tea were purchased.[14]

The extent to which the Leighs were typical is hard to establish with certainty. Other elite households were more conservative in the groceries they bought. In 1716, Grace Nettleton came to keep house for her nephew-in-law, Sir Francis Leicester, at Tabley House in Cheshire, and subsequently kept detailed accounts of her expenditure.[15] Most of the outgoings were on various sorts of meat and fish, and there were also payments to the herb woman, the milk woman, and the baker, as well as for cream, butter, and eggs. In the summer, she bought strawberries, cherries, raspberries, cucumbers, and cauliflowers among a range of other fresh produce. Her purchases of groceries in the first half of 1720 reveal a distinctly narrower range than the Leighs at a similar date, being dominated by plum cakes and biscuits (Table 8.2). Although various spices appear in the accounts, they were purchased only rarely and in small quantities: 8*d.* of cinnamon, 16*d* (8 oz) of pepper, 8*d.* of cinnamon, 1*s.* 8*d.* of mace and 1*s.* 6*d.* of nutmegs.[16] Perhaps most striking is the complete lack of tea and very occasional mention of coffee. It is possible that Sir Francis was responsible for such purchases, but Grace's accounts appear to cover most other consumables, so it is more likely that tea and coffee were rarely served in the house. Almost the exact opposite can be seen in another member of the Cheshire elite. Here, the evidence is

[14] The former included Lisbon sugar, Bristol loaves, and Barbados sugar (SCLA, DR18/5/2188, 2217, 5992). This range contradicts the assertion that sugar was not 'branded' by island or linked to production regions (Bickham, 'Eating the Empire', 92).

[15] CALS, DLT/B51.

[16] CALS, DLT/B51, entries for 15 Apr. and 26 May 1721.

Table 8.2. Edible groceries purchased by Grace Nettleton, by type, 1720

Product	No. of varieties	No. of purchases	
		No.	%
Cakes, biscuits, and pies	7	50	46.7
Dried fruit	3	17	15.9
Spices and seeds	7	11	10.3
Oil and vinegar	2	11	10.3
Sugars	5	14	13.1
Tea, coffee, chocolate	1	2	1.9
Total	25	105	

Source: CCA, DLT/B51, account book of Grace Nettleton.

drawn from an anonymous early eighteenth-century account book, probably of a Cheshire gentleman,[17] which notes his everyday purchases in the form of a simple list. The cost of each purchase is noted, but no dates are given other than annually at the 13 November, which presumably was the day on which he (or someone else) appraised his spending for the year. His purchases included no culinary groceries and only occasional mention of cakes or tarts. Candles, soap, and tea were purchased in some quantity; but sugar and coffee predominated, between them accounting for about 60 per cent of the grocery items listed. The implication is that the man was in lodgings, with his meals provided, but the accounts show how such an individual could still engage in regular shopping for groceries and, more generally, how individuals' shopping habits were shaped by their domestic regime.

Perhaps more typical of gentry spending were the gentlemen and esquires who used Dickenson's shop in Worcester. Edmund Taylor, esquire, of Welland made twelve purchases during 1741 and 1742, buying tea and coffee; pepper, mace, and Jamaica pepper; sugar and rum; nuts, soap, starch, and hair powder.[18] Such shopping patterns were not very different from those of professionals and some tradesmen, certainly in terms of the range of goods being bought (see Table 8.3). Individuals varied considerably in what they acquired from Dickenson, but in aggregate clergymen and attorneys purchased rum, tobacco, and various grades of sugar; tea, coffee, and chocolate; pepper, nutmeg, mace, ginger, cinnamon, cloves, long pepper, mustard, and aniseed; raisins, currants, and figs; anchovies, citron, and rice. Shopkeepers and artisans also bought a wide range of imported groceries from Dickenson, featuring strongly among those buying tea, coffee, and chocolate. The presence in this group of ordinary tradesmen—joiners, shoemakers, glovers, and the like—confirms McCants's suggestion that the consumption of these beverages had spread far beyond the elite and middling sorts by the mid-eighteenth century (see Chapter 9).[19] Moreover, while some were restricted to buying small quantities of

[17] CALS, DCB 1179/60. There are references to the expenses incurred at the races, bowling green, and barber, and for horses, hunting, and coursing.
[18] WSL, D1798 HM 29/2–4.
[19] McCants, 'Poor Consumers', 181–9.

Table 8.3. Purchasing behaviour of Thomas Dickenson's account holders by status, 1741–1742

Socio-economic group	No.	No. of visits	% > 5 visits	Mean no. of goods per individual
Gentry	11	3.3	27.3	2.5
Professionals	14	5.1	35.7	2.8
Shopkeepers	43	4.5	25.6	2.0
Craftsmen	33	3.8	18.2	1.9
Artisans	10	5.4	30.0	2.3
Others	4	2.5	25.0	1.5
Wholesale	2	93.5	100.0	10.5

Source: WSL, D1798 HM 29/2–4.

cheaper teas, others bought higher-quality teas and even chocolate—often seen as retaining luxury status into the second half of the eighteenth century. Thus, for example, Samuel Lucas (a soap boiler) bought 2 lb of best hyson tea on 21 November 1741, while the tailor, Thomas Cooke, combined purchases of best bohea tea with others of chocolate. This he bought in half-pound quantities on three occasions during December 1741 and January 1742. Only coffee appears to have marked social status, since, with one exception, buyers were either clergymen or gentlemen.

A similar pattern can be seen in the purchases of tea and coffee made during 1768–9 by customers of the Newcastle-under-Lyme mercers Fletcher and Fenton.[20] Although the greatest range and highest-quality teas were bought by the gentry, those given the title 'Mr', 'Mrs', or 'Miss' in the account books also made occasional purchases of costly teas such as fine hyson.[21] In general, however, they bought mid- or lower-grade teas: singlo, green, and bohea being the most popular. Customers not given the dignity of any title were more restricted, buying only green and bohea tea, and generally in quantities of only two or four ounces. They were, nonetheless, buying tea. So too were the customers of William Wood's shop in Didsbury. Even a small sample reveals purchases of at least twenty-five different kinds of goods, a typical basket comprising treacle, sugar, flour, meal, bread (often manchet loaves), candles, soap, cheese, and tea.[22] If Wood's customers were most often buying only basic groceries, at least half also bought salt, starch, and tobacco, and there were occasional purchases of green tea, coffee, tobacco, snuff, raisins, pepper, mustard, and rice.

How do we best understand these different purchasing patterns? In buying small amounts of higher-grade teas, it is possible that poorer consumers were seeking to

[20] WSL, D(W)1788/V/108-111.

[21] On the differential spending of those granted honorific titles, see Shammas, *Pre-Industrial Consumer*, 243–8.

[22] MCL, MS F942. The sample comprises James Cash, Joshua Barlow, Thomas Birch, Ann Bancroft, Samuel Holbrook, George Fletcher, David Wrocroft, and Ann Atkinson.

imitate and perhaps emulate their social superiors. Certainly, such small luxuries would help to bolster respectable status, especially as they were linked into bundles of material goods and domestic practices. More likely, they were occasional treats, similar to the annual purchases made from Thomas Dickenson by the joiner John Read. On 25 December 1740 and 26 December 1741 he bought sugar plums and spice to the value of 5*s.* 2*d.*—perhaps as a special Christmas treat for his family.[23] Such occasional purchases suggest that these consumers were motivated more by the physical and emotional pleasure that these commodities could bring rather than the ways in which they might bolster status. This would make utility not emulation the driving force behind these consumption choices, privileging Scitovsky's ideas of personal comfort and perhaps de Vries's notion of social comfort over McKendrick's emphasis on fashion.[24] Certainly, the evidence from Wood's account book shows how deeply the market had penetrated the lives of ordinary villagers.

Gender differences in the pattern of purchases are also apparent. At Dickenson's shop, female account holders were far more likely to buy tea and sugar, while their male counterparts were over-represented in purchases of rum, tobacco, and, to a lesser extent, coffee (Table 8.4). Of course, while a female account holder was probably acting for a household without a male head, many male account holders would also have been providing for their wife and perhaps daughters. Female patterns of spending might thus be expected to stand out more starkly in these records. This does, indeed, appear to be the case: two-thirds of Dickenson's female account holders purchased sugar and nearly one-third bought tea; whereas only one-quarter of male account holders bought rum, and less than one in ten bought either tobacco or coffee.[25] Although a little crude, these distinctions fit into gender norms of the time, matching Smith's cultural contexts wherein a female domestic realm of tea drinking is contrasted with a more public coffee-drinking and tobacco-smoking domain frequented by men.[26] They also mesh with the practices of the gentlewomen studied by Vickery, who notes that tea was drunk with social equals, visiting tradeswomen, and at socially inclusive tea parties (see Chapter 9).[27]

The centrality of tea and sugar to female shopping was particularly strong, emerging even when the account was held by a man. This can be seen at both ends of the social scale. William Wood noted the person who made each purchase under a particular account, presumably to avoid disputes when it came to reckoning up the amount owed. These confirm the broad gender distinctions that appear from Dickenson's accounts and suggest that wives were more likely to be the ones who purchased sugar and especially tea. For example, between September and November 1786, George Fletcher made two purchases of tea and six of sugar, but his wife

[23] WSL, D1798 HM 29/2–4.
[24] Scitovsky, *Joyless Economy*; de Vries, *Industrious Revolution*, esp. 20–5; McKendrick, 'Consumer Revolution'.
[25] WSL, D1798 HM 29/2–4.
[26] Smith, *Consumption*, 139–88.
[27] Vickery, *Gentleman's Daughter*, 207–8.

Table 8.4. Groceries purchased from Thomas Dickenson of Worcester, grocer, 1741–1742

Gender	No. of purchases	Percentage of shopping trips											
		Chocolate	Coffee	Tea	Sugar	Treacle	Spices	Fruit	Rum	Tobacco	Soap	Other
Male	720	3.6	4.4	12.4	31.5	4.0	9.4	6.3	10.1	6.4	11.8	29.4
Female	77	3.9	2.6	36.4	54.6	2.6	10.4	7.8	1.3	1.3	7.8	19.5
Total	797	3.6	4.3	14.7	33.8	3.9	9.5	6.4	9.3	5.9	11.4	28.5

Source: WSL, D1798 HM 29/2–4.

bought tea five times and sugar on fourteen separate occasions. She also made the only purchase of coffee on this account, while he alone bought tobacco. This gender divide was clearer still in the purchasing practices of the Gibbards in the 1820s: John dealt with the wine merchant and Mary with the tea merchant, Charles Hancock. She bought a variety of teas, but mostly souchong—a choice that brought approbation from Hancock, who wrote in 1827: 'You are certainly a lady of excellent taste and judgement and an ornament at the tea table, and show much discernment. Bessy [Hancock's wife] is a dear little thing but does not know Bohea from Congou.'[28] Mary was probably flattered by this, especially as Hancock was a personal friend of the family as well as a supplier: it underlined her position as a knowledgeable and tasteful consumer. What is perhaps more revealing, however, is that the comparison is made between two women and their taste in tea. Both Mary Gibbard and Charles Hancock appear to take it as read that it was the wife's role to choose as well as serve the tea, extending her control of this domestic ritual into the business of supplying the key ingredient. This takes Smith's idea of domestic femininity into a more public realm as the lady of the house formed the link between the commercial world of the shop (or the supplier) and the private world of the home.[29]

Despite its alluring fit with conceptualizations of emerging separate spheres, this picture of gender-related consumption is misleading in its simplicity. From Dickenson's account books we can see that few individuals were typical of their gender. The brazier John Rowell fits the stereotype, as he bought mostly best tobacco from Dickenson, generally in quarter-pound parcels. So too does Mrs Elizabeth Bates, who, on seven visits, bought three types of sugar and as many of tea. The only other thing she purchased was chocolate and that on only a single occasion. Miss Molly Brooks also made regular purchases of sugar and tea, but along with these she bought currants, nuts, mace, pepper, currants, candied oranges, mustard, and chocolate. Mrs Harris shopped mostly for hops, soap, and starch—goods that indicate household maintenance or domestic production. Conversely, George Woodcock, an innkeeper, had a rather female pattern of purchases, usually buying only a single sugar loaf on his monthly visits, occasionally adding coffee or best bohea tea. The apothecary John Clements, meanwhile, shopped every other week, buying mainly sugar candy, treacle, and brimstone.[30] This evidence, showing that gendered patterns of consumption were an aggregate norm to which only some consumers were aligned, offers an important challenge to the masculine and feminine cultural contexts outlined by Smith.[31] It reminds us that these were ideal types around which the behaviour of individuals and households might approximate, but which developed in a range of different ways—a point to which we will return later.

[28] BLA, GA93. See also Bailey, 'Maintaining Status', 23–4.
[29] Smith, *Consumption*, 175–8.
[30] WSL, D1798 HM 29/2–4.
[31] Smith, *Consumption*. See also Kowalski-Wallace, *Consuming Subjects*; Vickery, *Behind Closed Doors*, 106–28.

SHOPPING TRIPS: THE RHYTHMS OF CONSUMPTION

There was a well-established annual and weekly rhythm of shopping in most provincial towns. In Lancaster, Stout noted that many of his shop customers came on market days—a pattern confirmed in shopkeepers' account books from the mid-eighteenth century. Thomas Dickenson dealt with around 70 per cent more customers on a Saturday, the most important of Worcester's three market days, when visitors were drawn from a wide hinterland. Similarly, Fletcher and Fenton transacted over one-third of their business on a Monday, the main market day in Newcastle-under-Lyme.[32] Overlain on this weekly cycle were seasonal patterns of trade. Dickenson's accounts show peaks in the number of purchases during early March and mid-August, coinciding with Worcester's two Assizes; those of Fletcher and Fenton indicate that their busiest times coincided with the town's fairs. Into these general rhythms of trade were fitted the routines of individual households. Wealthy consumers are often seen as being able to buy in larger quantities and maintain a stock of foodstuffs, whereas poorer households relied on buying goods on a day-by-day basis. But to what extent is this borne out by the evidence?

The receipted bills of the Leighs of Stoneleigh Abbey show that many of their groceries were bought as part of large orders, but the picture is far from simple. Bills varied enormously in size and the Leighs were often granted long periods of credit, so that many large bills were the accumulation of several transactions. Four examples, taken during the period when the elderly and wealthy Mary Leigh was the owner of the estate, serve to illustrate the variety of arrangements. Perhaps the most straightforward case is that of the London grocers Wilson, Thornhill, and Wilson, who, on 28 August 1792, presented a bill for a single purchase of 'muscadella' raisins and Jordan almonds that amounted to just £1 8s. Here we see Mary making a simple purchase and being billed accordingly. Comparable in nature, but different in scale, was Thomas Ballard, who regularly supplied large quantities of tea, coffee, and chocolate. His bill of 13 June 1789 comprised 36 lb of tea, 10 lb of coffee, and 6 lb of chocolate and amounted to £18 1s. 6d. in total. Again, this was a single transaction, but reflected bulk purchasing of groceries, which would have been consumed over the following weeks or months. Of a similar magnitude was William Leaper's bill for £13 19s. 1d., presented and paid on 17 December 1789. Yet it incorporated forty-six separate transactions spread fairly evenly across the months since October the previous year. Relatively modest amounts were purchased on each occasion, the largest being £1 8s. for 56 lb of moist sugar. Although not a major supplier, Mary Leigh purchased goods from Leaper at least twice a month and often more frequently, perhaps using him to fill gaps in stores of goods as and when they arose. Another compound bill was presented by Frances Field, but here each transaction was sizeable. Between February and November 1789, Field supplied Mary with groceries on seven occasions, sometimes in relatively modest parcels and sometimes in much larger quantities, as

---

[32] Stout, *Autobiography*, 79; WSL, D1798 HM 29/2–4; WSL, D(W)1788/V/108–11.

with the £34 10s. 9d. of goods dispatched on 29 May.[33] If we bring together these various suppliers and transactions, and add the others with whom Mary had dealings, it is apparent that she was buying groceries at least once or twice a week. Unsurprisingly, staples such as coarse sugar, dried fruit, peas, and soap were purchased with greater frequency than were more exotic or luxury goods, but the latter were sometimes acquired in large batches rather than on a needs basis. This indicates that some purchases were more carefully planned than others, and that some grocers were used for such regular purchases while others were drawn on more to fill gaps in provision.

A similar pattern of frequent and more episodic purchasing characterized the shopping pattern of Grace Nettleton, who, on average, bought groceries three times a week. Her most regular purchase (plum cakes and biscuits) was made each Monday, but she rarely used this as an opportunity to buy other groceries. Indeed, while various goods were bought quite frequently, there is little to suggest much routine to her shopping—purchases were apparently made according to need. Soap was purchased every week to ten days, but the pattern varied considerably, as it did for other commonly bought items such as candles and dried fruit. Occasionally, a range of items were purchased on a single day (and presumably in a single transaction), as on 29 April 1720, when the following appear in her account book:

Salt (8d.), matches (1d.)	0–9
Three pd soap	1–4½
One loaf of fine sugar	5–1½
Six pd of coarse loaf sugar	3–6
Two pd for ye casters	1–8
Two pound of sixpenny	1–0
Six pd of raisins	2–0
one pint of claret (9d)	
cream for sillybabs (6d)	1–3
Flamery	0–2[34]

More often, however, groceries were bought in parcels of two or three items, seemingly as need dictated, as there are many entries in the accounts of purchases on several successive days. Thus, on 25 July, she bought codlings and sugar for preserving; the following day she purchased an ounce of coffee and some soap; the day after she had some vinegar; two days later she bought more sugar and soap and some candles; the following week, she purchased biscuits on 1 August, returning two days later for mustard, plum cakes, and more biscuits; and two days later again for more soap, vinegar, and salt.

A clearer idea of the relationship between the rhythm of purchases and an immediate or anticipated need for the goods can be gleaned from 'An Account of stores

[33] SCLA, DR18/5/5992, 5851, 5866a, 5865.
[34] CALS, DLT/B51.

expended every half year' kept in the 1750s for the Leigh family of Adlestrop in Gloucestershire.[35] This account includes an opening balance for each type of grocery; a note of any purchases made (arranged by month); a total for goods 'spent' (that is, consumed), and a closing balance for each six-month period. Comparing the timing and size of purchases with the amount of each commodity 'in store' for the period April 1757 to March 1759 gives an indication of whether goods were being bought because stocks were running low. Unsurprisingly, the picture is complex. Good supplies of some essential items were always maintained. For example, a minimum of 92 lb of candles was held in store at the end of each half year, and purchases were made to maintain this stock, most often in October, but also throughout the year. Stocks of other goods were allowed to dwindle, sometimes to nothing, before being replenished. Sugar and dried fruit were usually bought in bulk each half year in April and October, and there appears to have been little attempt to make additional purchases, even if stocks were running low. The closing balance for both moist and coarse or brown sugar was zero in three of the four accounting periods, as it was for best and common raisins. It is possible that other types of sugar or fruit might have been substituted when supplies ran out, but there was clearly a policy of buying these goods periodically rather than as needed. The reverse was true of tea and coffee, which were bought more frequently through the year—usually quarterly—with small quantities always held in the store. This may be a reflection of buying being more closely tied to consumption, but it was probably linked to a desire for these commodities to be fresh. This suggests that shopping for groceries was organized on a rational basis. However, stock management was far from perfect, and coffee was bought well ahead of need through the winter of 1757–8, resulting in a balance of 4½ lb being accumulated by April 1758 against a half-yearly consumption of only 1½ lb.

Lower down the social scale, consumers rarely bought a large range of goods in a single transaction. From a total of 853 transactions recorded in Thomas Dickenson's account between January 1741 and April 1742, only 27 involved purchases of 5 items or more and, of these, just 2 included more than 10 items.[36] Samuel Stephens, a surgeon, shopped on account roughly once a month, variously buying sugar, oil, paper, mace, cloves, ginger, cinnamon, pepper, currants, raisins, and anchovies; but he never purchased more than two or three items on each visit. Similarly, if slightly further down the social order, the barber George Saunders visited Dickenson's shop thirty-four times, but on only five occasions did he leave with more than a single item. These middling sort of consumers appear to have been buying for more immediate needs than were the Adlestrop Leighs. The limited range and relatively small volumes being bought did not betoken a hand-to-mouth existence, but neither do they suggest that such consumers held significant stores of groceries in their homes. Their pattern of shopping thus reflects their more direct day-to-day needs. This can be seen in the way that a number of Dickenson's customers came to the shop almost daily. John Clements, for example, bought treacle on 21 January 1742, returning

[35] SCLA, DR18/31/548.
[36] WSL, D1798 HM 29/2–4.

Sugar and Spice

Table 8.5. Typical customers of William Wood, 1785–1787

Customer	No. of transactions	Transactions per month	Range of goods	% of 'typical basket'
Ann Atkinson	47	15.7	12	100
Ann Bancroft	63	15.8	10	88.9
Joshua Barlow	58	11.6	12	77.8
Thomas Birch	54	12.0	13	88.9
James Cash	47	9.4	11	88.9
George Fletcher	84	21.0	10	66.7
Samuel Holbrook	23	5.75	6	44.4
David Wrocroft	39	6.0	12	88.9
Total and mean	415	11.5	11	80.5

Note: A 'typical basket' comprised: bread/manchet, candles, cheese, flour, meal, soap, sugar, tea, treacle.
Source: MCL, MS F942.

the next day for powder sugar, and the day after for brown and white sugar candy and figs. A fortnight later, on 10 February, he bought more sugar candy and then came back on the following two days for figs and aniseeds respectively.

This type of everyday shopping typified the poorer consumers who bought from William Wood (Table 8.5). Mui and Mui use the example of Martha Chase to illustrate the way in which goods were bought in small quantities, enough to last only a few days. Martha went to Wood's shop on 3 January 1787 and bought 1 lb of treacle; she returned later that day for currants and a clove pepper. On the following day she bought treacle, flour, and barm; the next day she had a manchet loaf, and the day after a further loaf, tea, and sugar. On 7 January, Martha bought sugar, coffee, and bread valued at 8*d.*, and two days later she had treacle and sugar for 7*d.*[37] Yet this was categorically not a hand-to-mouth existence. Martha was not returning to the shop with this frequency because she could afford only small quantities. We know about her shopping patterns because she and her husband, 'ould William Chase', had an account with Wood that ran for a number of years. They built up a bill before periodically settling it or, more usually, paying off a sum every quarter. Mui and Mui plausibly explain the need for such accounts in terms of the lack of small coinage,[38] but the reason for such regular trips to the shop were social and cultural as much as economic. Martha and William, and Wood's other customers, could have bought a range of goods or larger quantities of goods in a single visit. That they chose not to might be explained by a lack of suitable and secure storage of groceries in their homes or that they preferred to buy only what was needed at that particular time. This suggests a very different mindset from wealthy consumers with their store books and household accounts—one that was less influenced by the rhetoric of advice manuals and less troubled by concerns over the trustworthiness of servants.

[37] WSL, D1798 HM 29/2; Mui and Mui, *Shops and Shopkeeping*, 212–13.
[38] Mui and Mui, *Shops and Shopkeeping*, 215–16.

Some insight can be gained here by considering the frequency with which different goods were purchased. Flour or meal, loaves of bread or manchet, treacle,
sugar, and candles were the most frequent purchases, being bought in small quantities on a weekly or even daily basis. Soap and sand were also regular purchases, as
were salt and cheese; but they were rather less frequent, appearing in most accounts
between two and four times each month. This suggests that Wood's customers
were, indeed, buying goods as they needed them: daily bread perhaps for freshness,
and sugar, treacle, or candles as they ran out. The position of semi-luxuries is more
problematic. Mui and Mui suggest that only a handful of Wood's customers bought
tea on a regular basis; most made only occasional and often very small purchases:
an ounce or half an ounce at a time, often in combination with sugar.[39] Yet this
oversimplifies individual purchasing patterns. While David Wrocroft made
sporadic purchases of 1 oz of tea during May and June 1786, the following February saw 9 oz of tea being bought on his account in just ten days—two purchases
taking place on a single day. These amounts remain quite modest, but suggest
purchases beyond daily needs—perhaps an attempt to stock up or to cater for a
particular occasion. Significantly, these purchases were generally for tea on its own,
not with sugar. The coupling of tea and sugar plagues the historiography and, as we
shall see in the following chapter, oversimplifies the consumption of both commodities. In the real lives of Wood's customers, tea was grouped with other goods as
well. For example, James Cash or his wife bought tea on seven occasions in January
and February 1786, variously combined with bread, sugar, treacle, soap, cheese,
and salt.[40] As such, it was part of their everyday shopping, even if it was not quite
an everyday commodity itself. In terms of the rhythms of shopping, then, there is
again little evidence of imitative behaviour: class differences were, it seems, driven
primarily by personal circumstances. These were, in turn, shaped partly by purchasing power and the ability to maintain and manage domestic stores, but also by the
attractions of the grocer's shop as a place of sociability for the consumer. This
brings us to the important question of who actually went shopping for groceries.

MODES OF SHOPPING: WHO SHOPPED AND WHERE?

As part of her browse–bargain model of shopping, Berry argues that routine
purchases of everyday goods are precisely those that could be made by servants or
children.[41] However, Walsh suggests that there were often problems, real or perceived,
in trusting servants: they might not inspect goods sufficiently closely or secure the
best price; they might make arrangements with particular retailers despite consist-
ently high prices or poor quality,[42] or they might dawdle over the errand. Something

---

[39] Mui and Mui, *Shops and Shopkeeping*, 213.
[40] MCL, MS F942, fos 51–2, 97–100, 17–18.
[41] Stobart, Hann, and Morgan, *Spaces of Consumption*, 152–4.
[42] This practice was known as 'the market penny', from the commission made by the servant. See
Walsh, 'Shopping at First Hand', 19.

of these risks can be seen in a letter from Elizabeth Purefoy of Shalstone to a grocer in nearby Brackley. She acknowledged receipt of some goods and then noted that she had been given too much change, adding that 'had it been any servant but an ignorant boy you would have lost the money'.[43] Walsh discusses in detail the contemporary literature that sought to advise housewives over the use of servants for shopping and how best to regulate and monitor their behaviour.[44] Ultimately, though, the housewife would have needed to shop regularly to maintain her knowledge of the market and prices, especially for foodstuffs. The question of who shopped for groceries is important in determining the social and cultural significance of the processes of shopping: whose identity was (potentially) being constructed and how? If it was primarily servants who shopped for groceries, then this would erode any wider impact in terms of sociability, communicating taste, and cementing identity.

The evidence is equivocal and suggests that responsibility was split between various members of the household. Those going to Thomas Turner's village shop were usually there on their own account; they stayed for tea, to play cards and sometimes to eat and drink into the evening.[45] Clearly, these were not visits solely prompted by the need to stock up on certain items or even to make ad hoc purchases. But Turner's diary gives us only a glimpse of the comings and goings at his shop. A slightly fuller picture can be gleaned from William Wood's account book, which reveals that husbands, wives, children, neighbours, and servants all shopped for groceries. In the six months from January 1786, fifty-two purchases were made on the account of James Cash, around two-thirds of which are linked to a named individual. His wife made nine purchases, James made eight, and their son bought goods on six occasions. Most intriguing for a family that was not very wealthy, there are eight entries for items 'fetched' or 'had' by a maid or servant. A slightly different pattern emerges from the account of George Fletcher, with George himself being named in half of the sixty-six transactions itemized for May and December 1786. His wife made just eight purchases, while eleven were attributed to a maid and fourteen to Betty Walsh—most likely a neighbour, but possibly a servant, as there is no temporal overlap between the purchases made by Betty and the maid.[46] From this, it appears that maids or servants were an important part of the process of acquiring groceries, even in relatively modest households, and that husbands and wives were both heavily, if not equally, involved in provisioning the house. There was little to distinguish the purchases attributed to servants from those made by householders; but then—as we have already seen— most of the visits to Wood's shop involved buying a small range and quantity of goods. Thus we see James Cash variously buying tea and sugar, treacle and candles, or eggs; his wife buying tea and sugar, bread, or sugar, soap, and berm; his son getting treacle and salt, soap, or tea and sugar; and the maid bread, candles and

---

[43] Eland, *Purefoy Letters*, no. 102.
[44] Walsh, 'Shopping at First Hand', 17–25.
[45] Vaisey, *Thomas Turner*, 11 July 1764, 14 Jan. 1763.
[46] Betty Walsh did not have her own account with Wood and I have not found reference to her elsewhere in the account book.

salt, sugar and starch, or soap.[47] The entire household, it seems, might be trusted to buy from Wood.

A rather different picture emerges from the account book of Thomas Dickenson, servants accounting for around one-third of the 137 entries that identify the purchaser. This suggests that proxy shopping was somewhat less common among the customers of this higher-order provincial grocer: most purchases were made by the account holder or his wife. Moreover, servants generally bought only one or two specific items with a total value, on average, of about 6s. For example, Mrs Harris sent her maid to Dickenson's shop for $3\frac{1}{2}$ lb of 'best Bristol soap'; yet she bought $3\frac{1}{2}$ lb hard soap, 14 oz hops, $\frac{1}{2}$ oz green tea, and $\frac{1}{2}$ oz bohea tea when she visited the shop herself.[48] These distinctions are linked to the generally larger range of goods purchased by Dickenson's regular customers, but they also indicate that servants and children were often trusted with running small errands but were rarely involved in larger transactions.

Further up the social scale, the balance of activity shifted more. In aristocratic households such as Stoneleigh Abbey, most transactions with retailers were conducted through the steward or housekeeper.[49] Other elite consumers, however, played an active role in choosing groceries and dealing with suppliers. We have already noted that Mary Gibbard was responsible for purchasing tea; she placed orders and corresponded personally with the supplier.[50] Much the same was true of Elizabeth Purefoy and her son Henry, both of whom ordered a wide variety of groceries from shopkeepers in nearby Brackley and, more commonly, in London. These orders often comprised a range of goods, including sugar, dried fruit, and spices, and were repeated on regular occasions.[51] In a similar manner Judith Baker placed regular and almost unchanging orders with her London suppliers between 1766 and 1783.[52] Such practices strongly suggest the kind of stocking-up that characterized the purchasing practices of the Adlestrop Leighs and indicate that at least some elite consumers were systematic in their shopping practices and could trust the shopkeeper and carrier to select and transport such routine purchases.

This portrayal of mundane trips or orders to stock up on a range of necessaries suggests a certain set of consumer practices: customers had a clear idea of what they wanted before they entered the shop or corresponded with the shopkeeper; interaction between shopkeeper and customer was therefore largely structured around assembling the list of goods required. Yet this image of planned and functional shopping is doubly misleading. On the one hand, we have already seen that grocers went to considerable trouble actively to sell their wares.[53] On the other, the records

---

[47] MCL, MS F942, fos 17–18.
[48] WSL, D1798 HM 29/2–4.
[49] SCLA, D18/5 (Leigh bills and receipts).
[50] Bailey, 'Maintaining Status', 23–4.
[51] Eland, *Purefoy Letters*, nos 105, 106.
[52] Berry, 'Prudent Luxury', 147.
[53] For a fuller discussion of these practices, see Stobart, Hann, and Morgan, *Spaces of Consumption*, 126–9; Hann and Stobart, 'Sites of Consumption'.

include numerous seemingly unplanned visits to grocers and hurried orders being placed to meet unexpected needs. The former can be seen in the shopping practices of Wood's customers, the frequent, almost chaotic comings and goings of Martha Chase being typical of his clientele. For example, George Fletcher, having shopped on four of the five previous days, came to Wood's shop on 2 December 1786 and bought meal and sugar, returning later in the day for sugar. The following day his maid had treacle and George bought ale, his wife coming the day after for a loaf, soap, and candles, and the maid for soap and other goods. Much the same was true of a near contemporary of Wood, who kept shop in Greens Norton, Northamptonshire. Many customers came to this shop two or three times in a single day and some made an extraordinary number of visits. The account of Edward Williams, for example, records sixty-seven separate transactions for June 1798, including five on 13 June, when he bought sugar, tea, and worsted; candles; bread and butter, and bread and cheese, and paid for shoe mending.[54] These ad hoc practices were echoed forty years later in the behaviour of some well-to-do women who occasionally patronized the Islington shop of Edward Peacock. Giving evidence to a Select Committee, he reported that on Sundays 'respectable women will come in and say "Oh, dear me, I am so glad your shop is open; I do not know what I should have done if I had not found it open; I want several things"'.[55]

It is unlikely that shopping undertaken by the Leighs and Purefoys involved them entering grocers' shops. There is some evidence that London shops were visited in person, but most of their shopping was transacted through correspondence.[56] However, this did not mean that these consumers were disengaged from the process of shopping: notes written on bills and regular letters kept customer and shopkeeper in close contact with one another.[57] The attractions of what might be termed correspondence shopping are readily apparent from the purchases made by the Leighs. They show that the family drew a wide range of groceries from suppliers in Coventry and especially London—the latter providing superior quality goods or newer products that were less easily obtained in provincial towns. For example, when tea and chocolate were first purchased by the family in 1711, they were acquired from the London retailer George Dottin. Later, when these products became more widespread, they still went to London for the finer grades.[58] Similarly, it was a London grocer, Francis Field, who later supplied novelties such as ketchups, morels, truffles, soy sauce, vermicelli, and carouch.[59]

The problems of shopping in this way were manifold: the goods had to be transported safely, money transferred remotely and securely, quality assured when the goods could not be inspected in advance, and prices clearly agreed. Many of these could be offset to a degree by dealing with known and trusted suppliers with whom

---

[54] NRO, Y.Z.4040, fo. 60.
[55] Quoted in Alexander, *Retailing in England*, 174.
[56] Thomas Turner sold goods to the Duke of Newcastle, but did so through paying visits to his steward (see following section).
[57] Walsh, 'Shops, Shopping and the Art of Decision Making', 169.
[58] See, e.g., SCLA, DR18/5/1826, 5998.
[59] SCLA, DR18/5/5865.

the customer had built up a long-term relationship. There was inevitably some turnover in the suppliers provisioning the Leigh family, but they remained remarkably loyal to certain tradesmen. Judith Baker and the Purefoys also stuck with established suppliers. The former ordered her groceries from Blakiston, Myles & Co. in the Strand for over fifteen years, while the latter patronized Mr Cossins of St Pauls Churchyard in the 1730s and continued to do so when the same shop passed to Wilson and Thornhill in the 1740s.[60] Her correspondence with these men, and with the Brackley grocer Mr Yates, tells us much about the organization of such shopping. Most important was the need for clear instructions about precisely what goods were required. Thus, Elizabeth Purefoy wrote to Wilson on 21 December 1746 requesting:

a quarter of an hundred of sugar about 6 pence a pound...a quarter of an hundred of treble refined loaf sugar, one pound of the best Bohea Tea, half a pound of the best green tea, one pound of the best coffeeberries, 2 pounds of Ginger, a quarter of a pound of cloves, half a pound of nutmegs, one pound of cocoa, one pound of black pepper, a quarter of a pound of hyson tea by itself, half a quarter of an hundred of Currants, half a quarter of an hundred of Raisins—I doubt there is no Raisins in the sun so I desire you will send the large sort of raisins; 6 pounds of 6 penny sugar by itself, 8 pounds of common lump sugar, and 3 pounds of sego [*sic*]. Pray let these all be the best sorts & as cheap as you can afford them, & send your Bill with them & will order you payment. Send them by ye Buckingham carrier.[61]

While particularly lengthy, this letter was fairly typical of the orders placed with Wilson.[62] Quite apart from itemizing the precise nature of the goods that she required, Elizabeth gave detailed instructions about how and when they should be dispatched. The Buckingham carrier was almost invariably used, yet most letters end with the same instruction, no doubt in an attempt to avoid any delay or confusion, both of which appear to have been a constant concern.[63] For her part, Elizabeth paid with surprising promptness. She often requested bills to be sent with the goods, and, where they survive, these indicate that payment was generally made within two weeks, usually via the same carrier who brought the goods to Shalstone. Her reasons for doing this are made clear in another letter to Wilson where she notes: 'I allways pay you ready money because Mr Cossins told mee I should be better used for doing so.'[64] Whether she was treated better as a result is open to question; Elizabeth received her orders promptly, but she felt herself hard done by on several occasions, usually because the goods were seen as being inferior quality. She was particularly concerned about her tea, writing on 10 May 1741: 'pray don't let your Bohea tea be so full of Dust as your last was'; on 9 May 1744 that 'the pound of Bohea tea is almost all green tea', and on 6 February 1747 that 'the last Bohea Tea was so ordinary I could not drink it'. However, other goods were also

---

[60] Berry, 'Prudent Luxury', 147; Eland, *Purefoy Letters*, no. 65.

[61] Eland, *Purefoy Letters*, no. 105.

[62] See Eland, *Purefoy Letters*, nos 100, 103, 106, 107.

[63] Carriers were also used to take goods to corresponding customers of Thomas Dickenson (see Ch. 6).

[64] Eland, *Purefoy Letters*, no. 104.

subjected to a critical eye: raisins supplied by Wilson were 'so bad they spoiled the liquor they were made on', while Henry had to write to his wine merchant complaining that 'My mother desires to know if there was no mistake in making ye chocolate it is so bitter & high dried that she can't drink it'.[65]

Central to the process of shopping by correspondence was the knowledge held by the consumers and their trust in the supplier. Elizabeth continued to place regular orders with Wilson and Thornhill, despite her complaints. Indeed, complaining underpinned her credentials as a knowledgeable and businesslike consumer. These were manifest in a number of others ways. Elizabeth's letter of 21 December 1746 shows unusual awareness of the likely availability of raisins,[66] but her expertise extended further than awareness of the seasonality of dried fruit. She was also concerned about how the goods would be dispatched. Her tea was generally sent in canisters, but she seems to have picked up something of the debate over the best method for storing tea, because, in a letter of 26 September 1753, she requests that 'the teas may be put up in sheets of black Lead'.[67] This kind of correspondence also reveals how purchase decisions were never 'single-moment' events. Elizabeth's letters reflect the kind of careful appraisal of current and future need that indicates an awareness of domestic stores and bears a close relationship to the organized weekly shop often associated with the coming of the supermarket.[68] It is tempting to label this mode of shopping as 'modern' and to draw a contrast with the more 'traditional' modes of behaviour seen in the customers of William Wood. But relating these two sets of shoppers through a simple linear progression would ignore both the socio-economic differences between these groups of people and the different cultures of consumption within which they operated. The implications of this are potentially profound: if different sets of consumers engaged in different rhythms and practices of shopping, then linking them together through the kind of emulation suggested by McKendrick becomes more problematic. Yet there were common threads running through these varied experiences, not least the ability to exercise choice, in terms of both the groceries they purchased and where they went to acquire them. Shopping in different ways or buying at different shops gave consumers the potential to express their identity as respectable, rational, sociable, or discerning.

SHOPPING AROUND FOR GROCERIES

At Stoneleigh Abbey, the Leighs received groceries from at least four different retailers at any particular point in the eighteenth century.[69] They supplied an overlapping range of goods, which suggests that choices were most likely being made

---

[65] Eland, *Purefoy Letters*, nos 103, 104, 106, 111.

[66] Other elite consumers appear to have ordered goods regardless of season and sometimes received dusty replies from suppliers (see SCLA, DR18/5/5992; SCLA, DR18/31/548, loose bill inserted into Stores Account).

[67] Eland, *Purefoy Letters*, no. 107.

[68] Walsh, 'Shops, Shopping and the Art of Decision Making', 169; Stobart, *Spend, Spend, Spend*, 192.

[69] SCLA, DR18/5, Leigh bills and receipts.

on the grounds of quality, price, and service, rather than availability. In effectively shopping around for their groceries, the Leighs followed some of the practices and perhaps the motivations suggested by Miller.[70] The mechanics of this process, as well as some of the motivation, can be seen in a letter written to Sir John Morduant by one of his servants while in London: 'I went to Mr Mason and enquired the price of his best vinegar which is 18*d*. per gallon, the ordinary is 10*d*. best anchovies are 16*d*. per lb, capers 11*d*. per lb and their best oyle at 3*s*. 6*d*. per qt.'[71] Elizabeth Purefoy did much the same, but in person. In 1751 she wrote to Benjamin Rose in Denington to say: 'I understand by the People of Astrop that you sell pickled mushrooms, so desire a line or two from you to let mee know the price you sell 'em at'.[72] Both of these consumers were seeking market information, specifically prices, ahead of making decisions about purchases. It is impossible to know their precise motivations for doing so, but it seems most likely that they wanted to assess whether these retailers offered the kinds of goods required at what were judged to be reasonable prices. Elizabeth was keenly aware of what she should be paying for particular goods, often making reference to the price charged by other shopkeepers. She used this information to secure better goods or service from established suppliers, with the implicit threat that she might take her custom elsewhere. Thus, she wrote to Wilson and Thornhill on 9 May 1744 to complain that 'the sugar at 10½*d*. a pound is dearer than anybody else gives', and again on 21 December 1746 that 'I hope you will let me have a better pennyworth than the last, for my neighbours had a better sugar at that price'.[73]

It is more difficult to judge the extent to which consumers of the middling sort were able to exercise this level of choice, although some evidence can be drawn from shop accounts that suggest they were also able to spread their custom. Thomas Dickenson offered a wide variety of groceries, but many of his customers purchased only certain types of goods in his shop (Table 8.6). Molly Brookes only occasionally bought from Dickenson's shop, but she acquired a wide range of groceries, which suggests that he may have been her only supplier. While her most frequent purchase was tea, she also had chocolate, sugar, soap, and a range of dried fruit and spices for cooking—all bought in quantities that appear appropriate for a single consumer. The apothecary John Clements was a much more frequent visitor to Dickenson's shop, and bought a number of goods absent from Brookes's basket. In general, these reflected greater variety within categories: six different sorts of spices and seeds; molasses and brown sugar as well as more refined types. It is possible that Clements was using some of these goods in the remedies prepared in his own shop, yet many were bought only occasionally. No purchases of tea or coffee were recorded, probably because Clements bought these from another grocer. Much the same was true of Benson and Stephens, neither of whom had tea from Dickenson. They both bought sugar regularly and other goods more occasionally; but Stephens

[70] Miller, *Theory of Shopping*, 5–9.
[71] WRO, CR1368, vol. 4/57.
[72] Eland, *Purefoy Letters*, no. 139.
[73] Eland, *Purefoy Letters*, nos 104, 105.

Table 8.6. Range of purchases from Thomas Dickenson, selected customers, 1741–1742

	No. of visits to buy named goods						
Goods	Revd Benson (N = 19)	Molly Brookes (N = 11)	John Clements (N = 55)	Samuel Richards (N = 16)	George Saunders (N = 33)	Samuel Stephens (N = 16)	Total
Treacle, sugar, candy	7	3	37	3	3	10	63
Soap	4	1		9	16		30
Mace, cloves, nutmeg, pepper	2	3	6			10	21
Starch, blue, black, brimstone	1		6	7			14
Other spices		2	5			6	13
Rum	1			3	7		11
Chocolate	6	2	2				10
Figs, raisins, currants	3	2	3			2	10
Tea		6		1	2		9
Nuts, almonds	1	1	3			2	7
Hair powder			2		4		6

Source: WSL, D 1798 HM 29/2.

must have acquired his soap elsewhere, while Benson's purchases of spices were too infrequent to sustain even a modest table. However, it is the shopping practices of Richards (a joiner) and Saunders (a barber) that indicate most clearly that these ordinary consumers were spreading their custom and making choices in terms of where to acquire particular goods. Richards made sixteen purchases from Dickenson, but only regularly bought hard soap. Other items, including rum, tea, starch, sugar, and lamp black, were purchased on odd occasions and in small quantities. Saunders also bought large quantities of soap, usually in 7 lb lots and most often described as 'best', and sometimes rum and hair powder, but little else. Perhaps they did not use spices, dried fruits, or tobacco; more likely, they chose to buy these from another grocer.

This kind of shopping around would have been quite feasible in mid-eighteenth-century Worcester with its range of shops, but it also appears that choice was being exercised by poorer consumers in smaller settlements. If we take the 'typical basket' of goods bought from William Wood, it is clear that many consumers were either doing without key items or acquiring them from somewhere other than Wood's shop (see Table 8.5). George Fletcher, for example, might have gone without meal or flour if no baking was carried out at home, but the absence of soap is more difficult to understand. More striking is the lack of flour, meal, cheese, candles, or treacle in the purchases made by Samuel Holbrook.[74] The impression that Wood's customers had both the opportunity and the desire to exercise choice is still more apparent from his sale of bacon and butter. The former was bought by many customers, but only in small quantities, prompting Mui and Mui to argue that he

[74] MCL, MS F942, fos 57–8 63–4, 278.

was not their major source of supply. Wood acquired the latter from a shoemaker, Thomas Birch, whose account was credited for 73 lb of butter during three months in the autumn of 1786. Again, the modest quantities in which this was purchased and the fact that only half of Wood's customers bought butter from him indicate another source—possibly Birch himself.[75]

It is one thing to demonstrate that consumers were acquiring their groceries from a number of sources. It is quite another to suggest that their shopping practices involved browsing in the manner conceptualized by Berry and described by contemporary commentators such as Schopenhauer.[76] Such practices can be seen as a rational means of acquiring knowledge about goods or as a frivolous pastime. Either way, they helped to mould the individual as a consumer. Direct evidence of browsing in shops is very difficult to find in correspondence and contemporary accounts; yet, as Walsh argues, 'early-modern housewives were not shopping for standardized quality, but the best quality they could lay their hands on at a given time'.[77] Household manuals offered advice about choosing, trying, and buying fresh foods, particularly meat, flour, and bread. Attention centred on balancing up the quality and price of particular items, and the need for the buyer to do so using her own senses and skills, independent of any importuning by the retailer. Buying fresh food was thus a skilled business, and it was important not to rely on a single supplier.[78] This was true of groceries as well. Complaints made by Elizabeth Purefoy about the quality of goods were echoed by many others. Sir Roger Newdigate, for example, received an apology from Twinings in response to a complaint about a consignment of souchong.[79] Such correspondence reflects the close attention that consumers paid to the quality of the goods they were sold, but it also reveals one of the pitfalls of ordering goods remotely and thus being unable to inspect them in the shop.

Browsing groceries was useful in making informed decisions about the goods to be purchased and central to the sociability of shopping for groceries. Gibson's advertisement announcing that 'Gentlemen and Ladies may try the Teas'[80] brought these ideas together: the sociability of tea drinking being coupled with the serious business of assessing quality against price. And much the same can be seen in the stylized image constructed for Henry Lilwall's trade card, with the customers seated comfortably before the counter as the shopkeeper presents and packages their goods on the counter. With durable goods, browsing was linked to bargaining over price, bolts of cloth frequently carrying codes that told the shop assistant its cost, starting price, and any abatement that might be offered. In contrast, fixed prices were a common feature of the grocery trade from the early eighteenth century and formed a central theme of selling practices and newspaper advertisements. Moreover, there is strong evidence from shopkeepers' account books that prices varied little if at all between customers, excepting small discounts for buying

[75] Mui and Mui, *Shops and Shopkeeping*, 214.
[76] Berry, 'Polite Consumption'; Schopenhauer, *A Lady Travels*, 151.
[77] Walsh, 'Shopping at First Hand', 14.
[78] Walsh, 'Shopping at First Hand', 21.
[79] WRO, CR136/B/2626.
[80] *Newcastle Courant*, 15 Aug. 1752.

in bulk.[81] Yet prices were clearly not beyond the bargaining process. Elizabeth Purefoy could request a better pennyworth from her regular supplier, presumably in the expectation of a lower price or superior quality goods.[82] More telling, perhaps, is a letter written by Steele in a 1712 copy of the *Spectator*. This purported to be from a disgruntled shopkeeper, complaining about customers who, 'under Pretence taking their innocent Rambles forsooth, and diverting the Spleen, seldom fail to plague me twice or thrice a Day, to cheapen Tea or buy a Screen'. Shown the goods they enquired after, these people would declare: 'this is too dear, that is their Aversion, another thing is charming but not wanted: The Ladies are cur'd of the Spleen, but I am not a Shilling the better for it.'[83]

In these diatribes against undisciplined female shoppers, tea becomes another product whose price was open to negotiation. More generally, it is placed in the wider arena of shopping as a leisure activity. The tone is highly critical, but the practices described are clearly intended to strike a chord with readers—to be familiar as well as frivolous. It is uncertain whether such practices penetrated far into the realm of the provincial grocer's shop, but suggests that routine shopping for groceries did not occupy a wholly separate sphere from the pleasurable browsing of luxury goods. Central to both, of course, was the relationship between the shopkeeper and the customer. This links closely to ideas of trust and reputation, and to the reciprocal construction of respectability, but also to the wider mutuality of shopping, whether in person or by correspondence. The Gibbards enjoyed an unusually close relationship with their London tea merchant, Charles Hancock, who wrote, mostly to Mary, about personal as well as business matters. Indeed, their family lives appear to have overlapped considerably and intimately. Hancock asked about the health of the Gibbards' children and was close to Mary's nephew, writing in January 1824: 'My love pray to Johnny Harvey and tell him I fully expect to have the pleasure of his company for a week on his way to school, The Pantomimes he must see. He must write and fix the time and tell me all about his plans.'[84] Hancock was not simply a useful stopping-off point for young relatives visiting the metropolis; he was also entrusted with resolving some of the Gibbards' financial matters in London. Having being asked to enquire into a personal matter of some unpaid dividends due to John's uncle, the Reverend John Gibbard, Hancock replied in January 1819, agreeing to help and concluding with the promise of 'our united remembrances to Mrs G. and your sister, and offering you my very best services in the City'.[85] The trust that this intimacy both reinforced and reflected was useful to the Gibbards in that they had a reliable source of good-quality teas. It was also helpful to Hancock, facilitating sales to useful customers and assisting in smoothing over any disagreements that arose.[86]

---

[81] Mui and Mui, *Shops and Shopkeeping*, 215.
[82] Eland, *Purefoy Letters*, no. 105.
[83] Quoted in Mackie, *Commerce of Everyday Life*, 222–3. See also Kowalski-Wallace, *Consuming Subjects*, 85.
[84] BLA, GA93.
[85] BLA, GA25/35.
[86] Bailey, 'Maintaining Status', 22.

Thomas Turner also cultivated close relations with prime consumers, in his case the Duke of Newcastle at nearby Halland House. These were articulated through the duke's steward, Christopher Coates, who on one occasion came to Turner's shop with his wife and at least four other couples. They drank tea, 'spent the evening with us and played brag', before being treated to what was, for Turner, a fairly elaborate meal of 'salt fish, a dish of Scotch collops with force meat balls, a piece of cold roast beef, some potted beef, a cold baked rice pudding, bullace and gooseberry tarts, celery, watercresses, egg sauce, cold ham and parsnips'.[87] The following year, Turner records dining in similar company at Coates's expense, staying on after dinner again to play brag.[88] The mutuality of such dining was important in maintaining his connection at Halland House, but most of Turner's sociability was more modest in its scope and involved the ordinary folk of the village. He regularly sat and drank tea with his customers, as, for example, when 'Mrs Fuller, widow, buying some things in the shop in the morn, breakfasted with me, as did Miss Fanny in the afternoon, and drank tea with me'. Such hospitality was clearly unplanned, but some social visits to the shop were more premeditated—at least for some. One afternoon, Turner notes, 'Fanny Hicks, James Marchant, Fanny Weller and Bett. Mepham drank tea with me, and they stayed and spent the evening with me and played at brag. They all met by accident, coming to buy goods in the shop, Fanny Weller excepted.'[89] Importantly, this links the sociability of tea drinking with the business of buying and selling. The two were tied closely together, both in practice and in Turner's perception and enjoyment of his life. More broadly, these practices were important in the construction of social identity—a process that affected the lives of ordinary villagers as much as the middling sorts.

CONCLUSIONS

To observe that purchasing practices were shaped by status and gender is unremarkable. The type, quality, and quantity of groceries that people bought would clearly be influenced by their spending power and by gender roles in the house and beyond. But aggregate stereotypes rarely held good for individual consumers, underlining the importance of personal preference and habit in the purchase of consumable as well as durable goods. Indeed, the routine nature of grocery shopping is apparent for both wealthy and poorer consumers. Some elite families, like the Leighs of Adlestrop, carefully monitored their stores and bought accordingly; others appear to have operated on a day-to-day or week-to-week basis, buying groceries as need arose or perhaps (as with Grace Nettleton) as part of a weekly routine. Much the same was true of the people who bought from village shops, with individuals such as Martha Chase returning several times in a single day to

---

[87] Vaisey, *Thomas Turner*, 14 Mar. 1758.
[88] Vaisey, *Thomas Turner*, 9 Jan. 1758.
[89] Vaisey, *Thomas Turner*, 11 July 1764; 14 Jan. 1763.

make specific purchases. These variations suggest that shopping behaviour was shaped by factors other than imitation or distinction—it was not, in general, a process aligned with acquiring or markers of status. Consumers were driven by different motivations and displayed a corresponding variety of shopping behaviour, yet all relied on a stable and trusting relationship with the shopkeeper—a relationship that was crucial in framing the shopping process and, more broadly, the consumption of groceries. It was nuanced by the practice of buying from several different retailers, consumers choosing on the basis of price, quality, and service. Linked to this was the importance of market information, gathered in person, via servants or through correspondence with suppliers. This suggests that shoppers were rational consumers, responding in predictable ways to economic variables, but such a view is at odds with the sociability of shopping: the human interaction with the shopkeeper and fellow shoppers. Shopping for groceries may not have been central to polite consumption as modelled by Berry, but it could still be an important social activity, valued by shopper and shopkeeper alike—as Turner's diaries makes clear.

Shopping was largely shaped by considerations of utility. Among these were practical issues such as convenience and cost, considerations that impinged on the wealthy as well as on the poor. More important was the desire to enhance comfort and pleasure, priorities that align shopping for groceries more closely with de Vries's model of industrious revolution than McKendrick's emulation-driven consumer society, especially given the depth of market penetration among ordinary people. However, adopting either of these meta-narratives risks losing the nuances of shopping behaviour and the consumer identities that it helped to construct. For some, shopping for groceries helped to shape their identity as polite consumers; for others, it presented them as effective and efficient. The latter links back to the nature of shopping as an important and serious business as well as being an opportunity for sociability. It also underlines Miller's emphasis of shopping as being as much about others as self: 'good' shoppers being concerned with doing their best to supply the needs of those for whom they were buying.[90] This reminds us that consumption practices could be shaped by external considerations that privileged mutual regard and cooperation over the social competition emphasized by conspicuous consumption, politeness, and respectability.[91]

---

[90] Miller, *Theory of Shopping*, esp. 5–9.
[91] See de Vries, *Industrious Revolution*, 21–2.

9

Tea and Cakes: Consuming Groceries

INTRODUCTION

Food has long played an important part in shaping behaviour and identity, and unsurprisingly forms a central focus to several conceptions of consumer change. It was, for instance, crucial in hospitality and largesse in the premodern great house and to notions of the magnificence of table. In such contexts, food was closely linked to ideas of conspicuous consumption, not least because splendid meals involved deploying costly positional goods—the food itself, but also the cooks required in its preparation and the servants to bring it to the table. In these readings, food was used to strengthen claims of wealth and status, through what de Vries terms 'aggressive signalling'.[1] But it was also associated with more subtle or indirect assertions of social distinction, which drew on displays of taste as manifestations of cultural capital.[2] Taste could be communicated through a discerning palate (in terms of wine, for example, or tea, refined sugar, and cigars) and the consumption of fashionable food—from the courtly style of the Restoration period, through the mid-eighteenth-century fashion for *nouvelle cuisine* among the Whig elite, to the reassertion of English cooking towards the end of the century.[3] Alternatively, Smith and Schivelbusch, among others, see food as part of the normalizing agendas of politeness, respectability, and sobriety. Polite credentials could be cemented through the rituals of tea drinking, respectability through displays of virtuous moderation, and rational masculinity in the realm of the coffee house.[4]

The novel and luxury nature of certain foods was central to all these readings of eighteenth-century consumption. Novelty was one of the key attractions of the new groceries that appeared in Britain from the middle decades of the seventeenth century. Drinking tea, coffee, and chocolate afforded new physical experiences, and the wide range of teas available by the mid-eighteenth century provided variety and complexity. But novel goods also allowed for the construction of new consumption practices and, with them, new identities for individual or groups of consumers—a process discussed in detail by Smith and central to many conceptions

---

[1] De Vries, *Industrious Revolution*, 22; Veblen, *Theory of the Leisure Class*. Early modern dining practices are discussed in Heal, *Hospitality in Early-Modern England*; Dawson, *Plenti and Grase*, 208–19, 224–9; Colquhoun, *Taste*, 72–83.

[2] Bourdieu, *Distinction*.

[3] Lehmann, *British Housewife*, 169–289. On the link between cooking and national identity, see Anderson, *Imagined Communities*, 37–46.

[4] Smith, *Consumption*, 63–104, 108–18, 139–88; Schivelbusch, *Tastes of Paradise*, esp. 34–84; Hall, 'Culinary Spaces', 172–7.

of consumer revolution and social transformation.[5] These identities, values, and practices, like the goods themselves, are seen by Simmel as 'trickling down' the social hierarchy, their general uptake eased by the example of fashion leaders. But we should also recognize the upwards dynamic of this process, as lower social groups actively sought out the status markers of higher-status groups, and the possibility of independent cultures of consumption.[6]

Luxury is both a slippery and a relative term—a category that is contingent upon time and space, as well as culture and wealth.[7] Drawing on a lengthy debate over the virtues and vices of luxury, which ran through much of the early modern period, and on a growing body of empirical research, historians have broadened the scope of luxury consumption, moving beyond Sombart's emphasis on the gratification of individual sensuous desires to encompass a broad range of material goods.[8] These were identified by Veblen as the set of 'more excellent goods' central to his notion of conspicuous consumption.[9] This links to the idea of luxuries as 'social valuables', characterized by their high cost; 'the patron–client relations of production and trade, and the protection and reproduction of status systems'.[10] To these anthropological perspectives we might usefully add cultural definitions of luxury goods, which centre on them as 'incarnated signs' carrying broader meanings and associations. Understanding the social and cultural meaning of these signs depended on semiotic virtuosity, while consuming luxury in an appropriate manner drew on specialized knowledge.[11] This dual definition is useful in the context of groceries, Smith, for example, arguing that they 'fit into the context of luxury not only because their sensual qualities provided a variety of delightful tastes, but also because they came from the mysterious East'.[12] In other words, they were replete with cultural significance, but were also tangible and sensual, bringing pleasure to the consumer. This places groceries in the context, not only of fashion, discernment, and conspicuous consumption, but also of utility and comfort.

If we draw on these ideas to explore the consumption of groceries in the home, three areas are particularly worthy of further analysis. First is the way in which certain goods were viewed and consumed as novelties or luxuries. This involves considering how novelty might be defined for the individual consumer and how purchases of groceries might reflect a pursuit of the new. Leading from this is the question of how we best understand the processes whereby novelties such as tea and coffee spread between different social groups. Here, the notion of luxury is

[5] Smith, *Consumption*. For fuller discussion of the importance of novelty, see Ch. 1.

[6] Simmel, *On Individuality*, 293–323; McCracken, *Culture and Consumption*, 93–6.

[7] For discussion of the concept of luxury, see Berg, *Luxury and Pleasure*, 21–45; Berry, *Idea of Luxury*, 138–9; Peck, *Consuming Splendor*, 1–24.

[8] Peck, *Consuming Splendor*, 10–22; Berger, *Most Necessary Luxuries*; Sombart, *Luxury and Capitalism*.

[9] Veblen, *Theory of the Leisure Class*, 73–4.

[10] Berg, *Luxury and Pleasure*, 30.

[11] Appadurai, *Social Life of Things*, 3–63. See also Douglas, *Thought Styles*, p. iii; Miller, 'Consumption Studies', 267–74.

[12] Smith, *Consumption*, 93.

important, both as a signifier of distinction and as sensual pleasure. Assessing the relative importance of these two provides a better understanding of the motivations for and contexts of consumption. Second is the way in which groceries were used in producing meals. Recipe books can tell us much about shifts in culinary styles and the resulting changes in the consumption of a range of groceries. Of particular interest is the balance between continuity and change within recipes and ingredients, and the extent to which ideas of the exotic and imperial were incorporated into English cooking—is Bickham correct in seeing food as central to the British imperial experience? Third are the actual practices through which these foods were consumed and especially how the consumption of a range of groceries was interrelated within domestic routines.[13] This involves examining the meals served and consumed by elites in order to assess the changing balance of ingredients needed to create an elegant table. It also means looking beyond the ritual of tea drinking and established ideas of polite female sociability to consider the ways in which caffeine drinks were related to the consumption of a range of prepared foods.

NOVELTY, LUXURY, AND UTILITY: CONSUMPTION PATTERNS

Novelty involves newness, variety, and change, but measuring these and assessing their importance to consumers of groceries is by no means straightforward. At Stoneleigh Abbey, the Leigh's consumption of groceries changed quite markedly between the mid-seventeenth and late eighteenth centuries. Traditional culinary items such as dried fruit, spices, seeds, and sugar were being bought and consumed in the 1630s and still appeared in the bills 150 years later (see Table 8.1). Other goods vanished completely from the Leigh bills (ginger, prunes, and comfits, for example), while new categories of goods appeared for the first time: most obviously tea, coffee, and chocolate, but also ready-made sauces and ketchups. However, the extent to which goods should be viewed as novelties is open to question. Ketchups and pickles were familiar enough items when they started to be purchased by the Leighs in the 1760s. The shift here came in terms of buying such things ready-made, rather than preparing them at home: behaviour was novel rather than the product. Moreover, any switch to greater market orientation on the part of the Leighs was apparently partial, as two manuscript recipe books owned by the family and probably dating from the late eighteenth century include recipes for mushroom pickle and 'best Indian cavach'.[14] Similarly, while tea and coffee first appear in the Leighs' bills in 1711, they had been available for at least fifty years before this

---

[13] Coffee houses have been dealt with extensively elsewhere. See, e.g., Ellis, *Coffee House*; Cowan, *Social Life of Coffee*; Smith, *Consumption*, 140–61.

[14] SCLA, DR 98/167; SCLA, DR 762/55. Although it is not certain that these two pickles were actually made, their reproduction in family recipes books shows a continued interest and how they *might* be made. See Pennell, 'Perfecting Practice?'.

date. Furthermore, Edward, third Lord Leigh, drank tea, coffee, and chocolate while a student at Oxford University between 1702 and 1704. The first two pages of his pocket book show that he quickly set himself up with all the paraphernalia required to brew and serve hot drinks. Thereafter, it records at least eight purchases of chocolate (usually bought by the pound); six purchases of tea (in quarter- and half-pound packets), and three of coffee (in pound lots).[15] Whether these were new drinks for him is unclear, but his taste appears to have changed somewhat during his time at Oxford. Chocolate gave way to tea, three purchases of which were made during July 1704—a shift that might suggest that he was still deciding which drink he preferred.

Even while the future Lord Leigh was experimenting with caffeine drinks, they were already becoming popular among the lower orders. McCants and Blondé demonstrate that much poorer sections of society were also regular consumers of tea and coffee by the 1730s.[16] In Antwerp, tea drinking was sufficiently deep-rooted by 1747 for the Brabantine Estates to feel able to impose on everyone over the age of 7 a tax *Pour la Consommation du Thé*. In the Dutch Republic, the innovation spread rapidly to small provincial towns as well as larger cities, and did so in the face of growing impoverishment of the population. By the second half of the eighteenth century, around half of the very poorest families—many of whom did not possess even a single item of furniture—had equipment for making tea or coffee.[17] English inventory data do not extend quite so low down the social scale, but evidence from Kent and Cornwall suggests that as many as one-quarter of households had utensils specific to the preparation of hot drinks by the second quarter of the eighteenth century. Evidence of thefts from domestic property confirms that these included many poorer families (see Chapter 10).[18] Tea consumption by the poor was sufficiently widespread to produce a series of critiques from moralizing social commentators. In 1745, as part of the ongoing debate on the taxation of tea, Simon Mason complained about tea-drinking women who 'to be fashionable, and imitate their superiors, are neglecting their Spinning, Knitting and spending what their Husbands are labouring hard for...their Children are in Rags, gnawing at a brown Crust, while these gossips are conversing the affairs of the whole Town'. A generation later, the Reverend John Clayton criticized the poor of Manchester for their 'shameful extravagance' in buying tea (and gin) from shopkeepers. The problem was twofold: not only were these products wasteful fripperies; they were also bought 'on credit from shopkeepers', leaving little money to spend more worthily on food at the 'open market'.[19]

---

[15] SCLA, DR 18/29/6 Box 1.

[16] McCants, 'Poor Consumers', 179–87; Blondé, 'Think Local'.

[17] Many tea or coffee goods recorded in the inventories were damaged or old, and they were under-represented among goods taken to pawn shops, both of which suggests regular use (McCants, 'Poor Consumers', 192–4).

[18] Overton et al., *Production and Consumption*, 99; Weatherill, *Consumer Behaviour*, 168.

[19] Quoted, respectively, in White, 'Labouring-Class Domestic Sphere', 253–4; Wadsworth and Mann, *Cotton Trade*, 388. Cobbett was still complaining about the poor drinking tea in the early nineteenth century (Burnett, *Plenty and Want*, 35–7). See also Rees, *Grocery Trade*, ii. 14, 25; Mintz, *Sweetness and Power*, 115–17.

How are we best to understand the broadening consumption of these 'new' groceries? Simmelian trickle-down places the emphasis on the example of social elites, and it is clear that contemporaries such as Mason saw imitation of their betters as the key factor in female tea drinking. Some caution is needed here, however, because similar behaviour does not necessarily mean imitation, and imitation certainly does not imply emulation. Even if we assume that Mason's assessment was correct, it is the poor that were 'hunting' status markers of their social superiors, who had ample scope for 'flight' to new ones.[20] By and large, they did not—in part because the existence of different grades of tea (and of many other groceries) allowed for distinctions to be made within as well as between categories of goods. People could signal their wealth, distinction, and dignity by consuming higher-grade or luxury goods. Writing in 1712, Lady Strafford, for example, offered a stinging indictment of one Mr Marshall, who, rather than using wood and wax candles, had a 'Cole fire and Tallow candles which I know was made great jest on'.[21] Gradations in the quality and price of tea were often emphasized in the advertisements placed by dealers. In the 1770s, for example, Eagleton advertised nine different grades of tea, from superfine hyson at 14*s. 6d.* per pound, through superfine souchong at 9*s. 6d.*, to 'good common bohea' at 3*s. 10d.*[22] While poorer consumers might opt primarily for cheaper boheas or congous, the wealthy could distinguish themselves by purchasing 'luxury' varieties. A sample of fourteen bills presented to the Leighs between 1738 and 1792 record a total of thirty-eight purchases of tea. Most regularly bought were green and hyson teas, which both appeared in around two-thirds of purchases, although souchong was favoured after it was first purchased in the 1760s. All of these varieties might be considered premium blends and were probably consumed by the Leighs themselves. So too were the souchong and hyson bought by Mary Gibbard, but she also purchased significant quantities of the cheaper bohea, which was probably intended for the servants' hall.[23]

Similar distinctions were made through purchases of coffee and chocolate, and of culinary groceries such as sugar and dried fruit. What distinguished different grades of sugar and separated sugar from treacle was their price—a reflection of quality that might be measured, quite literally, in terms of refinement. In 1719, John Dryden was charged 7½*d.* per lb for single refined and 4½*d.* per lb for brown sugar. Nearly eighty years later, prices had increased, but the differential remained: a bill to the Leighs at Stoneleigh Abbey recorded purchases of single refined at 15*d.* per pound, finest Lisbon at 13*d.*, dry sugar at 9*d.*, and raw sugar at 8*d.* per lb.[24] Much the same was true of tobacco: the overseers of St John's workhouse in Chester paid 10*d.* per lb for tobacco, which must have been an inferior product to that being purchased around the same time by the Leighs, who were charged 2*s.* per lb for tobacco being given to their outworkers.[25] But distinctions of quality and lux-

---

[20] Campbell, 'Understanding Consumption', 41; McCracken, *Culture and Consumption*, 94.
[21] Quoted in Greig, 'Leading the Fashion', 299.
[22] *Adams Weekly Courant*, 18 Aug. 1778. See Ch. 7 for more detailed discussion.
[23] Bailey, 'Maintaining Status', 21–3.
[24] NRO, D(CA)142, bill to John Dryden, 1719; SCLA, DR18/5/6288.
[25] SCLA, DR18/5/2076, DR18/5/1782.

ury can also be found in less familiar guises. On Christmas Day 1720, Grace Nettleton bought six mince pies for a shilling apiece. These were probably for
consumption by the family, since they were distinguished from 'eight mince pies
for ye folks', which cost just 6*d.* each.[26]

It is possible, then, to identify some groceries as luxuries in terms of their price
and thus their exclusivity. Smith also suggests that their provenance could render
them luxuries, not least because of the discernment needed to understand the
implications for the quality of goods that were carried by a particular provenance
or label.[27] Jamaican rum had a reputation for high quality while Brazilian tobacco
was widely recognized as being cheap, but poor quality. Most distinctions were
more subtle and difficult to read, but were important nonetheless: as noted earlier,
the Leighs bought sugar as powder, lumps, loaves, raw and moist, but they were
also billed for Lisbon and Barbados sugar, which in 1738 sold at 6*d.* per lb—some
50 per cent more than simple 'sugar'.[28] Other labels were also guides to quality.
Most obvious were named chocolates such as Sir Hans Sloan's Milk and Churchman's Patent Chocolate, which Eagleton advertised at 5*s.* 6*d.* per lb—some 18 per
cent more than superfine and 50 per cent more than 'good' chocolate.[29] Coffee was
not 'branded' in the same way; quality distinctions being made instead through
place-name labels (see Chapter 2). While Mary Leigh bought Turkey and Mocha
coffee in the 1780s and 1790s, no bills mention West Indian coffee, despite its
availability from the 1730s.[30] Perhaps it was found among the ordinary coffee occasionally bought by Mary's father; if so, it is telling that it was not labelled as such,
probably because it was seen as an inferior product.[31] The labels attached to spices
and other flavourings were also significant. Many highlighted associations with
empire—for example, Jamaica ginger, Indian arrowroot, and Japan soy—but, as
argued earlier, their significance probably lay more in terms of communicating
authenticity than in linking the consumer to some grand imperial project.[32] Rather
more straightforward in their communication of luxury and differentiation from
the ordinary are labels such as fine, best, or superfine. With some groceries, the
adjective was as important as the noun: certain teas were better quality than others,
but each could be purchased in a variety of grades that allowed consumers with
money and discernment to differentiate themselves by buying the more expensive
finer grades.[33] The Leighs' consumption of tea, chocolate, and coffee mark this very
clearly, with over 60 per cent of purchases being labelled with a quality descriptor.

These gradations allowed consumers to mark their status and distinguish themselves from other social groups. In this sense, luxury equates with positional goods
and is deployed, as de Vries argues, as a defensive mechanism against the consumption practices of others.[34] The spread of luxury could thus be seen as profligate,
corrosive of social boundaries, and injurious to the moral fibre of the individual
and society as a whole—arguments that were regularly deployed in the debate over

---

[26] CALS, DLT/B51.   [27] Smith, *Consumption*, 93.   [28] SCLA, DR18/5/2128, 2217.
[29] *Adams Weekly Courant*, 18 Aug. 1778.   [30] SCLA, DR18/5/5851, 5998, 5999.
[31] See Ellis, *Coffee House*, 208–9.   [32] Bickham, 'Eating the Empire'; Hall, 'Culinary Spaces'.
[33] See e.g. *Adams Weekly Courant*, 18 Aug. 1778.   [34] De Vries, *Industrious Revolution*, 22.

luxury that surfaced in the seventeenth century and rumbled on through the early decades of the eighteenth.[35] And yet many 'luxury' groceries were clearly viewed and understood by contemporary consumers as everyday goods. We have already seen that the Sussex shopkeeper Thomas Turner treated tea as part of his regular social interaction with friends and customers in the mid-eighteenth century. It provided a reason for visiting his shop, an excuse to stay on after purchases had been made, and a lubricant to conversation. Around the same time, the overseers of St John's workhouse in Chester were buying a variety of groceries to supplement the inmates' diet. Between March 1731 and February 1732, they bought 6 lb of treacle and 1 lb of tobacco each week, and unspecified quantities of candles and soap roughly once a month.[36] There were also more occasional purchases of pepper, which was bought in 2 oz lots. By 1738 small quantities of sugar were being purchased, seemingly as an extra item, as the quantity of treacle remained unchanged. Oat cakes were also added to the inmates' diet, while pepper was being used rather more often, purchases increasing in frequency—at least during the early months of the year. There was some retrenchment by 1752, with sugar, pepper, and oatcakes all disappearing from the list of purchases. The quantities of treacle and tobacco remained unchanged, however, which suggests that this was seen as the acceptable level of 'luxury' that should be added to the diet of Chester's pauper population. Outside such institutions, workers were increasingly inclined to buy and consume imported groceries—a shift noted by Samuel Finney in the rural districts south of Manchester. He listed treacle, brown sugar, and tobacco among other 'small necessities' purchased locally in the mid-eighteenth century, but added tea, coffee and loaf sugar to this list by the 1770s.[37]

These 'customary luxuries', as Smith describes them, were things that even the poorest might expect to consume.[38] They were not markers of status or part of aspirational consumption—such ideas were meaningless for groups such as the inmates of the workhouse in Chester. Equally, while respectability may have been a broad aspirational characteristic of all classes by the early nineteenth century, this is unlikely to have been on the minds of the overseers of the poor. The fact that even involuntary consumers might be given such small luxuries suggests that these goods played a part in basic material and emotional comfort. This emphasis on utility as a motive and framework for consumption can also be seen in the tea-drinking habits of the poor. As Burnett argues, a hot sweet drink made an otherwise unappealing meal a little more bearable—it was a small comfort rather than an extravagant luxury.[39] Linking tea to meals invites us to consider the broader deployment of groceries within culinary processes. Cooking and eating were important in giving pleasure, constructing identity, and demonstrating wealth; and changes in diet and dining practices led to growth in demand for some groceries, while others languished in or disappeared from the kitchen cupboard.

---

[35] For a summary of these, see Peck, *Consuming Splendor*, 6–22; Berg, *Luxury and Pleasure*, 21–45.
[36] CALS, PC 51/22 Overseers' Accounts: St John's, Chester. The quantities of treacle and sugar suggest culinary rather than medicinal purposes.
[37] Quoted in Ashton, *Economic History*, 214–16. See also McCants, 'Poor Consumers', 184–7.
[38] Smith, *Consumption*, 99.   [39] Burnett, *Plenty and Want*, 44–5, 53–4, 67–8.

MODES OF CONSUMPTION: READING
RECIPE BOOKS

Traditionally, English cookery had made extensive use of a wide range of spices to produce richly flavoured dishes. This practice is seen by Colquhoun as a product of crusaders returning from the Near East with a taste for spiced and often sweetened food. Such tastes were reinforced by the ability of these dishes to signal the economic and cultural capital of elite consumers who could afford costly spices and exotic fruits, and had the ability to access such goods via overseas merchants.[40] Such tastes were not exclusive to England, but they do appear to have been more pronounced than in France. From analysis of mid-fifteenth-century manuscript cookery books, Flandrin identifies the most frequently used spices as saffron, ginger, cinnamon, pepper, cloves, and mace.[41] In each case, they feature in a greater proportion of English recipes. There was also a deep-rooted habit of mixing sweet and savoury, particularly seen in signature English dishes such as puddings and pies, but found in 26 per cent of dishes listed in the mid-fifteenth-century Beinecke manuscript cookery book. This often involved the use of raisins or other dried fruits, but increasingly meant adding sugar to savoury dishes, although this was often as a spice rather than overtly to sweeten the food.[42] Tastes gradually changed. Lehmann argues that, in the seventeenth century, and especially following the Restoration, there was a strong move against heavily spiced dishes and a shift towards courtly or French modes of cooking. This was manifest in a growing reliance upon sauces such as fricassées and ragouts, and a desire to separate sweet from savoury, perhaps most strongly expressed by La Varenne.[43] These tastes were communicated through a growing number of published recipe books written by eminent male cooks—often those employed at court or by the aristocracy: men such as Robert May, François Massialot, Patrick Lamb, Charles Carter, and Vincent La Chapelle. These deployed an extravagant mode of cooking that stressed novel combinations and preparations, especially in terms of sauces. In the middle decades of the eighteenth century, the French style reached its apogee in the exclusive and exclusionary *nouvelle cuisine* favoured by Whig grandees. Such modes of cooking were complex, costly, and time-consuming. Moreover, in the case of *nouvelle cuisine*, they were also seen as extravagantly wasteful—supreme examples of conspicuous consumption in that they deployed scarce and costly goods consciously to communicate wealth and status.[44]

This brought two reactions in the middle decades of the eighteenth century. Neither was imitative, but rather sought to construct counter-cultures of consumption. First was a move to offer simpler fare, more in touch with the needs and pockets of middling sort and gentry consumers. Recipe books written by ordinary

[40] Colquhoun, *Taste*, 3–6. See also Dawson, *Plenti and Grase*, 164–73; Schivelbusch, *Tastes of Paradise*, 7–8.
[41] Quoted in Lehmann, *British Housewife*, 22.
[42] Lehmann, *British Housewife*, 23; Hall, 'Culinary Spaces', 172; Mintz, *Sweetness and Power*, 82–4.
[43] Lehmann, *British Housewife*, 281–2; Colquhoun, *Taste*, 165.
[44] Veblen, *Theory of the Leisure Class*, 25.

women such as Martha Bradley and Hannah Glasse offered tips on economy as well as a host of more 'everyday' recipes. Second was a growing anti-French feeling, although this was often ambivalently expressed. The rhetoric in Hannah Glasse's books, for example, is clear enough, yet she still provided versions of complex French dishes.[45] Around the same time, Bickham argues, English recipes and recipe books became increasingly influenced by imperial connections, with recipes for curry, pilau rice, piccalilli, kebabs, New England pancakes, Carolina snowballs, and so on becoming established as standard elements in most cookery books. As well as forming another means through which food could demonstrate social distinction, it made cookery a kind of vicarious tourism as well as a celebration of imperialism and colonial goods.[46] Colquhoun also makes much of these new dishes, noting the growing use of curry powder from the 1780s, which, she argues, trounced the 'gentler flavours of mace and nutmeg' and led to a growing taste for heavily spiced dishes dominated by cayenne.[47] However, this seems to overstate the case and the novelty of these flavours: the mainstream of recipes took on an increasingly English character—a trend that Lehmann links most strongly to the influence of Elizabeth Raffald and the so-called tavern cooks of the late eighteenth century. This reassertion of English cookery involved a rejection of French sauces and an emphasis instead on 'honest' cooking, often with the appearance of the food taking precedence over its flavour. Simplicity was achieved through the growing use of ketchups—a move condemned by some as debasing the skills of the cook—while the importance of the visual placed even greater emphasis on dessert, which provided ample opportunities for display in the shape of centrepieces of spun sugar, jellies, and creams.[48]

These changes in culinary styles are widely recognized. Their importance to the present analysis comes in terms of the ways in which they influenced the consumption of groceries. To address this issue, I want to explore in detail four published cookery books reflecting different periods in the development of English (elite) cookery. The first is W.M.'s *The Compleat Cook*, published in 1663, which represents a bridge between early modern and the courtly style publications that followed. The second, *England's Newest Way in all Sorts of Cookery, Pastry and all Pickles*, by Henry Howard (1708) represents this French courtly style at its height; the third, Hannah Glasse's *The Art of Cookery, Made Plain and Easy* (1747; 7th edn 1760), exemplifies the subsequent reassertion of English cookery, and the fourth, John Farley's *London Art of Cookery* (1800), draws on the trend for fashionable dining at large London taverns.[49] These books were aimed at gentry or middling households, with the idea that they could re-create aristocratic dining according to their more modest means. This rationale points towards imitative if not emulative behaviour—an attempt to re-create and democratize the manuscript recipe books

[45] Lehmann, *British Housewife*, 283–6.   [46] Bickham, 'Eating the Empire', 94, 99–100.

[47] Colquhoun, *Taste*, 216.

[48] Lehmann, *British Housewife*, 287–9; Mennell, *All Manners of Food*; Mintz, *Sweetness and Power*, 93–4.

[49] The seventh edition of Glasse included an appendix of 150 'New and Useful Receipts' and thus forms a much larger collection than the original volume.

created in elite households. Lehmann argues that the latter declined in importance in the early eighteenth century as aristocratic women increasingly disengaged themselves from the processes of preparing food. However, as Pennell makes clear, manuscript recipe books were still being created by such women into the middle decades of the century and beyond, suggesting continued engagement with domestic culinary activities. The recipes that they recorded included those copied from published volumes; others given by friends, relatives, or servants, and attempts to capture favourite and/or traditional recipes for the benefit of themselves, their daughters, or their housekeepers.[50] For both the published and the manuscript volumes, the recipes provide a unique insight into the type of groceries used by respectable households and the ways in which they could be employed.

Of the overall trends noted above, the growing separation of sweet and savoury is perhaps the most evident in the cookery books sampled. The number of recipes combining meat, spices, and dried fruit had already declined since the Middle Ages, but still stood at 14 per cent in 1663 and only slightly less than that forty-five years later (Table 9.1). By 1760, however, this style of cookery had declined significantly, and it had all but vanished by the end of the century, appearing in just 1 per cent of Farley's recipes. Some recipes used sugar in place of fruit, but these were always less common and followed a similar downward trajectory over the century following the Restoration. Contrary to Colquhoun's assertion, there was no surge in the use of curry powder and cayenne. Indeed, the most common combination of spices remained remarkably constant: nutmeg, mace, and pepper appearing together in about 7 per cent of recipes throughout the period. The number of different groceries deployed in published recipe books displayed a similar stability through the later decades of the seventeenth century, but thereafter grew significantly, so that Farley's book includes more than twice the number found in Howard (Table 9.2). Assuming that practice followed this lead, it seems that a much broader palate of flavours was being used in domestic cooking by the end of the eighteenth century. Glasse's recipes called for 'new' ingredients such as cayenne, ketchup, and mushroom pickle, and also a widening variety of other, more delicate, flavourings including pistachios, bitter almonds, and cardamom. Farley continued this trend, again making use of cayenne and ketchups, but also other ready-made ingredients, such as oyster sauce. Moreover, a number of familiar groceries were deployed in an innovative manner in cooking, most notably hyson tea and coffee.

It would be wrong to draw too starkly any distinction between these periods of stability and change. While the number of groceries remained unaltered through the late seventeenth century, there was considerable flux in the type of ingredients being used. Indeed, only nineteen groceries were common to W.M. and Howard: saffron, fennel, gum Arabic, and verjuice, for example, were used by the former but not the latter, who instead drew on ingredients such as allspice, long pepper, citron, and isinglass. Subsequent growth in the number of groceries used is partly a product of the much larger number of recipes that appear in Glasse and Farley, the

---

[50] Lehmann, *British Housewife*, 33–58; Pennell, 'Perfecting Practice?', 241–5. Pennell further argues the practical nature of manuscript volumes and the need to validate recipes through use.

Table 9.1. Combinations of groceries used in four English recipe books, 1663–1760

Combination of groceries	W.M., 1663 (N = 161)		Howard, 1708 (N = 230)		Glasse, 1760 (N = 1,003)		Farley, 1800 (N = 863)	
	No.	%	No.	%	No.	%	No.	%
Meat, spice, fruit	23	14.3	26	11.3	34	3.4	9	1.0
Meat, spice, sugar	6	3.7	7	3.0	3	0.3	12	1.4
Nutmeg, mace, pepper	11	6.8	16	7.0	77	7.7	58	6.7
Nutmeg, sugar	14	8.7	25	10.9	47	4.7	64	7.4

Sources: W.M., *Compleat Cook* (1663); Howard, *England's Newest Way* (1708); Glasse, *Art of Cookery* (1760); Farley, *London Art of Cookery* (1800).

Table 9.2. Groceries included in four English recipe books, 1663–1760

W.M., 1663 (N = 161)		Howard, 1708 (N = 230)		Glasse, 1760 (N = 1,003)		Farley, 1800 (N = 863)	
Grocery	%	Grocery	%	Grocery	%	Grocery	%
Sugar	37.3	Sugar	42.6	Pepper	30.7	Sugar	34.5
Nutmeg	37.3	Nutmeg	40.4	Sugar	30.6	Pepper	29.7
Mace	32.3	Mace	37.0	Mace	28.9	Mace	27.5
Pepper	26.7	Pepper	32.2	Nutmeg	28.7	Nutmeg	26.5
Cloves	23.0	Cloves	27.4	Cloves	14.6	Cloves	13.6
Rosewater	17.4	Rosewater	17.8	Rosewater	8.4	Rosewater	8.5
Ginger	12.4	Anchovies	12.6	Currants	4.9	Anchovies	7.4
Anchovies	11.2	Currants	11.3	Anchovies	4.7	Ginger	6.1
Cinnamon	9.9	Cinnamon	10.0	Ginger	4.4	Almonds	6.1
Almonds	9.3	Almonds	7.0	Almonds	4.3	Currants	5.4
Currants	6.2	Candied lemon	4.3	Morels	4.0	Ketchup	5.0
Raisins	5.6	Ginger	3.9	Ketchup	3.3	Morels	4.9
Range	31	Range	30	Range	54	Range	67
Mean per recipe	2.6	Mean per recipe	2.7	Mean per recipe	1.9	Mean per recipe	2.2

Note: The twelve most frequently used groceries in each source are cited.
Sources: W.M., *Compleat Cook* (1663); Howard, *England's Newest Way* (1708); Glasse, *Art of Cookery* (1760); Farley, *London Art of Cookery* (1800).

average number of groceries per recipe falling quite markedly through the eighteenth century. In part, this decline reflects the changing character of recipe books, a large number of recipes that Glasse gives being for components of more complex dishes (there are, for example, recipes for pastry, fruit wines or cordials and sauces) and the way in which she describes basic skills such as roasting.

Despite such caveats, these four recipe books reveal important secular changes in taste, many of which become more apparent from the frequency with which particular ingredients were mentioned (Table 9.2). In 1663, sugar, nutmeg, and mace all appeared in about one-third of recipes; pepper and cloves were used in one-quarter; ginger, cinnamon, and anchovies in about one tenth, and currants and raisins in one-twentieth. This marks a considerable departure from medieval cookery, with ginger, cinnamon, and especially saffron being displaced by nutmeg and mace, while sugar had risen, most obviously at the expense of dried fruit. These trends were continued to 1708. The use of ginger declined still further, and candied lemon was included more often than raisins, but there was broad stability in the relative importance of different commodities. Manuscript recipe books confirm these broad patterns of consumption, but showed their own idiosyncrasies: a reflection of the ways in which they were assembled and their author's personal tastes and preferences. For example, Sarah Foley—a gentlewoman who probably assembled her recipe book in the middle or later decades of the eighteenth century—used cinnamon in almost one-fifth of her recipes, including both sweet and savoury dishes. A generation earlier, Mary Wise of The Priory in Warwick followed the old English tradition of favouring mace over nutmeg.[51] Glasse's *Art of Cookery* again marks a departure, with pepper assuming its modern place as the most commonly used spice and a range of 'new' groceries (ketchups, morels and truffles, and pickles) appearing alongside long-established ingredients such as ginger and anchovies. Farley perhaps marks something of a resurgence of stronger flavours, with a growing proportion of recipes requiring ketchups, pickles, and anchovies; but the overall pattern is remarkably similar to that seen a generation or more earlier.

These seventeenth- and eighteenth-century recipe books mark less of a retreat and more of a reorientation in the taste for spices from their medieval heyday. Pepper grew as a general as well as specific seasoning, while nutmeg emerged as a central feature of English cookery. Most telling was the frequent and enduring use of sugar—a reflection of the important place of desserts in English cookery. All four books contain a wide range of recipes for creams, jellies, cakes, pancakes, fritters, wafers, biscuits, and preserves. Significantly, these also formed an important element in manuscript recipe books. A small notebook forming part of the Stoneleigh Abbey archive lists numerous possibilities for drying and preserving fruit, and making jams, pastes, drops, and clear cakes.[52] Four or five recipes of this nature (most of them requiring several pounds of sugar) appear for a total of thirteen different fruits, from oranges to gooseberries. Interspersed with these are twenty-one recipes for various sweet dishes, including chocolate almonds, iced almond cakes, blancmange, pistachio creams and hartshorn flummery—the last being flavoured with almonds, mace and cinnamon and served in china cups.

This returns us to the ways in which groceries were combined in different recipes. Here, some important changes can be seen across the published cookery books sampled here. First is the combination of nutmeg and sugar in a wide variety of desserts, ranging from Devonshire white pot and quaking pudding, to cheesecake and snowballs.[53] The proportion of recipes combining these two ingredients fell

[51] SCLA, DR98/167; WRO, CR341/300, 301.   [52] SCLA, DR762/55 recipe book.
[53] W.M., *Compleat Cook*, 12; Howard, *England's Newest Way*, 8; Glasse, *Art of Cookery*, 222, 383.

considerably between the early and middle decades of the eighteenth century (Table 9.1) as a wider range of spices and seeds were deployed in sweet dishes. Sarah Foley used a sometimes bewildering variety of flavourings in her recipes. Her skirret pie, for example, contained mace, cinnamon, figs, gooseberries, candied lemon, and sugar.[54] Mary Wise, meanwhile, used caraway seeds to flavour many of her desserts, including pound cake, seed cake, and Tunbridge cakes.[55] From around the same time, sugar was increasingly being used on its own to create elegant and elaborate centrepieces, most notably in the spun-sugar confections produced and sold by Elizabeth Raffald and re-created in recipe form in her 1769 volume *The Experienced English Housekeeper*. These were complex luxuries: time-consuming and therefore costly to make, and requiring semiotic virtuosity to construct and decode the allusions in the intricate designs of desert islands or Chinese scenes.[56] The constant renewal of decorative features also allowed a similar reinvention of the genre as fashions changed or as fresh news stories could be celebrated in food. In many ways, they can be seen as classic example of novelty—a repackaging of the familiar to allow renewal within defined parameters. In this way, novelty regains some explanatory power in terms of the consumption of sugar and contests interpretations based on its combination with tea or coffee.[57]

Second, and also apparent from Table 9.1, is that the combination of nutmeg, mace, and pepper—seen by Colqhoun as a signature of Hannah Glasse—was already firmly established in the 1660s.[58] This apparent hallmark of English cooking was maintained despite the decline in the average number of groceries used in Glasse's recipes and the resurgence of stronger flavourings in the second half of the eighteenth century. As noted earlier, however, an important disruption to this trend was the emergence of dishes linked to Empire and especially to the orient.[59] While Bickham argues that their exoticism belied the frequent use of British ingredients, the 'exotic' recipes contained in the books sampled here often contained rather different combinations of spices from British or European dishes. Glasse's *Art of Cookery* includes five recipes with connections to India and another associated with Turkey. Her recipe for 'pellow rice the India way' sticks with a conservative combination of mace, cloves, and pepper, but her curry, piccalilli, and India pickle call for ginger, turmeric, and long pepper—the last two appearing in only a handful of her recipes.[60] These were exotic in terms of their flavours as well as their associations, and Bickham makes much of their significance, arguing that they signalled a growing awareness of and connection to Empire from the middle decades of the eighteenth century. He itemizes an expanding range of dishes, including 'West Indian pepper pot', 'ChinaChilo', and 'Mullagatawny or Currie Soup', and in particular highlights the growing imperial theme of table

<hr />

[54] SCLA, DR98/167.   [55] WRO, CR341/300, 301.

[56] See Day, *Royal Sugar Sculptures*.

[57] Smith, *Consumption*, 121–30; Mintz, *Sweetness and Power*, 115–18.

[58] Colquhoun, *Taste*, 199–204.

[59] Bickham, 'Eating the Empire', 99–100; Hall, 'Culinary Spaces', 177–84.

[60] Bickham, 'Eating the Empire', 100; Glasse, *Art of Cookery*, 101, 334, 376, 378. The manuscript recipe book belonging to the Leighs contained a recipe for best Indian cavach [*sic*].

centrepieces such as the 'floating desert island' produced by Raffald in the wake of Cook's South Sea voyages.[61]

For all their cultural currency, such dishes formed less than 1 per cent of Glasse's recipes (she gave more 'Jew's' recipes than those associated with India[62]) and a similar proportion in Farley's *London Art of Cookery*. They occasionally featured in mid- to late eighteenth-century manuscript recipe books, although the ingredients then had a tendency to be rather conservative. Thus, the recipe for 'best Indian cavach' contained in the Stoneleigh Abbey archive used only pepper, mace, and nutmeg.[63] Furthermore, while elaborate centrepieces may have taken the form of Chinese temples or desert islands, they were just as likely to comprise rural scenes or political figures. Walpole complained that the traditional components of dessert, such as 'jellies, biscuits, sugar plums and cream have long since given way to harlequins, gondoliers, Turks, Chinese and shepherdesses of Saxon china'.[64] A little later, parson Woodforde recorded his delight in the centrepiece that he had seen at a dinner given by the Bishop of Norwich in 1783. This comprised a garden scene with a temple in the centre; but he chose to buy plaster figures of the King of Prussia and Duke of York to adorn his own table.[65]

If food was indeed central to public engagement with empire in the later eighteenth century, then it is not apparent from the pages of recipe books, which focused very much on other geographical and cultural points of reference (Table 9.3). From 1663 to 1800 France was the country most commonly named, even discounting recipes described in French terms (à la daube, à la braise, and so on). In Restoration England, this is scarcely surprising; its persistence, despite the growing mood against France and French cookery, reflects the ambivalence seen in Glasse's book and her desire to present simplified versions of French dishes. Indeed, a more general cosmopolitan feel is created through recipes in the Spanish, Dutch, German, Italian, and Portuguese styles—a reminder of the continued importance of Europe as a key point of reference for British consumers, despite the geographically expanded horizons that came with the so-called commercial revolution. While specific references to France had diminished by 1800, this was part of a broader trend against geographical labels. Indeed, it is apparent from the titles that Farley gives to many of his dishes (à la mode, à la royale, à la bourgeois, and, most tellingly, à la Kilkenny) that French and English cookery had become thoroughly integrated by this date. Also striking is the persistence of British regional labels, from Shrewsbury cakes to Ipswich almond pudding. And yet there is little to distinguish these various European dishes in terms of the groceries they contained. Asparagus cooked in the Spanish way was seasoned only with pepper, as were Dutch red cabbage, Spanish cauliflower, and Dutch and German beans. Indeed,

[61] Bickham, 'Eating the Empire', 99, 101–2.

[62] These included recipes to pickle beef, preserve salmon, and stew green beans, and for a marmalade of eggs.

[63] SCLA, DR762/55. For further discussion of this 'domestication' of foreign dishes, see Pennell, 'Recipes and Reception'.

[64] Quoted in Colqhoun, *Taste*, 228.   [65] Beresford, *Diary*, 4 Sept. 1783.

there were few savoury recipes that went beyond some combination of pepper, mace, nutmeg, and cloves. Much the same was true of sweet dishes: Portugal, Shrewsbury, Banbury, and fine cakes contained very similar combinations of sugar, rosewater, and dried fruit.

Overall, then, this analysis of recipe books suggests that the essential ingredients in English cookery were established by the Restoration and changed only gradually in the century that followed. There was an expanding range of groceries incorporated into published recipes and occasional exotic departures into the empire-related dishes emphasized in Bickham, although these comprised a tiny fraction of the total. Yet most change was accommodated within established culinary styles and without recourse to a radically different set of imported ingredients. Indeed, the most pronounced change was probably the growing use of ketchups and pickles to give 'bite' to savoury dishes—perhaps a return to the piquancy of late-medieval food. What remains unclear, however, are the ways in which these groceries (and the dishes they helped to enliven) were actually consumed. This question comprises two elements: first, the extent to which the recipes included in cookery books were actually cooked and consumed in the home; and, second, the cultural and social practices that surrounded the consumption of food and drink.[66]

Table 9.3. Place names mentioned in titles of dishes in three English recipe books, 1663–1800

Geographical location	W.M. (1663)		Glasse (1760)		Farley (1800)	
	No.	%	No.	%	No.	%
British	4	20.0	10	13.7	16	36.4
French	8	40.0	21	28.8	6	13.6
Spanish	3	15.0	10	13.7	2	4.5
Italian	1	5.0	3	4.1	4	9.1
Portuguese	1	5.0	2	2.7	2	4.5
Dutch	0	0.0	7	9.6	3	6.8
German	0	0.0	5	6.8	4	9.1
Jewish	0	0.0	6	8.2	0	0.0
Turkish/Persian	2	10.0	1	1.4	2	4.5
Indian	0	0.0	5	6.8	2	4.5
North American	1	5.0	2	2.7	2	4.5
West Indian	0	0.0	1	1.4	1	2.3
	20		73		44	

Source: W.M., *The Compleat Cook* (1663); Glasse, *The Art of Cookery* (1760); Farley, *London Art of Cookery* (1800).

[66] The first is a key issue in Pennell, 'Perfecting Practice?'. The second is discussed at length in Dawson, *Plenti and Grase*, 205–19; Pennell, 'Material Culture of Food', ch. 5; Lehmann, *British Housewife*, 301–22; David, 'John Trot', 55–9.

GROCERIES, MEALS, AND THE RITUALS
OF CONSUMPTION

Bills of fare were presented in many cookery books during the eighteenth century, sometimes accompanied by elaborate copper plates showing their arrangement on the table. Lehmann argues that these were quite closely related to meals eaten by the elite, at least on grander occasions.[67] They confirm that the French or courtly style was favoured by aristocratic diners in the early to mid-eighteenth century, although there appears to have been a refocusing of attention onto the *petits plats* characteristic of *nouvelle cuisine*. Taking the bills of fare in Carter's *Complete Practical Cook* as exemplars of this style, we can identify the groceries drawn upon to produce a grand aristocratic dinner in the 1730s (Table 9.4). Overall, there was a fairly modest range of grocery ingredients required: fifteen for the first course, thirteen for the second, and eighteen for the meal as a whole. Pepper and nutmeg were by far the most important, with mace and cloves also appearing quite frequently, suggesting fairly lightly spiced, if quite rich food, especially in the first course. More complex and fuller flavours appear in the second course, ginger and cinnamon often being used in combination in cheesecakes, pies, and tansies. Perhaps most surprising is the sparing use of sugar, which appears in only one-fifth of dishes, mostly in the second course. It was generally combined with spices in custards, tarts, and so on rather than with fruit in puddings and pies. Indeed, dried fruit is remarkable in its absence, although it would, of course, have featured at dessert.

There is a close correspondence between the ingredients in Carter's bills of fare and the purchases of culinary groceries made by the Leighs in the early to mid-eighteenth century (see Table 8.1). Pepper was bought most frequently, but there were also regular purchases of cinnamon, mace, cloves, nutmeg, and ginger, and, more occasionally, anchovies and almonds. Tellingly, perhaps, both the range of dried fruit being bought and the frequency with which it was required seem to have declined during this period. We do not know their actual dining habits, but it was quite possible for the Leighs to have enjoyed the kind of dinners laid out by Carter and described by contemporaries such as Lady Grisell Baillie.[68] Yet such displays of novel and luxury dining were by no means ubiquitous among the elite. The food purchased by Grace Nettleton to supply her nephew's table in the 1720s displays a remarkable lack of spices and flavourings: there are very occasional purchases of cinnamon and pepper, and a few of mustard, but nothing else.[69] If this is a true reflection of the flavourings available in the kitchen at Tabley Hall, then very few of Carter's recipes could have been served at table. This stands in stark contrast with Smith's assertion of spices as a 'customary luxury' and reminds us that taste and pleasure were driven by individual preference as well as broader notions of utility or status.[70] Not everyone, it seems, pursued status through the 'luxury' of spices and fashionable dining.

---

[67] Lehmann, *British Housewife*, 350–4.
[68] See Scott-Montcrieff, *Household Book of Lady Grisell Baillie*, 281–301.
[69] CALS, DLT/B51.   [70] Smith, *Consumption*, 99; de Vries, *Industrious Revolution*, 20–2.

Table 9.4. Groceries needed to prepare the dishes in a 'courtly' bill of fare, 1730

Ingredient	First course (32 dishes)		Second course (40 dishes)		Total (72 dishes)	
	No.	%	No.	%	No.	%
Pepper	16	50.0	13	32.5	29	40.3
Nutmeg	10	31.3	12	30.0	22	30.6
Sugar	3	9.4	10	25.0	13	18.1
Mace	7	21.9	5	12.5	12	16.7
Ginger	3	9.4	9	22.5	12	16.7
Cloves	6	18.8	4	10.0	10	13.9
Cinnamon	3	9.4	4	10.0	7	9.7
Rosewater	0	0.0	5	12.5	5	6.9
Biscuits	1	3.1	3	7.5	4	5.6
Truffles	3	9.4	0	0.0	3	4.2
Pistachio	3	9.4	0	0.0	3	4.2
Anchovies	1	3.1	1	2.5	2	2.8
Hartshorn	1	3.1	1	2.5	2	2.8
Almonds	0	0.0	2	5.0	2	2.8
Citron	0	0.0	2	5.0	2	2.8
Candied lemon	1	3.1	0	0.0	1	1.4
Vermicelli	1	3.1	0	0.0	1	1.4
Eryngo root	1	3.1	0	0.0	1	1.4
	60		71		131	

Source: Carter, *Complete Practical Cook*.

Based on evidence from the bills of fare drawn up for the Duke of Newcastle, Lehmann argues that aristocratic dining remained fairly constant at least through to the 1770s.[71] Lower down the social hierarchy, however, there were significant shifts in the food eaten at dinner. Drawing on her experience in a busy Salford tavern, Elizabeth Raffald directed *The Experienced English House-keeper* of 1769 explicitly at middling sort and gentry consumers. Her bill of fare for a 'grand table' presents two courses each of twenty-five dishes. Analysis of the ingredients required in their preparation underlines both the change in taste and the impact that this had on the consumption of groceries (Table 9.5). The total number of groceries required for each course had changed very little since Carter's time: fourteen for the first course and sixteen for the second. However, the two courses were increasingly distinct from one another in terms of ingredients and flavours, with just six items in common: pepper, mace, cloves, nutmeg, anchovies, and sugar. Following the model of French cuisine, sweet dishes were found only in the second course. However, as we have already noted, these were very different sorts of confection, often in the form of intricate tableau rather than the dramatic piles of jellies, custards, and tarts that form the centrepiece of earlier grand tables. Raffald's second

[71] Lehmann, *British Housewife*, 360–1.

Table 9.5. Groceries needed to prepare the dishes in an 'English' bill of fare, 1769

Ingredient	First course (25 dishes)		Second course (25 dishes)		Total (50 dishes)	
	No.	%	No.	%	No.	%
Mace	4	16.0	6	24.0	10	20.0
Pepper	6	24.0	3	12.0	9	18.0
Sugar	0	0.0	8	32.0	8	16.0
Nutmeg	5	20.0	2	8.0	7	14.0
Lemon pickle	6	24.0	0	0.0	6	12.0
Cayenne	5	20.0	0	0.0	5	10.0
Truffles	4	16.0	0	0.0	4	8.0
Ketchup	4	16.0	0	0.0	4	8.0
Anchovies	3	12.0	1	4.0	4	8.0
Cloves	1	4.0	3	12.0	4	8.0
Almonds	1	4.0	3	12.0	4	8.0
Rosewater	0	0.0	4	16.0	4	8.0
Bitter almonds	0	0.0	3	12.0	3	6.0
Walnut ketchup	2	8.0	0	0.0	2	4.0
Ginger	1	4.0	0	0.0	1	2.0
Jamaica pepper	1	4.0	0	0.0	1	2.0
Walnut pickle	1	4.0	0	0.0	1	2.0
Cinnamon	0	0.0	1	4.0	1	2.0
Biscuits	0	0.0	1	4.0	1	2.0
Pistachio	0	0.0	1	4.0	1	2.0
Candied lemon	0	0.0	1	4.0	1	2.0
Vermicelli	0	0.0	1	4.0	1	2.0
Currants	0	0.0	1	4.0	1	2.0
Raisins	0	0.0	1	4.0	1	2.0
	44		40		84	

Source: Raffald, *Experienced English House-Keeper* (1769).

course includes 'moonshine', a floating island, and a rocky island, as well as a centrepiece decorated with spun sugar.[72] Despite the considerable change that these creations had upon the look of the dinner table, the most dramatic culinary shift was the heavy use of ketchups, pickles, and cayenne. These displaced older favourites such as ginger, cinnamon, and cloves, and created more strongly flavoured dishes, including the first course centrepiece: mock turtle, a dish that was fiendishly complex in its making. They appear in around one-fifth of dishes in the first course, but none in the second, thus heightening the contrast between the two courses. Again, these trends are reflected in the grocery purchases made by the

[72] Man of these involved flummery and jellies, but the emphasis was very much on presentation, with detailed instructions about how to create artificial snow from whisked egg white, how to arrange the individual moulds, and even the direction in which the model ducks and swans should face for maximum effect. See Raffald, *Experienced English House-Keeper*.

Leighs. From the 1760s, they bought ginger only once and cloves just twice; increasingly common, though, were purchases of pickles, ketchups, truffles, and morels, and even soy sauce. Once more, while their own menus are unknown, the Leighs' consumption of groceries certainly shifted away from those needed for courtly dinners and towards those of Raffald's reasserted English style. Given the intended market of this recipe book among the middling sorts, this might suggest 'trickling-up' of consumption practices, as some of the aristocracy at least adopted apparently middle-class taste.[73]

Further down the social scale, the adherence to these changing styles was somewhat looser. For the early eighteenth century, Lehmann suggests that gentry meals were simpler versions of those eaten by the aristocracy, but—as we have already seen—there was a growing rejection of French dishes, which were seen to represent luxury and decadence.[74] By the closing decades of the century, therefore, gentry dining was characterized by relatively plain and uncomplicated dishes. The ingredients for E. Smith's bills of fare 'for Every Season of the Year' probably give us a fair approximation of the ingredients used, although with two important caveats. First, the lists remain unchanged through the numerous editions of this book—a warning to read these as representative more of the 1720s than later periods, but perhaps also an indication of stability in the dining habits of the middling sorts. Second, the six to ten dishes per course that she suggests made them considerably grander than most of the meals enjoyed by Parson Woodforde and others.[75] Smith's menus suggest a fairly modest palate of grocery ingredients: nine for the first course and twelve for the second (Table 9.6). Yet this is not dramatically fewer than that required for Carter's altogether grander bills of fare. Nutmeg, pepper, mace, and sugar dominate; cloves, cinnamon, and anchovies were very much secondary, and ginger was absent. The impression that most dishes were quite lightly flavoured is underlined by the fact that long lists of ingredients were rare and usually appear in sweet dishes such as cheesecakes and tansies. This finds its reflection in Woodforde's later descriptions of dinners, which rarely enumerate dishes with rich sauces, centring instead on roast and boiled meat, puddings, pies, and custards. A typical if large meal shared with his clergy friends on 23 June 1783 comprised: boiled leg of lamb with carrots and turnips, roast beef with cucumbers, ham, peas and beans, four roast chickens, gooseberry tarts and custards; followed by a dessert of oranges, almonds, raisins, and strawberries with cream.[76] Few middling sort or gentry diners appear to have found much pleasure in 'frenchified' cookery and its unpronounceable and unknown dishes. The Reverend Stotherd Abdy shared the relief of his fellow guests when the French cook ('Monsieur Hash Slash'), who had been hired to cater for the wedding of his patron's relative, left the house. Food reverted to 'good eatable dishes, and [one] could really tell what they were'.[77] Far from

[73] See McCracken, *Culture and Consumption*, 95.   [74] Lehmann, *British Housewife*, 356.
[75] Smith, *Compleat Housewife*. See Beresford, *Diary*, passim; Lehmann, *British Housewife*, 366–8.
[76] Beresford, *Diary*, 23 June 1783.
[77] Beresford, *Diary*, 28 Aug. 1783; Houblon, *Houblon Family*, ii. 135.

emulating their social superiors, these middle-ranking consumers forcibly rejected the excesses and pretensions of elite modes of consumption. This not only challenges any straightforward trickle-down effect, but demonstrates the existence of strong and independent cultures of consumption.[78]

Humbler households relied on an even narrower range of dishes and ingredients. Thomas Turner's meals were characterized by boiled or roast meat and puddings. Fairly typical were the 'pork, light pudding and greens' that he had on 9 March 1756 or the 'buttock of beef and ham, plum pudding and greens' he enjoyed around a month later. But he frequently ate the remainder of earlier meals, sometimes enlivened with an additional dish, as on 2 July 1756, when he 'dined on the remains of Monday's dinner with a butter pudding cake'.[79] If we look across to Hannah Glasse's recipes, these two meals probably required the use of pepper, sugar, currants and raisins, nutmeg, and perhaps mace and almonds.[80] Neither was taken at home, where even the more elaborate meals that Turner records called for few additional flavourings. In August 1756 he entertained his mother and brother, along with Mr Beard and his wife, on '2 roasted ducks (of our own breed), a piece of bacon, a leg of mutton, cauliflowers and carrots, with a currant pond pudding boiled'.[81]

Table 9.6. Groceries needed to prepare the dishes in two 'gentry' bills of fare, 1727

Ingredient	First course (total of 18 dishes)		Second course (total of 14 dishes)		Total (total of 32 dishes)	
	No.	%	No.	%	No.	%
Nutmeg	5	27.8	6	42.9	11	34.4
Mace	6	33.3	4	28.6	10	31.3
Sugar	2	11.1	7	50.0	9	28.1
Pepper	6	33.3	2	14.3	8	25.0
Cloves	3	16.7	2	14.3	5	15.6
Anchovies	3	16.7	0	0.0	3	9.4
Almonds	1	5.6	2	14.3	3	9.4
Rosewater	1	5.6	2	14.3	3	9.4
Biscuits	0	0.0	3	21.4	3	9.4
Cinnamon	0	0.0	3	21.4	3	9.4
Candied lemon	1	5.6	0	0.0	1	3.1
Truffles	0	0.0	1	7.1	1	3.1
Hartshorn	0	0.0	1	7.1	1	3.1
Currants	0	0.0	1	7.1	1	3.1
Saffron	0	0.0	1	7.1	1	3.1
	28		35		63	

Source: Smith, *Compleat Housewife*.

[78] McCracken, *Culture and Consumption*, 93–6; de Vries, *Industrious Revolution*, 189, 199.
[79] Vaisey, *Thomas Turner*, 9 Mar. 19 Apr., 2 July 1756. For a fuller discussion of Turner's dining, see Pennell, 'Material Culture of Food', ch. 5.
[80] Glasse, *Art of Cookery*, passim.   [81] Vaisey, *Thomas Turner*, 8 Aug. 1756.

Despite the attempt by Smith, Glasse, Raffald, and others to present menus and recipes that were within the financial and time budgets of gentry and middling-sort households, it appears that only elite dining and consumption of groceries were closely related to the ideals presented in cookery books. Rather than fashion and taste trickling down, as Simmel argued (or up, as others have suggested), there appears to have been a disconnect between elite and other consumers, each being situated within their own culture of consumption and eating according to their own means and tastes.[82] This does not mean that less privileged consumers were unconcerned with the quality and presentation of their food. Turner often noted the way in which food was prepared and was quick to note poor standards of cooking. After one particularly irksome meal at his uncle's house he noted that they had been served

a leg of very ordinary ewe mutton half boiled, very good turnips, but spoiled by almost swimming in butter, a fine large pig roasted, and the rind as tough as any cowhide (and it seemed as if it had been basted with a mixture of flour, butter and ashes), and sauce which looked like what is vomited up by sucking children, a butter pond pudding, and that justly called, for there was almost enough in it to have drowned the pig, had it been alive.[83]

Woodforde's meals did, on occasions, resemble the dishes outlined in published works, but he was more interested in unusual foods and, more generally, in the meal as an event.[84] His account of a dinner given by the Bishop of Norwich on 4 September 1783 is telling. He describes the number of diners; the organization of the meal ('2 Courses of 20 Dishes each Course, and a Desert [*sic*] after 20 Dishes'), and the wines consumed. He then lists some of the main dishes, but finishes with a detailed description of the table centrepiece discussed earlier: 'a most beautiful artificial garden...about a yard long, and about 18 inches wide, in the middle of which was a high round Temple supported on round pillars...wreathed round with artificial Flowers—on one side was a Shepherdess on the other a Shepherd...'.[85]

Such concerns invite us to consider some of the rituals surrounding the consumption of culinary and other groceries. In this context, much attention has focused on tea, which is closely associated with women and the domestic realm. Smith has argued that it was central to the construction of a particular mode of femininity, while Vickery has emphasized the connection between tea parties, scandalous conversation, and female sociability.[86] Crucial to both of these constructions is the way in which tea was served to her guests by the hostess, largely without recourse to servants. Moreover, with its reliance upon complex equipage—which itself was the subject of changing fashions and the dictates of good taste—tea parties retained their social cachet, despite the spread of tea drinking among the lower orders from an early

[82] Simmel, 'Fashion'; McCracken, *Culture and Consumption*, 93–103.
[83] Vaisey, *Thomas Turner*, 17 Oct. 1756.   [84] Lehmann, *British Housewife*, 372–3.
[85] Beresford, *Diary*, 4 Sept. 1783.
[86] Smith, *Consumption*, 171–88; Vickery, *Behind Closed Doors*, 273–5. See also Congreve, *The Double Dealer*, Act I, scenes i and vii; Pennell, 'Material Culture of Food', ch. 5.

date.[87] This was reinforced by the availability of a range of different qualities as well as different types of tea, which, as discussed earlier, allowed the differentiation of rank and status as well as the display of discernment and taste.

These practices were important, but we need to place the consumption of tea into a rather broader context. Although it might stand alone as a social engagement within polite circles, the ritualistic drinking of tea was an afternoon event, placed after dinner, but before supper. It was therefore frequently seen as part of a wider set of social or familial activities. For example, in the 1770s Elizabeth Shackleton noted in her diary several visits of the shopkeeper Betty Hartley wherein she 'drank tea and suppd here'. More formally, Woodforde gave his guests tea or coffee after dinner before serving supper later in the evening, the intervening time often being spent playing cards.[88] At grander gatherings, the company might separate: men staying in the dining room to continue drinking, while women retired to tea in the drawing room.

Tea was also drunk at other times of the day. By the early eighteenth century, it was consumed by the elite alongside coffee and chocolate at breakfast—a practice that had spread to the middling sort by the middle of the century at the latest.[89] For example, in inviting himself to breakfast, Jonathan Swift exhorted Sir Andrew Fountaine thus: 'Pray get all things ready for Breakfast. Have the Coffee Tee and Chocolate cut and dry in so many Pots, for I will most infallibly come this morning.'[90] In this context, the associations of tea drinking were rather different. Smith argues that breakfast as a meal combined the consumption of what were seen by contemporaries as healthy foods with others that were associated with the exotic—a combination that held good well into the nineteenth century.[91] Thus, when visiting Stoneleigh Abbey in 1806, Cassandra Austen wrote: 'At nine in the morning we say our prayers in a handsome chapel . . . then follows breakfast, consisting of chocolate, coffee, and tea, plum cake, pound cake, hot rolls, cold rolls, and dry toast for me.'[92] This was clearly a meal that gathered together the family at the start of the day, but some breakfast encounters appear to have been less formal, as when Henry Prescott, the notary and deputy registrar of Chester diocese, recorded that 'after prayers Mr Davies takes a dish of tea with mee, wee discourse matters'. On another occasion, he noted that he had called on Lady Soames, where his wife 'Suzy meets mee. Wee are treated with good Coffee, thence to dinner.'[93] Prescott's consumption of these drinks was a routine part of his day, rather than a ritual intended to inform his (gender) identity, something that was achieved instead through the more traditional sociability of heavy drinking with his male friends in local inns. Much the same was true of Thomas Turner, who frequently drank tea with friends, both in his shop and at their houses. It appears to have accompanied informal sociability and on occasions was linked to

---

[87] Kowalski-Wallace, 'Women, China and Consumer Culture'; Pennell, 'Material Culture of Food', ch. 4.
[88] Quoted in Vickery, *Gentleman's Daughter*, 208; Beresford, *Diary*, 23 June 1783.
[89] Lehmann, *British Housewife*, 301–2.   [90] Quoted in Lehmann, *British Housewife*, 302.
[91] Smith, *Consumption*, 184–5.   [92] Quoted in Tyack, *Warwickshire Country Houses*, 182–3.
[93] Addy, 'Henry Prescott', 15 Nov. 1706, 26 Jan. 1709.

rational discussion as in November 1756, when 'my wife went down to Whyly to pay Mrs French a visit, and I drank tea at Mrs Weller's and talked with her about my leaving the shop'.[94]

A similar informal inclusiveness can be seen in Elizabeth Shackleton's habit of serving tea to a wide variety of visitors to her house. Vickery notes that she produced her china for the benefit of ex-servants, the mothers of servants and tenants, and visiting tradeswomen, as well as her social equals. In these contexts, 'tea facilitated the process of exchange', be it social, patronage, or business.[95] What is also apparent from the pages of Elizabeth Shackleton's diary, but is often neglected in analyses of tea drinking, is that serving 'tea' also involved offering food as well. When she invited her tenants' wives to tea in 1779, she noted: 'They were civilly Entertain'd. Had wine, coffee, tea, muffins, toast, Punch and great pieces of Iced rich Plumb cake.'[96] The association of tea and cake links directly to notions of femininity, both in the ritual of tea drinking, and in the production and consumption of sweet dishes. This reinforces, but extends, Smith's argument about the role of 'tea and sympathy' in domestic feminity.[97] It also ties the drinking of tea (and other hot drinks) to the consumption of a wide range of other groceries—not just sugar. For example, the plum cake served by Shackleton would have required 2 lb of flour, 1 lb of butter, and 16 eggs, plus 1 lb of sugar, 2.5 lb of currants, 1 lb of candied orange peel, 1 lb of sweet almonds, 0.25 oz of nutmeg, the same of mace, and 3 spoonfuls of orange flower water.[98] As Smith and others have noted, this links to the grouping of exotic goods on the breakfast table,[99] but it extends the association to other times of day and other forms of social encounter and embeds these goods more deeply into the everyday practices of a wide range of consumers.

CONCLUSIONS

Conventional narratives of consumer change in the long eighteenth century have emphasized the role of luxury and novelty in structuring individual and collective consumption. Both qualities have been seen as playing an important part in the rising demand for groceries, especially exotic imports such as tea, coffee, chocolate, and sugar. When newly introduced, such goods afforded the opportunity for wealthy consumers to distinguish themselves from others, either through conspicuous consumption or by leading new and fashionable forms of consumption. However, the novelty of particular commodities passed quickly and was difficult to re-create in a way that was possible for textiles, toys, or chinaware, where regular changes in fashion might be seen as driving forward consumption. Mintz stresses the revolutionary moment when sugar was first mixed with tea, but the spread of

[94] Vaisey, *Thomas Turner*, 4 Nov. 1756.   [95] Vickery, *Gentleman's Daughter*, 208.
[96] Quoted in Vickery, *Gentleman's Daughter*, 208.
[97] Lehmann, British Housewife, 321; Smith, *Consumption*, 121–30, 171–5.
[98] Raffald, *Experienced English House-Keeper*, 245.
[99] Smith, *Consumption*, 183–8; de Vries, *Industrious Revolution*, 20–1; Berg, *Luxury and Pleasure*, 229; Vickery, *Gentleman's Daughter*, 207, 209.

the practice and the sustained demand for both commodities cannot be explained in terms of the novelty of the experience.[100] The significance of this is twofold. First, novelty per se cannot have sustained growth in consumption of things like tea or sugar—once their use had spread through different social groups, something else was needed to keep them attractive to consumers. Second, and much more broadly, it further questions the explanatory power of fashion-driven emulative consumption. Even if we assume that the poor drank tea in imitation of their social superiors (and this itself seems a poor explanation), then how do we account for the lack of 'flight' on the part of middling or elite consumers to some new marker of status?[101]

One possibility is that distinctions could be maintained through luxury, gradations of quality (more costly blends of tea, for example) helping to distinguish the discerning and wealthy consumer from the common order. This idea could be extended to the number, complexity, and cost of elaborate dishes for the table—a very conspicuous form of consumption. In this way, serving high-quality tea and rich plum cake could signal status and taste, both to social equals and to those lower down the social hierarchy in receipt of periodic largesse. There is a danger here of eliding luxury with positional goods. We have seen, for instance, that 'customary luxuries' were an important part of the diet of even the very poorest. For the inmates of the workhouse, treacle and tobacco did not mark status. Rather, they offered comfort and pleasure, linking consumption to ideas of utility and drawing it into everyday practices of cooking and eating.[102]

There were remarkable continuities in the culinary use of groceries over the course of the eighteenth century. Undoubtedly, it is significant that recipes associated with empire begin to appear in cookbooks from the middle of the century, but neither their number nor the ingredients that they contained suggest a radical shift in the values or mindset of their authors or readers. Britain and Europe remained the dominant points of cultural reference, with social rather than imperial concerns resonating through recipes and menus. Keeping abreast of the taste for courtly French dishes was important to the social standing and political identity of the new Whig elite, but their example was not followed by everyone. Indeed, the gentry and middling sorts increasingly rejected 'Frenchified' cooking, and a distinct English culinary identity was reasserted through a new breed of recipe books. This might be seen as an example of the trickle-up of fashion, but it points more convincingly to the existence of distinct cultures of consumption of the kind suggested by Campbell.[103] Within these, food and eating held different meanings for different groups who were motivated by different concerns. The elite can be seen as communicating their status through the quality of their food and drink, the complexity of their dishes, and the abundance of their table. This was conspicuous consumption tempered, as Veblen himself argued it should be, by the moderating influence of taste.[104] The middling sorts were more concerned with 'defensive

---

[100] Mintz, *Sweetness and Power*, 214.   [101] See McCracken, *Culture and Consumption*, 94.
[102] See de Vries, *Industrious Revolution*, 21–2; Burnett, *Plenty and Want*, 35–7.
[103] Campbell, 'Understanding Consumption', 41.   [104] Veblen, *Theory of the Leisure Class*, 49.

consumption', characterized by Smith as the search for respectability. For some, this may have involved a championing of English cooking; for others, it focused more on the virtues of rational and sober habits, and, for others again, it focused on the useful and pleasurable activities of polite sociability.[105] Smith argues that respectability increasingly shaped the consumption of all classes, but the evidence of eating and drinking practices suggests altogether more modest ambitions. These people regularly ate the leftovers of previous meals (reheated or repackaged by the addition of a few extra ingredients) and sought comfort in the small luxuries of sweetened tea, cheap tobacco, and white bread. Although diverse in their motivations and meanings, all these practices involved 'consumption bundles', which linked consumables to sets of material objects that facilitated their preparation and presentation.[106] It is to the material culture of consuming groceries that we turn in the final chapter.

[105] De Vries, *Industrious Revolution*, 22; Schivelbusch, *Tastes of Paradise*, 34–71; Smith, *Consumption*, esp. 171–88; Vickery, *Gentleman's Daughter*, 196–7, 204–5.

[106] De Vries, *Industrious Revolution*, 31.

10

Cups, Caddies, and Castors: Groceries and Domestic Material Culture

INTRODUCTION

The growing consumption of a range of new groceries within the home is often seen as being causally linked to the transformation of domestic material culture across much of Europe. In material terms, this involved a shift to less durable goods: china and glass replaced pewter; lighter furniture often made from tropical hardwoods appeared in place of traditional heavier designs made from oak; wallpapers were hung instead of tapestries, and window curtain superseded bed hangings.[1] In economic terms, the lower unit price of many of the new goods facilitated the ownership of more and/or a greater variety of items, even though their less durable nature meant that they needed to be replaced more often. Conceptually, goods became less important as stores of economic capital and more important in terms of their symbolic value—as markers of status and identity.[2] Empirical evidence for this transition has come principally from large-scale studies of probate inventories. In her pioneering research, Weatherill traced the growing ownership of items such as window curtains, pictures, books, saucepans, china, and utensils for hot drinks. More recent studies by Shammas, Estabrook, Overton, and others have confirmed these broad trends, adding nuance to the argument in terms of regional and rural–urban differences in the nature and timing of change.[3] At the same time, research on other European countries has revealed similar changes elsewhere, challenging the notion of English exceptionalism, and pointing towards a wider transformation in material culture and consumer attitudes.[4]

Through all these studies there runs an understanding that new foods—and particularly hot drinks—played a pivotal role in the construction of a 'modern' consumer culture. They were central to the consumption bundles that form part of

---

[1] See, e.g., de Vries, *Industrious Revolution*, 122–80; Shammas, *Pre-Industrial Consumer*, 181–8; Blondé, 'Tableware'; Overton et al., *Production and Consumption*, 87–120.

[2] Nijboer, 'Fashion'; de Vries, *Industrious Revolution*, esp. 20–39; Smith, *Consumption,* 41–3; Vickery, *Gentleman's Daughter*, 13–37, 161–4; Shammas, *Pre-Industrial Consumer*, 62; Mintz, 'Changing Roles of Food'.

[3] Weatherill, *Consumer Behaviour*; Shammas, *Pre-Industrial Consumer*; Estabrook, *Urbane and Rustic England*; Overton et al., *Production and Consumption*; Beckett and Smith, 'Urban Renaissance'.

[4] For a good summary of this work, see de Vries, *Industrious Revolution*, 123–33.

de Vries's industrious revolution, but also impacted on the mental categories through which they were perceived and valued.[5] Here, practical issues of use and supply are sometimes seen as important, as are notions of comfort and pleasure, and shifting modes of cooking and sociability. However, most analyses centre on the growing importance of fashion and novelty.[6] The former could signify rank and dignity, but might also connote modishness and goods that appealed because of their novelty—expressed through style and decoration, or new materials and manufacturing processes.[7] The last of these is especially emphasized by Berg, who argues that changes in production were crucial in allowing British manufacturers to imitate imported goods and offer these at a lower price—a process that both responded to and fuelled demand for semi-luxury goods among the growing middling sort.[8] The desire for such novelties is most obviously linked into emulative models of consumption, but they could serve to defend current status as well as support aspirations to higher things. We see this in the series of cultural contexts surrounding the consumption of novel groceries that are the centrepiece of Smith's account of the rise of respectability. He argues that tea and sugar in particular were associated with the home, and with a specific form of domestic femininity.[9] In this way, we can see the eighteenth-century home as gendered or, more subtly perhaps, as a series of gendered spaces, the identity of which was shaped around a material culture linked to the consumption of certain novel goods, especially groceries. Thus, the parlour might be regarded as particularly feminine, linked with rituals of tea drinking and female sociability, while the dining room was more male and associated with smoking and drinking.[10] Yet both were linked to exotic goods and were subject to attempts to integrate something of the orient and the exotic into the domestic environment—for example, through the growing use of mahogany or a taste for Chinese porcelain.

To gain a better understanding of the relationship between (new) groceries and changing domestic material culture, we must start by reviewing the shifting patterns in the ownership of novel goods linked to hot drinks as revealed in large-scale studies. Of particular interest is the extent to which social status and gender (central concerns of Weatherill, Smith, Vickery, and others) impacted on the ownership and nature of such goods. Building on this, two lines of argument are usefully pursued. The first comes through broadening the analysis to examine the ownership of a wider set of items linked to the consumption of groceries within the home: tea tables, sugar bowls, pepper boxes, casters, snuff boxes, and the like. The second involves focusing on the association of these goods within the home. At one level, this means noting the rooms in which these goods were located and

[5] De Vries, *Industrious Revolution*, 31–7; Blondé, 'Think Local'.
[6] Practicality and utility are discussed in Weatherill, *Consumer Behaviour*, 137–65, but are dealt with more fully in Pennell, 'Material Culture of Food', ch. 4.
[7] Greig, 'Leading the Fashion'; Berg, *Luxury and Pleasure*, 250–2.
[8] Berg, 'New Commodities', 63–85; Berg, *Luxury and Pleasure*, 85–110. More generally, see also Fairchilds, 'Production and Marketing of Populuxe Goods'; Crowley, *Invention of Comfort*.
[9] Smith, *Consumption*, 105–38, 171–88. See also Herman, 'Tabletop Conversations'.
[10] See, e.g., Kross, 'Mansions, Men, Women'; Vickery, *Behind Closed Doors*, 257–90.

assessing the extent to which front-stage/back-stage dichotomies are helpful in understanding distribution and use in the home. At another, it involves examining the ways in which these goods were grouped with other objects, particularly familiar markers of changing material culture such as pictures and window curtains. In peering closer at the domestic interior, this kind of analysis gives due weight to the small details of ownership emphasized by Pennell.[11] It also facilitates a critical examination both of gendered uses of space within the home, and the extent to which shifts in material culture were related to developing ideas of exoticism and empire. More broadly, analysing the spatial and mental links between material goods provides a lens through which to examine the importance of consumption bundles in explaining consumer transformation.

THE MATERIAL CULTURE OF TEA AND COFFEE DRINKING

A number of durable goods were associated with the consumption of new groceries, but it is only 'utensils for hot drinks' that can be unambiguously linked to specific consumables.[12] Weatherill argues that, being 'new and obvious', items such as teapots, tea kettles, coffee pots, and teaspoons were well recorded in probate inventories, making it possible to trace with some confidence changing patterns of ownership.[13] That said, a strong culture of earthenware ownership and use had long been established in England and elsewhere in Europe. More specifically, Ellis notes that small drinking vessels known as 'tea-cups' were being regularly imported by the Dutch East India Company from 1624—decades before there was any market for tea.[14] They were valued for their delicate appearance and were used for drinking wine and spirits. The novelty of such items might be questioned, therefore; but Weatherill's analysis suggests that ownership of objects specific to hot drinks was still restricted in the late seventeenth century to a small proportion of the wealthy individuals represented in the sample of the London Orphan's Court and just a handful of 'ordinary' consumers (Table 10.1). Subsequent growth in ownership was steady to begin with and then increasingly rapid, especially as the price of tea dropped in the 1720s.[15] By the middle decades of the century, about half the people leaving inventories owned equipment for making tea or coffee,

[11] Pennell, 'Material Culture of Food', ch. 4.

[12] *Earthenware, china*, and even *silverware* might include teapots, cups, sugar basins, or teaspoons without these being separately itemized, and *tables* could include tea tables and other smaller tables used for serving tea. Yet all these groups also included many other items that were less closely linked with new groceries. Similarly, *saucepans* were needed for new cooking practices associated with different flavourings bought from grocers, but it is more difficult to see the latter as the driving force behind these changes and the material objects implied.

[13] Weatherill, *Consumer Behaviour*, 206.

[14] Blondé, 'Tableware'; Overton et al., *Production and Consumption*, 103; Ellis, *Coffee House*, 129.

[15] Overton et al., *Production and Consumption*, 106. These trends were also seen elsewhere in Europe (see de Vries, *Industrious Revolution*, 152–4).

Table 10.1. Ownership of 'utensils for hot drinks', 1675–1725 (%)

Weatherill	1675	1685	1695	1705	1715	1725		
Main series	0	0	1	2	7	15		
London Orphan's	2	0	8	48	78	96		
Overton et al.	*1660–89*			*1690–1719*		*1720–49*		
Kent	0			4		27		
Cornwall	0			0		6		
Pennell	*1650–70*			*1690–1710*		*1720–45*		
Westmorland	2			0		12		
Thames Valley	0			0		16		
Barnett	*1673–99*			*1700–19*		*1720–39*	*1740–59*	*1750–91*
Norwich	3			5		24	47	95

Sources: Weatherill, *Consumer Behaviour*, 26–7; Overton et al., *Production and Consumption*, 99; Pennell, 'Material Culture of Food', table 4.1; Barnett, 'In with the New', 83.

although the likelihood of possessing such items varied according to wealth and status, geographical location, type of settlement, and gender.

These patterns are familiar. What is less apparent from the literature is the variation in adoption of different goods within this category. This is significant, because it can tell us much about the relative importance of different groceries in transforming material culture, and is explored here through a sample of inventories taken from across provincial England (Table 10.2). Coffee pots (mostly made from copper) were already widely owned at the start of the eighteenth century, and they became gradually more common, appearing in about half of the sample inventories by the middle decades of the century. In contrast, teapots were rarely listed, perhaps because they were included within general valuations for china, earthenware, pewter, or silverware. Equally, there is little evidence that other items needed for preparing and serving tea were widely owned before the 1720s.[16] The subsequent spread of kettles, teaspoons, and cups links well with the upsurge in tea consumption from this date, but real growth in ownership of teapots appears to date from the third quarter of the eighteenth century. A survey of cases brought to the Old Bailey reveals fifteen teapots and sixteen coffee pots reported as stolen during the 1750s, suggesting broadly equal ownership at this time. Thirty years later, there were 21 cases involving the theft of coffee pots, but 37 of teapots, plus 62 of tea kettles, and 179 of teaspoons, mostly silver.[17] The last of these, of course, reflects the high value to weight ratio of such goods and the ease with which they might be sold on. It also indicates the widespread ownership of such semi-luxuries as part of the equipment needed in everyday processes and rituals of consuming small luxuries such as tea and sugar.

[16] It is likely that generic kettles were used for boiling water for both tea and coffee—a multiple use of the type emphasized by Pennell, 'Material Culture of Food', ch. 4.
[17] OBP, 1750–9, 1780–9.

Table 10.2. Ownership of selected 'utensils for hot drinks', 1675–1775 (%)

Date	Coffee pots	Coffee mills	Teapots	Cups	Teaspoons	Tea kettles
1675–1719 (N = 25)	32.0	4.0	12.0	12.0	4.0	8.0
1720–1739 (N = 47)	34.0	14.9	8.5	14.9	21.2	36.2
1740–1775 (N = 24)	48.1	22.2	18.5	40.7	33.3	59.3
Total (N = 99)	37.3	14.1	12.1	22.2	20.2	34.3

Source: probate inventories.

Outside London, silver teaspoons, teapots, and the like were less widely owned, Weatherill demonstrating both a geographical and a hierarchical diffusion of such goods. Areas close to or well connected to London took up new modes of consumption (including tea and coffee drinking) more quickly than did those that were relatively isolated—a pattern confirmed in the contrasting domestic material cultures of Kent and Cornwall. Equally, townspeople, especially those in large provincial centres, were more likely to own novel goods than their country cousins.[18] Weatherill explains such differences in terms of systems of supply, an argument that fits well with the importance of towns in the provision of groceries, and the production and distribution of the china-, earthen-, and metalware that facilitated their consumption.[19] Yet, focusing simply on supply overlooks the cultural differences between town and country that both Estabrook and Pennell see as being more important in shaping urban and rural consumption patterns.[20] Such contrasts also relate to occupational differences, Weatherill noting that yeomen and husbandmen were slow to take up new forms of consumption, whereas urban tradesmen were often innovative consumers. With the exception of farmers, however, wealth was a more important factor in determining the ownership of utensils for hot drinks: 22 per cent of inventories with household goods worth over £100 included such items—a figure that fell to 8 per cent where household goods were worth £26–£100, and just 1 per cent for inventories with lower valuations.[21]

Ownership of coffee pots, teaspoons, and cups helped to distinguish wealthier individuals as innovative consumers in the early decades of the eighteenth century. As consumption and ownership spread more widely, however, such distinctions became blurred—a process that placed heightened emphasis on the quality, complexity, and completeness of the equipage for tea and coffee drinking. Important distinctions can be seen in the materials from which these objects were made.

[18] Weatherill, *Consumer Behaviour*, 43–90; Overton et al., *Production and Consumption*, esp. 106–7, 159.
[19] Weatherill, *Consumer Behaviour*, 84–7; Berg, *Luxury and Pleasure*, 139–49, 162–8; McKendrick, 'Josiah Wedgwood'; Clifford, 'Commerce with Things'; Popp, 'Building the Market'.
[20] Estabrook, *Urbane and Rustic England*, 128–63; Pennell, 'Material Culture of Food', ch. 4.
[21] Weatherill, *Consumer Behaviour*, 172–3, 180, 108. Overton et al., *Production and Consumption*, 159–61, confirm the conservative nature of farmers, but find the evidence for the innovative nature of tradesmen and the gentry more equivocal.

Styles has argued convincingly that silverware was important in making the culture of tea drinking recognizable among wealthy Londoners in the late seventeenth century—novelty being set within an existing set of goods.[22] Moreover, silver was expensive and thus exclusive; it added lustre to the tea tables of wealthy consumers and reflected their wealth and status on its polished surfaces.[23] Those less well heeled made do with copper, tin, and pewter, although a growing number of teapots were of earthenware or porcelain. Two things are significant here. First, the material culture of tea drinking was shifting in line with more general changes in domestic material culture: pewter teapots, which had comprised about one-quarter of those reported stolen in the Old Bailey during the 1750s, were absent by the 1780s.[24] Second, there were distinctions to be drawn between the various types of ceramic. At the start of the eighteenth century, when all china had to be imported, the price difference with earthenware was considerable; once British manufacturers perfected the art, prices fell, but the differential remained. Indeed, while men such as Wedgwood cleverly exploited the growing market by producing earthenware of a quality and finish that made it appealing to the middle ranks, they were also careful to maintain the exclusivity of their chinaware.[25] In some ways, Wedgwood went a stage further and sought to create an image of his goods as more exclusive than those of his competitors, not least through deliberate policies that priced his tableware two or three times higher than prevailing prices.[26] He never attained the status of some of the great European porcelain works, but it is significant that catalogues for country-house sales from the late eighteenth century onwards note Wedgwood wares, but no other British manufacturers.[27] Provenance was important in giving these goods extra value and meaning. This was certainly the case where pieces were linked to the Orient and thus, perhaps, to cultures of 'authentic' tea-drinking rituals. At Stanwick Hall in 1788, the catalogue included 'twelve India cups'; that at Sudborough Hall in 1836 itemized 'Indian china tea pots', and there is reference to Nankeen and Japan china at Wollaton Hall in 1805. More unusual were the two 'antique teapots' offered at Welton Place in 1830, the attraction being their venerable character—oldness and rarity making them more attractive as markers of distinction.[28] Whereas porcelain from Meissen, Sèvres, and, to a lesser extent, Wedgwood might be seen as positional goods, these 'genuine' eastern goods and antiques linked their owners into more esoteric tastes and cultures of collecting, distinguishing them as connoisseurs as well as consumers.[29]

Status could also be marked through the complexity of the paraphernalia. My sample of inventories includes a range of items such as sugar basins, slop basins,

---

[22] Styles, 'Product Innovation'.

[23] Stobart, 'Gentlemen and Shopkeepers'.

[24] OBP, 1750–9, 1780–9. See also Vickery, *Behind Closed Doors*, 272; Blondé, 'Think Local'.

[25] See Berg, *Luxury and Pleasure*, 126–53.

[26] Berg, *Luxury and Pleasure*, 148–50.

[27] For example, the catalogue for the sale at Brixworth Hall in 1797 listed two Wedgwood table services (NCL, M0005646NL/15, 8).

[28] NCL, M0005646NL/9, Stanwick Hall (1788), 9; M0005645NL/22, Sudborough Hall (1836), 12; M0005644NL/5, Wollaston Hall (1805), 22; M0005644NL/13, Welton Place (1830), 29.

[29] See Bourdieu, *Distinction*, esp. 2, 228; McCracken, *Culture and Consumption*, 31–43, 113.

and tongs as well as cups, saucers, teaspoons, and teapots, but very few of these middle-ranking consumers owned more than two or three 'specialist' items. In 1720 Joseph Yardley, a starcher from Coventry, had a 'hatchet and hammer for tea', and about twenty years later the widow Elizabeth Wells had teaspoons, 'tea tongs and strainer' listed among her silverware. Neither appears to have owned any other items relating to hot drinks. The grocer Benjamin Wright was exceptional in owning two pairs of salts, a set of casters, a chocolate pot, canisters and nippers, a tea urn and stand, as well as a tea chest, and two waiters.[30] Yet this variety was fairly typical of wealthy professionals and the gentry. Sale catalogues from the late eighteenth century frequently included full sets of equipage, often in silver—a trend seen in earlier paintings, most famously Colious's *Family at Tea* of 1732.[31] These appeared alongside matching sets of chinaware, which were sometimes differentiated according to the type of beverage or meal for which they were intended. At the 1823 sale at Geddington House, for example, we see:

13 *A Handsome tea and coffee set*, containing 12 cups and saucers, 8 coffee ditto and saucers, tea pot and stand, cream ewer, sugar vase, 2 basons, butter tub, cover and stand, and 2 bread and butter plates

14 Eleven breakfast cups and 12 saucers, egg stand with 5 cups, 2 basons, cream ewer, sugar vase, 2 butter tubs, covers and stands, 1 other, 2 muffin plates and covers, 4 oval dishes, 12 small plates and 2 large ditto, *to match the last lot*[32]

Even though they were matching, the different purpose of the two sets is clear from the range and type of pieces each comprised: tea was taken with bread and butter; breakfast comprised eggs, muffins, and rolls.

The ownership of such a variety and range of silver and chinaware reveals both the importance of tea and breakfast in transforming domestic material culture, and the ways in which individuals could use the consumption of these meals to mark their status. They could signal both taste and wealth in performances of conspicuous consumption. Surprisingly, perhaps, this did not preclude the retention of damaged, repaired, and non-matching goods. When she died in 1760, the Birmingham spinster Sara Dicken had '1 china slop basin 4 saucers and 3 cups old and crack'd'. Despite their poor state of repair and odd number, Dicken had clearly chosen to keep the cups alongside her other chinaware. This again reminds us of the significance of small items to the individual, in terms of both the utility and the construction of self-image.[33] Further up the social scale, and as late as 1823, the chinaware owned by Henry Fryer Esq. of Stamford Baron

[30] LiRO, B/C/11, Joseph Yardley (1720); KAS, 11.82.16, Elizabeth Wells (1743); LiRO, B/C/11, Benjamin Wright (1778).

[31] This is reproduced in many places, including Weatherill, *Consumer Behaviour*, 35.

[32] NCL, M0005644NL/8, Geddington House (1823), 20. See also NCL, M0005647NL/2, Rollaston Hall (1801), 24–5.

[33] LiRO, B/C/11 Sara Dicken (1760); Pennell, 'Material Culture of Food', ch. 4.

included a 'tea pot with silver spout', indicating a repair had been undertaken in the past.[34] Such examples are comparatively rare among sales from gentry houses, but it is clear that even wealthy consumers had goods repaired rather than always buying new ones. Vickery notes that a brazier's bill paid in 1739 by the Arderne family in Cheshire recorded, among other things, 'soldering a coffee-pot cover and fixing a new handle onto a teapot'.[35] Even when repairs were impossible, the rest of a set was often retained, sometimes to be sold on at a later date. Sale catalogues regularly included tea services where there were fewer cups than saucers, and at Stanford Hall in 1792 some of these oddments seem to have been assembled into a single lot, number 20: 'Twenty tea and coffee cups, 17 saucers, various, 3 stands, 2 plates, 14 chimney ornaments, various, and some odd pieces'.[36] The fact that old items and oddments retained some monetary value strongly suggests that the new material culture (characterized by goods such as china) was not simply about the meaning of goods. Any shift in consumer mentalities was thus partial and contingent.[37]

Tea drinking and its material objects were often associated with women. Kowalski-Wallace has argued that the tea table can be seen as a kind of disciplinary apparatus that shaped female behaviour and identity—an instrument of self-construction and display.[38] But this ignores the wide range of social groups who 'took tea' and the variety of social engagements that might be lubricated by tea drinking (see Chapter 9). Acknowledging this diversity allows us to recognize how women at all social levels were associated with the equipment needed for preparing and serving tea. As Barnett argues, 'women, literate in the visual language of material culture, would have manipulated their setting to the best social effect, perhaps regardless of the limitations of space'.[39] Evidence from probate records is problematic in this regard, since it is often difficult to distinguish the specific role of women in acquiring and using utensils for hot drinks. Comparing the houses of bachelors with those of spinsters and widows, Ponsonby finds extensive equipment for tea drinking only in the inventories of the latter. Indeed, all the women in her sample had quantities of tea-ware that far exceeded the needs of what were often small households, suggesting that they engaged in domestic sociability that involved tea.[40] Further, she notes changes in the contents of houses before and after the death of a male householder. The 1761 probate inventory of John Marrion, a Staffordshire farmer, included six delftware plates, a mahogany tea chest with silver tongs, tea dishes, and saucers. Nine years later, when his wife Susannah died, her inventory listed additional delftware, cups, and saucers, while the twenty trenchers that had seemingly formed the main way of serving food in her husband's time were gone.

[34] NCL, M0005644NL/9, Stamford Baron (1823), 39.
[35] Vickery, *Behind Closed Doors*, 271.
[36] NCL, M0005646NL/11, Stanford Hall (1792), 12.
[37] This ties in with the conclusions of Blondé, 'Think Local'.
[38] Kowalski-Wallace, *Consuming Subjects*, 19–36.
[39] Barnett, 'In with the New', 88. See also Vickery, *Behind Closed Doors*, 272–3, 142; Smith, *Consumption*, ch. 6.
[40] Ponsonby, *Stories from Home*, 134–6, 146.

These small differences are underscored by Vickery's suggestion that tea and china-ware were often viewed as the possessions of the woman of the house. She cites the example of a case heard at the Old Bailey in 1775, when a china teapot, seven cups and saucers, a basin, and a sugar dish were taken from the dining room of a wine merchant called John Filks. In giving evidence, his wife referred to the goods as 'my china'—a clear indication of gendered ownership.[41]

Women were enthusiastic buyers of tea services and the like, even when their personal circumstances did not promise many visitors. Vickery notes that the wealthy Yorkshire spinster Diana Eyre, who lodged with her sister and brother-in-law from the 1750s to the 1770s, still chose to purchase in 1764 a tea table, tea waiter, two teapots, and a coffee mill, as well as jelly glasses and other items of tableware. Two decades later, the chronically ill Mary Hartley fitted out a Bath apartment with genteel furniture and an assortment of goods from Matthew Boulton, including tea canisters, and chocolate and coffee pots with matching lamps for warming the contents.[42] Both women were buying in accordance with their own tastes, setting themselves up to engage in the sociability of the tea table. But men also bought and used equipment for preparing and serving hot drinks. Between 1702 and 1704, Edward, the future third Lord Leigh, was a student at Oxford University and kept a careful account of expenditure in his pocket book. This included purchases linked to his studies (books, matriculation, and stationery), leisure activities (theatre tickets, admission to the University Press and the physic garden, and lessons from a dancing master), and personal appearance (hair powder, gloves, and a watch chain). One of the first things he set about doing, however, was equipping himself with the paraphernalia needed to serve hot drinks in his rooms. Thus, on 20 June 1702 he bought a tea table for 10*s.* a sugar box for 1*s.*, and six teacups for 13*s.* Two months later, he bought seven more teacups at 1*s.* apiece and a coffee mill for 15*s.* The following month he bought six teaspoons, a coffee pot, a boiler, and a chocolate pot at a total cost of £2 5*s.*[43] Given the number of cups and spoons, and the quantity of tea, coffee, chocolate, and sugar that he also bought, he was clearly equipping himself to serve a range of hot drinks to friends in his private rooms. That sociability over the tea table could flourish in the all-male domain of university is also apparent from the account books of his distant relative, the future Reverend Thomas Leigh, who made similar purchases in the late 1750s, and Sam Turner (also a future clergymen), who spent lavishly on furnishings for his room, including china, a tea chest, and tea board.[44] While the link, drawn by Smith and others, between tea and female domesticity was undoubtedly close, it would be wrong to see it as axiomatic or exclusive. There were other contexts and motivations for tea drinking in the domestic realm—not least male sociability.

---

[41] See Vickery, *Behind Closed Doors*, 273.
[42] Vickery, *Behind Closed Doors*, 214, 217. Vickery cites several other examples of women spending in this way.
[43] SCLA, DR 18/29/6/1.
[44] SCLA, DR 18/31/856; Vickery, *Behind Closed Doors*, 272.

A WIDER MATERIAL CULTURE FOR CONSUMING GROCERIES

The purchases made by these men and women show how the 'bundling' of goods could be quite encompassing and prompts consideration of the wider set of durable goods linked to the domestic consumption of groceries. Some of these formed part of the more general equipage of tea and coffee drinking, often drawn together in inventories under the generic heading of 'chinaware'—a category that might include teacups and sugar bowls, but also the plates, dishes, and jugs needed for serving milk, cakes, bread and butter, and the tables upon which these things were served.[45] Although the style of a piece was often mentioned (tables, for instance, might be described as oval), probate inventories rarely made explicit the use to which they were put. It is significant, then, that appraisers felt it useful to record the presence of tea tables in seventeen houses, suggesting that these pieces were particularly noteworthy. Initially, they were restricted to higher-status individuals, being listed only in the homes of gentlemen, merchants, and clergymen between 1698 and 1720; but thereafter they spread to tradesmen, including a brewer, a baker, an apothecary, and an upholsterer. Tea tables were not hugely costly items: the guinea paid by Elizabeth Purefoy for one at a local house sale in January 1742 appears to have been towards the top end of the scale, inventory valuations ranging from 6s. 8d. down to a mere 1s. 6d.[46] Whether this variation reflected differences in materials, quality, or size is impossible to know. Indeed, it is difficult to tell exactly what appraisers meant when they used the term 'tea table'. It seems likely that it reflected intrinsic qualities of the furniture, yet the term appears to have lost its resonance in the later eighteenth century. The last inventory in my sample to mention a tea table dates from 1743, while sale catalogues dating from the 1760s onwards never described furniture in this way, despite the abundance of other paraphernalia for tea drinking. Of course, both these catalogues and the earlier inventories include plenty of other tables that could be used for serving tea: perhaps the practice was so widespread that the particular adjective was redundant, replaced by Pembroke or breakfast table, for instance.[47]

Other groceries also required specific durables for their polite consumption, especially as dining habits changed. Silver salts were an established feature of the dining table and were listed in the inventories of a range of different tradesmen, including a tailor and a mercer as well as merchants and grocers. Unsurprisingly, though, they were most prominent in the homes of elite consumers, where they often featured alongside cruets. In January 1765, Edward, fifth Lord Leigh, was billed by the London silversmith Thomas Gilpin for a wide variety of silverware, including a cruet

[45] It is noteworthy that the first appearance of a sugar bowl in the probate inventories sampled here pre-dates any mention of tea or coffee by twenty—five years, Robert Baldwin of Canterbury having in his possession a silver sugar dish when he died in 1672 (KAS, 11.34.9, Robert Baldwin (1672)).

[46] Eland, *Purefoy Letters*, i. 110; CALS, WS 1709, Peter Williams; LiRO, B/C/11, Joseph Yardley (1720).

[47] The multi-functional nature of particular objects is emphasized by Pennell, 'Material Culture of Food', ch. 4.

frame and castors, four large cruets, and six large oval salts at a combined cost of £48 2s. 8d.[48] Along with sauce boats, waiters, candlesticks, and silver cutlery, these were crucial elements in the display of a fine dinner table—just as important as the food being served. They remained a central feature of the sets of silverware advertised in country-house sales through the late eighteenth and nineteenth centuries, in many cases being joined by an array of other artefacts used for serving various condiments. At Wollaston Hall, for example, the silverware offered for sale in 1805 included: 'three pair of salts with *gilt insides*, and 6 spoons'; a 'soy frame with 6 cruets', and 'a preserving spoon, a nutmeg grater, a pepper box, a salad fork, and a mustard spoon'.[49] Such items reflect developments in the practices of elite dining, which meant that flavourings bought at the grocer's shop were offered to guests at the table. That these practices were not restricted to the very wealthy is apparent from an early nineteenth-century print entitled *The Dinner Locust*. The focus of attention is on the couple about to dine and their uninvited guest, but on the table is a set of cruets sat on small wooden frame.[50] Moreover, there are occasional references to casters in the probate inventories: Thomas Yardley of Coventry owned '3 old castors' and John Ward of Tarporley had two silver castors.[51] It is unclear whether these were for sugar or pepper; either way, their presence indicates that at least some lower-status consumers were serving condiments at the table from the early eighteenth century. This suggests that any transformation of domestic material culture was a long, drawn-out process and, as Blondé, Overton, and others have argued, questions the revolutionary nature of any change.[52]

A greater number of householders were using spices and salt in their cooking, as is clear from the presence in over one-third of the inventories of spice, pepper, or salt boxes. Few details are given, but most of these boxes were wooden and worth just a few pence—Samuel Baker's pepper box being valued at 4d. and John Pollard's 'old salt box' at 6d.[53] It is likely that such boxes were more widely owned, but are either hidden under general headings of 'lumber' or listed simply as boxes. Also widespread, but largely invisible, are clay pipes for smoking tobacco, which were so cheap that they were effectively disposable. Unsurprisingly, then, while appearing in the stock of many shops, they are not recorded in any of the inventories within the sample surveyed here. Their presence can be inferred in some homes from the appearance of tobacco boxes. Mostly these were heavy wooden items, lined with lead and designed to keep the tobacco from losing its flavour. Only occasionally do we see silver boxes, which were more closely linked to the display rituals involved in serving tobacco to guests.[54]

---

[48] SCLA, D/R/18/5/4215. All the items were engraved with Lord Leigh's crest and coronet.
[49] NCL, M0005644NL/5, Wollaston Hall (1805).
[50] Anon., *The Dinner Locust*, 1826 (reproduced as plate 5 in Vickery, *Behind Closed Doors*).
[51] LiRO, B/C/11, Thomas Yardley (1720); CALS, WS 1715, John Ward.
[52] See Blondé, 'Tableware'; Overton et al., *Production and Consumption*, esp. 87–120.
[53] LiRO, B/C/11, Samuel Baker (1730); LiRO, B/C/11, John Pollard (1730). See also Pennell, 'Material Culture of Food', ch. 4.
[54] Lead-lined boxes were recorded in CALS, WS1709, Peter Williams; CALS, WS 1736, Abner Scholes; LiRO, B/C/11, Jonathan Nichols (1743). Silver tobacco boxes were found in KAS, 11.40.251, George Reeve (1677); KAS, 11.77.190, Richard Johnson (1725).

It is difficult to know how these were used by their owners, but we can be more certain about the silver snuff boxes owned by Jonathan Nichols, a Coventry tinman, and William Bastard, a Cornish merchant, and the '2 pearl snuff boxes [with] silver rims' listed among the possessions of the Birmingham spinster Sara Dicken.[55] Snuff taking grew rapidly in popularity in the first decade of the eighteenth century and became a leitmotif of polite and fashionable society in the 1720s.[56] Snuff boxes were, therefore, important, both as symbols of taste and elegance, and as props in the performance of social and cultural propriety.[57] Taking snuff in public involved an elaborate ritual that had to be mastered—a knowing and conscious display of status. In 1711, the *Spectator* informed its readers that Charles Lily, a London toy dealer, would be offering lessons on the 'ceremony of the snuff box, rules for offering snuff to a stranger, a friend, or mistress; with an explanation of the careless, the scornful, the politic & the surly pinch, and the gestures proper to each of them'.[58] Although clearly satirical, this advertisement points to the importance of deportment and gesture when taking snuff. These performances were given extra meaning by the deployment of handkerchiefs, tiny spoons, and, above all, the snuff box itself, which was seen as being powerfully shaped by the vicissitudes of fashion. In March 1710 the *Tatler* announced of gold boxes that

a new edition will be put out on Saturday next, which will be the only one in fashion until after Easter. The gentleman that gave £50 for the box set with diamonds may show it till Sunday, provided he goes to church, but not after that time, there being one to be published on Monday which will cost four score guineas.[59]

Again, this should be understood as satire, but snuff boxes were, in many ways, perfect examples of the novelties that so irked many contemporary commentators, including Adam Smith.[60] They were positional goods (defined by cost), luxuries (being made from gold, silver, or pearl), and yet utterly amenable to the constant changes in form and detail that made them exemplars of fashionable consumption. And yet silver snuff boxes were found among the possessions of tradesmen and artisans, even in quite remote parts of the country. It is unlikely that Nichols, Bastard, or Dicken had lessons in how to take snuff or that they were concerned about the fashionability of their boxes. Indeed, it is possible that those belonging to Dicken were heirlooms, listed in her inventory alongside a gold watch valued at £8 and two old silver watches, together worth £1. Certainly, her snuff boxes were exactly the kind of small personal item bequeathed to loved ones as mementos.[61] Rather later and also removed from the febrile atmosphere of

[55] LiRO, B/C/11, Jonathan Nichols (1743); CRO, William Bastard (1720); LiRO, B/C/11, Sara Dicken (1760).
[56] Quoted in Corbellier, *Snuff Boxes*, 7. See also MacArthur, 'Material Culture and Consumption', 204–8.
[57] Fennetaux, 'Toying with Novelty', 24.
[58] Reproduced in Bond (ed.), *The Spectator*, ii. 297.
[59] Quoted in Hughes, *Snuff Boxes*, 19.
[60] Smith, *Theory of Moral Sentiments*, pt 4.
[61] See Berg, 'Women's Consumption'. The exchange of snuff boxes also became a symbol of fraternity (Schivelbusch, *Tastes of Paradise*, 144–5).

London society, snuff boxes occasionally appear in sales from country houses, where they take the form of curios or collectors' items. At the 1823 sale of the property of Henry Fryer Esq., a wide range of decorative items, from a 'Curious silver filigree honeysuckle, enclosed in a glass case' to a 'china scent jar, ornamented with beautifully painted birds' were listed in a 'Cabinet of Miscellaneous Articles'.[62] They included:

120 Chrystal snuff box, mounted in gold, taken from the carriage of Napoleon Bonaparte at the Battle of Waterloo
121 Amber snuff box
122 Curious small snuff box, mounted in silver
123 Shell snuff box, mounted in silver

In the same cabinet was another container that may once have been useful, but was by then seen as decorative: an 'Agate tea caddy, mounted in silver gilt, ornamented with precious stones'. Containers for keeping it fresh and perhaps safe from thieving hands were an important part of storing and serving tea.[63] The most basic form of container was the canister. Generally made from tin and with tight-fitting lids, canisters were supplied by a growing number of tea dealers (see Chapter 7). Tin could be burnished like silver, but canisters were essentially functional rather than decorative, sometimes being placed within tea caddies or chests in order to make them more presentable and also more secure, the outer boxes being fitted with locks. The term 'caddy' is not used in any of the inventories sampled and appears in the records of the Old Bailey only from the 1780s onwards, when it usually described a wooden box, sometimes with a silver lid or matching silver spoon. 'Chests' were listed in a small number of inventories, but only from the 1730s—about the time they appear in the Old Bailey Records. These may have referred to the boxes in which tea was shipped, but, to judge from their value, the tea chests owned by the Birmingham salesman Thomas Chapman and the Northamptonshire grocer Thomas Mee were probably purpose built to contain canisters of tea.[64] The caddies and chests listed in sale catalogues were certainly of this style. Those offered at the 1761 sale at Cottingham and the 1815 sale at Thorp Malsor were dressed in respectable mahogany to complement the dining room or parlour furniture. The reserve price of 3*s.* attached to the tea chest at Cottingham is broadly in line with valuations found in probate inventories, suggesting quite modest pieces. Rather more ornate, though still some way short of Henry Fryer's agate caddy, was the 'maple wood tea chest, with 2 cut-glass tea canisters, and sugar basin' listed at the 1836 sale at Hollowell.[65] These details carry a wider significance. Tea combined with canisters, caddies, and so on to form a set of goods that, through their quality and price, could operate as markers of status. This bundling also made the consumption of groceries

---

[62] NCL, M0005644NL/9, Stamford Baron (1823), 49.
[63] For a fuller discussion, see Vickery, 'Englishman's Home'.
[64] LiRO, B/C/11, Thomas Chapman (1760); NRO, Thomas Mee (1775).
[65] NCL, M0005644NL/7, Thorp Malsor (1815), 11; M0005644NL/20, Hollowell (1836), 20.

more susceptible to fashion changes: the tea remained the same, but the paraphernalia might change regularly to match prevailing tastes.

LOCATION WITHIN THE HOME

Material possessions are both functional objects and receptacles of meaning. Their placement in the home and alongside other goods is, therefore, profoundly significant to the ways in which they were used, the messages they sent about taste, wealth, and fashion, and how they might shape personal identity. Discussion of the placement of goods within the home can usefully be framed around Goffman's notion of front and back stage. The former comprised those spaces in which an individual 'performed' a public character—material objects constituting the set on and through which the performance could unfold. The latter were more private spaces to which the person might withdraw from the gaze of the audience and in which they would prepare for their more public performances.[66] Historians have been wary of applying these ideas too directly in the domestic realm, preferring to nuance the dichotomy by emphasizing multiple publics, gendered spaces, and diurnal changes in the character and status of rooms within the house.[67] Novel goods were especially important in this context, since they helped to articulate the distinction between different spaces, not least because they were often linked to new social practices and socio-symbolic value systems.[68] In short, the location within the home of coffee pots, pepper boxes, cups and saucers, and tea tables is profoundly significant in understanding both the consumption of groceries and the character of different rooms in the house.

Salt, pepper, and spice boxes were mostly found in the kitchen or more occasionally the 'house', if that was the room in which cooking took place (Table 10.3).[69] This made a great deal of practical sense, as salt and spices would be on hand to add to food as it was being prepared.[70] If the family owned pepper castors or salts, then these could be filled in the kitchen and taken to the table. In larger houses, this would have involved collecting such tableware from its place of storage, usually with other silverware in the butler's pantry or a closet in the kitchen. Probate inventories often reveal little about the location of such items in modest households, since they were mostly listed with other silver goods outside the room-by-room itinerary followed by most appraisers. Occasional references suggest secure locations, such as the room over the kitchen where John Ward of Tarporley

---

[66] Goffman, *Presentation of Self*.

[67] Weatherill, *Consumer Behaviour*, esp. 8–9; Overton et al., *Production and Consumption*, 134–6; Kross, 'Mansions, Men, Women'; Andersson, 'A Mirror of Oneself'; Vickery, *Behind Closed Doors*, *passim*; Barnett, 'In with the New', 84–91.

[68] Smith, *Consumption*, esp. 171–88; Barnett, 'In with the New', 85; Vickery, *Behind Closed Doors*, 207–30.

[69] Stobart, 'Accommodating the Shop', 359–62.

[70] Pennell, 'Material Culture of Food', ch. 4, suggests that pepper and spice boxes had previously been kept in bedchambers—a reflection of the value of their contents and the popularity of spiced drinks.

kept his '4 silver salts' or the closet apparently leading off the dining room, which, among other things, contained William Preeson's six silver salts (valued at £2 8*s*.).[71] Other receptacles for storing groceries, including tea chests and canisters, were also found in the kitchen. This suggests that they were functional rather than decorative items, an impression that is reinforced by the absence of such items from paintings of ladies or families at tea, which instead focus on the porcelain or silver tea sets, trays, and tables.[72] If true, this pattern of behaviour appears to have changed in the later decades of the eighteenth century. Rather than in the kitchen, chests and caddies were found in parlours, dining rooms, and drawing rooms—the places in which the tea itself would have been consumed. The elegant maple wood tea chest listed in the dining room at Hollowell and the 'neat mahogany tea caddie with sliding canisters, cut-glass sugar vase, lock and key' found in the drawing room at Geddington House were clearly items of display.[73] Unlocking this caddie, removing one of the glass canisters, and spooning out the tea would have formed an important part of the ritual of serving tea. Equally important, though, was the permanent presence of these chests and caddies in public spaces, where they served as an ornament to the room and a constant reminder of both the tea stored within and the practices of its consumption.

Other items never made this kind of permanent transition from back to front stage. In the probate inventories, tea kettles are listed in the kitchen or occasionally in the brew house or buttery, and this is where they are invariably found in later sale catalogues. Coffee and the very much rarer chocolate pots were slightly more widely dispersed through different rooms, but most were found in the kitchen, 'house', buttery, or pantry, sometimes grouped with other copper- or tin-ware. Again, there were practical reasons for this, not least the presence of a fire on which to boil the kettle or warm the coffee pot.[74] Kettles were essential in the process of making hot drinks, but ephemeral to consumption rituals. Thus, in wealthy households, a footman or maid would carry the kettle into the drawing room and deliver the boiling water to his or her mistress, who presided over tea while servant and kettle retreated from the room.[75] In less privileged homes, the journey from kitchen to table was undoubtedly shorter, but a similar distinction between preparation and consumption was apparent. When made from silver, coffee and chocolate pots could appear front stage and proclaim the wealth and status of the owner. Shortly before his death in 1738, Edward, third Lord Leigh, paid £10 4*s*. for a silver coffee pot and a further 1*s*. 6*d*. to have his crest and coronet engraved on it. In his youth and away from the family home at Oxford, his outlay of 7*s*. on a coffee pot and 11*s*.

---

[71] CALS, WS 1715, John Ward; LRO, WCW 1705, William Preeson.

[72] See, e.g., anon., *A Family Being Served with Tea* (*c*.1740–5), Yale Center for British Art, B.1981.25.271; anon., *The Tea Table* (*c*.1710), Lewis Walpole Library, 766.0.37 (reproduced as plate 34 and figure 53 respectively in Vickery, *Behind Closed Doors*), and R. Colius, *Family at Tea* (1745), V&A, P.9&:1–1934 (reproduced as plate 3 in Weatherill, *Consumer Behaviour*).

[73] NCL, M0005644NL/20, Hollowell, 1836, 20; M0005644NL/8, Geddington House (1823), 16.

[74] Ellis, *Coffee House*, 127–8.

[75] See, e.g., anon, *Family Being Served with Tea*.

Table 10.3. Location of grocery-related objects within the home, *c.*1670–1770 (%)

Object	Kitchen	House	Parlour	Chamber	Other	Unknown
Salt or spice boxes (N = 35)	66	20	0	0	3	11
Tea chests and canisters (N = 7)	57	0	29	0	0	14
Tea kettles (N = 32)	66	6	0	0	19	9
Coffee pots (N = 38)	47	21	0	8	11	13
Teapots (N = 10)	40	20	20	10	0	10
Cups and saucers (N = 21)	14	5	33	29	5	14
Teaspoons (N = 19)	11	5	21	26	16	21
Tea tables (N = 20)	0	0	70	0	5	25

Source: probate inventories.

on a chocolate pot suggests that he chose copperware, which was practical rather than showy.[76] Further down the social scale, however, an array of copperware could still make an impressive display. A coffee pot appears on the mantelpiece in Van Aken's *Grace before a Meal* (*c.*1720) and in the parlour of Thomas Bell, a Norwich baker who died in 1738. His chimney piece was decorated with '2 enamelled chocolate pots, 12 tea cups, ditto Burntin basins, 6 ditto coffee pots, 3 ditto tea cups and other china'.[77]

In general, coffee and chocolate pots were not part of the tableware or the polite rituals that surrounded the consumption of hot drinks; nor did they feature in elaborate 'tea sets'. Teapots were rather different. While probate inventories indicate that they were most commonly kept in the kitchen, some were found in the parlour and even in bedchambers, often placed alongside cups and saucers (Table 10.3). In prints and paintings, they regularly appear on a mantelpiece or table, even in the dwellings of the poor or down-at-heel. In Hogarth's *The Distressed Poet*, the cupboard is bare, the milkmaid is demanding payment, and the wife is mending cloths; but a teapot and cups stand on the mantel. The solace found in Bigg's *Poor Old Woman's Comfort* might be read as the warmth of the fire, but is more likely seen in the customary luxury of the teapot, cup and saucer, tea caddy, and white bread and butter on the table behind her.[78] Such visual representations are echoed in probate inventories. As well as the coffee and chocolate pots ranged along Thomas Bell's mantelpiece, his parlour contained '2 Burntin china tea pots and saucers, a ditto sugar dish, a basin, 8 cups and sau-

[76] SCLA, DR 18/5/2000; SCLA, DR 18/29/6 Box 1. See also Stobart, 'Gentlemen and Shopkeepers'.

[77] Joseph Van Aken, *Grace before a Meal*, Ashmolean Museum, WA1962.17.4 (reproduced as plate 1 in Weatherill, *Consumer Behaviour*); NoRO, ANW 23/22A/44 (I am grateful to Amy Barnett for this reference).

[78] William Hogarth, *The Distressed Poet* (1736), BM, 1868,0822.1541 (reproduced as figure 11 in Vickery, *Behind Closed Doors*); William Bigg, *Poor Old Woman's Comfort* (1793), V&A, 199–1885 (reproduced as figure 1 in Styles, *Dress of the People*).

cers'. These were described as being 'upon the tea table'—a location that suggests a desire to play on their decorative qualities and socio-cultural significance, as well as making them ready for use.[79] The parlour, of course, was the usual place in which to receive visitors, its association with tea drinking being close and axiomatic: even when tea or coffee was prepared elsewhere, it would be carried into the parlour to be consumed.[80] This might be undertaken in a variety of ways, but was most appropriately facilitated by use of a tea tray or tea board. Along with pots, cups, and saucers, these regularly feature in depictions of polite tea drinking, either set on the table or in the hands of servants.[81] Indeed, their mode of carriage was seen by some as being just as important as the goods with which they were laden. In the detailed instructions that she wrote out for her various servants, Miss Anne Boulton of Birmingham told her male servant to see that the tea tray was correctly laid and carried to the drawing room, before waiting on the company there.[82]

Drawing rooms and parlours are often seen as feminine, refined, and intimate; but they were also regarded as public.[83] A similar tension was seen in the presence of tea tables, pots, and cups in a number of bedchambers. Occasionally, this might be explained by the absence of a suitable room downstairs (a common problem for shopkeepers), but it is best understood as part of the trend towards the construction of 'great' or 'best' chambers. This drew on a process already well established in noble houses in the late Middle Ages; the lord of the house increasingly using his great chamber as a combined private reception room and bedchamber. This habit was spreading to ordinary households in the early decades of the seventeenth century and was common by the second quarter of the eighteenth century—a transition that again questions the transformative power of tea drinking on domestic arrangements.[84] What it produced was a room that had much in common with the parlour, but that was upstairs and thus much less public. Most rooms of this nature appear to have been used for entertaining close friends or family, so it is unsurprising that some would contain the paraphernalia for drinking tea and coffee. The contrasting feel of parlour and great chamber is apparent from the inventory of the Cornish merchant Stephen Lawrence (d. 1721). Other than a bed and cupboard (typical features of the great chamber), the furnishing of the two rooms was remarkably similar: they both contained tea tables, chinaware, and a large number of chairs. The distinction came in the up-to-date character and value of the furniture,

---

[79] NoRO, ANW 23/22A/44. For similar examples, see Ponsonby, *Stories from Home*, 120, 142–9.
[80] Overton et al., *Production and Consumption*, 132–3.
[81] See e.g. anon., *Family Being Served with Tea*; anon., *The Morning Visit; or The Fashionable Dresses for the Year 1777* (1778), BM, J,5.108 (reproduced as figure 4 in Vickery, *Behind Closed Doors*); Thomas Rowlandson, *A Tea Party* (*c.*1790–5), Yale Center for British Art, and 'Tea Tray Painted with Tea-Party Scene' (1743), V&A 3864.1901 (reproduced as figures 5.15 and 5.7 respectively in Greig, 'Eighteenth-Century English Interiors').
[82] Ponsonby, *Stories from Home*, 120.
[83] Herman, 'Tabletop Conversations'; Smith, *Consumption*, 171–87; Kross, 'Mansions, Men, Women'; Vickery, 'Englishman's Home'; Barnett, 'In with the New', 89.
[84] Girouard, *English Country House*, 88; Overton et al., *Production and Consumption*, 133–4; Blondé, 'Think Local'.

and the detail of the decoration. Lawrence's parlour chairs were cane-bottomed and worth £3 12*s.*, whereas those in the chamber were plain ones valued at just £1 4*s.*; the tea tables were worth 5*s.* and less than 2*s.* respectively. In the parlour were five maps valued at 12*s.* 6*d.*, while the chamber contained more personal, but lower-value items—two patchwork stools and a 'Venice glass'.[85] We can imagine Lawrence's business contacts being entertained in the rather formal parlour, while his friends were welcomed to the intimacy of the upstairs room. Such distinctions offered a range of spaces that might be accessible to some but closed to others and thus cut across any simple dichotomy of public and private, front and back stage.[86]

CONTEXTS AND ASSOCIATIONS

The idea of consumption bundles has been influential in thinking about which goods were conceived, bought, and used together, but it has rarely been applied in spatial terms. While Weatherill touched on the grouping of goods within the home, this has received surprisingly little attention since then, except in the form of the equipage for tea.[87] Taking this as a starting point, it is possible to see how tables, pots, cups, and basins came together both functionally and spatially in many eighteenth-century homes. In the 1715 inventory of John Ward, the rector of Tarporley, his tea table, hand tea table, and some chinaware are grouped together and given a collective value of 12*s.* A generation later, Elizabeth Wells of Bridge in Kent had a wide range of tea-related objects: five china cups and six saucers; an earthenware dish, two basins and three plates; one pewter and one earthenware teapot, and four more cups plus another saucer.[88] This assemblage of goods represents the output of a range of different manufacturers and craftsmen whose skills were drawn upon and drawn together in order to consume tea and coffee, sweetened with sugar and accompanied by cakes or bread and butter. However, to fully appreciate the way in which the consumption of groceries linked into the wider transformation of domestic material culture, we need to look beyond the tea table and inspect the rest of the room and, indeed, the house.[89]

John Molyneux was a prosperous merchant, engaged in the West Indian and North American trade. His inventory, taken on 1 March 1699,[90] details shares in seven ships, together worth £3,287; ten cargoes of tobacco valued at over £2,800, plus ginger, indigo, raisins, and goods bound for Virginia worth £237; £6,038 of debts owing to him, including £600 in 'transport money due from the King for

[85] CRO, L1249, Stephen Lawrence (1721).

[86] Andersson, 'A Mirror of Oneself'. For a fuller discussion of the complexities of boundaries within the home, see Vickery, *Behind Closed Doors*, 25–48.

[87] Weatherill, *Consumer Behaviour*, 32–6, 179–82.

[88] CALS, WS 1715, John Ward; KAS, 11.82.116, Elizabeth Wells (1743).

[89] For detailed discussion of assemblages of culinary wares, see Pennell, 'Material Culture of Food', ch. 4.

[90] LRO, WCW 1699, John Molyneux.

sundry ships'; and £696 in ready money. With a total estate of £15,240, he was one of wealthiest men in Liverpool. His house reflected his status, being furnished with a wide variety of luxurious and exotic goods, including many of the novel goods highlighted in Weatherill's study. Looking glasses, paintings, window curtains, books, silverware, table linen, saucepans, and cane-bottomed chairs all feature on the inventory, but especially notable is the frequent appearance of japanned furniture—a highly fashionable and exotic commodity at this date.[91] Perhaps surprisingly, objects linked with imported groceries were not found in Molyneux's dining room or parlour, which were both elegantly furnished, but quite traditional. Instead, they were grouped together in the kitchen (where coffee pots and a chocolate mill sat alongside mustard boxes, apple roasters, funnels and a large amount of pewter ware) and in the 'plate case', which contained three casters and five salts along with tankards, cups, salvers, spoons, forks, and porringers. In both settings, novel goods were placed alongside older items, signalling the coexistence of new and traditional consumption practices. However, it was in the more intimate space of Mrs Molyneux's chamber where such items were most closely linked with the construction of a fashionable interior and 'modern' modes of consumption. In addition to a bed furnished with silk damask and worth £60, this room contained damask curtains for the windows and doors, seven chairs to match the bed, a dressing box inlaid with mother of pearl, gilt-framed pictures, and a walnut chests of drawers. An exotic feel was given by the extensive use of japanned furniture and toiletries: a trunk, a cabinet, powder boxes, patch boxes, brushes, pin cushions, and a tea table. There were also some special pieces of silverware: two porringers, two tumblers, a jug, two cups, a candlestick, two spoons, a basin, and a teapot. Here Mrs Molyneux could have sat around the tea table with her particular friends, surrounded by a mix of elegant and exotic goods, and serving tea from her silver pot. In this, she was the epitome of Smith's respectable feminine domesticity; but this relied not just on tea and sympathy, but also on the assemblage of material objects in her room.[92]

Few homes could match this kind of opulence, but fashion and novelty also characterized more modest interiors, often with the equipage for serving drinks sitting centre-stage. The Reverend John Ward's tea tables and china were found in his parlour. While the walls were hung with tapestries, much of the rest of the furniture was characteristic of a newer domestic material culture. There were twelve cane chairs, an oval table, a large looking glass, three window curtains, and five pictures including two family portraits and a landscape.[93] With its large number of chairs and tables, and careful embellishment with textiles, paintings, and chinaware, this was a room in which the elite of the parish might be received. Much the same could be said of the parlour of Robert Wilkinson, a tailor from Nantwich. This contained a clock, a looking glass, twelve pictures, thirty books and a book

---

[91] Coquery, 'Semi-Luxury Market'; Berg, 'Asian Luxuries'.
[92] See Smith, *Consumption*, 181–3.
[93] CALS, WS 1715, John Ward. Landscape paintings have particular significance, since they suggest awareness of and interest in a wider world.

desk, window curtains, six cane chairs and two oval tables, along with a teapot and dishes, three glasses, and cruet.[94] Grouping together his 'modern' goods in this room created a sharp contrast with 'the house', which served as both a kitchen and an informal living room, and created an appropriate space for Wilkinson to treat favoured customers.

Such parlours formed archetypes of the new material culture—the equipment associated with the consumption of tea, coffee, sugar, and condiments being an integral part of the ensemble of novel goods. But it would be wrong to see this as the only way in which groceries and their associated material objects were tied into the domestic environment. Just as often, they were set within more traditional assemblages of goods. William Preeson was another wealthy Liverpool merchant who died six years after John Molyneux. He owned a plantation in Virginia; extensive real estate in Liverpool; three ships engaged in the Atlantic trade (worth a total of £925), and a half share in another.[95] His house was comfortably furnished and contained a range of novel goods, including window curtains and mirrors in most of the bedchambers. His 'great parlour' could accommodate many visitors, having twelve cane chairs and a 'large oval table', as well as a smaller tea table. With six pictures in gilded frames on the walls, it was also quite showy. Surprisingly, then, what little chinaware he owned was kept in a closet off the dining room, itself furnished quite traditionally with a dozen leather chairs, a table, and a mirror (which the appraisers noted as 'broke'). The closet contained an eclectic mix of valuable and modest items, some of which were very traditional, while others were novel and linked with serving condiments at the dinner table. There were:

Six whiteware dishes	0-6-0
Two Decanters	0-3-0
Six drinking Glasses	0-1-0
One Doz'n of Sweetmeat Glasses	0-2-0
Two Cruetts	0-0-6
One Large Silver Tankard	8-0-0
One Small Tankard	4-0-0
One Large Salver	5-0-0
Two Small Salvers	4-0-0
One Set of Silver Casters	4-0-0
Eight Silver Spoons	3-4-0
Six Silver Salts	2-8-0
One pair of silver Canns	5-10-0[96]

Greater informality in the consumption of tea and coffee is apparent from the inventory of the Birmingham salesman Thomas Chapman, who died in 1760.[97] His two bedchambers contained mahogany furniture, including a tea board, and window curtains. One had a mirror and some decorative tiles, while the other contained nineteen small prints; but neither was furnished with a table. Visitors

[94] CALS, WS 1721, Robert Wilkinson.
[95] LRO, WCW 1705, William Preeson.
[96] LRO, WCW 1705, William Preeson.
[97] LiRO, B/C/11, Thomas Chapman (1760).

were probably entertained in the kitchen, which was crowded with a diverse range of equipment for cooking, eating, and socializing. At the top of the inventory— and perhaps at one end of the room—was the fire, complete with jack, spits, pots, and pans, in among which we find a copper coffee pot, a brass dredger, a pepper box, and a salt box. Once these goods were noted, the appraisers turned their attention to the other function of the room and listed:

1 Square Table	0-18-0
1 Round Table	0-6-0
1 Small Ironing Board	0-3-0
1 Corner Cubbard	0-18-0
1 Tea Chest	0-7-0
2 Mahogany Bottle Stands, 1 small waiter	0-2-0
1 Japanned Waiter	0-2-0
13 Delph plates	0-3-0
8 China dishes, 8 Saucers, 2 Sauce boats, Basins & Glasses	0-12-0
6 leather Chairs	0-15-0
1 Armed Chair, 1 low Chair	0-4-0
2 Blinds, 1 Mapp	0-4-0[98]

In Chapman's house at least, the sociability of tea and coffee appears to have been informal and everyday, and reflects the arrangement illustrated in the *Poor Old Woman's Comfort*.[99] This might be seen as a reflection of the broadening market for these drinks through the middle decades of the eighteenth century. Long before this, however, there are indications that the material culture of consuming hot drinks was neither novel nor new. Joseph Yardley, the Coventry starcher (d. 1720), left an estate valued at £110 16s. 3d. He lived comfortably enough, owning a range of linen and the odd piece of high-quality furniture, such as a walnut chest of drawers valued at £1 1s.[100] His parlour resembled those of his near contemporaries John Ward and Robert Wilkinson, containing cane chairs, a black framed mirror, eight window curtains, and a small tea table. Yet the image of a refined and fashionable interior jars somewhat with the last item listed: a 'parcell of Old China'. Opening the closet door, the appraisers then found '2 Old hand Tea boards, hatchet & hammer for tea, an Old Chocolate pot, a Glass Decanter, 3 Old Castors, a Brass Collar for a dog' with a collective value of just 6s. 6d. The significance of these descriptions is twofold. First, it demonstrates that, even at the start of the eighteenth century, an artisan in provincial England might own equipment to prepare and serve the full range of hot drinks.[101] Second, it reminds us that novelty does not remain: new goods grow old and innovative practices become established behaviour. Thus, while fashion might prompt the initial purchase, goods were

[98] LiRO, B/C/11, Thomas Chapman (1760).
[99] William Bigg, *Poor Old Woman's Comfort* (1793).
[100] LiRO, B/C/11, Joseph Yardley (1720).
[101] His back kitchen contained, among other things, a tea kettle and coffee pot, and '1 doz Old knives, 1 doz Old forks'.

often retained for other reasons: they remained fit for purpose, became objects of sentimental attachment, or perhaps were simply kept because of inertia—forgotten in the cupboard, like so many modern-day applicances.

The contents of Yardley's closet, and that of Preeson, also suggest that these goods were not always an omnipresent centrepiece of domestic material culture; they might also be useful items brought out when needed, but otherwise stored out of sight. And yet their influence could be felt even without their physical presence in a room. Most obviously, the tea table remained as a reminder of the rituals and pleasures of taking tea; but symbolism could extend into the name given to rooms, the significance of which was sufficient for them to be singled out in advertisements of property to let. Thus we see a house in Holywell, north Wales, described in 1780 as being 'Fit for the Residence of Gentleman's Family,—It consists of two good Parlours, a Kitchen, Larder and Servants' Hall on the first Floor; a very large and elegant Tea Room, and three Bed Chambers on the second Floor; and four good Bed Chambers in the Attic storey'.[102] Significantly, the tea room appears in addition to the parlours and is the only room singled out for particular comment. Moreover, it is placed on the second floor, suggesting a degree of privacy and intimacy in its use and perhaps reflecting the kind of internal thresholds and differential access to various parts of the house described in detail by Vickery.[103]

The precise nature of the decoration in this town house is unclear, although 'elegant' suggests respectability and taste rather than opulence. It may also have been quite conservative, as there was a growing tendency in the closing decades of the eighteenth century to furnish private tea rooms in an oriental style. This was a reflection of both the exotic associations of tea drinking and the experiences of the travellers on a Grand Tour, which was, by the 1790s, taking in Greece, Turkey, and the Levant, as traditional destinations became more difficult to visit because of war. A restrained exoticism can be seen in the 'Breakfast and Tea-Room' at Hazlebeach Hall in Northamptonshire. The catalogue for the contents sale in 1802 lists a predictable and fairly traditional assemblage of chintz window curtains and matching sofa, mahogany bookcases, writing desk and Pembroke table, and ladies' work and reading tables. In this, it matched the breakfast rooms seen in many minor country houses at this time. What made it different were the range and quantity of objects linked to India: a sixfold Indian screen, two mahogany fire screens with Indian figures, 'six pictures of Indian birds, in Japan frames', and ten chairs with 'Japan (*Indian cane*) Frames'.[104] This rather eclectic mix was continued in the pictures hung on the walls, which included country seats and gardens, views of Coalbrookdale, naval victories, and an interior of Antwerp cathedral; but also an engraving of 'Sir W. Penn's Treaty with the Indians'. There are echoes here of Mrs Molyneux's late-seventeenth-century bedchamber, although at Hazlebeach the impression is of a more deliberate attempt to create an Indian or perhaps a broader imperial theme

---

[102] *Adams Weekly Courant*, 20 June 1780. See also *Adams Weekly Courant*, 12 Dec. 1780, 22 Jan. 1782.
[103] Vickery, *Behind Closed Doors*, 25–48.
[104] NCL, M0005647NL/7, Hazlebeach Hall (1802), 18 (emphasis in the original).

to the room. This was certainly the intention of J. Morritt, who was determined to create in his Yorkshire home a version of the Turkish coffee houses that he saw on his travels. As he wrote to his mother in 1794: 'when I return I mean to fit up a tea-room à la kiosk, that is, like a Turkish summer-house, for your own self, as I am sure it would suit you'.[105] This would produce a very particular kind of domestic space—one that was both private and intimate, and yet linked through material objects and consumption practices to a wider world of goods and cultures. Tea, and its exotic associations, were here prompting more general shifts in the character of domestic material culture. More subtly, we might see groceries as prompting shifts in the style rather than type of material culture.

CONCLUSION

For many historians, the growing consumption of imported groceries lay at the heart of a dramatic transformation in domestic material culture in the late seventeenth and eighteenth centuries. This comprised new sets of goods and fundamentally different consumer mentalities. Material objects became commodities to be valued for their symbolic rather than economic worth. Blondé's recent challenge to this orthodoxy seeks to establish a longer chronology to these changes; what I have attempted here is a broadening of perspective to encompass goods other than those linked to the consumption of hot drinks—the most obvious and widely discussed consumption bundle.[106] In this way, my analysis has linked back to Weatherill's pioneering analysis and Pennell's more recent work on a range of culinary practices, cultures, and objects.[107] The evidence presented suggests that the ownership of objects related to hot drinks did indeed grow significantly in the early eighteenth century. This undoubtedly built on an established tradition of owning and using ceramics and was facilitated by the incorporation of new items into recognized sets of goods (for example, silverware). However, there were important quantitative and qualitative differences, particularly in terms of the range of goods involved: tea, coffee, and chocolate encouraged the acquisition of pots, cups and saucers, sugar basins and tongs, plates and dishes, canisters and chests, tables, and boards. These were large consumption bundles, often loosely associated and most probably assembled over a period of time. Within particular households as well as society as a whole, any grocery-inspired transformation in material culture was a gradual process. The range of new objects grew considerably and became increasingly widespread in eighteenth-century homes in Britain, Europe, and North America, but they were often incorporated into existing sets of goods and consumption practices. While Smith's new cultural contexts were important in helping to encourage the uptake of new groceries, the location of novel grocery-related

---

[105] Morrit, *A Grand Tour*, 98. See also Bickham, 'Eating the Empire', 80.
[106] See de Vries, *Industrious Revolution*, 31–7, 149–54.
[107] Blondé, 'Think Local'; Weatherill, *Consumer Behaviour*, 137–65; Pennell, 'Material Culture of Food'.

goods in the home suggests that they were being slotted into established social and domestic practices as much as facilitating new ones. The parlour and kitchen emerge as the most important rooms for keeping and using these objects. However, simple dichotomies of front-and back-stage, or public and private space, do not capture the nuances of domestic routines or the interactions between the domestic and the world beyond the threshold. Some goods were closely associated with displays of wealth, taste, and modernity (ensembles of silver tableware and the refined equipage of the tea table being good examples); but they could also be linked to notions of intimacy: tea taken in the bedchamber or the family breakfast.

To an extent, all these practices link to Smith's suggestion that consumers sought to construct a respectable identity through the consumption of new and imported groceries.[108] These were material and durable goods that people of all status groups could afford and there was, at least in some measure, a common language in the routines and rituals of consumption. Yet there were more complex motivations that cut across the normalizing agenda of respectability and limited evidence that people consciously strove for such status. Fashion was important to some consumers and with some goods: snuff boxes and the equipage for tea, for example, were both subject to the vagaries and scrutinizing eye of taste. Practicality could be a key consideration when acquiring goods—boiling water from kettles could be used a number of ways; tea could be taken on any table, and spices stored in anonymous but reasonably airtight boxes. Pleasure was also important, the enjoyment of drinking tea, taking snuff, or eating food being enhanced by the sensory attractions of the associated material objects. Writ large, this might mean constructing the material culture of an entire room around the joys of consuming exotic goods. Oriental-style tea rooms might represent mental links to empire; they could equally be seen as attempts to recapture something of the exoticism of consuming what were, after all, everyday goods. The bundling of goods around the consumption of imported groceries was clearly important in transforming domestic material culture, but the relationship was complex and changing. It involved a mixing of new and old goods and practices within the home, and was inspired by a range of motivations rather than a single socially inclusive cultural shift such as respectability.

[108] Smith, *Consumption*, 189–222.

Conclusion

When they began to earn higher wages, Samuel Finney noted, the industrial workers around the Cheshire village of Wilmslow looked to spend their money on tea, coffee, sugar, and spices, as well as printed cottons, silk waistcoats, and laced caps. This world of goods was made available by local shopkeepers, who 'increased amazingly' in number in the third quarter of the eighteenth century.[1] What had been novel or luxury goods two generations previously were made everyday—a normal part of workers' lives and routine items on the shelves of modest country shops. These processes of change have been the core concern of this book. My starting point was the link between the introduction of a set of new colonial groceries and a series of profound changes in material culture and cultures of consumption. This axiomatic association is central to many interpretations of consumer transformation, from Weatherill to Smith to de Vries,[2] yet it both underplays and overemphasises the significance of groceries to these changes. In *Sugar and Spice* I have shown the importance of retailing and shopping in engendering wider changes in consumption: the grocery trade was dynamic and responsive to consumer demand, and was an active agent in making shopping an everyday activity, effectively tying consumers into the market. In these ways, the impact of groceries went beyond that envisaged in many established interpretations. At the same time, new groceries were sold, bought and consumed alongside a more established set of goods, especially other groceries. This mixing of new and old tempered the revolutionary impact of colonial groceries, in both the shop and the home, and added layers of nuance to the practices and attitudes of consumers. To put more meat on to the bones of this argument, we can usefully return to the five key themes highlighted in the introduction.

RETAILING AND SHOPPING

At the heart of this book is a concern with the ways in which retailers responded to changes in consumption. At a basic level, the grocery trade was quicker than other branches of retailing to respond to shifts in the economic and population geography of the country. A lag between demographic growth and retail provision often left new industrial towns poorly served in terms of shops, but trade directories

---

[1] See Ashton, *Economic History*, 214–16.
[2] Weatherill, *Consumer Behaviour*; Smith, *Consumption*; de Vries, *Industrious Revolution*.

indicate that grocers were most numerous in counties experiencing industrial and urban growth. In part, this reflects the tendency noted by Samuel Finney for relatively well-paid industrial workers to spend their earnings in shops. This meeting of opportunity and motivation is central to de Vries's conception of industrious revolution,[3] but for workers to consume in the way he envisaged there had to be locally available supplies in the shape of grocers' and other shops. Rapid development of the grocery trade in a particular area was thus crucial in facilitating the broader uptake of the new groceries that helped to usher in a consumer society. Growth was further facilitated by the relatively low set-up costs for grocers. A large urban business might require upwards of £100 capitalization, but the stock of a village or back-street shop could amount to little more than a few pounds' worth of goods, much of which could be had on credit from wholesaling grocers in London or larger provincial towns. Perhaps crucial, however, was the high turnover of groceries compared with durable goods: contemporary commentators such as Defoe were clear that regular purchases of small items could sustain a steady income for any shopkeepers who were attentive to their business. Within towns, most grocers were initially concentrated onto and around the main streets—often clustered around the market. Dispersal, when it came in the late eighteenth and early nineteenth centuries, took grocers either out along the principal arterial routes or, more occasionally, into expanding residential districts.

All this suggests a retail sector that responded to and facilitated new patterns of consumption, but that was ultimately driven by changes in the level and geography demand. From this perspective, retailing becomes emasculated, following dutifully in the wake of demand and adapting as best it could to the profound changes in consumer and material cultures seen in the eighteenth century. Any retail revolution is thus secondary and responsive to the transformation of consumption.[4] But this denial of independent agency severely underplays the significance of retail change. Grocers were caught up in wider processes of retail modernization, which were important in promoting and shaping the consumption of a variety of new and traditional goods to an increasingly wide range of social groups. Grocers' shops contained specialist equipment necessary for the storage and sale of perishable goods: there were bags, barrels, bottles, canisters, and boxes, plus mills, engines, weights and scales, and paper for packing. There was also an expanding array of fitments linked to displaying or selling wares: counters, shelves, nests of drawers, and glazed windows—the last being particularly important in projecting the shop onto the street. This emphasis on display and the visual did not preclude other senses, of course: goods could be touched, smelled, and even tasted, which all helped to promote their sale and consumption. Shopkeepers further promoted their goods by using the shop to create an image of themselves as knowledgeable and businesslike, and they made serving customers more efficient by storing goods in an orderly manner and pre-packaging loose items such as tobacco, raisins, or tea. Other 'modern' practices included

[3] De Vries, *Industrious Revolution*, esp. 25–31.
[4] See Blondé and Van Damme, 'Retail Growth'.

the use of fixed prices. Far from being a nineteenth-century innovation, these were sufficiently well established in the early decades of the eighteenth century for them to be advertised in provincial newspapers alongside notes that sales were for ready money only. The implication, and sometimes the explicit suggestion, was that these prices were low and made possible by the efficiencies that resulted from the time saved in not haggling and not extending credit. In many respects, groceries lent themselves to such sales techniques: they were relatively standardized (although the range of qualities and types could be bewildering) and could be bought pre-packaged, some in containers branded by a particular tradesman—a practice most common with tea. These techniques offered potential advantage in a sector that could be extremely competitive, and it is no accident that tea dealers were the most active in these areas. Men such as Eagleton, Gye, and Sparrow cut margins and marketed their wares aggressively, placing frequent advertisements in the press and sometimes decrying their competitors. Yet this was not simply a zero-sum game: promoting tea through printed advertisements and price cutting helped to encourage growth in overall consumption.

Of course, these modern practices were not the whole story. Most grocers did not advertise and those that did often emphasized traditional values, addressing polite notices to their friends and the public and assuring potential customers that they would be well served. This reflected the persistence of traditional forms of selling, which placed emphasis on service and establishing long-term relationships with customers. In the shop, this was manifest in the construction of a sociable environment—something that often spilled over into the shopkeeper's parlour, used to entertain valued customers. It was also apparent in the centrality of credit in selling to customers of all social ranks. Grocers, like other retailers, took great care to manage credit and cultivate customers through the provision of helpful information. As supply lines to the shop became more diverse and widespread, there was an increased use of agents and published market information—both especially well developed in the tea trade. However, individual contacts and, above all, trust remained central to systems of supply. This was built up over time and through the mutuality of information exchange, sometimes conducted in person, but often through correspondence—forms of communication that remained in place, despite the growth of printed media.

What we have, then, is a blending of traditional and modern practices, although neither of these terms held any real meaning for grocers themselves. They were simply developing their businesses as best they could: promoting their wares, trying to retain and augment their customer base, and responding to wider changes in supply and demand. Whether this amounted to a retail revolution is perhaps less important than recognizing shopkeepers as active agents in consumer change. This point is well made by Blondé and Van Damme, who argue that established retail practices (most importantly a close relationship with a trusted supplier) were *necessary* to guide consumers through upheavals in consumption. This marrying of stability with change is intriguing, but problematic: grocers adjusted their practices in ways that responded to and actively promoted changes in consumption—something that they surely needed to do in order to supply a growing proportion of the population with a widening range of goods. Just as they helped to make fashion, shopkeepers also moulded consumer tastes and shopping practices.[5] They made new goods available, contextualizing them in a range of more familiar items, offered cash and credit sales to serve customers' needs and convenience, and provided a growing range of market information about availability, price, and quality. Their advertisements drew on urban landmarks and established fixtures within the retail landscape to locate them in space and give directions to potential customers. Coupled with trade directories and town guides, these helped to create a virtual landscape of consumption through which shoppers and others imagined and negotiated the retail geography of the town. Most importantly, their provision of a wide variety of relatively inexpensive and desirable goods, often available on credit, was central in making shopping an everyday activity for all but the very poorest.

For the shopkeeper, the most important people were, as Cox argues, their customers.[6] Modern historians have often assumed that it was women who were principally responsible for buying groceries.[7] It is true that much of the burden of everyday shopping fell onto wives, but grocers' account books clearly show that husbands, children, maids, and even neighbours also shopped. Sometimes, these visits appear to have been unplanned and even chaotic. Some of the plebeian customers who patronized the village shop in Greens Norton came several times a day, buying an assortment of goods on each occasion. It is difficult to explain this solely in terms of buying as need arose or returning for things forgotten on an earlier trip. The sociability of the shop assuredly played some part, as it did for the women who came to Thomas Turner's shop to drink tea and play cards.[8] Such practices mesh closely with the popular image of the village shop as the centre of the community: a place to meet, socialize, and gossip as much as to buy and sell. It is easy to dismiss this image as a rosy view of a lost world constructed through the pages of popular fiction or fashionable prints.[9] These certainly sanitized the shop, but nonetheless provided a fair reflection of its importance to village life. Those at the opposite end of the wealth spectrum experienced grocery shopping in very different ways, not least because they rarely entered the shop itself, preferring to order goods by letter and have them delivered. This practice relied on a considerable level of trust and offers insight into the customer's ability and willingness to complain about poor-quality goods or high prices. In between these extremes, the urban middling sorts shopped with varying frequency, patronizing a number of shops in order to supply their needs and wants. They were served civilly in the shop and entertained in the shopkeeper's parlour as valued customers and friends.

Overall, the rhythms of shopping for groceries were complex and varied, linked not just to wealth but also to the structure and organization of household management. Whether they were also shaped by a desire to browse and window shop is

[5] Blondé and Van Damme, 'Retail Growth'; Berg, *Luxury and Pleasure*, 255.
[6] Cox, *Complete Tradesman*, 116–46.
[7] See Berry, 'Polite Consumption'; Walsh, 'Shopping at First Hand?'.
[8] NRO, Y.Z.4040, fo. 60; Vaisey, *Thomas Turner*, 11 July 1764; 14 Jan. 1763.
[9] See, e.g., Thompson, *Lark Rise to Candleford*; the various images reproduced in Brown and Ward, *Village Shop*; Cox and Dannehl, *Perceptions of Retailing*, 36–42.

less certain. In this respect, groceries were not the same as drapery, chinaware, or toys: there is limited evidence that people engaged in leisurely shopping for tea or tobacco. Such items fall explicitly outside Berry's browse–bargain model of polite consumption,[10] and yet it is clear that polite and plebeian consumers could exercise some choice when it came to buying groceries, shopping around for the best prices and quality or, more prosaically, as availability dictated. Moreover, while they were everyday purchases, groceries were far from mundane, and some care was taken to select the right goods—for example, by Mary Gibbard when buying tea. Most importantly, the sociability of the grocer's shop should not be overlooked. Indeed, it is possible that the introduction of new groceries heightened the need for browsing and the attractions of the shop as a social space. Sugar, tea, and tobacco came in a wide range of grades, and, as shopkeepers themselves were keen to point out, the quality of some consignments was better than that of others. The shopper might reasonably want to test these in person, and we know that at least some shopkeepers were willing to oblige. Furthermore, tea became increasingly important in lubricating social interaction in the shop or the shopkeeper's parlour.

In this way, shopping can be best understood, not as a reflection of social ambition or idle fecklessness, but in terms of utility. It was, as Walsh and Miller have both argued in very different contexts, a serious business that served the practical purpose of acquiring goods.[11] At the same time shopping provided pleasure. This arose partly out of the satisfaction derived from securing good-quality groceries at the best price or from providing effectively for the needs of others, but it also derived from the comfort found in the sociability of the shop. Viewed in this way, shopping meshes with, but extends the market-engagement that de Vries sees in commercialized household economies. Looking to grocers as points of supply for a growing range of goods was only part of the story, albeit an important one; consumers also went shopping to supply emotional and psychological needs. This was true of poor workers as well as the wealthier middling sorts. A growing range of commodities was consumed by everyone—most dramatically tea and sugar, but also tobacco, spices, dried fruit, white bread, and so on. Marked changes in the preferences of consumers helped to transform diet, material culture, and modes of domestic living (points to which we will return later), but also made shopping and shops central to the everyday lives of many households. In short, shopping was a central, but underemphasized aspect of the industrious revolution, de Vries himself recognizing only the role of shops as points of supply.[12]

Of course, not all consumers were the same, either in the goods they bought or in their shopping practices. There were obvious dividing lines between different social strata, but gender was also marked and constructed through consumption. However, we should be wary of pushing too far the seemingly axiomatic association of men with coffee and tobacco, and women with tea and sugar, which is

---

[10] Berry, 'Polite Consumption'.
[11] Walsh, 'Shopping at First Hand?'; Miller, *Theory of Shopping*.
[12] De Vries, *Industrious Revolution*, 169–77.

made by Smith in particular.[13] In terms of both domestic consumption practices and groceries purchased, the link between gender and consumption was partial and contingent. This reflected the mixed nature of many households, which meant that much consumption and certainly many meals and social engagements were moulded around the family rather than single-gender groupings. But it also arose from the wide range of groceries bought for and consumed within the house: tea and sugar might thus be part of a basket of goods that also contained coffee, tobacco, spices, fruit, soap, candles, hair powder, lamp black, and so on. The consumption bundles that so forcibly struck Smith, de Vries, and especially Mintz, and that appear so clear in economic models and even the rhetoric of contemporary commentary, become more subtle and blurred in everyday practice.[14] Certainly tea and sugar were consumed together, but in a much wider variety of ways than simply adding one to the other.

IDENTITIES, ATTITUDES, AND MOTIVATIONS

Identities were constructed through consuming groceries, but in more nuanced ways than Smith allows: they were built through what was purchased and where, but also how it was consumed and with whom. Sometimes they were the product of everyday routine and practice; at other times they were conscious constructions. With the latter, Walvin, Mintz, and more recently Smith and Bickham have made much of the link between groceries imported from colonial plantations and consumers' identification with empire and the imperial project.[15] *Sugar and Spice* has considered this through three related sets of evidence: stock lists, advertisements, and the recipes and ingredients listed in cookery books. Each of these indicates the growing importance of colonial goods, imagery, and associations, especially in the second half of the eighteenth century. Importantly, these pointed both east and west. There were references to West Indian sugar, coffee, and spices, but also India soy and rice; advertising images of native Americans smoking pipes and of Chinese people picking or drinking tea; and recipes for Carolina snowballs and Indian piccalilli. Numerically, however, colonial place names formed only a small proportion of the total, Europe being far more important as a point of reference on both the grocer's shelf and the consumer's table. Naturally, colonies dominated in terms of the new groceries, but people did not simply drink sweetened tea and smoke tobacco. Moreover, many colonial goods were badged with a European place name, reflecting where they were imported and processed. Perhaps the most pervasive of these was Scotch snuff, which quickly came to signify the type of product rather than its provenance.

---

[13] Smith, *Consumption*, 139–88.
[14] Smith, *Consumption*, 122–3; de Vries, *Industrious Revolution*, 31–7; Mintz, *Sweetness and Power*, 214.
[15] Walvin, *Fruits of Empire*; Mintz, *Sweetness and Power*; Smith, *Consumption*; Bickham, 'Eating the Empire'.

This throws up the question of what meaning colonial references had for shop-keepers and consumers. After all, identifying the existence of imperial references is very different from demonstrating their significance to ordinary people. In some cases, provenance mattered a great deal, as with the late-eighteenth-century campaigns to boycott slave-produced West Indian sugar. More often, the label was important in terms of what it said about the nature and quality of the product: distinguishing grades rather than suggesting moral choices. Even where the point of reference was unequivocal, the purpose behind promoting the connection needs to be carefully considered. Images of Chinese people dominated grocers' trade cards by the early nineteenth century. Bickham interprets these in terms of imperial ambitions, but in reality they spoke to consumers more about the authenticity of the product and their own consumption practices; they provided reassurance that the tea they were drinking was pure and unadulterated, and somehow linked them to a simpler yet more exotic place. As with emulation theory, there is a danger of interpreting behaviour as motivation. Empire was clearly important in bringing a wide range of groceries to England, but we need to be wary of reading into colonial imagery and place names a series of connections and meanings that reflect historians' rather than contemporary attitudes. Wilson, Bowen, and others have demonstrated that the public was becoming increasingly interested in Empire during this period, but Bickham's assertion that food lay at the heart of this process does not sit easily with the evidence presented here.[16] Empire was just one point of reference for consumers and, it seems, not one of overweening importance. People were more concerned with issues such as status, pleasure, and the practicalities of acquiring and consuming groceries; they consumed growing quantities of colonial goods, but without their provenance necessarily being of particular importance.[17]

Much has been made of novelty in making goods appealing to consumers and driving their dispersal across the country and to different social groups. Tea, coffee, and chocolate were genuinely novel items in the mid-seventeenth century, and, if sugar and tobacco were more familiar commodities, they were spreading to a greater range of consumers as new supplies made them more affordable. Novelty is theorized as the driving force behind fashion's 'valorization of ephemerality' and offered a succession of new sensory experiences.[18] It is also seen as central to the construction and reconstruction of identity, providing the opportunity to define and project 'self'—for example as a sober coffee-drinking man of business.[19] But it is easy to overplay the importance of novelty: it quickly passes as the new becomes familiar. Groceries were less amenable to the small changes that produced endless variety in chinaware or printed textiles. For all but a brief period, fashion therefore

---

[16] Wilson, *Sense of the People*; Bowen, 'British Conceptions of Global Empire'; Bickham, 'Eating the Empire'.

[17] This links to the controversial argument put forward by Porter, *Absent-Minded Imperialists,* about the relative unimportance of empire to a large section of the population in nineteenth-century Britain. It invites a similar re-evaluation of the eighteenth-century experience.

[18] Berg, *Luxury and Pleasure*, 250.

[19] Campbell, 'Understanding Consumption'; Styles, *Dress of the People*, 8–16; Cowan, *Social Life of Coffee*, 10–12, 16–47; Schivelbusch, *Tastes of Paradise*, 34–9.

had mainly an indirect influence on their consumption, being mediated through changes to material objects, such as snuff boxes or tea services, or through new ways of serving or consuming food and drink. The latter is seen in the development of breakfast and tea as new and distinctive meals; the emergence of recipes for 'Indian' dishes in English cookbooks, and the construction of elaborate decorative centrepieces made from spun sugar or ornamented with carved figurines. All these helped to maintain the attraction of tea, sugar, and spices, but they show that novelty on its own cannot have sustained growth in consumption of such commodities, not least as they ceased being markers of status because of their newness.

Returning to our newly prosperous Cheshire textile workers, we see their consumption characterized by novel, colonial items (tea, coffee, and cotton), and others that were more familiar (spices, lace, and silk). The latter were traditional luxuries—'social valuables' defined by their high cost, the complexity of their production and acquisition, and 'the protection and reproduction of status systems'.[20] This links luxury with Veblenian positional goods, social distinctions being maintained by gradations of quality (more costly blends of tea, for example) or the richness of table (measured in the quantity and complexity of dishes). Grace Nettleton differentiated between her family and her servants in terms of the cost and quality of food provided, but the Christmas mince pies formed luxuries for both sets of people. These were luxury goods in terms of their intrinsic qualities and because of their symbolic importance as part of the Christmas celebrations at Tabley Hall. Consuming such victuals brought physical and emotional pleasure. More generally, drinking sweetened tea or allowing inmates in the workhouse small amounts of treacle and tobacco suggests that these fell into Smith's category of customary luxury.[21] That they retained something of the aura of luxury is apparent from the criticisms levelled by moralizing patricians who berated the poor for wasting their money in such unnecessary items. However, to the poor themselves they were small comforts rather than extravagant luxuries, making otherwise unappealing meals a little more bearable.[22]

The idea of physical comfort offers a useful way of understanding the attraction of various groceries, especially when linked to pleasure—the second aspect of Scitovsky's conception of utility.[23] As with luxury, both terms are relative and contingent, and can thus apply to any social group, regardless of wealth or status. Physical and emotional comfort could be found in cheap, sweetened tea or in expensive blends consumed from fine porcelain; in a clay pipe of tobacco or a pinch of snuff from a silver box, and from a reheated meal enlivened with a little pepper or an elaborately flavoured dish of mock turtle. Pleasure, seen in terms of arousal and stimulation, links closely to the intrinsic qualities of many of the new imported groceries. Indeed, it was as stimulants that they were drawn into the world of medicine, and the same qualities shaped their association with certain character traits and cultural environments—most famously the sobriety and thoughtfulness

---

[20] Berg, *Luxury and Pleasure*, 30.
[21] Bigg, *Poor Old Woman's Comfort*; Smith, *Consumption*, 99.
[22] See Burnett, *Plenty and Want*, 35–7.   [23] Scitovsky, *Joyless Economy*.

of the coffee-drinking and tobacco-smoking man of business. Yet the associations drawn by Smith, Schivelbusch, and others overlook the more basic pleasures of the everyday sociability of eating and drinking with friends, or visiting the grocer's shop for fresh supplies, to catch up with the gossip or simply to pass the time. These pleasures link most directly to the notion of personal comfort, but they also form an important part of what de Vries terms social comfort—the use of consumption as a sign to mark and defend social position.[24]

This leads us to a wider consideration of consumer motivation and the nature of consumer transformation in eighteenth-century England. There is widespread acceptance of a Europe-wide shift in material culture around this time—one in which the consumption of groceries played an important part. De Vries sees this in terms of consumption bundles, with assemblages of related goods becoming established around key commodities.[25] The evidence for this is strong, but points to a rather more complex relationship. Bundles of goods could be large and diverse, and the connections indirect. De Vries uses the example of tea and sugar, but the association was not enacted simply by adding one to the other—they were also combined through serving cake with tea and were often purchased along with a variety of other groceries. Indeed, it is significant that the bundling of goods generally meant that tea, coffee, and the like were bought from the grocer (linking them to other groceries), rather than the china dealer or toyshop (where they might be bundled with the material objects necessary for their consumption). The latter occurred primarily in the home, but spread far beyond the equipage of tea drinking that has fascinated many historians. While kettles, teapots, cups, and teaspoons became more widespread, so too did tea tables, cruet sets, sugar hammers, and spice boxes. Importantly, many groups of goods were established well before the revolutionary changes of the late seventeenth and eighteenth centuries. This produced the kind of continuities in material culture highlighted by Overton and others, and suggests a similar attenuation of any shift in attitudes towards material goods.[26] This can be seen in the way that silver teapots, sugar basins, cruets, and so on were often kept together, along with the rest of the household's silverware. Their physical proximity indicates a mental bracketing of these goods as valuable, in both social and economic terms. More generally, we should not forget that tea services, coffee pots, and sugar castors had practical as well as symbolic value, and their appearance in sale catalogues confirms that they also retained economic value.

These continuities and practicalities question generalizations about the relationship between changing material culture and the consumption of a new set of groceries. Smith's attempt to do this by elaborating various cultural contexts adds much to our understanding of the processes involved, but there are problems in squaring these with the practicalities of everyday consumption. Domestic

[24] Smith, *Consumption*, 139–70; Schivelbusch, *Tastes of Paradise*, 34–9;. De Vries, *Industrious Revolution*, 22.
[25] De Vries, *Industrious Revolution*, 31–7.
[26] Overton et al., *Producers and Consumption*, esp. 87–120; Blondé, 'Think Local'.

femininity, for example, is discussed with little reference to what women actually *did* in terms of buying and consuming tea, serving breakfast, and so on.[27] Part of the problem here is the existence, or otherwise, of a knowing consumer: to what extent did people shop for, purchase, and consume goods in a manner that was conscious or premeditated? The evidence is equivocal. Some shopping trips were carefully planned, but others appear to have been ad hoc or even chaotic. Some domestic spaces were laid out to produce a particular impression (as polite or fashionable) and to facilitate associations between goods and practices (tea sets permanently displayed on tables); others reflected the gradual accretion of goods or the practicalities of everyday life. While consumers were clearly aware of abstract concepts such as luxury, virtue, or femininity, it is less apparent whether or how these ideas came to the fore in shaping their day-to-day consumption practices. Respectability does emerge as an important ideal, for both shopkeepers and their customers. Grocers went to some trouble to construct their shops as respectable environments and themselves as reliable and reputable tradesmen, projecting their credentials through advertisements couched in the language of polite deference. In this way, respectability formed an important bridge between shop and home, but it is less apparent that it formed an overarching framework for all consumer behaviour, especially as Smith attempts to spread this ideal into the homes of the working classes.[28] In reality, different cultures of consumption coexisted alongside one another. These were seen in the gentry's reaction against the Frenchified excesses of elite dining practices, the diverse shopping practices of rich and poor, and the different rituals and meanings associated with tea drinking—sometimes as part of social display and sometimes as an intimate or individual experience.

These differences remind us that consumers did not have a single identity but rather constructed and reconstructed self-identity through their everyday actions. They also question how far it is possible to generalize about the motivations of those consuming such goods. McKendrick's emulation model offers little in this context.[29] The rhetoric of contemporary commentators was loud and vociferous, complaining that poor women took up tea drinking 'to be fashionable, and imitate their superiors'. Furthermore, this emulative behaviour involved not merely drinking, but also 'conversing the affairs of the whole Town' in much the same way as their social superiors were seen as doing.[30] However, the reality was rather different. The taste for tea, sugar, or spices might have trickled down from the rich to the poor and some of the rituals and material culture surrounding their consumption undoubtedly followed a similar route. But this does not mean that the old woman in Bigg's painting of the *Poor Old Woman's Comfort*, with her simple three-legged table laid with tea, white bread, and butter, was seeking to emulate a grand lady of the *beau monde* or even a housewife from the middling sort. That these things formed her 'comfort' suggests a very different set of motivations, more in line with her physical and mental well-being. Much the same

[27] Smith, *Consumption*, 171–87.   [28] Smith, *Consumption*, 204–10.
[29] McKendrick, 'Consumer Revolution'.
[30] Quoted in White, 'Labouring-Class Domestic Sphere', 253–4.

was true of the small luxuries comprised by Christmas purchases of sugar plums or shopping practices that brought poorer customers to the shop to enjoy its sociability rather than engage in polite consumption. Other groups went as far as rejecting rather than emulating the example set by their social betters, a point best illustrated by the gentry's reassertion of honest English cooking in the middle decades of the eighteenth century.

Assertions of taste were more usually deployed by the elite to distinguish themselves from the lower orders. Evidence of this 'flight' as cultural markers were chased down by poorer consumers can be found in the consumption of finer grades of tea, more refined sugar, and more complex forms of cooking. Together, these give some credence to McCracken's reworking of trickle-down theory.[31] More subtly, perhaps, the messages conveyed by the provenance of groceries or chinaware, and by serving dishes that echoed colonial connections or political currency, allowed the cognoscenti to distinguish themselves from ordinary consumers. As Veblen noted, these were subtleties that had to be learned and that therefore comprised and reflected the cultural capital of the consumer.[32] In this, they were assisted by a close personal relationship with the shopkeeper or dealer who could provide detailed information as well as high-quality goods. However, distinctions were most often drawn between grades of goods. Taste is thus useful in understanding consumption as a contingent process and in explaining the differences between the consumption practices of different social groups, especially those further up the social hierarchy. It is less powerful as an explanation for consumption in general or what might have motivated consumers from various social strata to drink sweetened tea, smoke tobacco, or add spices to their cooking.

In focusing on social comfort and thus on the behaviour of groups, all these theories divert attention from what made goods attractive to individual consumers. If we concentrate instead on the individual, we can see behaviour shaped by a complex blend of motivations. In terms of material goods, for instance, their location and context in the home speaks of display and fashion, on the one hand, and intimacy and utility, on the other. In reality, these differences probably reflected the varied ways in which tea and other groceries were consumed: sometimes as part of an elaborate social display and sometimes as an intimate or individual experience. Turning this around, we can see how the appeal of new and more familiar groceries varied according to the context and combination in which they were consumed. Sugar, for example, might be seen as virtuous when taken with tea or coffee; a luxury when consumed in the form of subtleties or comfits; a display of virtuosity when spun into elaborate confections; a necessity when preserving summer fruits, or an everyday ingredient when cooking. This reminds us that consumption did not take place in a single material or conceptual context, but occurred in a contingent and relational manner. We can better understand this complexity by appreciating three things: that consumers had to engage with a market that was in tune with their needs; that the goods served some need, often in relation to the

---

[31] McCracken, *Culture and Consumption*, 93–103.   [32] Veblen, *Theory of the Leisure Class*, 49.

comfort of self or others, and that the consumer and retailer were active agents in consumer change, shaping their own practices rather than caught up in some monster process beyond their control.

In sum, groceries were deeply embedded in the economic, social, and cultural life of provincial England. They were central to the lives of polite and plebeian consumers, in some ways drawing lines of connection between the two. By the second half of the eighteenth century, tea drinking was an experience shared by many. So too was a taste for sweetened foods and tobacco smoke; the use of candles to light and soap to clean the home; and the possession of a range of durable goods for storing, serving, and eating imported foods. Central to the process of acquiring these things, and at the heart of this book, was a retail system that was flexible and dynamic, responsive to demand, and active in shaping consumer preferences. Supply systems operated at a national scale, making goods from across the world available in even remote village shops. They were displayed on shelves and in windows, advertised in the press, and imagined through illustrations on trade cards and bill heads. Visits to the grocer's shop thus opened up a world of goods, but also a more local world of sociability and mutuality based on regular social interaction, credit, and trust. Shopping for groceries was an everyday activity—part of people's daily and weekly routines, and thus important in shaping their identity as consumers, but also as members of the community. In many ways, the eighteenth-century grocer's shop was a stepping stone to the modern world of mass consumption and mass retailing. Yet it carried with it many practices from an earlier age—ones that remained central to the grocer's trade well into the twentieth century. In searching for what is new and distinctive, then, we need to be attentive to such long-term continuities. Selling tea and coffee helped to reshape the grocery trade, but we should not forget that it was also shaped by the need to supply a wide variety of other foods, not least sugar and spice.

Bibliography

ARCHIVAL SOURCES

Bedfordshire and Luton Archive
GA25/35, Letter from Charles Hancock to John Gibbard, 21 January 1819
GA5, Bill from Charles Hancock, undated
GA93, Letter from Charles Hancock to Mary Gibbard, 15 September 1827

Bodleian Library, University of Oxford
John Johnson Collection of Printed Ephemera

British Library, London: Manuscripts
Add. 36,666, Walthal Fenton Order Book, 1770s

British Museum, London: Department of Prints and Drawings
Banks Trade Card Collection
Heal Trade Card Collection

Cheshire Archives and Local Studies
CR/63/2/133/17, Peter Broster's Sketch Plan of Eastgate Street, *c.*1754
DCB 1179/60, Domestic Account Book, 1713–18
DLT/B51, Account Book of Grace Nettleton, 1720
PC 51/22, Overseers' Accounts: St John's, Chester, 1731–52
Probate Records

Cornwall Record Office
Probate Records

Hanley Reference Library
D4842/14/4/7, Receipts of John Wood of Burslem, 1797–98

John Rylands Library
Eng MS 703, Diary of George Heywood

Kent Archive Services
Probate Records

Lancashire Record Office
Probate Records

Lichfield Record Office
B/C/5, Probate Records for the Diocese of Lichfield, peculiars
B/C/11, Probate Records for the Diocese of Lichfield, regular series

London Metropolitan Archives
MS 8251, Apothecaries Ordinance Book

Manchester Central Library
MS F942, Customer Ledger of William Wood of Didsbury, 1786–91

The National Archives
C5/582/120, Inventory of Thomas Wootton of Bewdley, d. 1667
E182, Shop Tax Returns, 1785

Norfolk Library and Information Service
NP00012331, Robert Kitton's Trade Card, no date

Norfolk Record Office
ANW23/3/209, Probate Inventory of Elizabeth Neale, 1706
MC50/23/5, Sir Martin Foulkes, Bill and Catalogue from Joshua Long, 17 February 1775
Poll Book, 1714

Northamptonshire Central Library
M0005644–47NL, Assorted Sale Catalogues
M0000533NL, Catalogue for the Sale of the Belongings of John Campion of Kettering, Grocer and Chandler, 1816
Uncatalogued Trade Ephemera: Trade Cards and Bill Heads

Northamptonshire Record Office
Probate Records
NRO, D(CA)142, Bill to John Dryden, 1719
NRO, O(N) 30, Grocery Wholesale Price List, 1814
NRO, YZ 4040, Shopkeeper's Account Book, 1797–8
NRO, ZB 34/1, Shop Ledger of Richard Linnell of Silverstone, 1833–9

Old Bailey Papers
http://www.oldbaileyonline.org/

Oxfordshire Record Office
Probate Records
OA/B/118, Daybook of Ann Gomm, 1792–1813

Parliamentary Papers
First Report, Royal Commission on Excise Establishment (Tea Permits), 21:417, 1833
Report on the Recovery of Small Debts, Journal of the House of Commons, 4, 1823

Shakespeare Central Library and Archive
DR 18/29/6 Box 1, Pocket Book of Edward Leigh, 1702–3
DR 18/31/856, Household, Stables, Garden, Servants, Personal and Extraordinary Expenses of the Reverend Thomas Leigh, 1758–62
DR 98/167, Recipe Book of Mary Foley, no date
DR 762/55, Leigh Family Recipe Book, no date
DR 18/31/548, Loose Bill Inserted into Stores Account, 1757
DR 18/31/548, An Account of Stores Expended every Half Year, beginning Lady Day, 1757
DR 18/5—Bills and Vouchers of the Leigh family, Stoneleigh Abbey

Shropshire Archives
Attingham Collection, 112/6/Box 34/36

Warwickshire County Record Office
CR1368, Morduant Family Letters
CR136/B/2626, Receipted Bills to Sir Roger Newdigate
CR341/300, CR341/301, Household Books of Mary Wise, no date

William Salt Library
D1798 HM 29/2–4, Day Books and Account Books of Thomas Dickenson of Worcester, 1740–52
D1798 HM 27/5, Purchasing Book of Thomas Dickenson of Worcester, 1740–52
D (W) 1788/V/108–11, Sales ledgers of Fletcher and Fenton of Newcastle-under-Lyme, 1768–83

NEWSPAPERS, JOURNALS, AND DIRECTORIES

Adams Weekly Courant
Aris's Birmingham Gazette
Barfoot P., and Wilkes, J., *Universal British Directory* (London, 1793–8)
Bristol Mercury
Chase, W., *The Norwich Directory; or, Gentlemen and Tradesmen's Assistant* (Norwich, 1783)
Gore, J., *The Liverpool Directory for the Year 1766...* (Liverpool, 1766)
Gore's Liverpool Advertiser
Leeds Mercury
Liverpool Chronicle
Liverpool Mercury
London Morning Advertiser
Morning Post
Newcastle Courant
Norwich Gazette
Norwich Mercury
Pearson and Rollason, *The Birmingham Directory or Merchant and Tradesman's Useful Companion* (Birmingham, 1777)
Pigot & Co., *National Commercial Directory...* (London, 1828–9)
Pigot & Co., *National Commercial Directory...* (London, 1839)
Poor Man's Guardian
The Tatler

OTHER PUBLISHED PRIMARY SOURCES

Addy, J. (ed.), 'The Diary of Henry Prescott, LL.B., Deputy Registrar of Chester Diocese', *Record Society of Lancashire and Cheshire*, 127 (1987).
Anon., *Wine, Beer, Ale and Tobacco, Contending for Superiority* (London, 1629).
Anon., *The Women's Petition against Coffee...* (London, 1674).
Beresford, J. (ed.), *The Diary of a Country Parson, 1758–1802. By James Woodforde* (Oxford, 1935).
Birkett, M., *A Poem on the African Slave Trade. Addressed to her Own Sex* (Dublin, 1792).

Blome, R., *Britannia or a Geographical Description of the Kingdoms of England, Scotland, and Ireland* (London, 1673).

Blundell, N., *The Great Diurnal of Nicholas Blundell of Little Crosby, Lancashire*, ed. F. Tyrer (3 vols; Liverpool, 1968–72).

Bond, D.(ed.), *The Spectator*, ii. *1711–1712* (Oxford, 1965).

Burney, F., *Evelina: The History of a Young Lady's Introduction to the World* (1778; new edn, London, 1821).

Campbell, R., *The London Tradesman: Being a Compendious View of all the Trades...* (London, 1747).

Carter, C., *The Complete Practical Cook; or, a New System of the Whole Art and Mystery of Cookery...* (London, 1730).

Clare, M., *Youth's Introduction to Trade* (8th edn; London, 1758).

Clayton, J., *Friendly Advice to the Poor, Written and Pubish'd at the Request of the Late and Present Offices of the Town of Manchester* (Manchester, 1755).

Cleland, J., *Memoirs of a Woman of Pleasure* (Harmondsworth, 1985).

Coleridge, S. T., 'On the Slave Trade', *Watchman*, 26 Mar. 1796.

Collyer, J., *Parent's and Guardian's Directory and Youth Guide* (London, 1761).

Congreve, W. *The Double Dealer* (London, 1694).

Crafton, W. B., *Short Sketch of the Evidence for the Abolition of the Slave Trade...* (London, 1792).

Defoe, D., *The Compleat English Tradesman: Directing him in the Several Parts and Progressions of Trade...* (1726; 4th edn, London, 1745).

Defoe, D., *Tour through the Whole Island of Great Britain* (1724–7; new edn, Harmondsworth, 1971).

Duncan, M. D., *Wholesome Advice against the Abuse of Hot Liquors* (London, 1706).

Eland, G. (ed.), *Purefoy Letters, 1735–1753* (London, 1931).

Farley, J., *The London Art of Cookery, and Housekeeper's Complete Assistant...* (London, 1800).

Glasse, H., *The Art of Cookery Made Plain and Easy by a Lady* (7th edn; London, 1760).

Houblon, A., *The Houblon Family, its Story and Times* (London, 1907).

Houghton, J., *Husbandry and Trade Improv'd: Being a Collection of Many Valuable Materials Relating to Corn, Cattle, Coals, Hops, Wool, &c...* (London, 1727–8).

Howard, H., *England's Newest Way in All Sorts of Cookery, Pastry, and All Pickles that are Fit to be Used* (London, 1708).

Hughes, T., *Ancient Chester: A Series of Illustrations of the Streets of this Old City* (London, 1880).

James I., *A Counter-Blaste to Tobacco* (London, 1604).

Lackington, J., *Memoirs of the Forty-Five First Years of the Life of James Lackington, Bookseller* (London, 1827).

Lowe, R., *The Diary of Roger Lowe of Ashton in Makerfield*, ed. W. Sasche (London, 1938).

Markham, G., *The English Housewife*, ed. M. Best (Montreal and Kingston, 1986).

Moryson, F., *An Itinerary Containing his Ten Yeeres Travell...* (4 vols; Glasgow, 1907–8).

Morrit, J. B. S., *A Grand Tour: Letters and Journeys, 1794–96*, ed. G. E. Marindin (London, 1985).

Owen, R., *The Life of Robert Owen Written by Himself* (1857; new edn, 2 vols, London, 1967).

Pepys, S., *The Diary of Samuel Pepys*, ed. R. Latham and W. Matthews (11 vols; London, 1970–83).

Postlethwayt, M., *The Universal Directory of Trade and Commerce* (2nd edn; London, 1757).

Raffald, E., *The Experienced English House-Keeper: Consisting of near 800 Original Recipes* (Manchester, 1769).

Roberts, H., *The Chester Guide* (Chester, 1851).

Roberts, L., *Merchant's Mappe of Commerce* (London, 1638).

Schopenhauer, J., *A Lady Travels: Journeys in England and Scotland from the Diaries of Johanna Schopenhauer* (London, 1988).

Scott-Montcrieff, R. (ed.), *The Household Book of Lady Grisell Baillie, 1692–1733* (Edinburgh, 1911).

Smith, A., *Theory of Moral Sentiments* (London, 1759).

Smith, A., *The Wealth of Nations* (London, 1776; Oxford, 1976).

Smith, E., *The Compleat Housewife, or, Accomplished Gentlewoman's Companion...* (London, 1727).

Stout, W., *Autobiography of William Stout of Lancaster, 1665–1752* (Manchester, 1967).

Stubbes, H., *The Natural History of Coffee, Thee, Chocolate and Tobacco* (London, 1682).

Thompson, F., *Lark Rise to Candleford* (London, 1945).

Twining, R., *An Answer to the Second Report of the East India Company Directors, Respecting the Sale and Prices of Tea* (London, 1785).

Twining, S., *Two Hundred and Twenty-Five Years in the Strand, 1706–1931* (London, 1931).

Vaisey, D. (ed.), *The Diary of Thomas Turner, 1754–1765* (Oxford, 1984).

Venner, T., *Via Recta ad Vitam Longam, or a Plaine Philosophical Discourse* (London, 1620).

W. M., *The Compleat Cook: Expertly Prescribing the Most Ready Wayes, Whether Italian, Spanish, or French, for Dressing of Flesh, and Fish, Ordering of Sauces, or Making of Pastry* (London, 1663).

West, W., *The History, Topography and Directory of Warwickshire* (Birmingham, 1830).

Whittock, N., *On the Construction and Decoration of the Shop Fronts of London* (London, 1840).

SECONDARY SOURCES

Addison, W., *English Fairs and Markets* (London, 1953).

Alexander, D., *Retailing in England during the Industrial Revolution* (London, 1970).

Anderson, B., *Imagined Communities: Reflections on the Origin and Spread of Nationalism* (London, 2006).

Andersson, G., 'A Mirror of Oneself: Possessions and the Manifestation of Status among a Local Swedish Elite, 1650–1770', *Cultural and Social History*, 3 (2006), 21–44.

Angiolini, A., and Roche, D. (eds), *Cultures et formations négociantes dans l'Europe moderne* (Paris, 1995).

Appadurai, A. (ed.), *The Social Life of Things: Commodities in Cultural Perspective* (Cambridge, 1986).

Ashton, T. S., *An Economic History of England: The 18th Century* (London, 1955).

Ashworth, W., *Customs and Excise: Trade, Production and Consumption in England, 1640–1845* (Oxford, 2003).

Bailey, L., 'Maintaining Status: Consumption in the Nineteenth-Century Household. The Gibbard Family of Sharnbrook, Bedfordshire' (unpublished MA thesis, University of Northampton, 2010).

Barker, H., *The Business of Women: Female Enterprise and Urban Development in Northern England, 1760–1830* (Oxford, 2006).

Barnett, A., 'In with the New: Novel Goods in Domestic Provincial England, *c.*1700–1790', in B. Blondé, N. Coquery, J. Stobart, and I. Van Damme (eds), *Fashioning Old and New: Changing Consumer Patterns in Western Europe, 1650–1900* (Turnhout, 2009), 81–94.

Barnett, A., 'Shops, Retailing and Consumption in Eighteenth-Century Provincial England: Norwich, 1660–1800' (unpublished Ph.D. thesis, University of Northampton, 2011).

Beckett, J., and Smith, C., 'Urban Renaissance and Consumer Revolution in Nottingham 1688–1750', *Urban History*, 27 (2000), 31–50.

Bennett, A., *Shops, Shambles and the Street Market: Retailing in Georgian Hull, 1770–1810* (Wetherby, 2005).

Ben-Porath, Y., 'The F-Connection: Families, Friends and Firms, and the Organisation of Exchange', *Population and Development Review*, 6 (1980), 1–30.

Berg, M., 'Women's Property and the Industrial Revolution', *Journal of Interdisciplinary History*, 24 (1993), 233–50.

Berg, M., 'Women's Consumption and the Industrial Classes of Eighteenth-Century England', *Journal of Social History*, 30 (1996), 415–34.

Berg, M., 'New Commodities, Luxuries and their Consumers in Eighteenth-Century England', in M. Berg and H. Clifford (eds), *Consumers and Luxury: Consumer Culture in Europe, 1650–1850* (Manchester, 1999), 63–87.

Berg, M., 'Asian Luxuries and the Making of the European Consumer', in M. Berg and E. Eger (eds), *Luxury in the Eighteenth Century: Debates, Desires and Delectable Goods* (Basingstoke, 2003), 228–44.

Berg, M., 'Consumption in Eighteenth- and Early Nineteenth-Century Britain', in R. Floud and P. Johnson (eds), *The Cambridge Economic History of Britain*, i. *Industrialisation, 1700–1860* (Cambridge, 2004), 357–87.

Berg, M., *Luxury and Pleasure in Eighteenth-Century Britain* (Oxford, 2005).

Berg, M., and Clifford, H., 'Commerce and the Commodity: Graphic Display and Selling New Consumer Goods in Eighteenth-Century England', in M. North and D. Ormrod (eds), *Art Markets in Europe, 1400–1800* (Aldershot, 1998), 187–200.

Berg, M., and Clifford, H., 'Selling Consumption in the Eighteenth Century: Advertising and the Trade Card in Britain and France', *Cultural and Social History*, 4 (2007) 145–70.

Berger, R. M., *The Most Necessary Luxuries: The Mercers' Company of Coventry, 1550–1680* (Philadelphia, 1993).

Berry, C., *The Idea of Luxury: A Conceptual and Historical Investigation* (Cambridge, 1994).

Berry, H., 'Polite Consumption: Shopping in Eighteenth-Century England', *Transactions of the Royal Historical Society*, 12 (2002), 375–94.

Berry, H., 'Promoting Taste in the Provincial Press: National and Local Culture in Eighteenth-Century Newcastle-upon-Tyne', *British Journal for Eighteenth-Century Studies*, 25 (2002), 1–17.

Berry, H., 'Prudent Luxury: The Metropolitan Tastes of Judith Baker, Durham Gentlewoman', in P. Lane and R. Sweet (eds), *Out of Town: Women and Urban Life in Eighteenth-Century Britain* (Aldershot, 2005), 130–54.

Bianchi, M., 'The Taste for Novelty and Novel Tastes', in M. Bianchi (ed.), *The Active Consumer: Novelty and Surprise in Consumer Choice* (London, 1998), 64–86.

Bickham, T., 'Eating the Empire: Intersections of Food, Cookery and Imperialism in Eighteenth-Century Britain', *Past and Present*, 198 (2008), 71–109.

Black, J., *The British Abroad: The Grand Tour in the Eighteenth Century* (Stroud, 1997).

Blackburn, R., *The Making of New World Slavery: From the Baroque to the Modern, 1492–1800* (London, 1997).

Blackman, J., 'The Development of the Retail Grocery Trade in the Nineteenth Century', *Business History*, 9 (1967), 110–17.

Blondé, B., 'Tableware and Changing Consumer Patterns: Dynamics of Material Culture in Antwerp, 17th–18th centuries', in J. Veeckman (ed.), *Majolica and Glass from Italy to Antwerp and Beyond: The Transfer of Technology in the 16th–Early 17th Century* (Antwerp, 2002), 295–311.

Blondé, B., 'Think Local, Act Global? Hot Drinks and the Consumer Culture of 18th-Century Antwerp' (forthcoming).

Blondé, B., Briot, E., Coquery, N., and Van Aert, L. (eds), *Retailers and Consumer Changes in Early-Modern Europe* (Tours, 2005).

Blondé, B., Stabel, P., Stobart, J., and Van Damme, I. (eds), *Buyers and Sellers: Retail Circuits and Practices in Medieval and Early-Modern Europe* (Turnhout, 2006).

Blondé, B., and Van Damme, I., 'Fashioning Old and New or Moulding the Material Culture of Europe', in B. Blondé, N. Coquery, J. Stobart, and I. Van Damme (eds), *Fashioning Old and New: Changing Consumer Patterns in Western Europe, 1650–1900* (Turnhout, 2009), 1–14.

Blondé, B., and Van Damme, I., 'Retail Growth and Consumer Changes in a Declining Urban Economy: Antwerp (1650–1750)', *Economic History Review*, 63 (2010), 638–63.

Borsay, P., *The English Urban Renaissance: Culture and Society in the English Provincial Town, 1660–1770* (Oxford, 1989).

Bourdieu, P., *Distinction: A Social Critique of the Judgement of Taste* (London, 1984).

Bourdieu, P., 'The Forms of Capital', in J. Richardson (ed.), *Handbook of Theory and Research for the Sociology of Education* (New York, 1986).

Bowen, H., 'British Conceptions of Global Empire', *Journal of Imperial and Commonwealth History*, 26 (1998), 1–26.

Bowen, H., *The Business of Empire: The East India Company and Imperial Britain, 1756–1833* (Cambridge, 2006).

Bowlby, R., *Carried Away: The Invention of Modern Shopping* (New York, 2001).

Breen, T. H., 'An Empire of Goods: The Anglicization of Colonial America, 1690–1776', *Journal of British Studies*, 25 (1986), 467–99.

Brewer, J., *The Pleasures of the Imagination* (Chicago, 1997).

Brooks, J., *The Mighty Leaf: Tobacco through the Centuries* (Boston, 1952).

Brown, D., and Ward, S., *The Village Shop* (Newton Abbot, 1990).

Brown, S., 'The Complex Model of City Centre Retailing: An Historical Application', *Transactions of the Institute of British Geographers*, NS 12 (1987), 4–18.

Burnett, J., *Plenty and Want: A Social History of Diet in England from 1815 to the Present Day* (Harmondsworth, 1968).

Burt, R., 'The Network Entrepreneur', in R. Sedburg (ed.), *Entrepreneurship: The Social Science View* (Oxford, 2000), 281–307.

Campbell, C., *The Romantic Ethic and the Spirit of Modern Consumerism* (Oxford, 1987).

Campbell, C., 'The Desire for the New: Its Nature and Social Location as Presented in Theories of Fashion and Modern Consumerism', in R. Silverman and E. Hirsch (eds), *Consuming Technologies: Media and Information in Domestic Spaces* (London, 1992), 48–65.

Campbell, C., 'Understanding Traditional and Modern Patterns of Consumption in Eighteenth-Century England: A Character-Action Approach', in J. Brewer and R. Porter (eds), *Consumption and the World of Goods* (London, 1993), 40–58.

Carlton, K., 'James Cropper and Liverpool's Contribution to the Anti-Slavery Movement', *Transactions of the Historical Society of Lancashire and Cheshire*, 123 (1972), 57–80.

Carter, H., *The Study of Urban Geography* (4th edn; London, 1995).

Carter, P., *Men and the Emergence of Polite Society* (Harlow, 2002).

Casson, M., 'Institutional Economics and Business History: A Way Forward?', *Business History*, 39 (1997), 151–71.

Chaudhuri, K. N., *The English East India Company: The Study of an Early Joint-Stock Company, 1600–1640* (New York, 1965).

Chaudhuri, K. N., *The Trading World of India and the English East India Company, 1600–1760* (Cambridge, 1978).

Clifford, H. (1999). 'A Commerce with Things: The Value of Precious Metalwork in Early Modern England', in M. Berg and H. Clifford (eds), *Consumers and Luxury: Consumer Culture in Europe 1650–1850* (Manchester, 1999), 147–68.

Coe, S., and Coe, M., *The True History of Chocolate* (London, 1996).

Colquhoun, K., *Taste: The Story of Britain through its Cooking* (London, 2007).

Coquery, N., 'The Semi-Luxury Market, Shopkeepers and Social Diffusion: Marketing Chinoiseries in Eighteenth-Century Paris', in B. Blondé, N. Coquery, J. Stobart, and I. Van Damme (eds), *Fashioning Old and New: Changing Consumer Patterns in Western Europe, 1650–1900* (Turnhout, 2009), 121–32.

Corbellier, C., *European and American Snuff Boxes, 1730–1830* (New York, 1966).

Corfield, P. J., 'The Rivals: Landed and Other Gentlemen', in N. Harte and R. Quinnault (eds), *Land and Society in Britain, 1700–1914* (Manchester, 1996), 1–33.

Corfield, P. J., and Kelly, S., 'Giving Directions to the Town: The Early-Modern Town Directories', *Urban History Yearbook* (1984), 22–35.

Cowan, B., *The Social Life of Coffee: The Emergence of the British Coffeehouse* (New Haven, 2005).

Cox, N., *The Complete Tradesman: A Study of Retailing, 1550–1820* (Aldershot, 2000).

Cox, N., and Dannehl, K., *Perceptions of Retailing in Early Modern England* (Aldershot, 2007).

Crang, M., *Cultural Geography* (London, 1998).

Crowley, J., *The Invention of Comfort: Sensibilities and Design in Early Modern Britain and Early America* (Baltimore, 2001).

David, E., 'The John Trot Fault: An English Dinner Table in the 1750s', *Petits Propos Culinaires*, 15 (1983), 55–9.

Davies, K., 'A Moral Purchase: Femininity, Commerce and Abolition, 1788–1792', in E. Eger, C. Grant, C. O Gallchoir, and P. Warburton (eds), *Women, Writing and the Public Sphere, 1700–1830* (Cambridge, 2001), 133–59.

Davis, D., *A History of Shopping* (London, 1966).

Davis, R., 'English Foreign Trade, 1660–1700', *Economic History Review*, 7 (1952), 150–66.

Dawson, M., *Plenti and Grase: Food and Drink in a Sixteenth-Century Household* (Totnes, 2009).

Day, I., *Royal Sugar Sculptures: 600 Years of Splendour* (London, 2002).

De Vries, J., 'Between Purchasing Power and the World of Goods', in J. Brewer and R. Porter (eds), *Consumption and the World of Goods* (London, 1993), 85–132.

De Vries, J., *The Industrious Revolution: Consumer Behaviour and the Household Economy, 1650 to the Present* (Cambridge: Cambridge University Press, 2008).

Dean, P., and Cole, W. A., *British Economic Growth: 1689–1959* (2nd edn; Cambridge, 1962).

Dennis, C., *Objects of Desire: Consumer Behaviour in Shopping Centres* (Basingstoke, 2005).

Dictionary of Traded Goods and Commodities http://www.british-history.ac.uk/report.aspx?compid=58801 (accessed 11 Mar. 2011).

Douglas, M., *Thought Styles: Critical Essays on Good Taste* (London, 1996).

Douglas, M., and Isherwood, B., *The World of Goods* (New York, 1979).

Earle, P., *The Making of the English Middle Class: Business, Society and Family Life in London, 1660–1730* (London: Methuen, 1989).

Edelson, S. M., 'The Characters of Commodities: The Representation of South Carolina Rice and Indigo in the Atlantic World', in P. Coclanis (ed.), *The Atlantic Economy during the Seventeenth and Eighteenth Centuries* (Columbia, SC, 2005), 344–60.

Ellis, M., *The Coffee House: A Cultural History* (London, 2004).

Estabrook, C., *Urbane and Rustic England: Cultural Ties and Social Spheres in the Provinces, 1660–1780* (Manchester, 1998).

Evans, W., and Lawson, A., *A Nation of Shopkeepers* (London, 1981).

Everitt, A., 'The Marketing of Agricultural Produce', in J. Thirsk (ed.), *The Agrarian History of England and Wales*, iv. *1500–1640* (Cambridge, 1967).

Fairchilds, C., 'The Production and Marketing of Populuxe Goods in Eighteenth-Century Paris', in J. Brewer and R. Porter (eds), *Consumption and the World of Goods* (London, 1993), 228–48.

Fennetaux, A., 'Toying with Novelty: Toys, Consumption and Novelty in Eighteenth-Century England', in B. Blondé, N. Coquery, J. Stobart, and I. Van Damme (eds), *Fashioning Old and New: Changing Consumer Patterns in Western Europe, 1650–1900* (Turnhout, 2009), 17–28.

Farmer, D., 'Marketing the Produce of the Countryside, 1200–1500', in E. Miller (ed.), *The Agrarian History of England and Wales*, III: *1348–1500* (Cambridge, 1991), 324–430.

Ferdinand, C., 'Selling it to the Provinces: News and Commerce Round Eighteenth-Century Salisbury', in J. Brewer and R. Porter (eds), *Consumption and the World of Goods* (London, 1993), 393–411.

Fine, B., and Leopold, E., *The World of Consumption* (London, 1993).

Finn, M., 'Men's Things: Masculine Possession in the Consumer Revolution', *Social History*, 25 (2000), 133–55.

Fowler, C., 'Changes in Provincial Retail Practice during the Eighteenth Century, with Particular Reference to Central-Southern England', *Business History*, 40 (1998), 37–54.

Fukuyama, F., *Trust: The Social Virtues and the Creation of Prosperity* (Harmondsworth, 1995).

Gieszinger, S., *The History of Advertising Language: The Advertisements in the Time from 1788 to 1996* (Oxford, 2001).

Girouard, M., *Life in the English Country House: A Social and Architectural History* (Harmondsworth, 1978).

Glennie, P., and Thrift, N. J., 'Consumers, Identities and Consumption Spaces in Early-Modern England', *Environment and Planning A*, 28 (1996), 25–45.

Goffman, E., *The Presentation of Self in Everyday Life* (New York, 1956).

Goldthwaite, R., *Wealth and the Demand for Art in Italy, 1300–1600* (Baltimore, 1993).

Goodman, J., *Tobacco in History: The Cultures of Dependence* (London, 1993).

Gotti, M., 'Advertising Discourse in 18th-Century English Newspapers', in J. Skaffari, M. Peikola, and R. Caroll (eds), *Opening Windows on Texts and Discourses in the Past* (Amsterdam, 2005), 23–38.

Granovetter, M. (1973), 'The Strength of Weak Ties', *American Journal of Sociology*, 78 (1973), 1360–80.

Greig, H., 'Leading the Fashion: The Material Culture of London's *Beau Monde*', in J. Styles and A. Vickery (eds), *Gender, Taste and Material Culture in Britain and North America* (New Haven, 2006), 293–313.

Greig, H., 'Eighteenth-Century English Interiors in Image and Text', in J. Aynsley and C. Grant (eds), *Imagined Interiors: Representing the Domestic Interior since the Renaissance* (London, 2006), 102–27.

Hägerstrand, T., 'What about People in Regional Science?', *Papers and Proceedings of the Regional Science Association*, 24 (1970), 7–21.

Haggerty, J., and Haggerty, S., 'Visual Analytics of an Eighteenth-Century Business Network', *Enterprise and Society*, 11 (2010), 1–25.

Haggerty, S., 'Women, Work and the Consumer Revolution: Liverpool in the Late Eighteenth Century', in J. Benson and L. Ugolini (eds), *A Nation of Shopkeeper: Five Centuries of British Retailing* (London, 2003), 106–26.

Haggerty, S., *The British–Atlantic Trading Community, 1760–1810: Men, Women and the Distribution of Goods* (Leiden, 2006).

Hall, K., 'Culinary Spaces, Colonial Spaces: The Gendering of Sugar in the Seventeenth Century', in V. Traub, M. Lindsay Kaplan, and D. Callaghan (eds), *Feminist Readings of Early-Modern Culture: Emerging Subjects* (Cambridge, 1996), 168–90.

Hancock, D., *Citizens of the World: London Merchants and the Integration of the British Atlantic Community, 1735–85* (Cambridge, 1995).

Hancock, D., 'Self-Organized Complexity and the Emergence of an Atlantic Market Economy, 1651–1815', in P. Coclanis (ed.), *The Atlantic Economy during the Seventeenth and Eighteenth Centuries* (Columbia, SC, 2005), 30–71.

Hancock, D., 'Trouble with Networks: Managing the Scots' Early-Modern Madeira Trade', *Business History Review*, 79 (2005), 464–91.

Hann, A., 'Industrialisation and the Service Economy', in J. Stobart and N. Raven (eds), *Towns, Regions and Industries: Urban and Industrial Change in the Midlands, c.1700–1840* (Manchester, 1995), 42–61.

Hann, A., and Stobart, J., 'Sites of Consumption: The Display of Goods in Provincial Shops in Eighteenth Century England', *Cultural and Social History*, 2 (2005), 165–87.

Harding, V., 'Shops, Markets and Retailers in London's Cheapside, c.1500–1700', in B. Blondé, P. Stabel, J. Stobart, and I. Van Damme (eds), *Buyers and Sellers: Retail Circuits and Practices in Medieval and Early-Modern Europe* (Turnhout, 2006), 155–70.

Harley, C. K., 'Trade: Discovery, Mercantilism and Technology', in R. Floud and P. Johnson (eds), *The Cambridge Economic History of Britain*, i. *Industrialisation, 1700–1860* (Cambridge, 2004), 175–203.

Heal, F., *Hospitality in Early-Modern England* (Oxford, 1990).

Herman, T., 'Tabletop Conversations: Material Culture and Everyday Life in the Eighteenth-Century Atlantic World', in J. Styles and A. Vickery (eds), *Gender, Taste and Material Culture in Britain and North America* (New Haven, 2006), 37–59.

Hirsch, F., *The Social Limits to Growth* (London, 1977).

Hughes, G. B., *English Snuff Boxes* (London, 1971).

Jefferys, J. B., *Retailing in Britain 1850–1950* (Cambridge, 1954).

Keene, D., 'Sites of Desire: Shops, Selds and Wardrobes in London and Other English Cities, 1100–1550', in B. Blondé, P. Stabel, J. Stobart, and I. Van Damme (eds), *Buyers and Sellers: Retail Circuits and Practices in Medieval and Early-Modern Europe* (Turnhout, 2006), 125–54.

King, S., and Timmins, G., *Making Sense of the Industrial Revolution: English Economy and Society, 1700–1850* (Manchester, 2001).

Klein, L., 'Politeness for Plebes: Consumption and Social Identity in Early Eighteenth-Century England', in J. Brewer and A. Bermingham (eds), *The Culture of Consumption: Image, Object, Text* (London, 1995), 362–82.

Kowalski-Wallace, E., 'Women, China and Consumer Culture in Eighteenth-Century England', *Eighteenth-Century Studies*, 29 (1995–6), 195–67.

Kowalski-Wallace, E., *Consuming Subjects: Women, Shopping and Business in the Eighteenth Century* (New York: Columbia University Press, 1997).

Kross, J., 'Mansions, Men, Women, and the Creation of Multiple Publics in Eighteenth-Century British North America', *Journal of Social History*, 33 (1999), 385–408.

Labarge, M. W., *A Baronial Household of the Thirteenth Century* (London: Eyre and Spottiswoode, 1965).

Lambert, J., *A Nation of Shopkeepers. Trade Ephemera from 1654 to the 1860s in the John Johnson Collection* (Oxford: Bodleian Library, 2001).

Langton, J., 'Liverpool and its Hinterland in the Late Eighteenth Century', in B. L. Anderson and P. Stoney (eds), *Commerce, Industry and Transport: Studies in Economic Change on Merseyside* (Liverpool: Liverpool University Press, 1983), 1–25.

Lawton, R., 'The Age of Great Cities', *Town Planning Review*, 43 (1972), 199–224.

Lefebvre, H., *The Production of Space* (Oxford: Blackwell, 1991).

Lehmann, G., *The British Housewife: Cookery Books, Cooking and Society in 18th Century Britain* (Totnes: Prospect Books, 1999).

Lesger, C. 'Patterns of Retail Location and Urban Form in Amsterdam in the Mid-Eighteenth Century', *Urban History*, 38 (2011), 24–47.

Lilja, K., Murhem, S., and Ulväng, G, 'The Indispensable Market: Auctions in Sweden in the Eighteenth and Nineteenth Centuries', in B. Blondé; Coquery, J. Stobart, and I. Van Damme (eds), *Fashioning Old and New. Changing Consumer Patterns in Western Europe, 1650–1900* (Turnhout: Brepols, 2009), 185–202.

Lyna, D. and Van Damme, I., 'A Strategy of Seduction? The Role of Commercial Advertisements in the Eighteenth-Century Retailing Business in Antwerp', *Business History*, 51 (2009), 100–21.

MacArthur, R., 'Material Culture and Consumption on an English Estate: Kelmarsh Hall, 1687–1845' (unpublished Ph.D. thesis, University of Northampton, 2011)

Mackie, E. (ed.), *Commerce of Everyday Life. Selections from The Tatler and The Spectator* (Basingstoke: Macmillan, 1998).

MacKenzie, J. M., *Imperialism and Popular Culture* (Manchester: Manchester University Press, 1986).

Mathias, P., *Retailing Revolution. A History of Multiple Retailing in the Food Trades* (London: Longmans, 1967).

McCants, A., 'Poor Consumers as Global Consumers: The Diffusion of Tea and Coffee Drinking in the Eighteenth Century', *Economic History Review*, 61 (2008), 172–200.

McClintock, A., *Imperial Leather: Race, Gender and Sexuality in the Colonial Context* (London: Routledge, 1995).

McCracken, G., *Culture and Consumption. New Approaches to the Symbolic Character of Consumer Goods and Activities* (Bloomington and Indianpolis: Indiana University Press, 1988).

McKendrick, N., 'George Packwood and the Commercialisation of Shaving: The Art of Eighteenth-Century Advertising' in N. McKendrick, J. Brewer, and J. Plumb (eds), *The Birth of a Consumer Society* (London: Hutchinson, 1982), 146–96.

McKendrick, N., 'Josiah Wedgwood and the Commercialization of the Potteries', in N. McKendrick, J. Brewer, and H. H. Plumb (eds), *The Birth of a Consumer Society* (London: Hutchinso, 1982), 100–45.

McKendrick, N., 'The Consumer Revolution of Eighteenth-Century England', in N. McKendrick, J. Brewer, and J. H. Plum (eds), *The Birth of a Consumer Society* (London: Hutchinson, 1982), 9–33.

Mennell, S., *All Manners of Food: Eating and Taste in England and France from the Middle Ages to the Present* (Oxford: Blackwell, 1985).

Midgeley, C., *Feminism and Empire. Women Activists in Imperial Britain, 1790–1865* (London: Routledge, 2007).

Miller, D. *Material Culture and Mass Consumption* (Oxford: Blackwell, 1987).

Miller, D., 'Consumption Studies as the Transformation of Anthropology', in D. Miller (ed.), *Acknowledging Consumption: A Review of New Studies* (London: Routledge, 1995), 264–95.

Miller, D., *A Theory of Shopping* (Cambridge: Polity, 1998).

Miller, D., Jackson, P., Thrift, N., Holbrook, B., and Rowlands, M., *Shopping, Place and Identity* (London: Routledge, 1998).

Miller, M., *The Bon Marchér Bourgeois Culture and the Department Store, 1869–1920* (Princeton: Princeton University Press, 1981).

Minchinton, W., 'Bristol—Metropolis of the West in the Eighteenth Century', *Transactions, Royal Historical Society*, 5th series, 4 (1954), 69–89.

Mintz, S., *Sweetness and Power. The Place of Sugar in Modern History* (London: Penguin Books, 1985).

Mitchell, I., 'The Changing Role of Fairs in the Long Eighteenth Century: Evidence from the North Midlands', *Economic History Review*, 60 (2007), 545–73.

Mitchell, I., 'The Development of Urban Retailing, 1700–1815', in P. Clark (ed.), *The Transformation of English Provincial Towns 1600–1800* (London: Hutchinson, 1984), 259–83.

Mitchell, I., 'Supplying the Masses: Retailing and Town Governance in Macclesfield, Stockport and Birkenhead, 1780–1860', *Urban History*, 38 (2011), 256–75.

Morrison, K., *English Shops and Shopkeeping. An Architectural History* (New Haven: Yale University Press, 2003).

Mui, H.-C. and Mui, L., 'Smuggling and the British Tea Trade Before 1784', *American Historical Review*, 74 (1968), 44–73.

Mui, H.-C. and Mui, L., *Shops and Shopkeeping in Eighteenth-Century England* (London: Routledge, 1989).

Mui, L., 'The Commutation Act and the Tea Trade in Britain, 1784–93', *Economic History Review*, 16 (1963), 234–53.

Muldrew, C., *The Economy of Obligation: The Culture of Credit and Social Relations in Early-Modern England* (Basingstoke, 1998).

Nef, J., *The Cultural Foundations of Industrial Civilisation* (Cambridge, 1958).

Nenadic, S., 'Middle-Rank Consumers and Domestic Culture in Edinburgh and Glasgow 1720–1840', *Past and Present*, 145 (1994), 122–56.

Nijboer, H., 'Fashion and the Early-Modern Consumer Evolution: A Theoretical Exploration and Some Evidence from Seventeenth-Century Leeuwarden', in B. Blondé, E. Briot, N. Coquery, and L. Van Aert (eds), *Retailers and Consumer Changes in Early-Modern Europe* (Tours, 2005), 21–9.

North, D., 'Transaction Costs in History', *Journal of European Economic History*, 3 (1985), 557–76.

Norton, M., 'Tasting Empire: Chocolate and the European Internalization of Mesoamerican Aesthetics', *American Historical Review*, 111 (2006), 660–91.

Overton, M., 'Prices from Probate Inventories', in T. Arkell, N. Evans, and N. Goose (eds), *When Death Do Us Part: Understanding and Interpreting the Probate Records of Early Modern England* (Oxford, 2000), 120–43.

Overton, M., Dean, D., Whittle, J., and Hann, A., *Production and Consumption in English Households, 1600–1750* (London, 2004).

Parkinson, A., *Nature's Alchemist: John Parkinson, Herbalist to Charles I* (London, 2007).

Patten, J., *English Towns, 1500–1700* (Folkestone, 1978).

Pearson, R., and Richardson, D., 'Business Networking in the Industrial Revolution', *Economic History Review*, 54 (2001), 657–79.

Peck, P., *Consuming Splendor: Society and Culture in Seventeenth-Century England* (Cambridge, 2005).

Pennell, S., 'Material Culture of Food in Early-Modern England, *c.*1650–*c.*1750' (unpublished D.Ph. thesis, University of Oxford, 1997).

Pennell, S., 'Perfecting Practice? Women, Manuscript Recipes and Knowledge in Early Modern England', in V. Burke and J. Gibson (eds), *Early Modern Women's Manuscript Writing* (Aldershot, 2004), 327–58.

Pennell, S., 'Recipes and Reception: Tracking "New World" Foodstuffs in Early Modern British Culinary Texts, *c.*1650–1750', *Food and History*, 7 (2009), 11–33.

Plumb, J., 'The Commercialisation of Leisure in Eighteenth-Century England', in N. McKendrick, J. Brewer, and J. Plumb (eds), *The Birth of a Consumer Society* (London, 1982), 266–88.

Ponsonby, M., *Stories from Home: English Domestic Interiors, 1750–1850* (Aldershot, 2007).

Popp, A., 'Building the Market: John Shaw of Wolverhampton and Commercial Travelling in Early Nineteenth-Century England', *Business History*, 49 (2007), 321–47.

Porter, B., *The Absent-Minded Imperialists: Empire, Society and Culture in Britain* (Oxford, 2004).

Powers, A., *Shop Fronts* (London, 1989).

Pred, A., *Lost Words and Lost Worlds: Modernity and the Language of Everyday Life in Late Nineteenth-Century Stockholm* (Cambridge, 1990).

Pred, A., 'The Choreography of Existence: Comments on Hägerstrand's Time-Geography and its Usefulness', in J. Agnew, D. Livingstone, and A. Rogers (eds), *Human Geography: An Essential Anthology* (Oxford, 1996), 636–49.

Priestly, U., and Fenner, A., *Shops and Shopkeepers in Norwich, 1660–1730* (Norwich, 1985).

Purvis, M., 'Co-Operative Retailing in Britain', in J. Benson and G. Shaw (eds), *The Evolution of Retail Systems, 1800–1914* (Leicester, 1992), 107–34.

Putnam, R., *Bowling Alone: The Collapse and Revival of American Community* (London, 2000).

Rappaport, E., *Shopping for Pleasure: Women in the Making of London's West End* (Princeton, NJ, 2000).

Rappaport, E., 'Packaging China: Foreign Articles and Dangerous Tastes in the Mid-Victorian Tea Party', in F. Trentman (ed.), *The Making of the Consumer: Knowledge, Power and Identity in the Modern World* (London, 2006), 125–46.

Reed, M., 'The Cultural Role of Small Towns in England 1600–1800', in P. Clark (ed), *Small Towns in Early Modern Europe* (Cambridge, 1995), 121–47.

Rees, J. A., *The Grocery Trade: Its History and Romance* (2 vols; London, 1932).

Richards, T., *The Commodity Culture of Victorian England: Advertising and Spectacle, 1851–1914* (Stanford, CA, 1990).

Riello, G., and Parthasarathi, P. (eds), *The Spinning World: A Global History of Cotton Textiles, 1200–1850* (Oxford, 2009).

Salzman, L., *English Trade in the Middle Ages* (Oxford, 1931).

Schivelbusch, W., *Tastes of Paradise: A Social History of Spices: Stimulants and Intoxicants*, trans. D. Jackson (New York, 1993).

Scitovsky, T., *The Joyless Economy: An Enquiry into Human Satisfaction and Consumer Dissatisfaction* (New York, 1976).

Shammas, C., *Pre-Industrial Consumer in England and America* (Oxford, 1990).

Shammas, C., 'Changes in English and Anglo-American Consumption from 1550 to 1800', in J. Brewer and R. Porter (eds), *Consumption and the World of Goods* (London, 1993), 177–205.

Shaw, G., *British Directories as Sources in Historical Geography* (Lancaster, 1982).

Shaw, G., and Alexander, A., 'Directories, and the Local Historian III: Directories as Sources in Local History', *Local History*, 46 (1994), 12–17.

Shields, R., 'Spaces for the Subject of Consumption', in R. Shields (ed.), *Lifestyle Shopping: The Subject of Consumption* (London, 1992), 1–20.

Simmel, G., 'Fashion', *International Quarterly*, 10 (1904), 130–55.

Simmel, G., *On Individuality and Social Forms* (Chicago, 1971).

Smith, J., *Men and Armour for Gloucestershire in 1608* (Stroud, 1980).

Smith, W. D., 'Complications of the Commonplace: Tea, Sugar and Imperialism', *Journal of Interdisciplinary History*, 23 (1992), 259–78.

Smith, W. D., *Consumption and the Making of Respectability, 1600–1800* (London, 2002).

Sombart, W., *Luxury and Capitalism* (1922; Michigan, 1967).

Stabel, P., 'From the Market to the Shop: Retail and Urban Space in Late Medieval Bruges', in B. Blondé, P. Stabel, J. Stobart, and I. Van Damme (eds), *Buyers and Sellers: Retail Circuits and Practices in Medieval and Early-Modern Europe* (Turnhout, 2006), 79–108.

Stobart, J., 'Shopping Streets as Social Space: Leisure, Consumerism and Improvement in an Eighteenth-Century County Town', *Urban History*, 25 (1998), 3–21.

Stobart, J., 'City Centre Retailing in late Nineteenth- and Early-Twentieth-Century Stoke-on-Trent: Structures and Processes', in J. Benson and L. Ugolini (eds), *A Nation of Shopkeepers: Five Centuries of British Retailing* (London, 2003), 155–78.

Stobart, J., *The First Industrial Region: North-West England 1700–1760* (Manchester, 2004).

Stobart, J., 'Personal and Commercial Networks in an English Port: Chester in the Early Eighteenth Century', *Journal of Historical Geography*, 30/2 (2004), 277–93.

Stobart, J., 'Information, Trust and Reputation: Shaping the Merchant Elite in Eighteenth-Century England', *Scandinavian Journal of History*, 30 (2005), 61–82.

Stobart, J. 'Accommodating the Shop: The Commercial Use of Domestic Space in English Provincial Towns, c.1660–1740', *Citta e storia*, 2 (2007), 351–63.

Stobart, J., 'Food Retailers and Rural Communities: Cheshire Butchers in the Long Eighteenth Century', *Local Population Studies*, 79 (2007), 23–37.

Stobart, J., 'Selling (through) Politeness: Advertising Provincial Shops in Eighteenth-Century England', *Cultural and Social History*, 5 (2008), 309–28.

Stobart, J., *Spend, Spend, Spend: A History of Shopping* (Stroud, 2008).

Stobart, J., 'Gentlemen and Shopkeepers: Supplying the Country House in Eighteenth-Century England', *Economic History Review*, 64 (2011), 885–904.

Stobart, J. 'Who were the Urban Gentry? A Social Elite in an English Provincial Town, c.1680–1760', *Continuity and Change*, 26/1 (2011), 89–112.

Stobart, J., and Hann, A., 'Retailing Revolution in the Eighteenth Century: Evidence from North-West England', *Business History*, 46 (2004), 171–94.

Stobart, J., Hann, A., and Morgan, V., *Spaces of Consumption: Leisure and Shopping in the English Town, c.1680–1830* (London, 2007).

Stobart, J., and Schwarz, L. D., 'Leisure, Luxury and Urban Specialization in the Eighteenth Century', *Urban History*, 35 (2008), 216–36.

Stone, S., 'Grocers and Groceries: The Distribution of Groceries in Four Contiguous English Counties *c.*1660–1750' (unpublished M.Phil. thesis, University of Wolverhampton, 1994).

Styles, J., 'Product Innovation in Early Modern London', *Past and Present*, 168 (2000), 124–69.

Styles, J., *The Dress of the People: Everyday Fashion in Eighteenth-Century England* (New Haven, 2007).

Sweet, R., 'Topographies of Politeness', *Transactions of the Royal Historical Society*, 12 (2002), 355–74.

Trentmann, F., 'Beyond Consumerism: New Historical Perspectives on Consumption', *Journal of Contemporary History*, 39 (2004), 373–401.

Tyack, G., *Warwickshire Country Houses* (Chichester, 1992).

Van Aert, L., and Van Damme, I., 'Retail Dynamics of a City in Crisis: The Mercer Guild in Pre-Industrial Antwerp (*c.*1648–*c.*1748)', in B. Blondé, E. Briot, N. Coquery, and L. Van Aert (eds), *Retailers and Consumer Changes in Early-Modern Europe* (Tours, 2005), 139–68.

Veblen, T., *The Theory of the Leisure Class: An Economic Study of Institutions* (Basingstoke, 1912).

Vickery, A., *The Gentleman's Daughter: Women's Lives in Georgian England* (New Haven, 1998).

Vickery, A., *Behind Closed Doors: At Home in Georgian England* (New Haven, 2008).

Vickery, A., 'An Englishman's Home is his Castle? Thresholds, Boundaries and Privacies in the Eighteenth-Century London House', *Past and Present*, 199 (2008), 147–73.

Wadsworth, A., and de Lacy Mann, J., *The Cotton Trade in Lancashire, 1600–1780* (Manchester, 1931).

Walker, R., 'Advertising in London Newspapers, 1650–1750', *Business History*, 16 (1973), 112–30.

Wallis, P., 'Consumption, Retailing and Medicine in Early Modern London', *Economic History Review*, 61 (2008), 26–53.

Walsh, C., 'Shop Design and the Display of Goods in Eighteenth-Century London', *Journal of Design History*, 8 (1995), 157–76.

Walsh, C., 'The Newness of the Department Store: A View from the Eighteenth Century', in G. Crossick and S. Jaumain (eds), *Cathedrals of Consumption: The European Department Store, 1850–1939* (Aldershot, 1999), 46–71.

Walsh, C., 'The Advertising and Marketing of Consumer Goods in Eighteenth-Century London', in C. Wischermann and E. Shore (eds), *Advertising and the European City: Historical Perspectives* (Aldershot, 2000), 79–95.

Walsh, C., 'Social Meaning and Social Space in the Shopping Galleries of Early-Modern London', in J. Benson and L. Ugolini (eds), *A Nation of Shopkeepers: Five Centuries of British Retailing* (London, 2003), 52–79.

Walsh, C., 'Shops, Shopping and the Art of Decision Making in Eighteenth-Century England', in J. Styles and A. Vickery (eds), *Gender, Taste and Material Culture in Britain and North America* (New Haven, 2006), 151–77.

Walsh, C., 'The Social Relations of Shopping in Early-Modern England', in B. Blondé, P. Stabel, J. Stobart, and I. Van Damme (eds), *Buyers and Sellers: Retail Circuits and Practices in Medieval and Early-Modern Europe* (Turnhout, 2006), 331–51.

Walsh, C., 'Shopping at First Hand? Mistresses, Servants and Shopping for the Household in Early-Modern England', in D. Hussey and M. Ponsonby (eds), *Buying for the Home: Shopping for the Domestic from the Seventeenth Century to the Present* (Aldershot, 2008), 13–26.

Walsh, C., 'Stalls, Bulks, Shops and Long-Term Change in Early-Modern England', in C. Lesger and J.-H. Furnee (eds), *The Landscape of Consumption. Shopping Streets and Shopping Cultures in Western Europe, 1600–1900* (Basingstoke, forthcoming 2012).

Walvin, J., *Fruits of Empire: Exotic Produce and British Taste, 1660–1800* (New York, 1997).

Wanklyn, M., 'The Impact of Water Transport Facilities on the Economies of English River Ports, *c.*1660–*c.*1760', *Economic History Review*, 49 (1996), 20–34.

Weatherill, L., *Consumer Behaviour and Material Culture* (2nd edn; London, 1996).

Webster, A., 'The Strategies and Limits of Gentlemanly Capitalism: The London East India Agency Houses, Provincial Commercial Interests and the Evolution of British Economic Policy in South and South-East Asia, 1800–50', *Economic History Review*, 59 (2006), 743–64.

Welch, E., 'The Fairs of Early Modern Italy', in B. Blondé, P. Stabel, J. Stobart, and I. Van Damme (eds), *Buyers and Sellers* (Antwerp, 2006), 31–50.

Welford, J., 'Functional Goods and Fancies: The Production and Consumption of Consumer Goods in Northumberland, Newcastle upon Tyne and Durham *c.*1680–1780' (unpublished Ph.D. thesis, University of Durham, 2010).

White, J., 'The Labouring-Class Domestic Sphere in Eighteenth-Century British Social Thought', in J. Styles and A. Vickery (eds), *Gender, Taste and Material Culture in Britain and North America* (New Haven, 2006), 247–63.

Wild, M. T., and Shaw, G., 'Locational Behaviour of Urban Retailing during the Nineteenth Century: The Example of Kingston upon Hull', *Transactions of the Institute of British Geographers*, 61 (1974), 101–18.

Wilhelmsen, L. J., *English Textile Nomenclature* (Bergen, 1943).

Willan, T., *An Eighteenth-Century Shopkeeper: Abraham Dent of Kirby Stephen* (Manchester, 1970).

Willan, T., *The Inland Trade: Studies in English Internal Trade in the Sixteenth and Seventeenth Centuries* (Manchester, 1976).

Williams, R., *Dream Worlds: Mass Consumption in Late Nineteenth-Century France* (Berkeley and Los Angeles, 1982).

Wilson, J., and Popp, A., 'Introduction', in J. Wilson and A. Popp (eds), *Industrial Clusters and Regional Business Networks in England, 1750–1970* (Aldershot, 2003).

Wilson, K., *Sense of the People: Politics, Culture and Imperialism in England, 1715–1785* (Cambridge, 1995).

Wischermann, C., 'Placing Advertising in the Modern Cultural History of the City', in C. Wischermann and E. Shore (eds), *Advertising and the European City: Historical Perspectives* (Aldershot, 2000), 1–31.

Wrigley, E. A., 'English County Populations in the Later Eighteenth Century', *Economic History Review*, 60 (2007), 35–69.

Young, C., and Allen, S., 'Retail Patterns in Nineteenth-Century Chester', *Journal of Regional and Local Studies*, 16 (1996), 1–18.

Index